BEYOND
THE DECADE

OF THE

BRAIN

Volume 3

Neuroprotection in Parkinson's disease

Editors:

C. Warren Olanow, MD, FRCP(C)
Professor and Chairman
Department of Neurology
Mount Sinai Medical Center
New York
USA

Peter Jenner, PhD, FRPharmS
Head of Pharmacology
Kings College London
London
UK

Published by:
Wells Medical Limited, Speldhurst Place, Speldhurst Road,
Royal Tunbridge Wells, Kent TN4 0JB, UK

ISBN 1859390765

ACKNOWLEDGMENT

The chapters in this book are based on papers published in Supplement 3 to *Annals of Neurology* 1998, volume 44, no. 3. The figures herein are reproduced with kind permission of The American Neurological Association and Lippincott Williams and Wilkins (formerly Lippincott-Raven Publishers).

This publication has been sponsored by an educational grant from SmithKline Beecham Pharmaceuticals

CONTENTS

Section V – Neuroprotection

Section VI – Future Directions

PARTICIPANTS

Professor S.-M. Aquilonius	University Hospital, Uppsala, Sweden
Professor E. Auff	University Hospital for Neurology, Vienna, Austria
Dr. M.F. Beal	Massachusetts General Hospital, Boston, USA
Dr. P.J. Bédard	Hôpital de l'Enfant-Jésus, Quebec City, Canada
Professor U. Bonnuccelli	University of Pisa, Pisa, Italy
Dr. K.L.B. Borden	Mount Sinai Medical Center, New York, USA
Professor D.J. Brooks	Hammersmith Hospital, London, UK
Professor R.E. Burke	Columbia University, New York, USA
Dr. P. Damier	Hôpital de la Pitié-Salpêtrière, Paris, France
Professor G. de Yebenes Justo	Fundacion Jimenez Diaz, Madrid, Spain
Professor A. Destee	CHU – Hôpital B, Lille, France
Dr. D.M. Gash	University of Kentucky Medical Center, Lexington, USA
Dr. T. Gasser	Klinikum Grosshadern, Munich, Germany
Dr. O. Hardiman	Beaumont Hospital, Dublin, Eire
Professor E.C. Hirsch	Hôpital de la Pitié-Salpêtrière, Paris, France
Dr. J. Hubble	Ohio State University Medical Center, Ohio, USA
Professor P. Jenner	Kings College London, London, UK
Dr. W.H. Jost	Deutsche Klinik für Diagnostik, Wiesbaden, Germany
Professor W.C. Koller	University of Kansas Medical Center, Kansas City, USA
Professor L. Lachenmayer	Allegemeines Krankenhaus Barmbek, Hamburg, Germany
Dr. J.W. Langston	The Parkinson's Institute, Sunnyvale, California, USA

Professor B. Lawlor	St. James' Hospital, Dublin, Eire
Professor K.L. Leenders	Paul Scherrer Institut, Villigen, Switzerland
Dr. O. Marinaki	Thriasion Hospital, Athens, Greece
Professor C.D. Marsden	Institute of Neurology, London, UK
Professor E. Melamed	Tel Aviv University, Tel Aviv, Israel
Professor Y. Mizuno	Juntendo University School of Medicine, Tokyo, Japan
Dr. J.H. Morrison	Mount Sinai Medical Center, New York, USA
Dr. J.A. Obeso	HOSPITEN, Tenerife, Spain
Professor N. Ogawa	Okayama University Medical School, Okayama, Japan
Professor C.W. Olanow	Mount Sinai Medical Center, New York, USA
Professor D. P. Perl	Mount Sinai Medical Center, New York, USA
Professor G. Pezzoli	Istituti Clinici di Perfezionamento, Milan, Italy
Professor W.H. Poewe	University of Innsbruck, Innsbruck, Austria
Dr. M.H. Polymeropoulos	NIH/NHGRI, Bethesda, USA
Professor N. Quinn	The National Hospital for Neurology and Neurosurgery, London, UK
Professor O. Rascol	Laboratoire de Pharmacologie Medicale et Clinique, Toulouse, France
Professor P. Riederer	University of Würzburg, Würzburg, Germany
Professor A.H.V. Schapira	Royal Free Hospital Medical School, London, UK
Dr. I. Shoulson	University Medical School, Rochester, USA
Professor F. Stocchi	Materia Medica, Rome, Italy
Dr. N.A. Tatton	Mount Sinai Medical Center, New York, USA
Dr. W.G. Tatton	Mount Sinai Medical Center, New York, USA
Dr. F. Tison	CHU – Hôpital Pellegrin, Bordeaux, France

Dr. J.J. van Hilten — Academisch Ziekenhuis Leiden, Leiden, The Netherlands

Professor A. Williams — The Queen Elizabeth Hospital, Birmingham, UK

Dr. N.W. Wood — Institute of Neurology, London, UK

Professor M.B.H. Youdim — Rappaport Institute, Haifa, Israel

GLOSSARY

Aβ	Alzheimer β protein
ACTH	adrenocorticotropic hormone
AD	Alzheimer's disease
ADP	adenosine diphosphate
AGE	advanced glycation endproducts
AIDS	acquired immune deficiency syndrome
AIF	apoptosis initiating factor
ALS	amyotrophic lateral sclerosis
AMPA	α-amino-3-hydroxy-5-methyl-4-isoxazole propionic acid
APP	amyloid precursor protein
ATP	adenosine triphosphate
BBB	blood–brain barrier
BCGS1	breast cancer susceptibility gene 1
BSO	buthionine sulfoximine
cdk	cyclin dependent kinase
CERAD	consortium to establish a registry for Alzheimer's disease
CNS	central nervous system
Cr	creatinine
CSF	cerebrospinal fluid
Cyt C	cytochrome C
DATATOP	deprenyl and tocopherol antioxidative therapy of parkinsonism
DBS	deep brain stimulation
DDC	dopa decarboxylase
DLBD	diffuse Lewy body disease (or dementia)
DNA	deoxyribonucleic acid
EAA	excitatory amino acid

EM	electron microscopy
EP	entopeduncular nucleus
^{18}F-dopa	^{18}fluorodopa
Fe^{2+}	ferrous iron
Fe^{3+}	ferric iron
GABA	gamma aminobutyric acid
GAPDH	glyceraldehyde 3-phosphate dehydrogenase
GDNF	glial derived neurotrophic factor
GFAP	glial fibrillary protein
GP	globus pallidus
GPe	globus pallidus externa
GPi	globus pallidus interna
GP	glutathione peroxidase
GSH	reduced glutathione
GSSH	oxidized glutathione
H_2O_2	hydrogen peroxide
ICE	interleukin-1β converting enzyme
IFN-γ	interferon gamma
IgG	immunoglobulin G
IL-1	interleukin-1
ILBD	incidental Lewy body disease
ISEL	*in situ* end-labeling
α-KGDHC	alpha ketoglutarate dehydrogenase complex
MAO-B	monoamine oxidase B
Mn	manganese
MPP+	1-methyl-phenylpyridinium ion
MPTP	1-methyl-4 phenyl-1,2,3,6 tetrahydropyridine
mRNA	messenger ribonucleic acid
MRS	magnetic resonance spectroscopy
MSA	multiple system atrophy
mtDNA	mitochondrial DNA
NAA	N-acetyl aspartate

NAC	non-amyloid component
NACP	non-amyloid component precursor protein
NAD	nicotinamide adenine dinucleotide
NADH	reduced form of NAD
NAT-2	n-acetyl transferase 2
NFkB	translocation factor NF kappa B
NFT	neurofibrillary tangle
NGF	nerve growth factor
7-NI	7-nitroindazole
3-NT	3-nitrotyrosine
NMDA	N-methyl-D-aspartate
NMR	nuclear magnetic resonance
NO	nitric oxide
NOS	nitric oxide synthase
eNOS	endothial nitric oxide synthase
iNOS	inducible nitric oxide synthase
nNOS	neuronal nitric oxide synthase
O_2-	superoxide
OH$^\bullet$	hydroxyl radical
6-OHDA	6-hydroxydopamine
ONOO$^-$	peroxynitrite
OXPHOS	oxidative phosphorylation
PBN	phenyl butyl nitrone
PC12 cells	pheochromocytoma 12 cells
PCD	programmed cell death
PD	Parkinson's disease
PDC	parkinsonism–dementia complex
PET	positron emission tomography
PML	promyelocytic leukemia protein
PND	post-natal day
PPN	pedunculopontine nucleus
PSP	progressive supranuclear palsy
PTP	permeability transition pore

ROS	reactive oxygen species
SN	substantia nigra
SNc	substantia nigra zona compacta
SND	striatonigral degeneration
SNr	substantia nigra zona reticulata
SOD	superoxide dismutase
SPECT	single photon emission computed tomography
STN	sub-thalamic nucleus
TBARS	thiobarbituric acid reactive substances
TdT	terminal deoxynucleotidyl transferase
TH	tyrosine hydroxylase
TIQ	tetrahydroisoquinolines
TNF-α	tumor necrosis factor alpha
tRNA	transfer ribonucleic acid
TUNEL	terminal deoxynucleotidyl transferase mediated dUTP nick end-labeling
UTP	uridine triphosphate
UPDRS	unified Parkinson's disease rating scale
VTA	ventral tegmental area

Parkinson's disease (PD) is set apart from other neurodegenerative diseases by our knowledge of its primary pathology and key biochemical defect and our ability to treat the major features of the illness. Nonetheless, the majority of patients eventually experience functional disability that cannot be satisfactorily controlled with existing therapy. Insight into the etiology of PD or the nature of the neurodegenerative process might permit the development of neuroprotective therapies that alter the natural progression of the disorder. However, it is becoming increasingly likely that the etiology of PD is complex, may be multifactorial, and may differ among individuals. Further, the nature of the pathological process underlying nerve cell death in PD remains a mystery as does the nature of Lewy bodies. Consequently, little can presently be done to prevent disease progression. The situation may, however, be beginning to change. Specific genetic and environmental factors have been identified to cause a PD-like syndrome and increasing evidence suggests that oxidative stress, excitotoxicity, and inflammatory factors are a component of the ongoing pathological process leading to degeneration of nigral dopamine-containing cells through an apoptotic process.

This current work is the proceedings of a meeting held in Cannes, France in October 1997 and is devoted to the current status and knowledge on the causes of neurodegeneration and the search for neuroprotection in PD. Authorities in each of these areas were invited to participate in this meeting and to present an up-to-date review on their selected topic. Specifically, advances related to etiology, pathogenesis, mechanism of cell death and prospects for therapy have been included in this volume.

Major new concepts were discussed at this meeting, including the role of α-synuclein, the idea that altered handling of abnormal or mutant proteins can lead to Lewy body formation and cell death, the concept that perhaps it is an abnormality of glial cell function rather than neuronal dysfunction which leads to cell degeneration, and the potential that dopamine agonists, NOS inhibitors, glutamate antagonists, and anti-apoptotic agents might prove to be neuroprotective. The topics are diverse and include comprehensive reviews and/or discussions related to the genetics of PD, the possible role of α-synuclein in the pathogenesis of PD, the current status of oxidative stress, glia, and trophic factors in the pathogenesis of cell death, the possibility that cell death occurs by an apoptotic mechanism, the significance of mitochondria in apoptotic cell death, and attempts to obtain neuroprotection with treatments ranging from dopamine agonists and anti-apoptotic agents to surgical interventions that interfere with STN overactivity. Finally, an overview is provided on the many different ways that one can hope to obtain neuroprotection in the future and what strategies should be pursued in order to permit so many new potential therapies to be tested in parkinsonian patients.

This volume reflects the changes in our understanding of the neurodegenerative process in PD that have occurred over the past decade. During this time the treatment of the disease has changed, in an attempt to avoid exacerbating its pathology and preventing the onset of dyskinesia. Now the wheel is turning again. Currently, we are on the threshold of gaining a clear understanding of why dopaminergic cells die in PD. With this, we hope, will come the ability to interfere directly with the cascade of events which lead to neuronal degeneration. If this can be accomplished it will lead to a revolution in the treatment of neurodegenerative illnesses such as PD. Disease progression will not be inevitable and, with the eventual introduction of predictive tests for PD, it may become possible to intervene before the initial symptoms appear. The dawn of neuroprotection as a treatment strategy has arrived and this is a key message addressed herein.

C. Warren Olanow, MD, FRCP(C)
Peter Jenner, PhD, FRPharmS
Editors

SECTION I

Introduction

CHAPTER ONE

The natural history of Parkinson's disease

WERNER H. POEWE AND G.K. WENNING
Department of Neurology, University Hospital, Innsbruck, Austria

Despite recent advances in the symptomatic treatment of Parkinson's disease (PD) there is still no realistic prospect for a cure. No neuroprotective candidate has yet emerged which has been demonstrated to have any long-lasting and dramatic impact on the course of the illness. Indeed, data on the natural course of PD are insufficient. Uncertainty surrounds the duration of a pre-clinical phase, whether progression of clinically overt disease is linear or exponential, how to recognise subtypes of the disease with different progression characteristics, and the risk factors and predictors for progression of disability. These issues are key to the design of treatments to restrain or decelerate the underlying disease process. This chapter reviews the available evidence on the natural history of PD.

PROGRESSION OF MOTOR DISABILITY IN UNTREATED PD

Hoehn and Yahr's study on PD, published before the introduction of levodopa, provides important information regarding the natural history of untreated parkinsonism.[1] The degree and progression of motor disability in a subgroup of 183 patients was assessed using the now well-established Hoehn-Yahr (HY) scale. Although the more severe HY stages (IV – severely disabling disease, patient still able to walk and stand unassisted, but markedly incapacitated; V – confinement to bed or to wheelchair unless aided) were associated with longer duration of disease, there was a remarkable variation in the rate of progression of disability. In patients with illness of less than five years' duration, 37% had reached stage III or beyond. In contrast, 34% of patients who had their illness for 10 years or longer were still in stages I and II. This suggests some heterogeneity of disease progression in PD, although a considerable proportion of patients with atypical parkinsonism may have been included. In a longitudinal follow-up survey of 271 patients, almost one-third of patients with a five-year disease duration became severely disabled or died. This proportion rose to 61% when the disease duration increased to 10 years, and to 90% when the disease had been present for more than 15 years.

A later study in southwest Finland showed that the time intervals between the different HY stages varied markedly thoughout the entire disease course, ranging for example from 0 to 30 years for the time to development of bilateral parkinsonism (HY stage I to stage II).[2] The speed of progression remained relatively constant for individual patients, and the time interval between HY stages I and II correlated with progression to advanced disability (HY stages III–V).

SOMATOTOPIC PROGRESSION OF PD

It is generally accepted that progression of motor symptoms in PD reflects advancing nigral pathology.[3] Neuronal loss within the substantia nigra in PD occurs unevenly with neurons in the ventrolateral tier being most severely depleted.[4,5] An uneven pattern of dopamine loss has also been observed in the striatum of PD patients with the loss being most pronounced in the dorsal and caudal parts of the putamen.[6] This might suggest that a disturbance of motor control in the leg should be the first clinical sign of PD, although this is not supported by clinical experience. Similar suggestions were made in a study of somatotopic progression of levodopa-induced dyskinesias.[7]

In a retrospective study involving 253 patients with a clinical diagnosis of PD, tremor was, as expected, the most common initial feature, being present in 63% of all patients. There was an unexpected laterality, initial complaints more often starting on the right side (61% *versus* 39% for the left side). In patients with unilateral arm involvement, spread of symptoms to the ipsilateral leg occurred between 0.8 to 1.4 years from onset while contralateral spread, corresponding to transition from HY stage I to II, took between 2.1 to 3.4 years. This might indicate an accelerated progression of nigral pathology once the symptomatic threshold has been reached, compared to the rate of progression during the presymptomatic stages of the disease. The preferential right-sided presentation is difficult to explain and warrants further studies of somatotopic disease progression in the initial phase of PD. Longitudinal follow-up studies do suggest that one side of the body is affected predominantly and persistently throughout the course of illness.[8]

RATES OF PROGRESSION IN EARLY PD

The potential to be able to provide neuroprotective treatment in PD has prompted careful monitoring of clinical indices of disease progression in studies of putative neuroprotective agents. The largest of these trials, the Deprenyl and Tocopherol Antioxidative Therapy of Parkinsonism (DATATOP),[9–13] was designed to examine the effects of deprenyl or tocopherol, or both, in patients with early PD who were not taking or requiring antiparkinsonian medications. Patients who did not reach the endpoint (requirement for levodopa) were termed 'survivors', and their annual rate of progression of motor disability as measured by UPDRS scores was unsurprisingly markedly slower than the rest of the patient cohort.

Similar observations have been made in patients with untreated early PD receiving treatment with levodopa or bromocriptine combined with placebo or deprenyl in a four-arm treatment study.[14] Excluding the deprenyl patients for possible neuroprotective effects of this drug, the calculated annual rates of decline in UPDRS motor scores were approximately 4% of the maximum score value in bromocriptine- or levodopa-treated patients, similar to the more slowly progressing survivors of the DATATOP study.

Slower rates of motor deterioration were observed in patients with PD treated with levodopa and/or bromocriptine, a small number also receiving deprenyl.[15] Given an average disease duration of 8.3 ± 5.8 years, the rate of progression of bradykinesia was 0.49% of the maximum attainable score. However, the bradykinesia score advanced rapidly initially with an annual rate of decline of 3.5% in the first year, falling to 1.5% in the tenth year after symptom onset. The available studies therefore indicate that the annual rate of progression of motor disturbance during the early stages of the disease may vary by a factor of 2–3.

It is intriguing to note that annual rates of decline of clinical motor indices were considerably slower in two studies examining patients on dopaminergic therapy[14,15] compared to untreated patients from the DATATOP trial, at least in those reaching the endpoint.[10] Whether this indicates a neuroprotective effect of dopamine replacement is open to speculation. Furthermore, most of the clinical evidence suggests that progression of motor disability may be more rapid early in the disease. Using sequential ^{18}F-dopa PET scans in groups of patients with short and long disease duration, evidence was found for a faster annual rate of reduction of putaminal fluorodopa uptake in patients with recent onset compared to those with longer duration of disease.[16]

RATES OF NIGRAL CELL LOSS AND DECLINE OF STRIATAL ^{18}F-DOPA UPTAKE IN PD

[18]F-Dopa PET measurements have been used to determine *in vivo* the rates of progression of the underlying pathology in sequential studies in PD patients. While it is well established that putaminal ^{18}F-dopa uptake correlates with clinical severity of symptoms,[16] the evidence that striatal ^{18}F-dopa uptake on PET reflects nigral cell counts is far from certain. It is therefore possible that rates of decline of ^{18}F-dopa putaminal uptake in PD represent a sensitive and objective means of studying progression of striatal dopaminergic dysfunction but do not actually reflect advancing neuronal attrition in the substantia nigra.[17]

Data from sequential ^{18}F-dopa PET studies in PD patients have produced conflicting results. In one study[3] the striatal/occipital ratio was found to have declined by 7.8% per decade in PD compared to 3% in healthy controls. In contrast, a much faster rate of progression of PET indices was observed in a sequential study of 10 patients with recent-onset PD with a mean duration of

18 months and seven patients with disease duration of 71 months.[16] The average left-to-right putaminal ^{18}F-dopa influx constant (Ki) was chosen as the most consistent and reliable measurement of striatal metabolism, and was found to decline at an annual rate of 7% of the normal mean in both patient groups.

PRECLINICAL DISEASE AND SYMPTOMATIC THRESHOLD

Early studies suggested that dopamine nerve cell counts were reduced by at least 50% at disease onset.[5,18,19] A back-analysis suggested that there was a relatively short preclinical phase of around 4.7 years, and this has since been supported by sequential ^{18}F-dopa PET scans, assuming a linear progression of PET indices.[16] The same assumption in another study, however, produced a considerably longer estimate of several decades,[3] and a similarly long latent phase has also been postulated by other workers.[20,21] More recently, evidence for a prodromal phase in PD patients was provided by comparing health records of 60 PD patients and 58 matched controls during the decade preceding onset of classical PD.[22] Prodromal symptoms occurred significantly more often in the PD group and included mood changes, limb pain, paresthesiasis and hypertension, and the duration of this prodromal phase was between four and six years.

While the exact duration of a latent phase of PD thus remains controversial there is little doubt about its existence and it is the prime target period for any neuroprotective treatment.

IMPACT OF DRUG TREATMENT ON DISEASE PROGRESSION

The introduction of levodopa has had a dramatic impact on the progression of disability and also – at least initially – on mortality.[23,24] However, there has been no detectable difference in the actual rate of disease progression between treated and untreated patients. More recently, drug development has focused on agents that might modify the natural progression of PD. To date, deprenyl is the only drug which has been demonstrated to have some potential to modify rates of progression of early PD in properly-controlled clinical trials.[12–15,25,26]

FACTORS INFLUENCING DISEASE PROGRESSION

Several authors have observed that the rate of disease progression is slower in tremor dominant cases.[2,27,28] In three recent clinical studies, age at onset was an important determinant of the rate of disease progression.[29–31] Faster disease progression was recognized in elderly PD patients and was associated with increasing levodopa-unresponsive features with axial motor disability, such as gait unsteadiness, freezing and dysarthria.[29–31] While Lewy body pathology in the substantia nigra appears to be similar in young- *versus* old-onset patients,[32] there is a striking difference in the prevalence of dementia between these groups with dementia being much more common in older-onset patients.[33–35]

Cognitive decline has been shown to be associated with faster progression of disability in PD. Longitudinal assessments of cognition, mood, and disability over 54 months in 87 PD patients and a control group of 50 matched healthy individuals showed an overall incidence of dementia of 19%, *versus* zero in the controls.[36] Patients who became demented were older, had a longer duration of disease, were more likely to be male, and disabled by PD at entry. PD patients with hallucinations related to dementia are at high risk of requiring nursing home placement and of death.[37,38] Nearly half of the demented patients in a study of 155 PD cases exhibited a predominantly akinetic-rigid syndrome, *versus* 19% of non-demented individuals.[39] Tremor-dominant cases were much less likely to develop dementia. In contrast, demented patients were older and had a shorter disease duration than the non-demented.[44] Mood disorder may thus be another risk factor for progression of disability.[40]

MORTALITY

In Hoehn and Yahr's series of 672 patients with primary 'parkinsonism',[1] 44% died during the follow-up period, yielding a mortality ratio of 2.9 times that expected in an age-matched population. Average age at death was 67 years and the average duration of life after diagnosis was 9.4 (1–33) years. This may not, however, have been representative of the entire parkinsonian population. Mortality was found to be increased by 1.6-fold in parkinsonian patients in Rochester, Minnesota, between 1935 and 1966,[41] while an earlier analysis of this same population found an even lower mortality rate of 1.41.[42]

The introduction of levodopa had a striking effect on the excess mortality observed in untreated patients with PD, bringing the life expectancy closer to that of the general population. Mortality in levodopa-treated patients appears to be positively correlated with the delay before starting treatment.[43] Several studies have shown that the beneficial effects of levodopa on mortality are most apparent in the early years of the disease but that mortality rises later in the disease course despite levodopa therapy.[43–45] However, all but one survival study in PD have recruited patients from specialist centres, and only three studies have compared the mortality of parkinsonian patients with matched control subjects.[46–48]

Analysis of mortality among the patients with early PD enrolled in the DATATOP trial showed an overall death rate of 17.1% over 8.2 years, or 2.1% per year.[13] This was substantially lower than in most of the previous studies and even lower than the expected mortality rate of an age-matched US population not affected by PD. Increased life expectancy due to deprenyl treatment has been reported in a retrospective study[49] but the DATATOP mortality rate was unaffected by deprenyl, tocopherol or combined treatment. In contrast, the Parkinson's Disease Research Group of the United Kingdom reported increased mortality associated with deprenyl treatment when given as adjunct to levodopa in an open label study in patients who were untreated at the time of entry.[31] There was no obvious explanation for this finding, but the UK study was characterized by its open label design and recruitment of slightly older, more disabled subjects requiring symptomatic antiparkinsonian therapy. In addition, there has been major criticism of its methodology.[50] In the recent SINDEPAR study, 101 untreated PD patients were randomized to receive deprenyl or placebo followed by symptomatic treatment with either levodopa or bromocriptine.[14] After a mean follow-up of 4.5 years there were six (12%) deaths in the placebo group and three (6%) deaths in the deprenyl group. This difference was not significant due to relatively small patient numbers, but was felt not to indicate increased mortality in deprenyl-treated patients.[50]

Available studies therefore provide confusingly heterogeneous mortality rates, probably due to discrepancies between patient populations with respect to co-morbidity, stage of disease at entry and diagnostic accuracy. The most recent data from DATATOP suggest that carefully selected patients with early and 'pure' PD without significant co-morbidity have 'super-normal' life expectancy when adequately treated and regularly followed at specialist centers. The impact of levodopa, while beneficial in the early years of treatment, does not seem to affect mortality in the long-term. Likewise, contrary to earlier claims, deprenyl treatment is not associated with increased life expectancy in PD, but there is also no convincing evidence that it contributes to excess mortality.

SUMMARY

- There are still insufficient data on the natural course of PD due to lack of standardized longitudinal follow-up studies.

- Reported progression rates in early PD vary considerably by a factor of 2 to 3. Likewise, data from sequential ^{18}F-dopa PET studies have produced variable decline rates of PET indices ranging between 7% and 70% per decade.

- Risk factors for rapid progression include old age at onset, concomitant major depression, dementia and akinetic-rigid symptom presentation.

- The introduction of levodopa into the routine treatment of PD patients had a dramatic impact on symptomatic control but does not seem to have affected the underlying rate of disease progression.

- There is as yet no firm evidence that deprenyl influences the rate of progression of PD but it does delay the need for levodopa which may represent a neuroprotective effect. However, deprenyl also failed to influence the development of levodopa-induced motor complications.

- Available studies on mortality in PD provide heterogeneous mortality rates probably resulting from discrepancies between patient populations with respect to comorbidity, disease stage at study entry and diagnostic accuracy. However, the most recent follow-up from the DATATOP cohort suggests normal life expectancy in carefully selected patients without significant comorbidity and adequate treatment and expert follow-up.

- Clinical data suggest that PD shows considerable heterogeneity when studying indices of progression and, indeed, mortality. While a number of modifying factors have been identified clinically it is worthwhile to define subgroups of PD with different progression characteristics.

ACKNOWLEDGMENT

We thank Dr L. Schelosky for analyzing the data on somatotopic disease progression

REFERENCES

1. Hoehn MM, Yahr MD. Parkinsonism: onset, progression, and mortality. Neurol 1967; 17: 427–442.

2. Marttila P.J, Rinne UK. Disability and progression in Parkinson's disease. Acta Neurol Scand 1977; 56: 159–169.

3. Vingerhoets FJG, Snow BJ, Lee CS, Schulzer M, Mak E, Calne DB. Longitudinal fluorodopa positron emission tomographic studies of the evolution of idiopathic parkinsonism. Ann Neurol 1994; 36: 759–764.

4. Hirsch E, Graybiel AM, Agid YA. Melanized dopaminergic neurons are differentially susceptible to degeneration in Parkinson's disease. Nature 1988; 334: 345–348.

5. Fearnley JM, Lees AJ. Ageing and Parkinson's disease: substantia nigra regional selectivity. Brain 1991; 114: 2283–2301.

6. Kish SJ, Shannak K, Hornykiewicz O. Uneven pattern of dopamine loss in the striatum of patients with idiopathic Parkinson's disease: pathophysiological and clinical implications. N Engl J Med 1988; 318: 876–880.

7. Vidailhet M, Bonnet AM, Marconi R, Guider-Khouja N, Agid Y. Do parkinsonian symptoms and levodopa-induced dyskinesias start in the foot? Neurol 1994; 44: 1613–1616.

8. Lee CS, Schulzer M, Mak E, et al. Patterns of asymmetry do not not change over the course of idiopathic parkinsonism: Implications for pathogenesis. Neurol 1995; 45: 435–439.

9. The Parkinson Study Group. DATATOP: a multicenter controlled clinical trial in early Parkinson's disease. Arch Neurol 1989; 46: 1052–1060.

10. The Parkinson Study Group. Effects of tocopherol and deprenyl on the progression of disability in early Parkinson's disease. N Engl J Med 1993; 328: 176–183.

11. Parkinson Study Group. Impact of deprenyl and tocopherol treatment on Parkinson's disease in DATATOP subjects not requiring levodopa. Ann Neurol 1996; 39: 29–36.

12. Parkinson Study Group. Impact of deprenyl and tocopherol treatment on Parkinson's disease in DATATOP subjects requiring levodopa. Ann Neurol 1996; 39: 37–45.

13. The Parkinson Study Group. Mortality in DATATOP: a multicenter trial in early Parkinson's disease. Ann Neurol 1998; 43: 318–325.

14. Olanow CW, Hauser RA, Gauger L, et al. The effect of deprenyl and levodopa on the progression of Parkinson's disease. Ann Neurol 1995; 38: 771–777.

15. Lee CS, Schulzer M, Mak K, et al. Clinical observations on the rate of progression of idiopathic parkinsonism. Brain 1994; 117: 501–507.

16. Morrish PK, Sawle GV, Brooks DJ. An ^{18}F-dopa PET and clinical study of the rate of progression in Parkinson's disease. Brain 1996; 119: 585–591.

17. Morrish PK. Parkinson's disease is not a long-latency illness. Mov Disord 1997; 12: 849–854.

18. Bernheimer H, Birkmayer W, Hornykiewicz O, Jellinger K, Seitelberger F. Brain dopamine and the syndromes of Parkinson and Huntington. Clinical, morphological and neurochemical correlations. J Neurol Sci 1973; 20: 415–455.

19. Paulus W, Jellinger K. The neuropathologic basis of different clinical subgroups of Parkinson's disease. J Neuropathol Exp Neurol 1991; 506: 743–755.

20. Gibb WRG, Lees AJ. The relevance of the lewy body to the pathogenesis of idiopathic Parkinson's disease. J Neurol Neurosurg Psychiatry 1988; 51: 745–752.

21. Duvoisin RC. The genetics of Parkinson's disease: a review. In, Rinne UK, Nagatsu T, Horowski R, eds, International Workshop Berlin Parkinson's Disease. Bussum, NL: Medicom 1991: 38–57.

22. Gonera EG, van't Hof M, Berger HJC, van Weel C, Horstink MWIM. Symptoms and duration of the prodromal phase in Parkinson's disease. Mov Disord 1997; 12: 871–876.

23. Hoehn MM. Parkinsonism treated with levodopa: progression and mortality. J Neurol Transm 1983; Suppl 19: 253–264.

24. Wenning GK, Ben Shlomo Y, Magalhaes N, Daniel SE, Quinn NP. Clinical features and natural history of multiple system atrophy: an analysis of 100 cases. Brain 1994; 117: 835–845.

25. Tetrud JW, Langston JW. The effect of deprenyl (selegiline) on the natural history of Parkinson's disease. Science 1989; 245: 519–522.

26. Lees AJ (Parkinson's Disease Research Group of the United Kingdom). Comparison of therapeutic effects and mortality data of levodopa and levodopa combined with selegiline in patients with early, mild Parkinson's disease. BMJ 1995; 311: 1602–1607.

27. Zetusky WJ, Jankowic J, Pirozzolo FJ. The heterogeneity of Parkinson's disease: Clinical and prognostic implications. Neurol 1985; 35: 522–526.

28. Roos RAC, Jongen CF, van der Velde EA. Clinical course of patients with idiopathic Parkinson's disease. Mov Disord 1996; 3: 236–242.

29. Goetz CG, Tanner CM, Stebbins GT, Buchman AS. Risk factors for progression in Parkinson's disease. Neurol 1988; 38: 1841–1844.

30. Blin J, Dubois B, Bonnet AM, Vidailhet M, Brandabur M, Agid Y. Does ageing aggravate parkinsonian disability? J Neurol Neurosurg Psychiatry 1991; 54: 780–782.

31. Diamond SG, Markham CH, Hoehn MM, McDowell FH, Muenter MD. Effect of age at onset on progression and mortality in Parkinson's disease. Neurol 1989; 39: 1187–1190.

32. Gibb WRG, Lees AJ. A comparison of clinical and pathological features of young- and old-onset Parkinson's disease. Neurol 1988; 38: 1402–1406.

33. Gershanik OS, Leist A. Juvenile Parkinson's disease. Adv Neurol 1986; 45: 213–216.

34. Lima B, Neves G, Nora M. Juvenile parkinsonism: clinical and metabolic characteristics. J Neurol Neurosurg Psychiatry 1987; 50: 345–348.

35. Quinn N, Critchley P, Marsden CD. Young onset Parkinson's disease. Mov Disord 1987; 2: 73–91.

36. Biggins CA, Boyd JL, Harrop FM, et al. A controlled, longitudinal study of dementia in Parkinson's disease. J Neurol Neurosurg Psychiatry 1992; 55: 566–571.

37. Goetz CG, Stebbins GT. Risk factor for nursing home placement in advanced Parkinson's disease. Neurol 1993; 43: 2227–2229.

38. Goetz CG, Stebbins GT. Mortality and hallucinations in nursing home patients with advanced Parkinson's disease. Neurol 1995; 45: 669–671.

39. Gerstenbrand F, Poewe WH. The classification of Parkinson's disease. In, Stern GM, ed, Parkinson's disease. London: Chapman and Hall, 1987: 315–331.

40. Starkstein SE, Mayberg HS, Leiguarda R, Preziosi TJ, Robinson G. A prospective longitudinal study of depression, cognitive decline, and physical impairments in patients with Parkinson's disease. J Neurol Neurosurg Psychiatry 1992; 55: 377–382.

41. Nobrega FT, Glattre E, Kurland LT, Okazaki H. Comments on the epidemiology of parkinsonism including prevalence and incidence statistics for Rochester, Minnesota, 1935–1966. In, Barbeau A, Brunette JR, eds, Progress in Neurogenetics. Amsterdam: Excerpta Medica 1967: 474–485.

42. Kurland LT. Epidemiology: Incidence, geographic distribution and genetic considerations. In, Field WJ, ed, Pathogenesis and treatment of parkinsonism. Springfield, Ill: Charles C. Thomas, 1958: 5–49.

43. Diamond SG, Markham CH, Hoehn MM, McDowell FI, Muenter MD. Multi-center study of Parkinson mortality with early versus later dopa treatment. Ann Neurol 1987; 22: 8–12.

44. Curtis L, Lees AJ, Stern GM, Marmot MG. Effect of L-Dopa on the course of Parkinson's disease. Lancet 1984; 2: 211–212.

45. Uitti RJ, Ahlskog JE, Maraganore DM, et al. Levodopa therapy and survival in idiopathic Parkinson's disease: Olmstead County Project. Neurol 1993; 43: 1918–1926.

46. Ebmaier Y.P, Calder SA, Crawford JR, Stewart L, Besson JAO, Mutch WJ. Mortality and causes of death in idiopathic Parkinson's disease: results from the Aberdeen whole population study. Acta Neurol Scand 1990; 81: 294–299.

47. Rajput AH, Offord KP, Beard CU, Kurland LT. Epidemiology of parkinsonism: incidence, classification and mortality. Can J Neurol Sci 1992; 19: 103–107.

48. Ben Shlomo Y, Marmot MG. Survival and cause of death in a cohort of patients with parkinsonism: possible clues to aetiology. J Neurol Neurosurg Psychiatry 1995; 58: 293–299.

49. Birkmayer W, Knoll J, Riederer P, et al. Increased life expectancy resulting from addition of l-deprenyl to Madopar treatment of Parkinson's disease: a long-term study. J Neural Transm 1985; 64: 113–127

50. Olanow CW, Fahn S, Langston JW, Godbold J. Selegiline and mortality in Parkinson's disease. Ann Neurol 1996; 40: 841–845.

DISCUSSION

Mizuno: How many neurons are remaining when the patient starts to show symptoms of PD? According to the traditional literature, more than 80% of neurons have to be lost to show initial symptoms of PD. However, according to Dr. Brooks' recent study, only 40–45% of neurons are lost when parkinsonism begins to develop. There is a considerable discrepancy between these two results, so what, therefore, is our current understanding?

Poewe: The Lees study showed a threshold of slightly less than 60% cell loss, which also differs from the 80% to which you refer. Those data came from early neurochemical studies and were derived, of course, from end-stage patients who had come to autopsy.

Melamed: It is very important to know how many neurons remain when the patient's first symptoms begin. If indeed some 80% of the neurons are lost, there will not be many neurons left to save in the substantia nigra compacta. I would also like to hear your views on whether disease progression is linear or non-linear. The dopaminergic neurons would be unable to continue the disease progression for 10 or 20 years, which would support the point that most of the progression initially occurs at a rapid rate and then reaches a plateau or a slower level of decline. Another possibility is that the progression of PD in the later stages is due to the participation of other, non-dopaminergic neurons in the degenerative process. We have much evidence to support this. A further point is that when at least 60% of the neurons in the substantia nigra compacta die, the remaining neurons become hyperactive and fire more rapidly than neurons in an intact system. There is some thinking that the wear and tear associated with this hyperactivity could itself contribute to the progression of the disease, thereby accelerating disease progression later on both within the nigra and in terminal sites. From what you say, however, this could be happening during the first few years, and not at the end-stages of the disease.

Poewe: Disease progression is probably not linear and it is important to recognize that other systems are contributing. On the basis of clinical data, not all of the progression of disability can be attributed to nigral pathology. Psychosis and cognitive decline are important problems contributing to disability and mortality. There is also good evidence to suggest that freezing, falls and gait disorder are non-dopaminergic.

Hirsch: As far as the number of surviving neurons in the substantia nigra is concerned, pathologically we have found great variability between patients. In some patients at the end-stage of the disease we have only 5% surviving neurons in the substantia nigra, whereas in other patients almost 50% survive. This means that many neurons can survive. From the earliest studies, which were biochemical, it appeared that 80% loss of neurons was needed but this is clearly not true. It is actually 80% loss of dopamine in the striatum that appears to be critical for onset of symptoms. I believe that the surviving neurons are perhaps 'sick' neurons and this is supported by the fact that they contain less tyrosine hydroxylase and less mRNA coding for tyrosine hydroxylase. Perhaps the best index, therefore, is not the number of neurons remaining but the activity of those remaining neurons, and this may be the key factor to analyse.

Perl: There has been a revolution in terms of counting neurons in the last few years with the introduction of non-biased sampling methods under the heading of stereology. This has taught us that many of our original concepts regarding neuronal loss may be wrong and have to be re-examined using unbiased sampling methods. There have been very few studies so far using these new techniques. A number of groups, including ours, are beginning to do this and I think we are going to find a great deal more variation than has been thought. The degree of nigral cell loss that occurs with normal aging may well also have to be revised.

Olanow: It is possible that the absolute number of cells is not the issue and that counting may not be the right direction in which to go. One of the things that came out of the DATATOP study is the notion that the clinical progression of the disease is probably not linear. We found a stable rate of progression in PD patients until a given time point when they experienced a rapid deterioration and then stabilized at a lower level, only to continue to progress over time. This points more towards clinical deterioration occurring as a result of the loss of a compensatory mechanism, rather than an absolute decline in a specific number of dopaminergic nerve cells.

Langston: The MPTP model in the squirrel monkey can be used to answer some of these questions. About 95% depletion of dopamine is required before we see what clinicians would call parkinsonism. There is some general slowing down in total activity but it is not a clinically obvious phenomenon. In those animals, there is typically between 50–60% cell loss, so there is a huge disparity between clinical symptoms, dopamine depletion, and cell loss. Secondly, the rate of disease progression is enormously important because it effects every aspect of what we think about. Dr. Forno has commented to me that her impression is that whatever is going on in the nigra in PD has burnt out at the end-stage of the disease. There is much less activity in terms of inflammatory response, raising the question that there may be multiple phases – perhaps a rapidly-accelerating early phase, followed by a slowing-down phase at the very end. If this is true, we are going to have to deal with a whole set of other pathogenic phenomena.

Koller: Non-motor signs are probably equally important, particularly the dementia. As we become more adept at treating the motor signs, we have begun to pay more attention to the cognitive signs and the dementia which appear to cause even more disability than the motor features. Are there any data on rate of progression of dementia? Perhaps we should be thinking about this in the same way as we have about motor progression.

Poewe: I am unaware of good data on the rate of cognitive decline in PD. It is well known that the prevalence of cognitive problems is greater in older patients and dementia is an age-dependent phenomenon. But PD is not a uniform disease. Pure nigral pathology in young-onset PD patients is probably different from combined nigral plus cortical plus other subcortical disease affecting an elderly patient who will become demented and will suffer from falling and gait disorder. These may not reflect the same disease or it may represent more than one disease.

Shoulson: It is not surprising to see variation in PD since we are dealing with human beings and we are following them over a period of time with relatively inexact measures. Moreover, there are likely to be many different etiologies for this common disorder. One semantic issue is that we should refer to alterations in clinical progression as a change in the course of the illness, rather than in the course of the underlying disease. The issue of age is very important when we describe a patient population. Besides the DATATOP study, we have now looked at the early course of disease prospectively over a period of one to two years in several populations, and age seems to be a very important issue in terms of progression. For example, the average age on entry into DATATOP, and a similar study we did with lazabemide, was 61 years. The progression of illness was about 8 UPDRS units per year as a mean with a standard deviation of the change being similar to the mean in that population. In a similarly disabled population with an average age of 63 years, just two years difference, a rather striking change occurred in the rate of decline. It was much more pronounced in the older patients than in the younger patients. If people who are not particularly disabled are selected for a clinical trial, we see no excess mortality in that population after ten years, compared to an age-matched population without PD followed over the same period of time. It is very important, therefore, to describe our observations as a clinical change in illness and to describe very carefully the characteristics of the population that are being studied.

Poewe: I quite agree. There are so many pitfalls and, even with carefully selected patients with virtually no or very little co-morbidity, we do not necessarily get the true picture.

Olanow: Older patients seem to progress at a faster rate than younger patients, yet we would expect that a younger patient with a larger population of nigral neurons would have to undergo a significantly greater depletion from baseline in the number of nigral cells and the level of striatal dopamine in order to begin developing PD. Why do you think they have a slower rate of progression?

Poewe: Perhaps the other factors such as extra-dopaminergic pathology which come into play in the elderly are contributing to the overall problem of progression, not just the classical motor signs.

Langston: Another obvious point is that the older nervous system is much less able to compensate and many of the typical compensatory mechanisms are less available to an aging nervous system, making it more vulnerable.

Shoulson: An autopsy study has been conducted at the University of Oklahoma, in which the investigators looked at the nigral loss at any point in time and compared it to the age of onset and their conclusion was, of course, that in an older individual much less nigral loss was required to give a comparable amount of illness or disability. Presumably this is related to the compensatory abilities of the rest of the brain in that study.

Marsden: This issue about whether accelerated cell death occurs at an early stage of the illness is obviously critical in terms of how we plan protective treatment. One explanation for all the clinical data is that a cohort of people with aggressive disease die early, leaving those with benign disease. Therefore we have to rely on the pathology and the PET scanning for hard data. We have in fact heard from Dr. Perl that we can no longer rely on the old pathology because stereology was not used then. One is then prompted to ask whether the PET data are really hard data.

Brooks: We have completed two different series and it appears in both series that those patients with clinical symptoms for less than two years are progressing significantly faster than those patients who have had clinical duration of greater than two years. So the hypothesis holds true in at least two series.

Melamed: Dr. Marsden, I have to understand you correctly. You say that we may have these results because patients who initially had a more incapacitating disease died and we are left with the others. But from our experience, once we have diagnosed patients with PD in the very early stages, they do not seem to die at an accelerated rate. So either they died before they developed signs of the disease or maybe I misunderstood you.

Marsden: No you understood, but you are not a geriatric neurologist. Taking a cohort of people based solely on duration of disease and not stratified for age, I think there will be an old age group who die very quickly. However, these patients are not in the hands of neurologists, but in the hands of community physicians and geriatric neurologists. Young-onset parkinsonians, under the age of 75 or 80, who are being treated by neurologists seem to do reasonably well, but the older ones in the community seem to die very quickly and may not get to see a PD specialist.

Olanow: Dr. Marsden, what about the 30–40-year-old PD patient who has a clinically slow rate of progression *versus* the 60-year-old who progresses more quickly based on our observations in our own practice?

Marsden: It depends entirely on the age stratification of the population under study and that, I would suggest, is the most critical issue in defining rate of progression.

Quinn: We have been looking at 150 young-onset patients and finding, as we suspected, that the rate of dementia is very slow while they remain biologically young. The incidences of freezing and falls are also low until the patients are many years into the illness, so young-onset PD seems to be a much purer disease. I am sure that the factor of aging itself interacting with PD is crucial in the development of extra disability.

Perl: We perform the neuropathology for a large geriatric nursing home, with care ranging from apartment living to full nursing care, and I am amazed at the frequency with which we see PD pathologically in this large cohort. Very frequently, the diagnosis has been suspected but never confirmed, or not considered at all. Patients may receive treatment but for a very short period of time, or sometimes they receive no treatment at all. Retrospective examination of the charts reveals indications in the nursing notes that there may be symptoms of the disease but there are no physician notes reflecting this. There are many such cases in these nursing homes and this is not an isolated experience.

Langston: We have touched upon an enormous issue here and that is, in terms of our practices, we are dealing with a very biased sample. In true population-based studies, the picture is very different. There are, however, very few good population-based studies so it is difficult to draw conclusions.

CHAPTER TWO

The early diagnosis of Parkinson's disease

DAVID J. BROOKS

MRC Cyclotron Unit, Hammersmith Hospitals, London, UK

The pathological hallmark of Parkinson's disease (PD) is generally accepted to be Lewy body degeneration of pigmented and other brainstem nuclei.[1] This eosinophilic inclusion body with its characteristic halo is found in the degenerating neurons, and is composed of neurofilaments and has ubiquitin immunoreactivity.

Clinically, PD is characterized by the presence of extrapyramidal rigidity, tremor, and bradykinesia.[2] A good response to levodopa and asymmetrical onset of limb involvement support the diagnosis. Atypical features include a supranuclear gaze disorder, cerebellar or pyramidal signs, and early onset of dementia, autonomic or gait problems. This definition is not specific to a single pathological entity but constitutes a clinical syndrome. About 25% of cases confidently diagnosed with PD had, on post-mortem, pathology other than brainstem Lewy body disease,[2,3] despite the fact that two-thirds of these patients had a good-to-excellent response to levodopa. Striatonigral degeneration (SND), progressive supranuclear palsy (PSP), multi-infarct disease and, occasionally, Alzheimer's disease may be erroneously identified as PD. Clinical examination is sensitive[4] but in isolation is no more than 75% specific for PD defined as brainstem Lewy body disease. Other biological markers have been sought.

BIOLOGICAL MARKERS OF PD

Patients with clinically typical PD have impaired detection and discrimination of odours, unlike those with PSP.[5] There remains an overlap with normality, however, suggesting that olfactory testing is unlikely to be sufficiently sensitive to detect early disease.

A more attractive approach is identification of specific systemic biochemical markers for the disorder. Mitochondrial complex I activity is selectively reduced in the substantia nigra of brainstem Lewy body disease cases at autopsy and is also low in the platelets of patients with clinically typical PD.[6,7] This deficiency is not seen in SND or PSP and is therefore a potential discriminator but control and PD ranges again overlap, precluding the use of this assay as a marker of early disease. An alternative biochemical approach has been to explore xenobiotic enzyme profiles. The activity of platelet monoamine oxidase B (MAO-B) has been reported to be abnormal but substrate dependent.[8] Again, normal and PD ranges of MAO-B activity overlap so this biochemical assay has not yet proved to be useful in the detection of early PD.

The discovery of a mutation in the α-synuclein gene on chromosome 4 in one large Italian and several smaller Greek PD kindreds has intensified the hunt for a genetic marker for PD.[9] The α-synuclein gene mutation is not present in the majority of kindreds or any of the sporadic cases of PD tested to date.[10] Searches for a mitochondrial gene defect in PD have not shown any specific findings to date and other candidate genes such as MAO-B, CYP2D6, tyrosine hydroxylase, dopamine-β-hydroxylase, GDNF, and BDNF have also been excluded.[11] A possible genetic marker may be the NAT2 slow acetylator genotype as this appears to be more strongly associated with familial PD.[12] A genetic marker for PD would be very exciting, but would not necessarily indicate active disease.

Certain behavioural tasks can discriminate PD patients from normal subjects.[13,14] This approach could, in principle, be used to detect early or pre-clinical PD but would not discriminate between typical and atypical forms of parkinsonism. PD patients are also known to be impaired at problem-solving tasks.[15] Some unmedicated patients with early disease can, however, perform at normal levels, so this task may be insufficiently sensitive to detect early PD reliably.[16]

FUNCTIONAL IMAGING

Functional imaging (PET, SPECT, MRS) provides a means of assessing the function of dopamine terminals and striatal neurons *in vivo* and of demonstrating characteristic patterns of dysfunction in PD. Measures of dopamine terminal integrity with PET and SPECT also allow pre-clinical disease to be detected in at-risk subjects for parkinsonian disorders.

Dopamine terminal function in PD

[18]F-6-fluorodopa PET was the first functional imaging modality used to assess dopamine terminal function in PD *in vivo*. Following intravenous administration ^{18}F-dopa is taken up by the terminals of the nigrostriatal dopaminergic projections and metabolized to ^{18}F-dopamine and subsequently ^{18}F-DOPAC and ^{18}F-HVA.[17] In early hemiparkinsonian cases, PET showed normal caudate ^{18}F-dopa uptake but putamen uptake was bilaterally reduced, particularly contralateral to the more affected limbs.[18] These observations have been subsequently confirmed.[19-22] PD patients have shown an average 50% loss of specific putamen ^{18}F-dopa uptake[20] compared with the 60–80% loss of

ventrolateral nigra compacta cells reported at post-mortem.[23,24] As putamen dopamine levels are reduced by over 90% in end-stage PD,[25,26] striatal uptake of ^{18}F-dopa is thought to reflect terminal density of nigrostriatal projections rather than endogenous dopamine levels. Pre-mortem striatal ^{18}F-dopa uptake correlates with subsequent nigral cell counts obtained at autopsy.[27] The finding that early hemi-PD cases show a 30% loss of ^{18}F-dopa uptake in the putamen contralateral to the affected limbs[28] suggests a threshold loss of nigral dopaminergic cells for onset of symptoms of about 30%.

Until recently, brain tracer uptake has been registered only within given transaxial slices (2D mode). Software developments now enable all activity in the brain volume to be detected simultaneously (3D mode). This leads to increased levels of scatter, but the six-fold increase in signal-to-noise ratio allows regions with low tracer uptake to be sampled more sensitively at increased resolution. Additionally, the crude images of ^{18}F-dopa uptake can be converted to parametric maps reflecting dopa decarboxylase activity. Consequently, ^{18}F-dopa PET can now discriminate PD cases from normal subjects even when patients have hemi-PD and only the 'asymptomatic' putamen is considered.[29]

Detection of preclinical PD

In seven kindreds with documented familial PD, 11 of 32 (34%) asymptomatic adult relatives had levels of putamen ^{18}F-dopa uptake more than 2.5 standard deviations below the normal mean.[30] This is significantly higher than the 15% prevalence normally associated with a positive family history in PD.

Putaminal ^{18}F-dopa uptake has also been found to be reduced in 50% of monozygotic and 13% of dizygotic asymptomatic co-twins of affected PD patients[31,32] (unpublished observations). The significantly raised concordance ($p=0.029$) in monozygotic co-twins of PD patients and the 34% prevalence of dopaminergic dysfunction in adult relatives of familial cases both support a role of inheritance in PD. These findings do not, however, exclude the possibility that nigral dysfunction can arise from an environmental agent in some cases of PD.

Diagnosis of atypical parkinsonism

Ten percent of patients initially thought to have PD eventually prove to have SND.[33] Up to 50% of SND patients can have a sustained response to levodopa[34] while 20% of brainstem Lewy body disease cases show a poor levodopa response[4] so the two conditions can be difficult to distinguish on clinical grounds alone. As in PD, putaminal ^{18}F-dopa uptake is reduced to 50% of normal in cases of probable SND and individual levels correlate with the degree of disability.[20,35] Patients with multiple system atrophy (MSA) show significantly lower mean caudate ^{18}F-dopa uptake compared with equivalently disabled PD patients. This helps to differentiate MSA from PD but the ranges overlap, and the reduced caudate ^{18}F-dopa uptake only discriminates MSA from PD with 70% specificity.[35–37]

Striatal dopamine D_1 and D_2 receptor binding has been studied with PET in SND and has been found to be reduced in comparison to PD,[38–40] but since the SND, PD, and normal ranges again overlap, putamen D_1 and D_2 binding is not a sensitive discriminator.

Patients with clinically probable SND show reduced resting levels of striatal glucose metabolism[36,41,42] unlike PD where resting striatal metabolism is normal or elevated. Frontal glucose metabolism may also be impaired in SND and, in MSA with ataxia, cerebellar metabolism is reduced. Using clinical definitions, 80% of probable SND cases could be discriminated from PD on the basis of striatal hypometabolism and fluorodeoxyglucose PET scans can help to differentiate PD from SND.[42] Proton magnetic resonance spectroscopy (MRS) also provides a potential means of discriminating SND from PD. N-acetylaspartate (NAA) is found in high concentrations in neurons and is believed to be a metabolic marker of neuronal integrity. Reduced NAA:creatinine ratios in the proton MRS signal from the lentiform nucleus have been reported in six of seven clinically probable SND cases while eight of nine clinically probable PD cases had normal levels of putamen NAA.[43]

Unlike PD, putamen and caudate ^{18}F-dopa uptake are uniformly reduced in PSP[20,44,45] and 90% of patients can be classified as atypical on the basis of their severe caudate involvement alone.[37] Mean caudate and putamen D_2 binding is also significantly reduced in PSP though there is an overlap with the normal range.[39,46,47] PET studies in patients with probable PSP have shown depressed basal ganglia metabolism.[44,48–52] Proton MRS studies have also found reduced lentiform nucleus NAA:Cr ratios in seven of nine patients with PSP.[53] Cortical metabolism is globally depressed in PSP but posterior frontal areas are particularly targeted.[49] While these techniques can sensitively distinguish PSP from PD, they are unable to discriminate PSP from SND.

Objective measurement of PD progression

Despite the continuing development of clinical rating scales, two problems undermine their use as measures of disease progression. First, subjective rating scores and objective task performance times can be influenced by medication, and the washout time required to obtain a true 'off' state following cessation of treatment is not known precisely and may be several weeks. Second, different aspects of the disease can progress at varying rates and any clinical rating must take this heterogeneity into account.

[18]F-dopa PET provides a means of monitoring PD progression objectively, and is free from the confounding effects of symptomatic therapy. The decline of striatal ^{18}F-dopa uptake in PD is more rapid than in controls[54] and an average annual decline in baseline putaminal ^{18}F-dopa Ki value of 9–12% has been reported.[55,56] Individual rises in UPDRS did not correlate well with individual reductions in putamen ^{18}F-dopa uptake, but this was not surprising since the UPDRS does not reflect dopaminergic dysfunction only.

[40]

Patients were scored after ceasing medication for 12 hours and the washout achieved in practice may have varied considerably from patient to patient. Both the PET and UPDRS measures in any case contain inherent variability. The lack of correlation between ^{18}F-dopa PET and UPDRS changes suggests that both measures should be used as independent markers of PD progression.

Assuming a linear relationship between decline in putamen ^{18}F-dopa uptake and disease duration, the preclinical window for PD has been estimated to be 6±3 years and clinical symptoms to arise after a 30% loss of terminal dopaminergic function.[56] In fact, loss of putamen ^{18}F-dopa storage appears to progress non-linearly since the earliest PD cases (clinical duration <2 years) had an annual rate of putamen Ki loss four times faster than those with more established disease. This suggests that the mean preclinical disease window is shorter than six years. These findings[56] fit well with the exponential relationship between nigral cell counts and pre-mortem clinical disease duration which suggests a mean preclinical disease period of approximately 4.6 years.[23]

SUMMARY

- Clinical assessment, although highly sensitive, cannot detect preclinical disease or reliably discriminate early PD, defined as brainstem Lewy body disease, from atypical variants such as MSA.

- To date, putative biochemical markers of PD have not proved sufficiently sensitive to be of value.

- Physiological and psychological approaches can provide sensitive markers of the presence of parkinsonism and may allow detection of preclinical disease but do not fully discriminate well between typical and atypical syndromes.

- Genetic markers for PD are becoming available. Mutations of the α synuclein gene have been reported.

- Currently, assessment of dopamine terminal function with PET and SPECT provides the most sensitive marker of PD and enables preclinical dopaminergic dysfunction to be detected in some at-risk relatives of patients with familial disease.

- Concomitant measurement of striatal metabolic function with PET, SPECT, or MRS can help discriminate atypical parkinsonian syndromes from PD with up to 80% specificity. These techniques have been used successfully to monitor PD progression.

REFERENCES

1. Jellinger K. The pathology of parkinsonism. In, Marsden CD, Fahn S, eds, Movement Disorders 2. London: Butterworths, 1987: 124–165.

2. Hughes AJ, Daniel SE, Kilford L, Lees AJ. The accuracy of the clinical diagnosis of Parkinson's disease: a clinicopathological study of 100 cases. J Neurol Neurosurg Psychiatr 1992; 55: 181–184.

3. Rajput AH, Rozdilsky B, Rajput A. Accuracy of clinical diagnosis in Parkinsonism - a prospective study. Can J Neurol Sci 1991; 18: 275–278.

4. Hughes AJ, Ben-Shlomo Y, Daniel SE, Lees AJ. What features improve the accuracy of clinical diagnosis in Parkinson's disease? A clinicopathological study. Neurol 1992; 42: 1142–1146.

5. Doty RL, Golbe LI, McKeown DA, Stern MB, Lehrach CM, Crawford D. Olfactory testing differentiates between progressive supranuclear palsy and idiopathic Parkinson's disease. Neurol 1993; 43: 962–965.

6. Schapira AHV, Cooper JM, Dexter D, Clark JB, Jenner P, Marsden CD. Mitochondrial complex I deficiency in Parkinson's disease. Ann Neurol 1989; 26: 17–18.

7. Parker WD, Boyson SJ, Parks KJ. Abnormalities of the electron transport chain in idiopathic Parkinson's disease. Ann Neurol 1989; 26: 719–723.

8. Williams A, Steventon G, Sturman S, Waring R. Xenobiotic enzyme profiles and Parkinson's disease. Neurol 1991; 41 (Suppl 2): 29–32.

9. Polymeropoulos MH, Lavedan C, Leroy E, et al. Mutation in the alpha-synuclein gene identified in families with Parkinson's disease. Science 1997; 276: 2045–2047.

10. Gasser T, Muller-Myhsok B, Wszolek ZK, et al. Genetic complexity and Parkinson's disease. Science 1997; 277: 388–389.

11. Bandmann O, Marsden CD, Wood NW. The genetics of Parkinson's disease. Mov Disord 1998; 13: 203–211.

12. Bandmann O, Vaughan J, Holmans P, Marsden CD, Wood NW. NAT2 slow acetylator genotype is associated with familial Parkinson's disease. Lancet 1997; 350: 1136–1139.

13. Benecke R, Rothwell JC, Dick JP, Day BL, Marsden CD. Disturbance of sequential movements in patients with Parkinson's disease. Brain 1987; 110: 361–379.

14. Watts RL, Mandir AS, Ahn KJ, Juncos JL, Zakers GO, Freeman A. Electrophysiologic analysis of early Parkinson's disease. Neurol 1991; 41 (Supp 2): 44–48.

15. Morris RG, Downes JJ, Sahakian BJ, Evenden JL, Heald A, Robbins TW. Planning and spatial working memory in Parkinson's disease. J Neurol Neurosurg Psychiatr 1988; 51: 757–766.

16. Owen AM, James M, Leigh PN, et al. Frontostriatal cognitive deficits at different stages of Parkinson's disease. Brain 1992; 115: 1727–1751.

17. Firnau G, Sood S, Chirakal R, Nahmias C, Garnett ES. Cerebral metabolism of 6-[18]fluoro-L-3,4-dihydroxyphenyl-alanine in the primate. J Neurochem 1987; 48: 1077–1082.

18. Nahmias C, Garnett ES, Firnau G, Lang A. Striatal dopamine distribution in Parkinsonian patients during life. J Neurol Sci 1985; 69: 23–230.

19. Leenders KL, Palmer A, Turton D, et al. DOPA uptake and dopamine receptor binding visualized in the human brain in vivo. In, Fahn S, Marsden CD, Jenner P, Teychenne P, eds, Recent developments in Parkinson's disease. New York: Raven Press, 1986: 103–113.

20. Brooks DJ, Ibañez V, Sawle GV, et al. Differing patterns of striatal ^{18}F-dopa uptake in Parkinson's disease, multiple system atrophy and progressive supranuclear palsy. Ann Neurol 1990; 28: 547–555.

21. Leenders KL, Palmer AJ, Quinn N, *et al.* Brain dopamine metabolism in patients with Parkinson's disease measured with positron emission tomography. J Neurol Neurosurg Psychiatr 1986; 49: 853–860.

22. Martin WRW, Stoessl AJ, Adam MJ, *et al.* Positron emission tomography in Parkinson's disease: Glucose and dopa metabolism. Adv Neurol 1986; 45: 95–98.

23. Fearnley JM, Lees AJ. Ageing and Parkinson's disease: Substantia nigra regional selectivity. Brain 1991; 114: 2283–2301.

24. Rinne JO, Rummukainen J, Lic M, Paljarvi L, Rinne UK. Dementia in Parkinson's disease is related to neuronal loss in the medial substantia nigra. Ann Neurol 1989; 26: 47–50.

25. Kish SJ, Shannak K, Hornykiewicz O. Uneven pattern of dopamine loss in the striatum of patients with idiopathic Parkinson's disease. N Engl J Med 1988; 318: 876–880.

26. Bernheimer H, Birkmayer W, Hornykiewicz O, Jellinger K, Seitelberger F. Brain dopamine and the syndromes of Parkinson and Huntington. Clinical, morphological, and neurochemical correlations. J Neurol Sci 1973; 20: 415–455.

27. Snow BJ, Tooyama I, McGeer EG, *et al.* Human positron emission tomographic [18F]fluorodopa studies correlate with dopamine cell counts and levels. Ann Neurol 1993; 34: 324–330.

28. Morrish PK, Sawle GV, Brooks DJ. Clinical and [18F]dopa PET findings in early Parkinson's disease. J Neurol Neurosurg Psychiatr 1995; 59: 597–600.

29. Rakshi JS, Uema T, Ito K, *et al.* Statistical parametric analysis of 18F-fluorodopa PET in early Parkinson's disease. Neurol 1996; 46 (Suppl): A452.

30. Piccini P, Morrish PK, Turjanski N, *et al.* Dopaminergic function in familial Parkinson's disease: A clinical and 18F-dopa PET study. Ann Neurol 1997; 41: 222–229.

31. Piccini P, Brooks DJ. The aetiology of Parkinson's disease: Contributions from 18F-dopa PET. Adv Neurol, in press.

32. Burn DJ, Mark MH, Playford ED, *et al.* Parkinson's disease in twins studied with 18F-dopa and positron emission tomography. Neurol 1992; 42: 1894–1900.

33. Quinn N. Multiple system atrophy - the nature of the beast. J Neurol Neurosurg Psychiatr 1989; 52: 78–89.

34. Fearnley JM, Lees AJ. Striatonigral degeneration: A clinicopathological study. Brain 1990; 113: 1823–1842.

35. Brooks DJ, Salmon EP, Mathias CJ, *et al.* The relationship between locomotor disability, autonomic dysfunction, and the integrity of the striatal dopaminergic system, in patients with multiple system atrophy, pure autonomic failure, and Parkinson's disease, studied with PET. Brain 1990; 113: 1539–1552.

36. Otsuka M, Ichiya Y, Hosokawa S, *et al.* Striatal blood flow, glucose metabolism, and 18F-dopa uptake: difference in Parkinson's disease and atypical parkinsonism. J Neurol Neurosurg Psychiatr 1991; 54: 898–904.

37. Burn DJ, Sawle GV, Brooks DJ. The differential diagnosis of Parkinson's disease, multiple system atrophy, and Steele-Richardson-Olszewski syndrome: Discriminant analysis of striatal 18F-dopa PET data. J Neurol Neurosurg Psychiatr 1994; 57: 278–284.

38. Shinotoh H, Inoue O, Hirayama K, *et al.* Dopamine D_1 receptors in Parkinson's disease and striatonigral degeneration: a positron emission tomography study. J Neurol Neurosurg Psychiatr 1993; 56: 467–472.

39. Brooks DJ, Ibanez V, Sawle GV, *et al.* Striatal D_2 receptor status in Parkinson's disease, striatonigral degeneration, and progressive supranuclear palsy, measured with 11C-raclopride and PET. Ann Neurol 1992; 31: 184–192.

40. Shinotoh H, Aotsuka A, Yonezawa H, *et al.* Striatal dopamine D_2 receptors in Parkinson's disease and striatonigral degeneration determined by positron emission tomography. In, Nagatsu T, *et al*, eds, Basic, Clinical, and Therapeutic Advances of Alzheimer's and Parkinson's

diseases. Vol 2. New York: Plenum Press, 1990: 107–110.

41. De Volder AG, Francard J, Laterre C, *et al.* Decreased glucose utilisation in the striatum and frontal lobe in probable striatonigral degeneration. Ann Neurol 1989; 26: 239–247.

42. Eidelberg D, Takikawa S, Moeller JR, *et al.* Striatal hypometabolism distinguishes striatonigral degeneration from Parkinson's disease. Ann Neurol 1993; 33: 518–527.

43. Davie CA, Wenning GK, Barker GJ, *et al.* Differentiation of multiple system atrophy from idiopathic Parkinson's disease using proton magnetic resonance spectroscopy. Ann Neurol 1995; 37: 204–210.

44. Leenders KL, Frackowiak RS, Lees AJ. Steele-Richardson-Olszewski syndrome. Brain energy metabolism, blood flow and fluorodopa uptake measured by positron emission tomography. Brain 1988; 111: 615–630.

45. Bhatt MH, Snow BJ, Martin WRW, Peppard R, Calne DB. Positron emission tomography in progressive supranuclear palsy. Arch Neurol 1991; 48: 389–391.

46. Baron JC, Maziere B, Loch C, *et al.* Loss of striatal [76Br] bromospiperone binding sites demonstrated by positron tomography in progressive supranuclear palsy. J Cereb Blood Flow Metabol 1986; 6: 131–136.

47. Wienhard K, Coenen HH, Pawlik G, *et al.* PET studies of dopamine receptor distribution using [18F] fluoroethyl-spiperone: findings in disorders related to the dopaminergic system. J Neural Transm 1990; 81: 195–213.

48. D'Antona R, Baron JC, Samson Y, *et al.* Subcortical dementia: frontal cortex hypometabolism detected by positron tomography in patients with progressive supranuclear palsy. Brain 1985; 108: 785–800.

49. Blin J, Baron JC, Dubois P, *et al.* Positron emission tomography study in progressive supranuclear palsy. Arch Neurol 1990; 47: 747–752.

50. Foster NL, Gilman S, Berent S, Morin EM, Brown MB, Koeppe RA. Cerebral hypometabolism in progressive supranuclear palsy studied with positron emission tomography. Ann Neurol 1988; 24: 399–406.

51. Goffinet AM, De Volder AG, Gillain C, *et al.* Positron tomography demonstrates frontal lobe hypometabolism in progressive supranuclear palsy. Ann Neurol 1989; 25: 131–139.

52. Otsuka M, Ichiya Y, Kuwabara Y, *et al.* Cerebral blood flow, oxygen and glucose metabolism with PET in progressive supranuclear palsy. Ann Nuc Med 1989; 3: 111–118.

53. Davie CA, Barker GJ, Machado C, Miller DH, Lees AJ. Proton magnetic resonance spectroscopy in Steele-Richardson-Olszewski syndrome. Mov Disord 1997; 12: 767–771.

54. Vingerhoets FJG, Snow BJ, Lee CS, Schulzer M, Mak E, Calne DB. Longitudinal fluorodopa positron emission tomographic studies of the evolution of idiopathic parkinsonism. Ann Neurol 1994; 36: 759–764.

55. Morrish PK, Sawle GV, Brooks DJ. An [18F]dopa PET and clinical study of the rate of progression in Parkinson's disease. Brain 1996; 119: 585–591.

56. Morrish PK, Rakshi JS, Sawle GV, Brooks DJ. Measuring the rate of progression and estimating the preclinical period of Parkinson's disease with [18F] dopa PET. J Neurol Neurosurg Psychiatr 1998; 64: 314–319.

DISCUSSION

Shoulson: Your data suggest that patients with PD with a duration of less than two years progressed at a rate of about 18% per annum. This contrasts with patients with a disease duration greater than two years where the progression was about 4% per annum. This suggests that there is a four-fold increase in the rate of progression in early PD. Is that correct?

Brooks: Those were the figures. One has to accept that there is a fair degree of variance of approximately 6 to 10% when PET scans are repeated in the same individual. There is a significant difference in the rate of progression between the early and later stages of the disease, but whether it is truly four-fold, I would hesitate to say. There is no doubt, however, that patients with disease duration less than two years are progressing faster than those in the later stages of the disease.

Shoulson: Was the interval between the first and second scan on average 18 months or at minimum 18 months?

Brooks: An average of 18 months.

Shoulson: So some patients might have had a shorter interval between scans and some longer?

Brooks: Yes.

Poewe: The imaging methods you have described are probably the best that are currently available for detection of preclinical disease. These studies of disease progression can be performed with both fluorodopa PET and SPECT. The SPECT method is more widely available and so may prove to be a better screening technique for defining at-risk populations, particularly in the elderly. You talked about some of the tests that could be used to detect at risk individuals such as motor tests, odor test, genetic markers and biochemical tests. What set of criteria could be used to define which populations should be screened with neuroimaging for at-risk disease? Also, should the relatives of PD patients be screened with neuroimaging?

Brooks: Without doubt, relatives of patients where two members have been affected in a kindred are clearly an at-risk group and could be considered for PET. Where only one member is affected, the situation is less clear. If β-CIT and similar techniques which are more widely available show similar kinds of results, this would be a very interesting cohort to examine with SPECT. A large survey in elderly patients is currently under way in Holland, where subjects with suspected bradykinesia have been screened with fluorodopa PET. I gather that, so far, all the subjects have actually had normal scans. This is clearly an impractical approach. I think it would be reasonable, resources

[45]

permitting, to screen subjects where there is already one affected member in a family. Unfortunately, I do not think any of the clinical tests or indices are as reliable as screening tests.

Koller: We are working on a paradigm with Dr. Erwin Montgomery, looking at indices such as sense of smell, neurobehavioral testing and physiologic measures of movement time to see if we can combine these into a formula that provides a sensitive and accurate screen for preclinical PD. It has the advantage of being relatively simple and cheap but we are not sure if it will work.

Melamed: With regard to the dopa decarboxylase imaging study you are doing, have you looked at this imaging technique in patients with very late-stage PD to see if there is any dopa decarboxylase left in the striatum? Are you looking at dopa decarboxylase present in surviving dopaminergic neurons or elsewhere, and what tracers are you using?

Brooks: We have looked at very end-stage patients and there is, as you might expect, a wide variation in the findings. Some have almost zero uptake of the tracer, while others still seem to have 20–30% retention in the striatum. As the tracer is being taken up and retained, one assumes that there is still dopa decarboxylase present in synaptic vesicles. We cannot, however, be certain exactly which neurons contain the decarboxylase that we are monitoring with this technique.

W. Tatton: Could you discuss the observation of increased striatal fluorodeoxyglucose uptake in PD?

Brooks: This is not fully understood. In the denervated striatum in which there is a loss of dopamine, you are in some ways taking the brake off the metabolism of striatal interneurons and the cortical input to the striatum. Glucose is a measure of synaptic activity, so it is primarily a measure of afferent input from the cortex and interneuronal function in the striatum. Why there is increased glucose activity in PD is still not fully understood. If you treat these patients with levodopa, it does not seem to alter glucose metabolism, even when they are in stages III and IV. David Eidelberg has shown that a pattern of increased striatal metabolism is maintained throughout the disease. This is in contrast to conditions in which there is striatal degeneration, where glucose metabolism is down. But I do not have a good explanation except that dopamine normally acts to inhibit activity and to put a brake on striatal metabolism in general. Therefore, when there is a loss of dopamine, there is a corresponding increase in striatal glucose metabolism.

W. Tatton: If I recall correctly, Professor Bédard in Quebec measured firing rates of striatal neurons in MPTP treated monkeys and showed that there was no increase in the activity of these neurons.

Brooks: That is correct, but those firing rates reflect the efferent output from the striatum rather than the afferent input. When we measure striatal glucose metabolism with PET, we are primarily providing information about interneuronal and afferent activity rather than efferent output.

W. Tatton: Also, you cannot distinguish between inhibitory and excitatory firing either?

Brooks: That is correct.

Aquilonius: Are there any firm indications of an increased rate of dopamine turnover in the remaining dopaminergic neurons or has this theory, which was based on animal experiments, been ruled out in humans? One would think that there should be an upregulation in firing and dopamine turnover in the remaining neurons to compensate for the dopamine deficiency in PD. If so, what happens to the influx rate of levodopa in these upregulated neurons? Does the animal model actually reflect the true situation in PD?

Brooks: In Uppsala there are some studies with ^{11}C-labeled dopa which suggest there may be a relative upregulation of dopa decarboxylase in long-standing PD, but strangely this upregulation is not seen with fluorodopa tracer studies. As far as the dopamine reuptake sites are concerned, the Yale group have shown in an animal model that β-CIT is not sensitive to levels of dopamine in the synaptic cleft and so does not provide a reflection of dopamine turnover. It simply provides information about terminal integrity.

Langston: The Yale group feel that β-CIT SPECT is comparable in sensitivity to FD-PET. Originally they showed a little overlap between PD patients and controls, but now, with more refined analyses, they see no overlap between these groups. This is good news because other techniques reveal considerable overlap between control and PD groups.

Olanow: The problem is not differentiating PD from normal controls but rather PD from the atypical parkinsonisms. Dr. Calne's group in Vancouver is now largely able to distinguish atypical parkinsonism from PD on fluorodopa PET based on the differential involvement of the caudate and putamen, with putamen being more involved in PD and both affected in parkinsonism. Are you doing that as well?

Brooks: Yes. We have about an 80% discrimination looking at caudate:putamen ratios.

Shoulson: Could you confirm the sample size in each group in terms of duration of illness? Also, what was the effect of age as a co-variant in terms of the duration of illness?

Brooks: Our pilot study had 32 PD patients, divided into two groups of 16. One group had a disease duration of less than 26 months and the other greater than 26 months. The approximate mean duration in the two sub-groups was one year and three years. The sample size was not large enough to have sufficient power to determine the effects of age. There were very few patients under the age of 50 in that cohort and to address that question we would need a sample going from 30 years of age right through to 70 years, with 8–10 subjects in each decade,. That would be a large study, and one that should be done, but is anyone yet in a position to do it?

Burke: For the present, we do not really know if this difference in rate of progression is a duration effect or an age effect, and that is an important issue to sort out.

Brooks: Although the age was common in the two sub-groups, we cannot extrapolate these results to a younger parkinsonian group.

Rascol: What is the correlation between neuroimaging and clinical evaluation in measuring the rate of progression of the disease?

Brooks: There is certainly a correlation. As the fluorodopa uptake drops, the UPDRS score correspondingly rises. It is not a close correlation in our hands, probably because treatment is a confounding variable. We did not have a sufficiently large population to do the sort of studies in which Drs. Lee and Calne showed a hyperbolic pattern of progression, so I could not comment on the actual shape of the progression curve in our group. It is interesting that back-extrapolation of the UPDRS data does not reveal a preclinical window, probably because the UPDRS is a non-linear scale.

Olanow: Transplant models may help in this regard. We have been able to count surviving dopamine neurons following transplantation in different regions of the striatum and correlate these numbers with fluorodopa uptake on PET scans. The correlation was extremely good (>0.9) and much greater than anticipated. In addition, both our group and the French group found a strong correlation (0.8) between fluorodopa uptake on PET and bradykinesia. Donald Calne's group also showed good correlation between striatal fluorodopa uptake and nigral cells in monkeys and between striatal fluorodopa uptake and bradykinesia in PD patients. I am therefore optimistic that PET will provide a good correlation of at least the bradykinesia component of UPDRS.

Brooks: Yes, that is our experience too.

Mizuno: I am interested in the asymmetry of the symptoms of PD patients. Your data also showed asymmetry on PET scans. Have you correlated the side of the initial symptoms with the handedness of the patient? I think the asymmetry may be related to the pathogenesis of neural cell death. If PD is a metabolic disease, one might expect symmetric manifestation of symptoms, but most of the patients show asymmetry in their symptoms. Do we have any idea why they have asymmetry in striatal fluorodopa uptake?

Brooks: I do not know why we see asymmetric PET scans or why the symptoms are frequently asymmetric. Whether this is a genetic or an environmental disorder, it is not at all clear why one set of dopamine fibers should be targeted ahead of the other. I have not correlated asymmetry with handedness, but nearly all our patients are right-handed.

Langston: We notice a degree of asymmetry in the MPTP monkeys as well, so it certainly does not rule out a systemic insult.

CHAPTER THREE

Alzheimer's disease and Parkinson's disease: distinct entities or extremes of a spectrum of neurodegeneration?

DANIEL P. PERL[1], C. WARREN OLANOW[2]
AND DONALD CALNE[3]

Departments of [1]Pathology and [2]Neurology, Mount Sinai Medical Center, New York, New York, USA, [3]Department of Neurology, University of British Columbia, Vancouver, British Columbia, Canada

There is increasing evidence that Parkinson's disease (PD) and Alzheimer's disease (AD) share many epidemiologic, clinical, neuropathologic, and etiopathogenic features. Both are age-related disorders in which approximately 5-10% of cases demonstrate an autosomal dominant pattern of inheritance. Each is characterized by the accumulation of cytoplasmic inclusions comprised of abnormally phosphorylated ubiquitinated cytoskeletal proteins. PD and AD show evidence of neuronal degeneration without overt inflammation that may occur *via* apoptosis, and evidence suggests that oxidative stress and excitotoxicity may contribute to the pathogenesis of cell death.

A degree of overlap has been considered to exist between PD and AD, occasionally making diagnosis difficult. Evidence now shows that this overlap is quite common, leading to the suggestion that neurodegeneration is a unified disease process with variable clinical expression.[1-5] This chapter reviews the evidence for both disorders occurring as a result of a common neurodegenerative process which affects vulnerable neurons in the substantia nigra and cerebral cortex to a varying degree based on the specific etiology and relative differences in neuronal vulnerability.

CLINICAL OVERLAP

Dementia in PD

The prevalence of dementia in PD is approximately 33%[6-8] but may be much higher, since the development of dementia is known to reduce survival in PD.[9] Problems in sampling and study design may also prevent accurate estimation of the true frequency of dementia in PD, as may the fact that physicians who care for PD patients do not perform formal tests of mental function routinely.

A community-based population study was designed to obtain a more complete picture of the prevalence of dementia in PD.[9] Here, a crude PD prevalence of 99.4 per 100,000 was found, ranging from 2.3 per 100,000 for those under 50 years of age to 1,145 per 100,000 for those over 80 years. Approximately 41.3% of PD patients suffered from dementia, and the prevalence increased from 12.4% in patients aged 50–59 years to 68.7% for those aged over 80 years. Importantly, the incidence of dementia in PD patients was 6–12 times greater than that in age-matched controls ($p<0.01$). Similar results were obtained in a case-control study[10] and in a hospital-based study of PD patients.[7]

To avoid problems associated with cross-sectional analyses, PD patients who were free of dementia, and age-matched controls, were studied prospectively at nine-month intervals.[11] Over 37 months, 10 (19%) PD patients, but no (0%) controls ($p<0.01$), developed a newly-diagnosed dementia meeting the restrictive DSMIII-R criteria. These patients were older, had a longer duration of PD, an older age at the time of onset, and a lower initial performance on the WAIS and MMSE. This 19% prevalence of dementia in PD patients followed for a relatively short time and diagnosed using such restrictive criteria would substantially underestimate the overall frequency and importance of dementia in PD.

Parkinsonism in AD

Clinical evidence of extrapyramidal dysfunction is detected in approximately one-third of AD patients,[12-16] characterized by rigidity and bradykinesia, with tremor occurring to a lesser degree.[17-20] These figures may also be an underestimate since they emanate from AD clinics which focus primarily on evaluating cognitive decline and usually lack expertise in assessing motor function.

As with dementia in PD, estimates of extrapyramidal involvement in AD are complicated by problems associated with study design and definition. In a prospective longitudinal study, the relative risk of developing extrapyramidal features was compared in 44 patients with mild AD and 58 age-matched controls.[21] AD patients with parkinsonian features at baseline were excluded from the study and only bradykinesia, cogwheel rigidity and resting tremor were evaluated, thus biasing the study towards underestimation of the true prevalence of extrapyramidal features in AD. Nevertheless, within the 66 months of follow-up, parkinsonian features developed in 36% of AD patients but in only 5% of controls (*p*<0.001). PD features could be detected at any stage of the dementing process. At autopsy, in addition to AD-related changes, nigral pathology consistent with PD was identified in 80% of these cases, suggesting that parkinsonism is a feature of the natural history of AD.

Neuropathologic Overlap

AD and PD are characterized pathologically by the progressive loss of specific neuronal populations and the accumulation of intraneuronal inclusions, on which morphologic criteria for diagnosis of PD and AD are based.[22–25] Even when these criteria are employed, the pathologic features of both PD and AD are encountered in the same individual in an exceptionally high number of cases.

Dementia in PD

In an evaluation of the clinical and pathological features of 36 individuals with 'autopsy-proven' PD,[26] 31% had severe dementia while 24% had mild cognitive impairment. Senile plaques and neurofibrillary tangles (NFTs) consistent with a pathologic diagnosis of AD were diffusely distributed throughout the cerebral cortex in 15 of these PD cases (42%). This was six times higher than the expected frequency of AD pathology in an aged-matched control population. In summary, 55% of patients with pathologically-confirmed PD had clinical features of dementia and 75% of these had AD pathology at post-mortem.

In a similar study, premorbid dementia was recorded in 19 of 34 (56%) PD cases, and at autopsy, senile plaques were found in 29 (85%) PD patients but in only 5 of 34 (15%) controls.[27] In the hippocampus of the PD patients, NFTs were present in 85%, granulovacuolar degeneration in 88% and cortical cell loss in 79%. In contrast, these AD-related features were detected in only 15–21% of controls. Only one of the pathologically-diagnosed PD cases did not have neuropathologic features of AD. In a prevalence study of AD pathology in 14 non-demented and 18 demented patients with 'pathologically-proven' PD, neocortical plaques and NFTs were present in 75% of the overall PD group and in 94% of those with dementia.[28] The frequency of AD findings was significantly greater in the PD cohort than in age-matched controls, and the pathological changes of AD were significantly greater in the demented PD patients than in non-demented PD patients. In contrast, there was no difference in the severity of the nigral changes seen in the two groups of PD patients. In another study, 44% of PD patients that came to autopsy had been demented during life,[25] of which 29% had findings of AD and 10% had cortical Lewy bodies consistent with a diagnosis of dementia with Lewy bodies (see below). The degree of cognitive impairment in PD patients correlated with the density of Lewy neurites in the CA2 field of the hippocampus.[29]

PD features in AD

There are numerous reports documenting a high prevalence of neuropathologic features of PD in the setting of AD. In 40 cases of 'autopsy-confirmed' AD, 20 (50%) had either clinical or pathologic features of PD, and 18 (45%) had neurodegenerative changes in the substantia nigra.[30] Eleven of 13 cases with extrapyramidal features had pathologic changes in the nigra consistent with a diagnosis of PD. In a study of the frequency of parkinsonian features in 20 cases of 'pathologically confirmed' AD, 11 (55%) had Lewy bodies and pathological features consistent with a diagnosis of PD.[31] Retrospective chart review revealed rigidity in 80% of these cases, bradykinesia in 33%, and masked facies in 50%. In a large series of AD patients selected because they met CERAD clinical and neuropathologic criteria for 'definite AD', 23% also had changes in the substantia nigra at post-mortem consistent with an 'additional' diagnosis of PD.[32]

Lewy bodies and NFTs

Neuropathologic criteria for the diagnosis of AD and PD have depended on the occurrence of cellular damage to particular neuronal populations, and specific cytoskeletal inclusions within the perikarya of remaining neurons which have traditionally been regarded as characteristic of each disorder. The diagnosis of AD is based on the presence of significant numbers of NFTs and senile plaques within limbic and neocortical structures,[22,23,33] and similarly, the presence of Lewy bodies in the substantia nigra has been a virtual requirement for the neuropathologic diagnosis of PD.[25,34] However, the concept that the NFT and the Lewy body are pathognomonic features of AD and PD does not hold true. Apart from the examples of overlap described above, these pathologic changes can be found in several other disorders, including post-encephalitic parkinsonism, dementia pugilistica, Pick's disease, progressive supranuclear palsy and long-term survival with subacute sclerosing panencephalitis.[35] In some cases, a clinical picture of typical levodopa-responsive PD has shown NFTs, but not Lewy bodies, confined to the substantia nigra at autopsy.[36] Lewy bodies are also encountered in Hallervorden-Spatz disease, infantile neuroaxonal dystrophy, and subacute sclerosing panencephalitis.[37]

TWO SYNDROMES SUPPORTING THE UNIFYING CONCEPT OF NEURODEGENERATION

Diffuse cortical Lewy body disease (dementia with Lewy bodies)

In 1961, Okazaki and coworkers[38] noted widespread Lewy bodies in the cerebral cortex in two elderly individuals with progressive dementia. With the advent of anti-ubiquitin immunohistochemistry, many more patients with progressive dementia have been identified who had extensive Lewy body formation in the cerebral cortex.[39] Generally, these cases also demonstrate Lewy bodies in the substantia nigra and the locus coeruleus and show AD-related changes in the hippocampus and cerebral cortex. The situation is confounded by the observation that these patients also frequently develop parkinsonian features and that virtually all PD cases have cortical Lewy bodies (D. Perl, unpublished observations.[24,25,40] A recent consensus conference proposed specific clinical and neuropathologic diagnostic criteria[41] for this condition which was entitled 'dementia with Lewy bodies' (DLB).

Most of the cases of DLB have been characterized in centers for research on dementia in the elderly and, as such, dementia is believed to be the initial and dominant feature which is then followed by development of parkinsonian features. However, a similar population of patients with extrapyramidal features followed by the development of dementia could well be generated from PD clinics. Indeed, 32 of 41 pathologically-established 'PD' cases examined in the UK[40] met the proposed criteria for DLB.[41] It thus remains unclear if DLB is a distinct disease entity, and how AD patients with extrapyramidal signs or PD patients with dementia differ from those with DLB, especially when the pathological features of AD, PD, and cortical Lewy bodies are all present within the same specimen.

Guam neurodegeneration

Another striking example of the overlap between parkinsonism and AD as well as amyotrophic lateral sclerosis (ALS), is the focus of neurodegeneration in Chamorro natives on the island of Guam. The coexistence of a cluster of ALS, parkinsonism, and dementia in a single population strongly suggests that clinical and pathological features of the major neurodegenerative disorders can result from a common etiologic process. The ALS form of neurodegeneration on Guam is clinically indistinguishable from western ALS.[42] Parkinsonism-dementia complex (PDC) was later described in the same population.[43] Bradykinesia is the most common parkinsonian feature, generally accompanied by speech and gait disturbance, impairment of fine motor movements, facial masking, and rigidity. Dementia is the presenting feature in approximately 30% of PDC cases and generally consists of memory deficits and disorientation.[44]

Patients with the ALS variant show changes in the spinal cord that are virtually identical to classical ALS cases seen elsewhere in the world. Patients with PDC have a loss of pigmented neurons in the substantia nigra as is seen in PD, but the remaining nigral neurons typically show NFT formation rather than Lewy bodies. Only 10% of cases have Lewy bodies, which occur in small numbers.[45,46] In both the ALS and PDC variants, NFTs are widespread and, while virtually identical to those encountered in classic AD,[47–50] are more numerous.[51–53] Granulovacuolar degeneration and cell loss in the basal forebrain are also seen in the Guam cases and are also more extensive than has been reported in AD.[54,55] Guamanian neurodegeneration may therefore represents an exaggerated form of aspects of AD-related pathology.[56]

Patients with the ALS or dementia variants frequently have pathologic involvement of the substantia nigra despite the absence of overt extrapyramidal dysfunction. In turn, cases of PDC frequently have anterior horn cell pathology in the absence of clinical features of amyotrophy.[44,46] Fluorodopa PET studies in Guam neurodegeneration demonstrate reduced striatal uptake even in clinically pure cases of ALS.[57] Similar observations have been made in cases with classic non-Guamanian ALS.[58] In fact, neuropathologic involvement of only the spinal cord, the extrapyramidal system, or the cerebral cortex is rarely seen in Guam neurodegeneration. These observations indicate that the neurodegenerative disorders of Guam, although originally described as separate entities, are probably a single condition in which amyotrophic, extrapyramidal, and dementing forms overlap extensively, both clinically and neuropathologically.

ETIOLOGY, PATHOGENESIS, AND MECHANISM OF CELL DEATH

Etiology

Genetic studies provide further evidence for shared vulnerabilities and common pathogenetic mechanisms. The majority of cases of PD and AD are sporadic, with 5-10% having an inheritance pattern indicative of autosomal dominant transmission. It is becoming apparent that AD and PD are likely to be associated with many different etiologies resulting from complex interactions between genetic determinants and the aging process and a variety of environmental factors. Mutations in the genes encoding for the amyloid precursor protein (APP) and α-synuclein have been identified in familial cases of AD and PD respectively.[59,60] Even in these genetically-based cases, overlap is evident. For example, one patient with familial AD related to a missense mutation at codon 717 of APP showed prominent Lewy body formation in the substantia nigra as well as in the cortex.[59] Recent information also links α-synuclein with both PD and AD. Linkage of PD to chromosome 4 in a large Italian family, the Contursi kindred, was recently reported.[61] Subsequently, a missense mutation· was discovered in the gene for α-synuclein.[60] The high correlation of this mutation with disease in the Contursi family and the lack of this gene defect in a large control population, suggested that the mutation was etiologic in nature. A fragment of the α-synuclein protein has been identified within the non-amyloid component [NAC] of senile plaques in AD.[62-64] This was subsequently found to be derived from the NAC precursor protein (NACP) which is homologous with α-synuclein.

Finally, the SOD-1 mutation discovered in patients with familial ALS[65] provides further support for overlap between different neurodegenerative conditions. Transgenic mice carrying the mutant SOD-1 gene have decreased numbers of nigral neurons and reduced striatal dopamine content,[66,67] and are sensitive to 1-methyl-4-phenyl-1,2,3,6-tetrahydropyridine (MPTP) and develop parkinsonism with doses that do not affect their wild type littermates.[67] Thus, a single gene mutation can induce different neurodegenerative phenotypes and the pattern is influenced by specific environmental agents.

[56]

Pathogenesis

While the precise mechanism of cell death in AD and PD is not known, oxidative stress has been implicated in both of these conditions.[68,69] Iron and aluminium, which promote oxidative stress, have been noted to accumulate within NFTs in AD, and in Lewy bodies and neuromelanin granules in SNc neurons of patients with PD.[70–73] Glutathione, a primary anti-oxidant in the brain, is reduced in PD[74] and upregulated in AD.[74,75] Levels of SOD are increased in both conditions.[76,77] These changes presumably reflect a compensatory response to oxidative stress, supporting the hypothesis that the brain is in a state of oxidant stress in both PD and AD. More recently, immunocytochemistry techniques have shown that 3-nitrotyrosine (3-NT) staining, a marker of nitric oxide (NO) formation, is increased in both NFTs in AD patients[78] and in the central core of Lewy bodies in PD patients.[79] NO can react with superoxide radical to form peroxynitrite which can nitrate tyrosine residues on proteins to form 3-NT. Increased levels of 3-NT in PD and AD are consistent with the possibility of a calcium-mediated activation of NO synthase activity with increased NO formation in both conditions.[80] These findings indicate that oxidative stress and NO-mediated damage contribute to the degenerative process in both AD and PD.

Cell death

There is evidence from *in situ* end-labeling [ISEL] studies that cell death occurs by apoptosis in both PD and AD.[81–90] Electron microscopy[82] and concurrent staining with dyes that mark chromatin condensation in individual neurons[84] have established that apoptosis has occurred. Moreover, a variety of toxins relevant to AD and PD, including the 25-35 fragment of β-amyloid protein, MPTP, 1-methyl-phenylpyridinium ion (MPP+), dopamine, levodopa, and excitotoxins can induce apoptosis of cultured neurons.[91]

Decreases in mitochondrial proton pumping and membrane potential, and opening of a mitochondrial permeability pore contribute to the cascade of events leading to apoptosis.[91–93] Impaired mitochondrial complex I and IV activity has been noted in PD and AD respectively,[94,95] and could lead to impaired proton pumping and a bioenergetic defect with consequent apoptosis. In the SOD-1 mutant mouse, neurodegeneration is prone to occur in cells containing phosphorylated neurofilament protein while cells containing calbindin are relatively resistant to the degenerative process.[96] Nerve cells that degenerate in PD and AD, as well as in ALS, contain phosphorylated neurofilament protein and there is evidence that calbindin-containing cells are relatively spared in both AD and PD.[97,98] Thus, motor cells in the cortex, SNc, and spinal cord that are rich in neurofilament and low in calbindin may be uniquely vulnerable to neurodegeneration induced by many different causes.

The unitary concept of neurodegeneration has profound implications for studies on AD and PD. Additionally, if AD and PD are part of a single disease process, then individual components of the neurodegenerative syndrome could serve as a biomarker to assess putative neuroprotection related to a particular intervention. The current classification of the neurodegenerative disorders is based on concepts developed almost 100 years ago, but many cases do not fit into these classic diagnostic compartments. It would be more reasonable to classify individual patients as having a 'neurodegenerative disorder' characterized by dementia or parkinsonism and morphologically by descriptive and quantitative measures of the distribution and extent of specific pathologic features. This approach would facilitate determination of which clinical features correlate with which pathologic lesions without the confines of a restrictive classification system. This review has compiled only some of the large amount of evidence available which demonstrates the overlap in AD and PD suggesting that these disorders are more closely linked than has been generally appreciated.

SUMMARY

- AD and PD are generally held to be separate and distinct disease entities. However, a considerable amount of evidence exists demonstrating that these disorders share common clinical and neuropathologic features and that overlap between the two conditions is extensive.

- A significant percentage of AD patients show extrapyramidal features, whereas many PD patients develop dementia. Similarly, many AD patients at autopsy show not only the neuropathologic features of that disorder but additionally demonstrate nigral pathology, including Lewy bodies. The vast majority of demented PD patients show widespread NFTs and senile plaques as well as Lewy body formation and nigral degeneration. The extent of such overlap is far greater than one would anticipate by chance alone.

- We argue that such overlap reflects a common pathogenic mechanism for the neurodegeneration encountered within specific vulnerable neuronal populations. Furthermore, we suggest that the current nosologic approach which attempts to separate AD from PD fails to properly deal with the issue of overlap and a new classification of the neurodegenerative disorders should be considered.

ACKNOWLEDGMENTS

Supported, in part, by grants AD-14382, AD-2210 and AD-5138 of the National Institutes of Health, and the National Parkinson Foundation.

REFERENCES

1. Calne DB, Eisen A. Parkinson's disease, motoneuron disease and Alzheimer's disease: Origins and interrelationship. Adv Neurol 1990; 53: 355–360.

2. Eisen A, Calne DB. Amyotrophic lateral sclerosis, Parkinson's disease and Alzheimer's disease: phylogenetic disorders of the human neocortex sharing many characteristics. Can J Neurol Sci 1992; 19S: 117–123.

3. Olanow CW. A radical hypothesis for neurodegeneration. Trends Neurosci 1993; 16: 439–444.

4. Olanow CW, Perl DP. Free radicals and neurodegeneration. Trends Neurosci 1994; 17: 193–194.

5. Uitti R, Berry K, Yasuhara O, et al. Neurodegenerative 'overlap' syndrome: clinical and pathological features of Parkinson's disease, motor neuron disease, and Alzheimer's disease. Park Rel Disord 1995; 1: 21–34.

6. Lieberman A, Dziatolowski M, Kupersmith, et al. Dementia in Parkinson's disease. Ann Neurol 1979: 6: 355–359.

7. Mayeux R, Chen J, Mirabello E, et al. An estimate of the incidence of dementia in idiopathic Parkinson's disease. Neurol 1990; 40: 1513–1517.

8. Aarsland D, Tandberg E, Larsen JP, Cummings JL. Frequency of dementia in Parkinson's disease. Arch Neurol 1996; 53: 538–542.

9. Mayeux R, Denaro J, Hemenegildo N, et al. A population–based investigation of Parkinson's disease with and without dementia. Arch Neurol 1992; 49: 492–497.

10. Rajput AH, Offord KP, Beard CM, Kurland LT. Epidemiology of parkinsonism: incidence, classification and mortality. Ann Neurol 1984; 16: 278–283.

11. Biggins A, Boyd JL, Harrop FM, et al. A controlled, longitudinal study of dementia in Parkinson's disease. Neurol 1991; 40: 566–571.

12. Chui HC, Teng EL, Henderson VW, Moy AC. Clinical subtypes of dementia of the Alzheimer type. Neurol 1985; 35: 1544–1550.

13. Mayeux R, Stern Y, Spanton S. Heterogeneity in dementia of the Alzheimer type: evidence of subgroups. Neurol 1985; 35: 453–461.

14. Molsa PK, Marttila RJ, Rinne UK. Extrapyramidal signs in Alzheimer's disease. Neurol 1984; 34: 1114–1116.

15. Pearce J. The extrapyramidal disorder of Alzheimer's disease. Eur Neurol 1974; 12: 94–103.

16. Sulkava R. Alzheimer's disease and senile dementia of Alzheimer's type: a comparative study. Acta Neurol Scand 1982; 65: 636–650.

17. Mayeux R, Stern Y. Intellectual dysfunction and dementia in Parkinson's disease. In, Mayeux R, Rosen WG, eds, The Dementias. New York: Raven Press, 1983: 2211–2227.

18. Mayeux R, Stern Y, Rosen J, Leventhal J. Depression, intellectual impairment, and Parkinson's disease. Neurol 1981; 31: 645–650.

19. Mortimer JA, Pirozzolo FJ, Hansch EC, Webster DD. Relationships of motor symptoms to intellectual deficits in Parkinson disease. Neurol 1982; 32: 133–137.

20. Zetusky WJ, Jankovic J, Pirozzolo FJ. The heterogeneity of Parkinson's disease: clinical and prognostic implications. Neurol 1985; 35: 522–526.

21. Morris JC, Drazner M, Fulling K, et al. Clinical and pathological aspects of parkinsonism in Alzheimer's disease. Arch Neurol 1989; 46: 651–657.

22. Khachaturian, ZS. Diagnosis of Alzheimer's disease. Arch Neurol 1985; 42: 1097–1105.

23. Mirra SS, Heyman A, McKeel D, *et al.* The Consortium to Establish a Registry for Alzheimer's Disease [CERAD]. Part II. Standardization of the neuropathologic assessment of Alzheimer's disease. Neurol 1991; 41: 479–486.

24. Hughes AJ, Ben–Shlomo Y, Daniel SE, Lees AJ. What features improve the accuracy of clinical diagnosis in Parkinson's disease: a clinicopathologic study. Neurol 1992; 42: 1142–1146.

25. Hughes AJ, Daniel SE, Kilford L, Lees AJ. Accuracy of clinical diagnosis of idiopathic Parkinson's disease: a clinico–pathological study of 100 cases. J Neurol Neurosurg Psychiat 1992; 55: 181–184.

26. Boller F, Mizutani T, Roessmann U, Gambetti P. Parkinson disease, dementia and Alzheimer disease: clinicopathological correlations. Ann Neurol 1980; 7: 329–335.

27. Hakim AM, Mathieson G. Dementia in Parkinson disease; A neuropathologic study. Neurol 1979; 29: 1209–1214.

28. Gaspar P, Gray F. Dementia in idiopathic Parkinson's disease: a neuropathological study of 32 cases. Acta Neuropathol 1984; 64: 43–52.

29. Churchyard A, Lees AJ. The relationship between dementia and direct involvement of the hippocampus and amygdala in Parkinson's disease. Neurol 1997; 49: 1570–1576.

30. Leverenz J, Sumi SM. Parkinson's disease in patients with Alzheimer's disease. Arch Neurol 1986; 43: 662–664.

31. Ditter SM, Mirra SS. Neuropathologic and clinical features of Parkinson's disease in Alzheimer's disease patients. Neurol 1987; 37: 754–760.

32. Hulette C, Mirra S, Wilkinson W, *et al.* The Consortium to Establish a Registry for Alzheimer's Disease [CERAD]. Part IX. A prospective cliniconeuropathologic study of Parkinson's features in Alzheimer's disease. Neurol 1995; 45: 1991–1995.

33. Hyman BT, Trojanowski JQ. Consensus recommendations for the postmortem diagnosis of Alzheimer's disease from the National Institute on Aging and the Regan Institute working group on diagnostic criteria for the neuropathological assessment of Alzheimer disease. J Neuropathol Exp Neurol 1997; 56: 1095–1097.

34. Oppenheimer DR, Esiri MM. Diseases of the basal ganglia, cerebellum and motor neurons. In, Adams JH, Duchen LW, eds, Greenfield's Neuropathology. New York: Oxford University Press, 1992: 988–1045.

35. Wisniewski K, Jervis GA, Moretz RC, Wisniewski HM. Alzheimer neurofibrillary tangles in diseases other than senile and presenile dementia. Ann Neurol 1979; 5: 288–294.

36. Rajput AH, Uitti RJ, Sudhakar S, Rozdilsky B. Parkinsonism and neurofibrillary tangle pathology in pigmented nuclei. Ann Neurol 1989; 25: 602–606.

37. Lowe J. Lewy Bodies. In, Calne DB, ed, Neurodegenerative Diseases. Philadelphia: W.B. Saunders, 1994: 51–69.

38. Okazaki H, Lipkin LE, Aronson SM. Diffuse intracytoplasmic ganglionic inclusions (Lewy type) associated with progressive dementia and quadriparesis in flexion. J Neuropathol Exp Neurol 1961; 20: 237–244.

39. Lowe J, Blanchard A, Morrell K, *et al.* Ubiquitin is a common factor in intermediate filament inclusion bodies of diverse type in man, including those of Parkinson's disease, Pick's disease, and Alzheimer's disease, as well as Rosenthal fibres in cerebellar astrocytomas, cytoplasmic bodies in muscle, and Mallory bodies in alcoholic liver disease. J Pathol 1988; 155: 9–15.

40. Quinn, NP. Dementia in Parkinson's disease. In, Wolters E, Scheltens P, eds, Mental Dysfunction in Parkinson's Disease. Amsterdam: Wrije Universiteit, 1993.

41. McKieth IG, Galasko D, Kosaka K, *et al.* Consensus guidelines for the clinical and pathologic diagnosis of dementia with Lewy bodies (DLB): Report of the

consortium on DLB international workshop. Neurol 1996; 47: 1113–1124.

42. Kurland LT, Mulder DW. Epidemiologic investigations of amyotrophic lateral sclerosis. 1. Preliminary report on geographic distribution, with special reference to the Mariana Islands, including clinical and pathologic observations. Neurol 1954; 4: 355–378.

43. Hirano A, Kurland LT, Krooth RS, Lessell S. Parkinsonism–dementia complex, an endemic disease on the island of Guam I. Clinical features. Brain 1961; 84: 642–661.

44. Elizan TS, Hirano A, Abrams BM, et al. Amyotrophic lateral sclerosis and parkinsonism–dementia complex of Guam. Neurological re–evaluation. Arch Neurol 1966; 14: 356–368.

45. Perl, DP. Amyotrophic lateral sclerosis and parkinsonism dementia complex of Guam. In, Markesbery W, ed, The Neuropathology of Dementing Disorders. London: E. Arnold, 1998: 268–292.

46. Rogers–Johnson P, Garruto RM, Yanagihara R, et al. Amyotrophic lateral sclerosis and parkinsonism–dementia on Guam: a 30–year evaluation of clinical and neuropathologic trends. Neurol 1986; 36: 7–13.

47. Hirano A. Progress in the pathology of motor neuron diseases. Prog Neuropathol 1973; 2: 181–215.

48. Shankar SK, Yanagihara R, Garruto RM, et al. Immunocytochemical characterization of neurofibrillary tangles in amyotrophic lateral sclerosis and parkinsonism–dementia of Guam. Ann Neurol 1989; 25: 146–151.

49. Buee–Scherer V, Buee L, Hof PR, et al. Neurofibrillary degeneration in amyotrophic lateral sclerosis/parkinsonism–dementia complex of Guam: immunochemical characterization of tau proteins. Am J Pathol 1995; 68: 924–932.

50. Mawal–Dewan M, Schmidt ML, Balin B, et al. Identification of phospho-rylation sites in PHF–tau from patients with Guam amyotrophic lateral sclerosis/parkinsonism–dementia complex. J Neuropathol Exp Neurol 1996; 55: 1051–1059.

51. Hirano A, Arumugasamy N, Zimmerman HM. Amyotrophic lateral sclerosis. A comparison of Guam and classical cases. Arch Neurol 1967; 16: 357–363.

52. Hof PR, Nimchinsky EA, Buee–Scherrer V, et al. Amyotrophic lateral sclerosis/-parkinsonism–dementia complex of Guam: quantitative neuropathology, immunohistochemical analysis of neuronal vulnerability, and comparison with related neurodegenerative disorders. Acta Neuropathol 1994; 88: 397–404.

53. Hof PR, Perl DP, Loerzel AJ, Morrison JH. Neurofibrillary tangle distribution in the cerebral cortex of parkinsonism–dementia cases from Guam: differences with Alzheimer's disease. Brain Res 1991; 564: 306–313.

54. Masullo C, Pocchiari M, Mariotti P, et al. The nucleus basalis of Meynert in parkinsonism–dementia of Guam: a morphometric study. Neuropathol Appl Neurobiol 1989; 15: 193–206.

55. Nakano I, Hirano A. Neuron loss in the nucleus basalis of Meynert in parkinsonism–dementia complex of Guam. Ann Neurol 1982; 13: 87–91.

56. Perl DP, Steele JC, Loerzel A, Kurland LT. Amyotrophic lateral sclerosis-parkinsonism dementia complex of Guam as a model of Alzheimer's disease. In, Iqbal K, McLachlan DRC, Winblad B, Wisniewski HM, eds, Alzheimer's Disease: Basic Mechanisms, Diagnosis and Therapeutic Strategies. Chichester: John Wiley, 1991: 375–381.

57. Snow BJ, Peppard RF, Guttman M, et al. Positron emission tomographic scanning demonstrates a presynaptic dopaminergic lesion in Lytico–Bodig. The amyotrophic lateral sclerosis-parkinsonism–dementia complex of Guam. Arch Neurol 1990; 47: 870–874.

58. Takahashi H, Snow BJ, Bhatt MH, Peppard R, Eisen A, Calne D. Evidence

for a dopaminergic deficit in sporadic amyotrophic lateral sclerosis on positron emission scanning. Lancet 1993; 342: 1016–1018.

59. Chartier–Harlin M–C, Crawford F, Houlden H, *et al.* Early–onset Alzheimer's disease caused by mutations at codon 717 of the beta–amyloid precursor protein gene. Nature 1991; 353: 844–846.

60. Polymeropoulos MH, Lavedan C, Leroy E, *et al.* Mutation in the alpha–synuclein gene identified in families with Parkinson's disease. Science 1997; 276: 2045–2047.

61. Polymeropoulos MH, Higgins JJ, Golbe LJ, *et al.* Mapping of a gene for Parkinson's disease to chromosome 4q21–q23. Science 1996; 274: 1197–1199.

62. Irizarry MC, Kim TW, McNamara M, *et al.* Characterization of the precursor protein of the non–A beta component of senile plaques [NACP] in the human central nervous system. J Neuropathol Exp Neurol 1996; 55: 889–895.

63. Iwai A, Masliah E, Yoshimoto M, *et al.* The precursor protein of non–A beta component of Alzheimer's disease is a presynaptic protein of the central nervous system. Neuron 1995; 14: 467–475.

64. Ueda K, Fukushima H, Masliah E, *et al.* Molecular cloning of cDNA encoding an unrecognized component of amyloid in Alzheimer's disease. Proc Natl Acad Sci USA 1993; 90: 11282–11286.

65. Rosen DR, Siddique T, Patterson D, *et al.* Mutations in Cu/Zn superoxide dismutase gene are associated with familial amyotrophic lateral sclerosis. Nature 1993; 362: 59–62.

66. Kostic V, Gurney ME, Deng HX, *et al.* Midbrain dopaminergic neuronal degeneration in a transgenic mouse model of familial amyotrophic lateral sclerosis. Ann Neurol 1997; 41: 497–504.

67. Good PF, Olanow CW, Hsu A, Gordon J. SOD–1 G86R transgenic mice have decreased striatal dopamine and a greater sensitivity to MPTP than control mice. Soc Neurosci Abs 1997; 23: 1877.

68. Markesbery WR. Oxidative stress hypothesis in Alzheimer's disease. Free Radic Biol Med 1997; 23: 134–137.

69. Jenner P, Olanow CW. Oxidative stress and the pathogenesis of Parkinson's disease. Neurol 1996; 47:161–170.

70. Good PF, Olanow CW, Perl DP. Neuromelanin–containing neurons of the substantia nigra accumulate iron and aluminium in Parkinson's disease: a LAMMA study. Brain Res 1992; 593: 343–346.

71. Good PF, Perl DP, Bierer LM, Schmeidler J. Selective accumulation of aluminum and iron in the neurofibrillary tangles of Alzheimer's disease: A laser microprobe [LAMMA] study. Ann Neurol 1992; 31: 286–292.

72. Hirsch EC, Brandel JP, Galle PJ, *et al.* Iron and aluminum increase in the substantia nigra of patients with Parkinson's disease: an X–ray microanalysis. J Neurochem 1991; 56: 446–451.

73. Jellinger K, Kienzl E, Rumpelmair G, *et al.* Iron–melanin complex in substantia nigra of parkinsonian brains: an x–ray microanalysis. J Neurochem 1992; 59: 1168–1171.

74. Sian J, Dexter DT, Lees AJ, *et al.* Alterations in glutathione levels in Parkinson's disease and other neuro-degenerative disorders affecting basal ganglia. Ann Neurol 1994; 36: 348–355.

75. Adams J, Klaidman L, Odunze I, *et al.* Alzheimer's and Parkinson's disease. Brain levels of glutathione, glutathione disulfide, and vitamin E. Mol Chem Neuropathol 1991; 14: 213–226.

76. Lovell MA, Ehmann D, Butler SM, Markesbery WR. Elevated thiobarbituric acid–reactive substances and antioxidant enzyme activity in the brain in Alzheimer's disease. Neurol 1995; 45: 1594–1601.

77. Saggu H, Cooksey J, Dexter DT, *et al.* A selective increase in particulate

superoxide dismutase activity in parkinsonian substantia nigra. J Neurochem 1989; 53: 692–697.

78. Good PF, Werner P, Hsu A, *et al.* Evidence of neuronal oxidative damage in Alzheimer's disease. Am J Pathol 1996; 149: 21–28.

79. Good PF, Hsu A, Perl DP, Olanow CW. Protein nitration in Parkinson's disease. J Neuropathol Exp Neurol, in press.

80. Beckman JS, Beckman TW, Chen J, *et al.* Apparent hydroxyl radical production by peroxynitrite: implications for endothelial injury from nitric oxide and superoxide. Proc Natl Acad Sci USA 1990; 87: 1620–1624.

81. Agid Y. Aging, disease and nerve cell death. Bull Acad Natl Med 1995; 179: 1193–203.

82. Anglade P, Vyas S, Javoy–Agid F, Herrero MT, Michel PP, *et al.* Apoptosis and autophagy in nigral neurons of patients with Parkinson's disease. Histol Histopath 1997; 12: 25–31.

83. Mochizuki H, Goto K, Mori H, Mizuno Y. Histochemical detection of apoptosis in Parkinson's disease. Neurol Sci 1996; 137: 120–123.

84. Tatton NA, Maclean–Fraser A, Tatton WG, Perl DP, Olanow CW, this volume.

85. Anderson AJ, Su JH, Cotman CW. DNA damage and apoptosis in Alzheimer's disease: colocalization with c–Jun immunoreactivity, relationship to brain area and the effect of postmortem delay. J. Neurosci. 1996; 16: 1710–1719.

86. Cotman CW, Whittemore ER, Watt JA, Anderson AJ, Loo DT. Possible role of apoptosis in Alzheimer's disease. Ann N Y Acad Sci 1994; 747: 36–49.

87. Cotman CW, Anderson AJ. A potential role for apoptosis in neurodegeneration and Alzheimer's disease. Mol Neurobiol 1995; 10: 19–45.

88. Dragunow M, Faull RL, Lawlor P, Beilharz EJ, Singleton K, Walker EB, Mee E. In situ evidence for DNA fragmentation in Huntington's disease striatum and Alzheimer's disease temporal lobes. Neuroreport 1995; 6: 1053–1057.

89. Lassmann H, Bancher C, Breitschopf H, Wegiel J, Bobinski M, Jellinger K, Wisniewski HM. Cell death in Alzheimer's disease evaluated by DNA fragmentation in situ. Acta Neuropathol Berl 1995; 89: 35–41.

90. Su JH, Anderson AJ, Cummings BJ, Cotman CW. Immunohistochemical evidence for apoptosis in Alzheimer's disease. Neuroreport 1994; 5:- 2529–2533.

91. Olanow CW, Jenner P, Tatton N, Tatton WG. Neurodegeneration in Parkinson's disease. In, Jankovic J, Tolosa E, eds, Parkinson's Disease and Movement Disorders, 3rd edition, in press.

92. Kroemer G, Petit P, Xamzami N, Vayssierre JL, Mignotte B. The biochemistry of programmed cell death. *FASEB* 1995; 9: 1277–1287.

93. Susin SA, Zamzami N, Kroemer G. The cell biology of apoptosis: evidence for the implication of mitochondria. Apoptosis 1996; 1: 231–242.

94. Schapira AHV, Cooper JM, Dexter DT, *et al.* Mitochondrial complex I deficiency in Parkinson's disease. J Neurochem 1990; 54: 823–827.

95. Simonian N, Hyman B. Functional alterations in Alzheimer's disease: Diminution of cytochrome oxidase in the hippocampal formation. J Neuropath Exp Neurol 1993; 52: 580–585.

96. Morrison BM, Gordon JW, Ripps ME, Morrison JH. Quantitative immuno-cytochemical analysis of the spinal cord in G86R superoxide dismutase transgenic mice: neurochemical correlates of selective vulnerability. J Comp Neurol 1996; 373: 619–631.

97. Morrison JH, Hof PR. Life and death of neurons in the aging brain. Science 1997; 278: 412–419.

98. Yamada T, McGeer PL, Baimbridge KG, McGeer EG. Relative sparing in Parkinson's disease of substantia nigra dopamine neurons containing calbindin–D_{28k}. Brain Res 1990; 526: 303–307.

DISCUSSION

Marsden: The non-specificity of the Lewy body is a well-known phenomenon. Approximately 10% of children with Hallervorden-Spatz disease and infantile neuroaxonal dystrophy have Lewy bodies in their substantia nigra. In addition, Lewy bodies are seen in a number of other neurodegenerative disorders including Alzheimer's disease and diffuse cortical Lewy body disease. It is obvious that the Lewy body is not specific for PD.

Perl: Interestingly, older patients with Hallervorden-Spatz disease have tangles.

Marsden: Absolutely. You have been referring to the overlap that can occur in which some patients have Lewy bodies in some cortical neurons along with neurofibrillary tangles in other cortical neurons. Have you ever seen this situation in the substantia nigra in which there are neurofibrillary tangles in some neurons and Lewy bodies in others?

Perl: Yes, but not in the same neuron.

Langston: To continue on a theme, you have to consider problems with sample bias. It is difficult to draw broad conclusions from this type of neuropathologic data. For example, much of our material comes from a large Alzheimer's disease center, which explains why we find the most common cause of Lewy bodies is Alzheimer's disease. It is hard to get an unbiased population for these type of studies.

Perl: I am fortunate to have not only an Alzheimer's center but also a Movement Disorder center at Mount Sinai. I have been able to see the same pathology in brains coming from the different centers and to see how differently they had been characterized clinically and nosologically. We do very few autopsies in the general community, but we have access to large numbers of patients from a nursing home population. While this is not an unbiased sample, people do enter the nursing home for a variety of reasons providing us with a wide range of samples. Another highly significant bias is that we see almost exclusively end-stage disease. We have very little information or insight into the early pathological phases of the disease and we desperately need to study this material. I suspect that many of the patients diagnosed as having incidental Lewy body disease cases might actually represent patients with early undiagnosed PD in the early stages of the illness. It is important that we study these cases in much greater detail.

Koller: There is an emerging concept of sick cells, which are dysfunctional or afunctional, but are still viable. Theoretically, through some intervention, these cells could be resuscitated. Can pathology shed some light on this concept?

Perl: Yes, I think so. We have counted neurons in serial sections of substantia nigra stained with antibodies for tyrosine hydroxylase (TH) as well as Nissl stains. To our surprise, substantial numbers of TH-negative neurons appear to be surviving in the nigra of these PD cases. I was surprised at the percentage of intact TH-negative neurons that appeared to be dopaminergic by morphologic criteria and I suspect that these may be the sick neurons to which you refer. It is these neurons that may be capable of being rescued and restored to a functional state.

W. Tatton: In our studies of experimental animals exposed to a variety of toxins, a significant number of neurons that meet morphological criteria for dopaminergic neurons, seem to turn their TH production on and off. TH production may be very cyclic in neurons and we do not know whether neurons that fail to stain for TH today might have stained for TH at a later time point. There is much we have to learn about the dynamics of TH staining in dopamine neurons.

Borden: Can you comment on the fact that you have seen ubiquitin associated with the Lewy bodies? Do you think this represents proteins that have not been degraded and could this be because the cells are too sick to undertake the normal protein degradation process?

Perl: I suspect not. A number of these inclusions are ubiquitinated and I think they have been cross-linked or stabilized and cannot be broken down further. There are more data on neurofibrillary tangles than on Lewy bodies, but biochemical studies suggest that in both cases they have been heavily cross-linked and cannot be broken down any further. The ubiquitin system is not capable of further degradation.

Olanow: The failure to break down or clear ubiquitinated proteins may be one of the factors leading to the cell death process. Alternatively, alterations in the ubiquitin process may itself be a contributory, if not initiating, event in cell death.

Langston: Were the TH-negative cells that you saw in your study melanized neurons?

Perl: Yes, some of them were melanized but were TH-negative. This was really remarkable.

Mizuno: We have seen an elderly lady with parkinsonism who had many tangles in nigral neurons but Lewy bodies in the cortex. We thought the patient had PSP or post-encephalitic parkinsonism although there was no history of encephalitis.

Perl: You need to publish this case.

Mizuno: When we look at the substantia nigra of a patient with PD, we see Lewy bodies in many neurons, but many neurons do not have Lewy bodies. Therefore, are Lewy bodies a factor leading to nigral neuronal death or do they represent nerve cells that have survived the parkinsonian process? With regard to the relationship between Alzheimer's disease and PD, although there are many similarities I believe these diseases are entirely different. The reason for this is that there are familial cases of Alzheimer's disease and PD in which a single gene mutation can cause either Alzheimer's disease or PD. In sick or aging neurons, the response to noxious stimuli may be similar, because there are only limited ways in which neurons can respond to a toxic stimulus. When we look at post-mortem brains, we are looking at the end result of many pathologic processes, so two patients with similar pathologies have not necessarily had the same or even a similar disease. Therefore, even diffuse Lewy body disease may be a different disease from idiopathic PD.

Perl: I think those are very relevant points. The answer to the nosologic questions will come when we understand more about the etiology, since this ultimately defines whether these diseases are separate entities. Pneumonia was pneumonia until we could identify the specific etiologies of the various types of pneumonia. There are undoubtedly specific genetic causes of some cases of Alzheimer's disease and PD. It is interesting that a patient with one of the APP mutations had extensive cortical Lewy bodies, indicating some overlap. There are, however, a vast majority of cases for which we have no explanation for the combination of pathologies, but I think they reflect shared mechanisms. The causes of Alzheimer's disease and PD are undoubtedly numerous but it is obvious that there is a great deal of clinical and pathologic overlap. If that is the case, then our approaches to investigation, intervention, and prevention need to take this into account. It may be a mistake to try and artificially keep these diseases separate.

Olanow: Studies in the SOD mutant mouse are very convincing in this regard. This is a mouse that carries the gene for familial amyotrophic lateral sclerosis (ALS). It develops a phenotype of ALS and dies within a very well-defined period of time. Yet when we study the substantia nigra of these rodents, we find that it is also abnormal. The animals have reduced numbers of nigral neurons, reduced striatal dopamine, and are extremely sensitive to toxins. This illustrates the fact that a gene for a specific disease may cause preferential degeneration of neurons in a specific region of the nervous system. But, the degenerative process induced by the gene mutation may be generic and cause vulnerability and perhaps subclinical degeneration in other locations as well. The specific etiology may determine which nerve cells preferentially degenerate, but the process itself may be capable of affecting multiple brain regions. The SOD model is extremely appealing in supporting the notion that there may be a generalized neurodegeneration that just happens to target a specific group of cells in a specific brain region.

Hirsch: We get our brains from a nursing home and our experience is that there is a difference in the distribution of the lesions in the substantia nigra in patients with PD and Alzheimer's disease. In Alzheimer's disease, there are pockets of neurons that degenerate in the substantia nigra with involvement of the ventral tegmental area. Is that also your experience? If this is the case, does it not mean that a sub-population of dopaminergic neurons are differentially vulnerable in PD and Alzheimer's disease, and would that not imply that different factors are involved in the pathogenesis of these diseases?

Perl: Our experience is not as extensive as yours. I do think there are factors which induce specific forms of neurodegeneration and other factors which protect against them. Obviously understanding these will be very important.

Marsden: To emphasize your view about the overlap between Alzheimer's disease and PD, you showed a list of the similarities between neurofibrillary tangles and Lewy bodies such as phosphorylated neurofilaments, nitrotyrosine residues, iron accumulation, and ubiquitination. Can you give me, from a pathologist's perspective, the differences between the two?

Perl: The neurofibrillary tangle has periodic filaments made of tau, the Lewy body does not. They both contain hyperphosphorylated neurofilaments but those in the neurofibrillary tangle are morphologically and chemically different.

Morrison: I think one dichotomy in neurodegenerative disorders associated with aging *versus* events associated with aging is that the latter do not require neuronal death to reveal a functional deficit. This meeting is concerned with neurodegeneration – how, why and where neurons die and how that can be related to a particular disease? There are many events in aging that we think may form the neurobiological basis for functional decline that do not require neuron death at all. These include serotonin and other receptor changes and possibly alterations in circuits. There are many things beside neuronal death that can lead to a functional deficit or compromise a neuronal system.

Melamed: Is there any correlation between the presence of a Lewy body within a neuron in the substantia nigra pars compacta and the presence or absence of TH immunoreactivity? This might indicate whether the presence of a Lewy body is a way in which the neuron protects itself against sickness and death.

Perl: In our hands these TH-negative neurons are primarily not Lewy body-positive neurons.

Hirsch: I agree. The TH-negative neurons which do contain neuromelanin, as far as we have seen, have never contained Lewy bodies. Nevertheless, they are located in the region in which the neuronal loss is the most severe in PD, so there is an association with the disease but we do not know the significance of it.

Perl: One of our problems is that we do not know when the Lewy body formation occurs in this process, whether its development is slow or rapid, or whether Lewy bodies are a transient event.

CHAPTER FOUR

Determinants of neuronal vulnerability in neurodegenerative diseases

BRETT M. MORRISON[1], PATRICK R. HOF[1,2,3],
AND JOHN H. MORRISON[1,2]

[1]Neurobiology of Aging Laboratories and Fishberg Research Center for
Neurobiology, Departments of [2]Geriatrics and Adult Development,
and [3]Ophthalmology, Mount Sinai School of Medicine,
New York, New York, USA

Neurons may be categorized according to regional and laminar location, connectivity, and neurochemical phenotype.[1] This approach is useful for understanding the determinants of selective vulnerability in neurodegenerative disorders. Alzheimer's disease (AD) and amyotrophic lateral sclerosis (ALS), which appear to be disparate disorders based on symptomatology and anatomic distribution of pathologic lesions, in fact share key attributes with respect to biochemical and cellular determinants of selective vulnerability. This chapter will focus on cell vulnerability in AD and ALS where we have performed most of our research. It is likely that the same principles will also prove to be true for Parkinson's disease (PD), where cell death has been found to occur preferentially within the substantia nigra pars compacta (SNc) and more specifically in ventral tier neurons that are relatively enriched in neurofilament and deficient in calbindin.

SELECTIVE VULNERABILITY IN AD

Distinct anatomic components of the hippocampus and neocortex show variable involvement in AD, with differential vulnerability to both cell death and neurofibrillary pathology.[1–16] The major cellular pathology in AD is the formation of neurofibrillary tangles (NFT), but not all neuron types are prone to NFT formation.[4,12,13,17] In the neocortex, NFT are preferentially associated with certain subgroups of pyramidal neurons.[13,18] Large pyramidal neurons in layers III and V are most affected, while smaller pyramidal neurons in layers II, VI, and in the upper part of layer III are moderately affected by NFT formation. In contrast, the small pyramidal cells and spiny stellate cells in layer IV are remarkably resistant in AD, as is the vast majority of inhibitory interneurons.[8] The vulnerability of neocortical neurons to NFT formation correlates with their morphology and connectivity, as all neurons at risk are large pyramidal cells that send long projections to other cortical regions and possibly to certain subcortical structures.

Vulnerable pyramidal neurons in AD
contain high levels of neurofilament protein

Neurofilament protein is a major component of the neuronal cytoskeleton which consists of three subunits – heavy, medium, and light – and has been shown to participate in NFT formation,[19–21] suggesting that neurons containing high levels of neurofilament may be particularly prone to NFT formation. In the primate cerebral cortex, the distribution of neurofilament-immunoreactive neurons closely matches that demonstrated for certain cortical efferent systems. Quantitative analyses in the monkey neocortex demonstrated that neurofilament-containing neurons constitute a subpopulation of corticocortically projecting neurons.[22–27] These neurofilament-enriched neurons are highly susceptible to NFT formation and cell death in certain regions of the neocortex and hippocampus in AD.[2–4,6,9,11] Furthermore, the densities of NFT and neurofilament-immunoreactive neurons are inversely related in AD, in that cortical layers with high NFT densities have severely reduced numbers of neurofilament-immunoreactive neurons.[3,4]

Analysis of NFT using thioflavine S stain or immunocytochemistry with antibodies to neurofilament and the microtubule-associated protein tau reveals progressive cellular alterations in vulnerable neuronal populations during normal aging. For example, layer II of the entorhinal cortex contains neurofilament-immunoreactive neurons that are also immunoreactive to tau protein and label with thioflavine S in the aging brain, suggesting the existence of transitional forms of NFT.[6] In patients with full cognitive abilities, rare NFT are seen in the frontal cortex but in AD, transitional forms of NFT are observed in the frontal cortex, and most NFT in the entorhinal cortex progress to an end-stage in which they are no longer immunoreactive to tau and neurofilament proteins, but are stained only with thioflavine S. A dynamic process may therefore govern the formation of NFT in certain neurofilament-containing neurons, the time course correlating with the development and progression of dementia.[6] High levels of neurofilament protein appear to be a prerequisite for NFT formation, since certain neurons which are prone to NFT formation in AD and do not normally express this protein in young adults, display increasing levels of immunoreactivity in elderly individuals.[9]

Possible role of glutamate receptors in neurodegeneration

Excitotoxicity may account for neurodegeneration in several neurologic disorders including brain ischemia, epilepsy, Huntington's disease, PD and ALS[28–42] *via* overactivity of glutamate receptors, including *N*-methyl-D-aspartate (NMDA), α-amino-3-hydroxy-5-methyl-4-isoxazole propionic acid (AMPA), and kainate receptors.[28,43] Overactivation results in an initial influx of Na^+, which causes cell swelling, and then Ca^{2+}, which appears to promote neurodegeneration.[31,44,45] Thus, analysis of the glutamate receptor profile of cortical neurons is key to correlating specific neurons and circuits with their potential vulnerability to degeneration through excitotoxicity. Such comprehensive analyses have been made possible through the development of subunit-specific glutamate receptor antibodies,[41,46] and permit construction of a neurochemical profile of putative vulnerability. For example, the density of AMPA-selective gluR1, 2, and 3 subunits is severely reduced in the neocortex and entorhinal cortex of demented cases, but increased in hippocampal regions that are relatively spared in AD, such as the dentate gyrus and CA2-3 fields.[47–51] Furthermore, glutamate toxicity has been linked to both neurodegeneration and cytoskeletal alterations similar to those underlying NFT formation.[52–55] Cultured neurons containing high levels of non-phosphorylated neurofilament protein are hypersensitive to AMPA/kainate receptor-mediated toxicity.[56,57] The regional, laminar and cellular distribution patterns of kainate receptor subunits in primate cortex correlate with the distribution of neuropathologic profiles in AD.[41,46,58] Specific splice variants of the NMDA R1 receptor subunit bind to the light subunit of the neurofilament protein, suggesting a crucial role of neurofilament in anchoring this class of glutamate receptor at the synaptic level,[59] a putative mechanism by which alteration in either glutamate receptors or neurofilament may influence each other.

Characteristic features of resistant neuronal subsets

Several classes of molecules have been observed in neurons resistant to the degenerative process of AD. Calcium-binding proteins, which provide intracellular calcium buffering and transport, and several regulatory enzymes, are useful markers for subsets of morphologically non-overlapping cortical interneurons that are generally resistant in AD and other neurodegenerative diseases.[8,60–65] The lack of significant levels of neurofilament protein and the rarity of NFT formation in these neurons may determine their resistance to degeneration.[65] Parvalbumin, calbindin, and calretinin are calcium-binding proteins that have been studied in the human neocortex and hippocampus. In the neocortex, these proteins subdivide the GABAergic interneurons into three major populations.[62]

Parvalbumin-immunoreactive interneurons display a well-preserved morphology even in severe cases of AD, and do not suffer a significant cell loss.[66–69] However, aberrant terminal sprouting of parvalbumin-immunoreactive terminals suggests an involvement in or reaction to the degenerative process. In contrast, parvalbumin-non-immunoreactive neurons are affected in the hippocampus and entorhinal cortex in AD, with significant loss and severe reduction of dendritic arborization in the CA1 field.[70]

Calretinin-immunoreactive neurons in prefrontal and inferior temporal cortices of control and AD cases have shown only marginal differences in laminar densities.[71,72] They also show some alterations in dendritic arbors in the absence of cell loss or association with NFT or senile plaques.[73] Hippocampal interneurons may be ultimately involved in AD, but only at late stages when there is severe loss of the projection neurons that constitute the local targets of these interneurons.

Calbindin-positive interneurons display some degree of differential vulnerability to degeneration. The main population in layers II and III is mildly vulnerable among AD cases,[67,74–76] while a smaller population in layers V and VI is affected only in AD cases displaying high NFT densities. This could reflect differential patterns of connectivity of calbindin-containing interneurons. Thus, calbindin-containing pyramidal cells could constitute a subset of the corticocortical projections that are vulnerable in AD, supported by the finding that neurofilament protein colocalizes with calbindin in a large number of neocortical pyramidal neurons.[77]

Consequently, while additional degenerative processes may also contribute to the symptomatology of AD, we propose that the degeneration of long corticocortical projections leads to a global neocortical isolation syndrome which may be the most devastating component of AD, and most directly related to dementia.

SELECTIVE VULNERABILITY IN ALS

ALS is a less common neurologic disease with an annual incidence rate of 1 in 100,000,[78] familial ALS accounting for approximately 5% of cases. The early symptoms of ALS are muscle atrophy, weakness, and fasciculations, and the disease progresses over an average of five years, leading to paralysis and premature death.[78,79] ALS is characterized by extensive loss of spinal, brainstem, and cortical motor neurons, corticospinal tract degeneration, somatic and axonal inclusions of aberrant neurofilament proteins, reactive astrocytosis, and atrophy of ventral roots in the spinal cord.[80–82] The linkage of mutations in the Cu^{2+}/Zn^{2+} superoxide dismutase (SOD-1) gene with the development of familial ALS revealed the first factor causally related to the disease, and permitted the development of transgenic mice expressing mutant forms of SOD-1 and an ALS phenotype.

The specificity of the neuron loss in ALS patients and SOD-1 transgenic mice is remarkable. In ALS patients, motor neurons in the spinal cord, brainstem, and motor cortex degenerate,[80–83] as do some interneurons within the spinal cord.[84,85] In contrast, neurons in the dorsal horn of the spinal cord, non-motor brainstem nuclei, and other regions of neocortex are not vulnerable. The pattern of vulnerability in SOD-1 transgenic mice is even more selective, neuron loss only being reported in the spinal cord and substantia nigra pars compacta.[86–93] Neuron loss in the substantia nigra is consistent with observations in ALS patients,[92,94] suggesting that dopamine neurons in the substantia nigra are susceptible to the same mechanisms of degeneration as motor neurons but to a lesser degree. Therefore, many of the conclusions about the vulnerability of motor neurons in ALS may also be applicable to dopaminergic neurons in PD.

To minimize the anatomical differences between mouse and human, we studied selective vulnerability of neurons in the spinal cord. Only half of all motor neurons and interneurons in the spinal cord have degenerated by endstage in G86R SOD-1 transgenic mice.[90,93] This raises the question of whether certain proteins found within motor neurons are specifically vulnerable or resistant to degeneration.

Alteration of SOD-1

SOD-1 is present in both neuronal and non-neuronal cells in the CNS,[95] and its main enzymatic function is clearance of superoxide radical. Approximately 50 mutations of the SOD-1 gene, mostly substitution of one amino acid, have been found in patients with familial ALS, and these account for approximately 20% of all familial ALS cases.[96] Many of the mutant forms of SOD-1 have shorter half-lives and reduced capacity for clearance of superoxide radical than the wild-type enzyme.[97–99] This does not, however, account for the motor system degeneration in patients with familial ALS, since transgenic mice expressing mutant SOD-1 develop symptoms and pathologies mimicking those found in ALS patients, without a reduction in clearance of superoxide radical.[86,88,89,91] Furthermore, SOD-1 knockout mice do not develop motor neuron degeneration despite the absence of SOD-1 enzymatic activity.[122] The mutant forms of SOD-1 may thus cause cell death by acquiring a toxic function that wild-type SOD-1 does not possess (the so-called 'gain of function' hypothesis). Ubiquitous expression of SOD-1 within virtually all neurons in the spinal cord suggests that SOD-1 does not, by itself, explain the selective vulnerability of motor neurons.[95]

Excitotoxicity

ALS patients appear to have altered metabolism and processing of glutamate,[101–104] which may be due to modification of glutamate transporters.[105–108] Neuronal degeneration following increased synaptic glutamate may depend upon binding or sequestering free intracellular calcium, and also the specific glutamate receptors present. Calcium-binding proteins are critical for buffering intracellular Ca^{2+} and may contribute to neuronal resistance to degeneration.[109,110] The number of calretinin-immunoreactive neurons was reduced by 40% in SOD-1 transgenic mice,[90] but the calbindin-immunoreactive neurons are spared. It is possible that calbindin protects neurons by buffering elevated intracellular calcium levels, secondary to an excitotoxic mechanism as discussed above.

Specific neurons in the spinal cord may be selectively vulnerable to excitotoxicity and degeneration via their unique combination of glutamate receptors. Recent studies have implicated AMPA and/or kainate receptors, but not NMDA receptors, in the excitotoxic mechanism of degeneration in ALS. Given the importance of Ca^{2+} flux in this mechanism, investigators have proposed that motor neurons are selectively vulnerable to excitotoxicity, due to a lack of gluR2 receptors. In spinal cord culture experiments, in response to kainate administration, *in vitro* motor neurons appear to be permeable to cobalt, a reflection of Ca^{2+} flux, and undergo degeneration.[57] In contrast, motor neurons *in situ* contain gluR2 mRNA.[111–116] We have shown that the presence or absence of gluR2 is not a determining factor of selective vulnerability.[117] The difference between *in vitro* and *in situ* results suggests that cell cultures may differ in important ways from neurons *in situ*.

Disruption of neurofilament

Accumulations of neurofilament are a hallmark of ALS pathology,[118–121] and transgenic mice with alterations in the gene encoding neurofilament develop motor neuron dysfunction and pathology.[122–124] Neurofilament is present within a vulnerable population of neurons (mean percentage loss of 51%) in the mutant SOD mouse. A subset of calretinin-immunoreactive interneurons and ChAT-immunoreactive motor neurons are also immunoreactive for neurofilament. In SOD-1 transgenic mice, the loss of both ChAT- and calretinin-immunoreactive neurons was accurately predicted by their degree of colocalization with non-phosphorylated neurofilament,[90] in contrast to calbindin-immunoreactive neurons. The presence of non-phosphorylated neurofilament in the cytoplasm of neurons is therefore a marker of vulnerability, just as calbindin is a marker of resistance. Neurofilament and intracellular calcium may contribute to the mechanism of degeneration in SOD-1 transgenic mice, and by extension, to ALS. This may also be true for cell vulnerability in PD, and studies already suggest that calbindin-containing neurons are spared in the SNc in PD.

SUMMARY

- AD and ALS differ in the regions of the nervous system affected and the resultant symptomatology, but they share key cellular and neurochemical determinants of vulnerability. In both cases, a subset of large projection neurons degenerates and is responsible for functional impairment.
- In both AD and ALS, the affected projection neurons contain high somatodendritic levels of neurofilament and, as degeneration progresses, develop characteristic neurofibrillary inclusions with the accumulation of neurofilament protein.
- Neurofilament appears to drive the vulnerability of spinal cord neurons in the SOD-1 transgenic mouse.

- Calbindin appears to play a protective role for motor neurons in ALS, SOD-1 transgenic mice, and AD.
- These data suggest that neurochemical correlates of cell vulnerability transcend brain region. Neurodegenerative disorders that differ fundamentally in their regional targets may in fact share important cellular and biochemical mechanisms of degeneration.
- It is likely that similar mechanisms and vulnerability factors will apply to PD where cell degeneration preferentially affects dopamine neurons in the ventral tier of the substantia nigra and calbindin-containing neurons are relatively spared.

ACKNOWLEDGMENTS

The authors thank Dr. Jon W. Gordon for providing the mice used in these experiments, and William G. M. Janssen for expert technical assistance. This work was supported by NIH grants AG06647 and AG05138, and the Amyotrophic Lateral Sclerosis Association.

REFERENCES

1. Morrison JH. Differential vulnerability, connectivity, and cell typology. Neurobiol Aging 1993; 14: 51–54.

2. Morrison JH, Lewis DA, Campbell MJ, *et al.* A monoclonal antibody to non–phosphorylated neurofilament protein marks the vulnerable cortical neurons in Alzheimer's disease. Brain Res 1987; 416: 331–336.

3. Hof PR, Morrison JH. Quantitative analysis of a vulnerable subset of pyramidal neurons in Alzheimer's disease: II. Primary and secondary visual cortex. J Comp Neurol 1990; 301: 55–64.

4. Hof PR, Cox K, Morrison JH. Quantitative analysis of a vulnerable subset of pyramidal neurons in Alzheimer's disease: I. Superior frontal and inferior temporal cortex. J Comp Neurol 1990; 301: 44–54.

5. West MJ, Gundersen HJG. Unbiased stereological estimation of the number of neurons in the human hippocampus. J Comp Neurol 1990; 296: 1–22.

6. Vickers JC, Delacourte A, Morrison JH. Progressive transformation of the cytoskeleton associated with normal aging and Alzheimer's disease. Brain Res 1992; 594: 273–278.

7. West MJ. Regionally specific loss of neurons in the aging human hippocampus. Neurobiol Aging 1993; 14: 287–293.

8. Hof PR, Morrison JH. The cellular basis of cortical disconnection in Alzheimer's disease and related dementing conditions. In, Terry R, Katzman R, Bick K, eds, Alzheimer's Disease. New York: Raven Press, 1994: 197–229.

9. Vickers JC, Riederer BM, Marugg RA, *et al.* Alterations in neurofilament protein immunoreactivity in human hippocampal neurons related to normal aging and Alzheimer's disease. Neurosci 1994; 62: 1–13.

10. West MJ, Coleman PD, Flood DG, Troncoso JC. Differences in the pattern of hippocampal neuronal loss in normal ageing and Alzheimer's disease. Lancet 1994; 344: 769–772.

11. Vickers JC, Chin D, Edwards AM, *et al.* Dystrophic neurite formation associated with age–related ß amyloid deposition in the neocortex: Clues to the genesis of neurofibrillary pathology. Exp Neurol 1996; 141: 1–11.

12. Gómez–Isla T, Price JL, McKeel Jr DW, *et al.* Profound loss of layer II entorhinal cortex neurons occurs in very mild Alzheimer's disease. J Neurosci 1996; 16: 4491–4500.

13. Gómez–Isla T, Hollister R, West H, *et al.* Neuronal loss correlates with but exceeds neurofibrillary tangles in Alzheimer's disease. Ann Neurol 1997; 41: 17–24.

14. Morrison JH, Hof PR. Life and death of neurons in the aging brain. Science 1997; 278: 412–419.

15. Simic G, Kostovic I, Winblad B, Bodganovic N. Volume and number of neurons of the human hippocampal formation in normal aging and Alzheimer's disease. J Comp Neurol 1997; 379: 482–494.

16. Vickers JC. A cellular mechanism for the neuronal changes underlying Alzheimer's disease. Neuroscience 1997; 78: 629–639.

17. Braak H, Braak E. Ratio of pyramidal cells versus non–pyramidal cells in the human frontal isocortex and changes in ratio with ageing and Alzheimer's disease. In, Swaab DF, Fliers E, Mirmiran M, Van Gool VA, Van Haaren F, eds, Aging of the brain and Alzheimer's disease. Amsterdam: Elsevier, 1986: 185–212.

18. Giannakopoulos P, Hof PR, Kövari E, *et al.* Distinct patterns of neuronal loss and Alzheimer's disease lesion distribution in

elderly individuals older than 90 years. J Neuropathol Exp Neurol 1996; 55: 1110–1120.

19. Ksiezak–Reding H, Dickson DW, Davies P, Yen SH. Recognition of tau epitopes by anti–neurofilament antibodies that bind to Alzheimer neurofibrillary tangles. Proc Natl Acad Sci USA 1987; 84: 3410–3414.

20. Zhang H, Sternberger NH, Rubinstein LJ, et al. Abnormal processing of multiple proteins in Alzheimer disease. Proc Natl Acad Sci USA 1989; 86: 8045–8049.

21. Trojanowski JQ, Schmidt ML, Shin R–W, et al. Altered tau and neuro-filament proteins in neurodegenerative diseases: diagnostic implications for Alzheimer's disease and Lewy body dementias. Brain Pathol 1993; 3: 45–54.

22. Hof PR, Nimchinsky EA, Morrison JH. Neurochemical phenotype of cortico-cortical connections in the Macaque monkey: Quantitative analysis of a subset of neurofilament protein–immunoreactive projection neurons in frontal, parietal, temporal, and cingulate cortices. J Comp Neurol 1995; 362: 109–133.

23. Campbell MJ, Hof PR, Morrison JH. A subpopulation of primate corticocortical neurons is distinguished by somatodendritic distribution of neurofilament protein. Brain Res 1991; 539: 133–136.

24. Hof PR, Ungerleider LG, Webster MJ, et al. Neurofilament protein is differentially distributed in subpopulations of corticocortical projection neurons in the macaque monkey visual pathways. J Comp Neurol 1996; 376: 112–127.

25. Hof PR, Nimchinsky EA, Ungerleider LG, Morrison JH. Morphologic and neurochemical characteristics of cortico-cortical projections: Emergence of circuit–specific features and relationships to degenerative changes in Alzheimer's disease. In, Hyman BT,

Duyckaerts C, Christen Y, eds, Connections, Cognition, and Alzheimer's Disease. Berlin: Springer, 1997: 59–82.

26. Hof PR, Ungerleider LG, Adams MM, et al. Callosally–projecting neurons in the macaque monkey V1/V2 border are enriched in nonphosphorylated neuro-filament protein. Vis Neurosci 1997; 14: 981–987.

27. Nimchinsky EA, Hof PR, Young WG, Morrison JH. Neurochemical, morpho-logic and laminar characterization of cortical projection neurons in the cingulate motor areas of the macaque monkey. J Comp Neurol 1996; 374: 136–160.

28. Choi DW, Koh J, Peters S. Pharmacology of glutamate neuro-toxicity in cortical cell culture: attenuation by NMDA antagonists. J Neurosci 1988; 8: 185–196.

29. Choi DW, Rothman SM. The role of glutamate neurotoxicity in hypoxic–ischemic neuronal death. Ann Rev Neurosci 1990; 13: 171–182.

30. Choi DW. Cerebral hypoxia: some new approaches and unanswered questions. J Neurosci 1990; 10: 2493–2501.

31. Meldrum B, Garthwaite J. Excitatory amino acid neurotoxicity and neuro-degenerative disease. Trends Pharmacol Sci 1990; 11: 379–387.

32. Olney JW. Excitotoxin–mediated neuron death in young and old age. In, Coleman P, Higgins G, Phelps C, eds, Molecular and cellular mechanisms of neuronal plasticity in normal aging and Alzheimer's disease. Amsterdam: Elsevier, 1990: 37–51.

33. Farooqui AA, Horrocks LA. Excitatory amino acid receptors, neural membrane phospholipid metabolism and neuro-logical disorders. Brain Res Rev 1991; 16: 171–191.

34. Meldrum B, Garthwaite J. Excitatory amino acid neurotoxicity and neuro-degenerative diseases. Trends Pharmacol Sci 1991; 11: 54–61.

35. Coyle JT, Puttfarcken P. Oxidative stress, glutamate, and neurodegenerative disorders. Science 1993; 262: 689–695.

36. Francis PT, Sims NR, Procter AW, Bowen DM. Cortical pyramidal neurone loss may cause glutamatergic hypoactivity and cognitive impairment in Alzheimer's disease: Investigative and therapeutic perspectives. J Neurochem 1993; 61: 1589–1594.

37. DeFelipe J, Huntley GW, del Río MR, *et al.* Microzonal decreases in the immunostaining for non–NMDA ionotropic excitatory amino acid receptor subunits GluR2/3 and GluR5/6/7 in the human epileptogenic neocortex. Brain Res 1994; 657: 150–158.

38. Ellison G. The *N*–methyl–D–aspartate antagonists phencyclidine, ketamine and dizocilpine as both behavioral and anatomical models of the dementias. Brain Res Rev 1995; 20: 250–267

39. Lipton SA, Rosenberg PA. Excitatory amino acids as a final common pathway for neurologic disorders. N Engl J Med 1995; 330: 613–622.

40. Blümcke I, Beck H, Scheffler B, *et al.* Altered distribution of a–amino–3–hydroxy–5–methyl–4–isoxazole propionate receptor subunit GluR2(4) and *N*–methyl–D–aspartate receptor subunit NMDAR1 in the hippocampus of patients with temporal lobe epilepsy. Acta Neuropathol 1996; 92: 576–587.

41. Morrison JH, Siegel SJ, Gazzaley AH, Huntley GW. Glutamate receptors: Emerging links between subunit proteins and specific excitatory circuits in primate hippocampus and neocortex. Neuroscientist 1996; 2: 272–283.

42. Ottersen OP, Laake JH, Reichelt W, *et al.* Ischemic disruption of glutamate homeostasis in brain: Quantitative immunocytochemical analyses. J Chem Neuroanat 1996; 12: 1–14.

43. Weiss JH, Choi DW. Slow non–NMDA receptor mediated neurotoxicity and amyotrophic lateral sclerosis. In, Rowland LP, ed, Amyotrophic lateral sclerosis and other motor neuron diseases. New York: Raven Press, 1991: 311–318.

44. Choi DW. Ionic dependence of glutamate neurotoxicity. J Neurosci 1987; 7: 369–379.

45. Tymianski M, Wallace MC, Spigelman I, *et al.* Cell–permeant Ca^{2+} chelators reduce early excitotoxic and ischemic neuronal injury in vitro and in vivo. Neuron 1993; 11: 221–235.

46. Huntley GW, Vickers JC, Morrison JH. Cellular and synaptic localization of NMDA and non–NMDA receptor subunits in neocortex: Organizational features related to cortical circuitry, function, and disease. Trends Neurosci 1994; 17: 536–543.

47. García–Ladona FJ, Palacios JM, Probst A, *et al.* Excitatory amino acid AMPA receptor mRNA localization in several regions of normal and neurological disease affected human brain. An in situ hybridization histochemistry study. Mol Brain Res 1994; 21: 75–84.

48. Greenamyre JT, Maragos WF. Neurotransmitter receptors in Alzheimer disease. Cerebrovasc Brain Metab Rev 1993; 5: 61–94.

49. Armstrong DM, Ikonomovic MD, Sheffield R, Wenthold RJ. AMPA–selective glutamate receptor subtype immunoreactivity in the entorhinal cortex of non–demented elderly and patients with Alzheimer's disease. Brain Res 1994; 639: 207–216.

50. Yasuda RP, Ikonomovic MD, Sheffield R, *et al.* Reduction of AMPA–selective glutamate receptor subunits in the entorhinal cortex of patients with Alzheimer's disease pathology: A biochemical study. Brain Res 1995; 678: 161–167.

51. Armstrong DM, Ikonomovic MD. AMPA–selective glutamate receptor subtype immunoreactivity in the hippocampal dentate gyrus of patients with Alzheimer's disease – Evidence for hippocampal plasticity. Mol Chem Neuropathol 1996; 28: 59–64.

52. De Boni U, Crapper McLachlan DR. Controlled induction of paired helical filaments of the Alzheimer type in cultured human neurons by glutamate and aspartate. J Neurol Sci 1985; 68: 105–118.

53. Sautière PE, Sindou P, Couratier P, et al. Tau antigenic changes induced by glutamate in rat primary culture model: A biochemical approach. Neurosci Lett 1992; 140: 206–210.

54. Mattson MP, Cheng B, Davis D, et al. β–amyloid peptides destabilize calcium homeostasis and render human cortical neurons vulnerable to excitotoxicity. J Neurosci 1992; 12: 376–389.

55. Yang Q, Wang S, Karlsson JE, et al. Phosphorylated and non–phosphorylated neurofilament proteins: Distribution in the rat hippocampus and early changes after kainic acid induced seizures. J Chem Neuroanat 1995; 9: 217–228.

56. Gottron F, Turetsky D, Choi D. SMI–32 antibody against non–phosphorylated neurofilaments identifies a subpopulation of cultured cortical neurons hypersensitive to kainate toxicity. Neurosci Lett 1995; 194: 1–4.

57. Carriedo SG, Yin HZ, Weiss JH. Motor neurons are selectively vulnerable to AMPA/kainate receptor–mediated injury in vitro. J Neurosci 1996; 16: 4069–4079.

58. Huntley GW, Vickers JC, Morrison JH. Quantitative localization of NMDAR1 receptor subunit immunoreactivity in inferotemporal and prefrontal association cortices of monkey and human. Brain Res 1997; 749: 245–262.

59. Ehlers MD, Fung ET, O'Brien RJ, Huganir RL. Splice variant–specific interaction of the NMDA receptor subunit NR1 with neuronal intermediate filaments. J Neurosci 1998; 18: 720–730.

60. Baimbridge KG, Celio MR, Rogers JH. Calcium–binding proteins in the nervous system. Trends Neurosci 1992; 15: 303–308.

61. Heizmann CW, Braun K. Changes in Ca^{2+}–binding proteins in human neurodegenerative disorders. Trends Neurosci 1992; 15: 259–264.

62. Andressen C, Blümcke I, Celio MR. Calcium–binding proteins: selective markers of nerve cells. Cell Tissue Res 1993; 271: 181–208.

63. Alexianu ME, Ho B–K, Mohamed AH, et al. The role of calcium–binding proteins in selective motoneuron vulnerability in amyotrophic lateral sclerosis. Ann Neurol 1994; 36: 846–858.

64. Iacopino AM, Quintero EM, Miller EK. Calbindin–D–28k: A potential neuroprotective protein. Neuro-degeneration 1994; 3: 1–20.

65. Sampson VL, Morrison JH, Vickers JC. The cellular basis for the relative resistance of parvalbumin and calretinin immunoreactive neocortical neurons to the pathology of Alzheimer's disease. Exp Neurol 1997; 154: 295–302.

66. Ferrer I, Soriano E, Tuñon T, et al. Parvalbumin immunoreactive neurons in normal human temporal neocortex and in patients with Alzheimer's disease. J Neurol Sci 1991; 106: 135–141.

67. Ferrer I, Tuñon T, Serrano MT, et al. Calbindin D–28k and parvalbumin immunoreactivity in the frontal cortex in patients with frontal lobe dementia of non–Alzheimer type associated with amyotrophic lateral sclerosis. J Neurol Neurosurg Psych 1993; 56: 257–261.

68. Hof PR, Cox K, Young WG, et al. Parvalbumin–immunoreactive neurons in the neocortex are resistant to degeneration in Alzheimer's disease. J Neuropathol Exp Neurol 1991; 50: 451–462.

69. Fonseca M, Soriano E, Ferrer I, et al. Chandelier cell axons identified by parvalbumin–immunoreactivity in the normal human temporal cortex and in Alzheimer's disease. Neuroscience 1993; 55: 1107–1116.

70. Chan–Palay V, Zetzsche T, Höchli M. Parvalbumin neurons in the hippo-

campus in senile dementia of the Alzheimer type, Parkinson's disease and multi–infarct dementia. Dementia 1991; 2: 297–313.

71. Hof PR, Nimchinsky EA, Celio MR, *et al*. Calretinin–immunoreactive neocortical interneurons are unaffected in Alzheimer's disease. Neurosci Lett 1993; 152: 145–149.

72. Fonseca M, Soriano E. Calretinin–immunoreactive neurons in the normal human temporal cortex and in Alzheimer's disease. Brain Res 1995; 691: 83–91.

73. Brion JP, Résibois A. A subset of calretinin–positive neurons are abnormal in Alzheimer's disease. Acta Neuropathol 1994; 88: 33–43.

74. Ichimiya Y, Emson PC, Mountjoy CQ, *et al*. Loss of calbindin–28k immunoreactive neurones from the cortex in Alzheimer–type dementia. Brain Res 1988; 475: 156–159.

75. Hof PR, Morrison JH. Neocortical neuronal subpopulations labeled by a monoclonal antibody to calbindin exhibit differential vulnerability in Alzheimer's disease. Exp Neurol 1991; 111: 293–301.

76. Nishiyama E, Ohwada J, Iwamoto N, Arai H. Selective loss of calbindin D28k–immunoreactive neurons in the cortical layer II in brains of Alzheimer's disease: A morphometric study. Neurosci Lett 1993; 163: 223–226.

77. Hayes TL, Lewis DA. Nonphosphorylated neurofilament protein and calbindin immunoreactivity in layer III pyramidal neurons of human neocortex. Cereb Cortex 1992; 2: 56–67.

78. Adams RD, Victor M, Ropper AH. Principles of Neurology. New York: McGraw–Hill, 1997.

79. Tandan R. Clinical features and differential diagnosis of classical motor neuron disease. In, Williams AC, ed, Motor neuron disease. London: Chapman and Hall, 1994: 3–28.

80. Hirano A, Kurland LT, Sayre GP. Familial amyotrophic lateral sclerosis. Arch Neurol 1967; 16: 232–243.

81. Hirano A. Cytopathology of amyotrophic lateral sclerosis. In, Rowland LP, ed, Amyotrophic lateral sclerosis and other motor neuron diseases. New York: Raven Press, 1991: 91–101.

82. Leigh PN, Swash M. Cytoskeletal pathology in motor neuron disease. In, Rowland LP, ed, Amyotrophic lateral sclerosis and other motor neuron diseases. New York: Raven Press, 1991: 115–124.

83. Schiffer D, Cordera S, Cavalla P, Migheli A. Reactive astrogliosis of the spinal cord in amyotrophic lateral sclerosis. J Neurol Sci 1996; 139 (Suppl.): S27–33.

84. Oyanagi K, Ikuta F, Horikawa Y. Evidence for sequential degeneration of the neurons in the intermediate zone of the spinal cord in amyotrophic lateral sclerosis: a topographic and quantitative investigation. Acta Neuropathol 1989; 77: 343–349.

85. Terao S, Sobue G, Hashizume Y, *et al*. Disease–specific patterns of neuronal loss in the spinal ventral horn in amyotrophic lateral sclerosis, multiple system atrophy and X–linked recessive bulbospinal neuronopathy, with special reference to the loss of small neurons in the intermediate zone. J Neurol 1994; 241: 196–203.

86. Gurney ME, Pu H, Chiu AY, *et al*. Motor neuron degeneration in mice that express a human Cu,Zn superoxide dismutase mutation. Science 1994; 264: 1772–1775.

87. Chiu AY, Zhai P, Dal Canto MC, *et al*. Age–dependent penetrance of disease in a transgenic mouse model of familial amyotrophic lateral sclerosis. Mol Cell Neurosci 1995; 6: 349–362.

88. Ripps ME, Huntley GW, Hof PR, *et al*. Transgenic mice expressing an altered murine superoxide dismutase gene provide an animal model of

amyotrophic lateral sclerosis. Proc Natl Acad Sci USA 1995; 92: 689–693.

89. Wong PC, Pardo CA, Borchelt DR, *et al.* An adverse property of a familial ALS–linked SOD-1 mutation causes motor neuron disease characterized by vacuolar degeneration of mitochondria. Neuron 1995; 14: 1105–1116.

90. Morrison BM, Gordon JW, Ripps ME, Morrison JH. Quantitative immuno-cytochemical analysis of the spinal cord in G86R superoxide dismutase trans-genic mice: neurochemical correlates of selective vulnerability. J Comp Neurol 1996; 373: 619–631.

91. Bruijn LI, Becher MW, Lee MK, *et al.* ALS–linked SOD-1 mutant G85R mediates damage to astrocytes and promotes rapidly progressive disease with SOD1–containing inclusions. Neuron 1997; 18: 327–338.

92. Kostic V, Gurney ME, Deng H–X, *et al.* Midbrain dopaminergic neuronal degeneration in a transgenic mouse model of familial amyotrophic lateral sclerosis. Ann Neurol 1997; 41: 497–504.

93. Morrison BM, Janssen WG, Gordon JW, Morrison JH. Time course of neuropathology in the spinal cord of G86R superoxide dismutase transgenic mice. J Comp Neurol 1998; 391: 64–77.

94. Wolf HK, Crain BJ, Siddique T. Degeneration of the substantia nigra in familial amyotrophic lateral sclerosis. Clin Neuropathol 1991; 6: 291–296.

95. Pardo CA, Xu Z, Borchelt DR, *et al.* Superoxide dismutase is an abundant component in cell bodies, dendrites, and axons of motor neurons and in a subset of other neurons. Proc Natl Acad Sci USA 1995; 92: 954–958.

96. Siddique T, Deng H–X. Genetics of amyotrophic lateral sclerosis. Hum Mol Genet 1996; 5: 1465–1470.

97. Borchelt DR, Lee MK, Slunt HS, *et al.* Superoxide dismutase 1 with mutations linked to familial amyotrophic lateral sclerosis possesses significant activity. Proc Natl Acad Sci USA 1994; 91: 8292–8296.

98. Tsuda T, Munthasser S, Fraser PE, *et al.* Analysis of the functional effects of a mutation in SOD1 associated with familial amyotrophic lateral sclerosis. Neuron 1994; 13: 727–736.

99. Fujii J, Myint T, Seo HG, *et al.* Characterization of wild–type and amyotrophic lateral sclerosis–related mutant Cu,Zn–superoxide dismutases overproduced in baculovirus–infected insect cells. J Neurochem 1995; 64: 1456–1461.

100. Reaume AG, Elliott JL, Hoffman EK, *et al.* Motor neurons in Cu/Zn superoxide dismutase–deficient mice develop normally but exhibit enhanced cell death after axonal injury. Nature Genet 1996; 13: 43–47.

101. Perry TL, Hansen S, Jones K. Brain glutamate deficiency in amyotrophic lateral sclerosis. Neurol 1987; 37: 1845–1848.

102. Plaitakis A, Caroscio JT. Abnormal glutamate metabolism in amyotrophic lateral sclerosis. Ann Neurol 1987; 22: 575–579.

103. Plaitakis A, Constantakakis E, Smith J. The neuroexcitotoxic amino acids glutamate and aspartate are altered in the spinal cord and brain in amyotrophic lateral sclerosis. Ann Neurol 1988; 24: 446–449.

104. Rothstein JD, Tsai G, Kuncl RW, *et al.* Abnormal excitatory amino acid metabolism in amyotrophic lateral sclerosis. Ann Neurol 1990; 28: 18–25.

105. Rothstein JD, Martin LJ, Kuncl RW. Decreased glutamate transport by the brain and spinal cord in amyotrophic lateral sclerosis. N Engl J Med 1992; 326: 1464–1468.

106. Rothstein JD, Van Kammen M, Levey AI, *et al.* Selective loss of glial glutamate transporter GLT–1 in amyotrophic lateral sclerosis. Ann Neurol 1995; 38: 73–84.

107. Rothstein JD, Jin L, Dykes–Hoberg M, Kuncl RW. Chronic inhibition of glutamate uptake produces a model of slow neurotoxicity. Proc Natl Acad Sci USA 1993; 90: 6591–6595.

108. Rothstein JD, Dykes–Hoberg M, Pardo CA, *et al.* Knockout of glutamate transporters reveals a major role for astroglial transport in excitotoxicity and clearance of glutamate. Neuron 1996; 16: 675–686.

109. Lledo P–M, Somasundaram B, Morton AJ, *et al.* Stable transfection of calbindin–D28k into the GH3 cell line alters calcium currents and intracellular calcium homeostasis. Neuron 1992; 9: 943–954.

110. Chard PS, Bleakman D, Christakos S, *et al.* Calcium buffering properties of calbindin D–28k and parvalbumin in rat sensory neurones. J Physiol 1993; 472: 341–357.

111. Sato K, Kiyama H, Tohyama M. The differential expression patterns of messenger RNAs encoding non–N–methyl–D–aspartate glutamate receptor subunits (GluR1–4) in the rat brain. Neuroscience 1993; 52: 515–539.

112. Tolle TR, Berthele A, Zieglgansberger W, *et al.* The differential expression of 16 NMDA and non–NMDA receptor subunits in the rat spinal cord and in periaqueductal gray. J Neurosci 1993; 13: 5009–5028.

113. Jakowec MW, Fox AJ, Martin LJ, Kalb RG. Quantitative and qualitative changes in AMPA receptor expression during spinal cord development. Neurosci 1995; 67: 893–907.

114. Jakowec MW, Yen L, Kalb RG. In situ hybridization analysis of AMPA receptor subunit gene expression in the developing rat spinal cord. Neurosci 1995; 67: 909–920.

115. Tolle TR, Berthele A, Zieglgansberger W, *et al.* Flip and flop variants of AMPA receptors in the rat lumbar spinal cord. Eur J Neurosci 1995; 7: 1414–1419.

116. Temkin R, Lowe D, Jensen P, *et al.* Expression of glutamate receptor subunits in alpha–motoneurons. Mol Brain Res 1997; 52: 38–45.

117. Morrison BM, Gordon JW, Janssen WG, Morrison JH. Distribution of the AMPA receptor subunit, GluR2, in the spinal cord of control and mutant superoxide dismutase transgenic mice. Soc Neurosci Abstr 1997; 23: 1914.

118. Manetto V, Sternberger NH, Perry G, *et al.* Phosphorylation of neurofilaments is altered in amyotrophic lateral sclerosis. J Neuropathol Exp Neurol 1988; 47: 642–653.

119. Munoz DG, Greene C, Perl DP, Selkoe DJ. Accumulation of phosphorylated neurofilaments in anterior horn motoneurons of amyotrophic lateral sclerosis patients. J Neuropathol Exper Neurol 1988; 47: 9–18.

120. Mizusawa H, Matsumoto S, Yen S–H, *et al.* Focal accumulation of phospho-rylated neurofilaments within anterior horn cell in familial amyotrophic lateral sclerosis. Acta Neuropathol 1989; 79: 37–43.

121. Troost D, Sillevis Smitt PAE, de Jong JMBV, Swaab DF. Neurofilament and glial alterations in the cerebral cortex in amyotrophic lateral sclerosis. Acta Neuropathol 1992; 84: 664–673.

122. Côté F, Collard J–F, Julien J–P. Progressive neuronopathy in transgenic mice expressing the human neuro-filament heavy gene: a mouse model of amyotrophic lateral sclerosis. Cell 1993; 73: 35–46.

123. Xu Z, Cork LC, Griffin JW, Cleveland DW. Increased expression of neuro-filament subunit NF–L produces morphological alterations that resemble the pathology of human motor neuron disease. Cell 1993; 73: 23–33.

124. Lee MK, Marszalek JR, Cleveland DW. A mutant neurofilament subunit causes massive, selective motor neuron death: implication for the pathogenesis of human motor neuron disease. Neuron 1994; 13: 975–988.

DISCUSSION

Langston: We have also seen, both in idiopathic PD and in the MPTP model, that calbindin bestows some protective effect and I wondered if you could speculate on the mechanism?

Morrison: The implication is that calbindin protects against high intracellular levels of free calcium, and if calbindin is missing then so too is this protective mechanism. Taking this a step further, one would think that the glutamate receptors that are particularly calcium-permeable should also correlate with cell vulnerability, but they do not. If we look at gluR2 which is the AMPA subunit that controls calcium permeability, one might suspect that gluR2 would be low in the motor neurons compared to interneurons because they are vulnerable to neurodegeneration, but it is not. One might also expect that GluR2 would have a distribution pattern in the cortex that correlates with areas of degeneration in Alzheimer's disease, but again it does not. I doubt that it has any pattern that correlates with sites of PD pathology in the nigra. So while calbindin shows very consistent correlations with resistance and implicates calcium in a significant way, it does not translate to other systems such as the glutamate receptors. We may have to look beyond calcium to get to the mechanistic answers.

Hirsch: I agree that in PD and in MPTP models, the neurons that survive express calbindin. The first question, then is as you have stated, is calcium really involved in the mechanism of nerve cell death? Have you seen any enzymes, which are known to be activated by calcium such as calpains or DNAses, upregulated in the SOD mutant model of neurodegeneration? If so, this could be another step towards the implication of calcium in nerve cell death.

Morrison: That is a great question and a great experiment. I think Dr. Lynch, in California, has looked at some of the calpains in the hippocampus in the context of Alzheimer's disease, but I am not quite sure what the answers have been. I do think you are absolutely right and that we need to look at the next steps down in the cascade.

Wood: The concept of a toxic gain-of-function is trendy and may be important for many dominant disorders. What I do not understand for the SOD mutation is how a toxic gain-of-function mutation applies in this disease when we see mutations throughout virtually all the exons and in many generic regions? I can understand it for the CAG repeat disorders. I am interested to know what could be going on with SOD-1 mutation.

Morrison: You raise another issue in terms of selective vulnerability. SOD-1 is widely distributed and if it leads to nitration of neurofilaments, why is this not occurring throughout the brain? There seem to be a lot of interacting molecular events which overwhelm the neuron. We also looked at a transgenic mouse into which the gene for human NFM was inserted into the genome. Thus, the mouse was expressing human NFM as well as mouse NFM. We found pathology in the cortex and brain stem with accumulation of neurofilaments in axons and Lewy body-like accumulation in the cortex. There were also tangle-like accumulations in the cortex, fitting well with what Dr. Perl presented, but nothing in the spinal cord as the transgene was not expressed in the spinal cord. How this relates to the regional pattern of degeneration in humans is unclear, but it could be that there are regional differences in genetic expression, and even if there is an SOD mutation we do not know whether it has the same penetrance in all regions and all cell types.

Melamed: With regard to calcium toxicity in ALS, I would like to add two pieces of information. Several years ago we felt that we could perhaps affect the progression rate of patients with ALS by giving them large amounts of nimodipine, a calcium channel antagonist that crosses the blood–brain barrier. So we performed a study and were disappointed to see that both placebo- and nimodipine-treated patients progressed in the same linear fashion and died without any features being affected by the treatment. That does not totally rule out the toxicity of calcium, but neither does it support it. On the other hand, there are some indications in patients with ALS that the calcium channel may be involved. We have found that purified immunoglobulins taken from patients with ALS, block calcium channels in pheochromocytoma cells quite dramatically. This could be an epiphenomenon that has nothing to do with the etiology, but it is interesting.

Morrison: Yes, that gives me an opportunity to mention a study by Dr. Appel involving transfection of the gene for calbindin. Following treatment with serum from ALS patients, neurons normally die, but if they were previously transfected with the calbindin gene, the cells were protected against the serum of the ALS patients. There is no question that calbindin can, in certain cases, be protective and can be linked to calcium influx, but the situation is complicated and involves more than just calcium binding.

Olanow: This is really a discussion of vulnerability factors and not specifically, etiology. It is hard to escape the idea that a deficiency of calbindin, which reduces calcium binding and results in increased levels of cytosolic free calcium, could be a contributory factor in these diseases. A striking fact is that in PD, AD and ALS, nerve cells that degenerate have low levels of calbindin. Dr. Appel has made the argument that motor cells may have reduced calcium buffering to enable them react to small fluxes in calcium. This might also explain why these nerve cells are vulnerable to the neurodegenerative diseases. The issue can be viewed in two ways. On the one hand, calbindin has been shown to protect against cell degeneration but on the other hand there may be very little calbindin in these cells to start with which makes them vulnerable to a variety of toxicities.

[84]

Morrison: I did show that in the spinal cord the motor neurons lack the known calcium binding proteins. In the cortex, the pyramidal cells for the most part also lack these calcium binding proteins. So it is a very good point. The lack of any mechanism may therefore be as important or more important than possessing it.

Shoulson: How model-dependent are these findings, since we know that the genetic models depend on the specific mutation? Secondly, you did not see any changes in neurofilament protein until the mice became sick. This may be a reflection of what you are not measuring. If you were to do the experiment are there measures you would now include in order to determine whether something is going on before the degenerative event occurs?

Morrison: Regarding the first question on models, we do have to be mindful of the variations between the different animal models. Firstly, there are strain issues. Certain strains have a natural resistance to calcium-mediated toxicity and others are highly vulnerable. Secondly, there is the question of where the transgene is being expressed. For instance, it appears that in the first neurofilament mouse we studied, if the human NFM gene had been expressed in the spinal cord we would have seen ALS pathology. With regard to the second question, we need to look more carefully at regulation. Let us take the example of gluR2 again since this is what we are working on. Is the presence of gluR2 in the normal condition or the absence of gluR2 in the normal condition enough to conclude that the AMPA receptors will be calcium permeable or not? We would like to see, at a higher resolution, if there are early changes in the glutamate receptor profiles of motor neurons on a synaptic level because this would never be reflected with our current level of resolution. To summarize, we should look at a higher levels of resolution and at regulation of these proteins, as opposed to simply their absence or presence in a given cell class.

Mizuno: We know that ocular muscles are spared in ALS and presumably have, in some way, a neuroprotective substance. It would be interesting to look at ocular motor neurons for the presence or absence of pathologic changes, and the presence or absence of calbindin in the SOD transgenic mice.

Morrison: We know that the facial motor nucleus has pathology in the SOD mutant mouse, and to look specifically at the ocular motor nuclei is an excellent idea. I should mention that in the SOD mouse there is little evidence of neocortical pathology, so in that sense it is a limited model of ALS. It is rather a model of lower motor neuron pathology, but we do see brain stem pathology, so I think we could use it to investigate your question.

Ogawa: We have reported the effect of immunosuppressants in inhibiting dopaminergic cell death. Until recently, many people believed that immunosuppressants bind to cyclosporin and NFK binding protein, and that this complex then binds to calcium to inhibit its movement. We have reported that the neuroprotectant effect of cyclosporin A may be different from its immunosuppressant effect. Dr. Snyder's group reported that immunophilins bind to a part of the cyclosporin receptor and have no immunosuppressive effect. These drugs can have strong neurotrophic and neuroprotective effects.

W. Tatton: The important question is what else changes with calbindin? We know calbindin is a low-capacity, high-affinity system that cannot handle calcium very well, and that most of the calcium comes out of the endoplasmic reticulum, not across the plasma membranes. The major buffer of calcium in cells is mitochondria. The agent BCL-2 has been shown to increase the capacity of mitochondria to buffer calcium while preserving the mitochondrial membrane potential and diminishing the risk of apoptosis. The mode of action of cyclosporin A is on the permeability transition pore of mitochondria. It maintains its closure and thereby increases the ability of the mitochondria to buffer calcium. Bongkregic acid, which does not share the immunophilin role has the same effect. It would be interesting to look at a whole range of other factors that affect calcium and might be involved with neuroprotection, together with calbindin-related factors. These could include calcium pumps and agents such as BCL-2 which control the ability of mitochondria to buffer calcium. These could be looked at as a package. One could also assess the transcriptional control of these agents. The broader question that you raise is if neuroprotection is based on calbindin.

Morrison: It is only recently that someone actually demonstrated that calbindin effectively buffers calcium in a cellular model. Until then, it seemed that calbindin would not buffer calcium very effectively, certainly not as well as mitochondria. We have gone back and looked for mitochondrial inclusions in our mice but did not see them, whereas they are the first reflection of pathology in some of the other SOD transgenics.

Brooks: We have followed a group of parkinsonian patients who had been transplanted on one side but not the other and who were on cyclosporin A throughout their first year of follow-up. The untransplanted side progressed as fast, if not faster than what we see in sporadic PD patients, so there was no evidence in that group that cyclosporin A was protecting them.

Schapira: We have looked at the effect of cyclosporin A on cultured cells and it can, in fact, protect against apoptosis induced by agents such as MPP+. This is, however, very concentration-dependent. The lowest concentrations of cyclosporin A protect while higher concentrations actually promote apoptosis. It is the N-valine part of cyclosporin which is the non-immunosuppressant part that protects. Consequently, we have an agent that is protective at very low concentrations without immunosuppressant properties.

Olanow: The real problem for clinicians in using these agents is not knowing what all of their effects might be, particularly in a clinical situation. Moreover, the effects are often dose-dependent and we do not know what concentration is present in specific cellular and sub-cellular regions. An example is cyclosporin. In our double-blind fetal transplant study, we used cyclosporin A in both our transplant and control patients because we did not know what effects it might have in PD. Since we started the study, it has become evident that cyclosporin has the capacity to promote or block apoptosis. We have also shown that it can induce and enhance dopaminergic behavioral effects. These factors must be considered in designing trials to test hypotheses in patients with these neurodegenerative disorders.

Etiology

Epidemiology versus genetics in Parkinson's disease: progress in resolving an age-old debate

J. WILLIAM LANGSTON

The Parkinson's Institute, Sunnyvale, California, USA

The debate over whether Parkinson's disease (PD) is caused by environmental agents, hereditary factors, or a combination of both, is a spirited controversy. James Parkinson suggested in 1817 that shock and fright might precipitate the disease,[1] but later in the century, Charcot argued that PD was inherited because many of his patients had positive family histories.[2]

Throughout the 20th century, opinion as to the cause of PD has swung to and fro.[2-6] The pendulum swung towards environmental causes in the mid 1980s, largely precipitated by an outbreak of parkinsonism in northern California due the production of a batch of tainted heroin.[7] A contaminant, 1-methyl-4-phenyl-1,2,3,6-tetrahydropyridine (MPTP) was found to be the offending agent. The fact that a very simple pyridine moiety could cause virtually all of the signs and symptoms of PD raised the tantalizing possibility the idiopathic disease might be due to a similar agent in the environment. The same year, a twin study indicated that PD did not appear to be an inherited disorder.[8] The power of these two observations triggered intensive investigations on the possible environmental origins of the disease.[9] However, further findings, including the identification of a large kindred with an autosomal dominantly inherited form of parkinsonism, again pointed to the possibility that parkinsonism may be inherited.[10,11]

IS PD INHERITED?

The identification of a large kindred of familial parkinsonism of Italian origin, the Contursi kindred,[12] re-kindled interest in the genetics of PD. This was followed by the localization of the gene responsible for parkinsonism in this family to chromosome 4q21–q23[13] and the mutation was identified in the gene encoding for α-synuclein.[14] This was a single missense mutation of G[209]A at exon 4. Parkinsonism in the Contursi kindred tends to develop at a younger age of onset. DNA from blood of 100 subjects with PD with younger onset (before age 51) was examined by PCR, but failed to reveal a single patient with the G[209]A missense mutation.[15,16] This suggests that the mutation in the α-synuclein gene is a rare cause of PD and is not the basis of typical PD. Brain tissue from 24 patients with clinically diagnosed PD during life was obtained from the Parkinson's Institute's tissue bank, and RT-PCR again showed no mutations in the entire gene coding region.[17] However, based on at least two pathologically studied patients from the Contursi kindred, the α-synuclein mutation is capable of inducing the two neuropathological hallmarks of PD – striking loss of nigral neurons, and the presence, albeit in small numbers, of classic Lewy bodies. Ubiquitin-positive neurites in the temporal cortex and in the hypothalamus have also been observed. This neuropathology had striking similarity to another interesting family with apparently dominantly inherited PD, the Spellman-Muenter kindred, [18,19] but this family is reported not to have the G[209]A missense mutation of the α-synuclein gene.[20]

If an abnormality in α-synuclein is etiologically important in the Contursi kindred, it represents an extraordinary model for PD. While mutation of the α-synuclein gene as a cause of typical sporadic PD appears to be ruled out, many other genes remain unexamined. To determine just how large a role heredity plays, we examined the NRC-NRC Twin Registry of World War II veterans.[21] Approximately 31,000 twins served in WW II, and this cohort has been followed since the early 1950s because of their potential value for medical research. By 1992, there were approximately 20,000 surviving twins, of whom 193 were diagnosed with PD at a mean age of 64 years.[22] The key issue is whether or not the concordance between monozygotic and dizygotic twins is the same or different. If the same, this provides strong evidence against an hereditary component in the disease. In this study, the risk ratio of concordance in monozygotic twins compared to dizygotic twins was 1.39 overall, a figure which was not statistically significant (hereditability 0.176). When we restricted analysis to twins in whom the disease began over the age of 50 years, the risk ratio was 1.02, indicating the two groups were virtually identical (hereditability 0.0096). Thus, based on this twin study, typical sporadic PD which generally occurs over the age of 50 years does not appear to be an inherited disease. However, in twins under the age of 50, all four monozygotic twin pairs were concordant for the disease, whereas only two of the 12 dizygotic twin pairs were concordant (risk ratio 6.00, hereditability approaching 1.0). Thus, there seems to be a higher familiar incidence in young onset cases, and a distinguishing feature of the Contursi kindred is the younger age of onset compared to that seen in typical PD. The twins in the registry were all born between 1917 and 1927. Since the average age of onset between concordant twins was approximately 10 years, there could be a 'ceiling effect' so this cohort should be followed for at least another five to 10 years to maximize the possibility of diagnosing all the affected co-twins. A conclusion from this study is that the best populations to study for gene identification may be those with a strong family history and young onset disease, rather than sib-pair analysis in older patients with apparently sporadic disease.

ENVIRONMENTAL FACTORS IN PD

MPTP is capable of inducing virtually all of the motor features of PD in human and non-human primates,[23] and a number of MPTP analogues cause similar damage to the nigrostriatal system.[24] Perhaps the most serious hurdle to any epidemiological investigation of living populations of patients with suspected PD is the absence of a diagnostic test or biomarker. Routine clinical diagnosis may be no more than 75% accurate,[25] so almost any study on parkinsonian patients will contain some individuals without the disease. Another factor is the long preclinical phase which can be enormously confounding. Because PD is a late-life disorder, mortality represents another barrier which prevents ascertainment of all cases. Thus if the preclinical period is long, exposure may be years before the disease begins and patients may die before they become symptomatic, thus confounding case control studies.

Identification of risk factors can assist the search for environmental causes. To date, the only unequivocally accepted risk factor for PD is increasing age. Population-based studies indicate that disease prevalence increases at least through the ninth decade of life.[27,28] Striatal dopamine declines with normal aging,[29] but the cause is not known, and may not be associated with cell loss in the substantia nigra, the cardinal neuropathological feature in PD. The effects of MPTP in experimental models of parkinsonism appear to be age-dependent in a manner similar to PD.[30]

Risk factors can be exogenous and endogenous. Working in a poorly ventilated manganese mine would be an exogenous risk factor for developing manganese-induced parkinsonism. Endogenous factors are more likely to be genetically determined. The body has an elaborate metabolic defense system to deal with exposure to unwanted and/or toxic compounds in the environment. If one or more of these systems carried a genetic mutation leading to defective enzyme production, affected individuals might be more susceptible to injury if exposed to an environmental toxin. Some groups have reported an association between PD and mutant alleles in the CPY2D6 gene,[31-36] a member of the cytochrome P450 superfamily of enzymes, which is a major detoxification system. However, the polymorphisms have proved to be relatively weak risk factors, increasing the risk for PD by only 2–5-fold.[37]

Abnormalities in both the activation and conjugation phases of the detoxification process might leave little room for compensation,[38] thereby greatly enhancing risk for the disease. Patients with mutant alleles in the Phase I enzyme CYP2D6 and the Phase II enzyme GSTM1[39] were examined, and those who were homozygous for the mutant allele of CYP2D6 and also carried the null allele for GSTM1 had a 10–14-fold increased risk for PD.[38, 39] This approach represents another potential avenue of research into the cause of the disease.

Factors emerging from epidemiological studies include rural living, farming, herbicide and pesticide exposure, and well-water consumption,[40] which could be surrogates for various chemical exposures. There also seems to be a north/south gradient[40] suggesting that factors in northern climates predispose to the disease, favoring an environmental etiology. However, most of these studies measured disease prevalence rather than incidence. Prevalence is the total number of cases in a population and is not a good marker for true occurrence. Incident cases provide a better measure, but these require follow-up examinations over time, so are expensive and time-consuming. This may explain why epidemiologic studies have pointed to very few specific compounds in the environment. Only two suspected agents have been identified using this approach. A case-control study from Germany identified organochlorine pesticides as possible offending agents[41] and dieldrin was found in six of 20 brains from parkinsonian patients compared to none of 14 controls.[42] A Canadian study pinpointed dithiocarbamates[43] as possibly being associated with PD. These agents enhance the toxicity of MPTP[44] and DDC enhances the effects of methamphetamine,[45] perhaps the only other relatively pure dopaminergic neurotoxicant.

Another condition that suggests an environmental cause is the amyotrophic lateral sclerosis/parkinsonism-dementia complex (ALS/PDC) in the western Pacific.[46] On Guam, the ALS component of the complex appears to be disappearing,[47,48] and the parkinsonism/dementia component seems to be occurring in older individuals. This change may relate to westernization of the diet. The cycad nut, which contains one or more potentially toxic compounds, was used as an alternative food source during WW II. While a specific compound in cycad has yet to be convincingly identified as an inducer of neurodegeneration, individuals have developed the disorder more than 30 years after leaving the island.[49] While the parkinsonism is clearly different from idiopathic PD, this observation presents the strongest evidence to date that early life exposure to an environmental toxin can lead to a progressive neurodegenerative process years later.

Finally, an inverse relationship between cigarette smoking and the risk for PD has been observed in 33 of 34 studies.[50] The assumption is that one or more compounds in cigarette smoke may protect against exposure to one or more neurotoxicants in the environment. Conversely, there could be an interaction between smoking and genetically determined risk factors, but this would be complex and difficult to elucidate. Nicotine is an obvious candidate, and has been shown to protect nigral neurons against degeneration after axotomy. Another compound found in cigarette smoke, 4-phenylpyridine, protects against MPTP toxicity in the mouse model.[51] This appears to mediated by its ability to inhibit MAO, the key metabolic step in activating MPTP to its toxic metabolite MPP+. Since there is suggestive evidence that chronic MAO-B inhibition in PD may be neuroprotective,[52,53] this may be worthy of further investigation.

SUMMARY

- Determining the relative contributions of environment and heredity to the cause of PD is more than an academic issue, since its resolution dictates future research directions torwards finding the pathogenesis of the disease and developing a neuroprotective treatment.

- The recent identification of the genetic mutation responsible for parkinsonism in a large Italian kindred indicates that some cases of PD can be genetically determined and provides exciting new research opportunities. However, this does not appear to be responsible for the vast majority of PD cases. A large twin study also points away from genetic influences, at least in patients with disease beginning after the age of 50 years. Conversely, genetic influences appear to be important in younger-onset disease.

- Epidemiological studies have indicated that rural living, well-water consumption, and exposure to pesticides are potential risk factors, but identification of specific agents has been wanting, and aging remains the only unequivocal risk factor for the disease.

- There is an inverse relationship between cigarette smoking and PD.

- The ALS/PDC complex in the western Pacific island of Guam suggests the possibility of long-latency toxins, but pinning down a specific causative agent for this syndrome has eluded investigators to date.

REFERENCES

1. Parkinson J. An Essay on the Shaking Palsy. London: Sherwood, Neeley, and Jones, 1817.

2. Charcot J. Lecons sur les Maladies du Systeme Nerveux. Paris: V.A. Delahaye et cie, 1867.

3. Friedman JH, Stern MB, Koller WC, eds, Parkinsonian Syndromes. New York: Marcel Dekker, Inc. 1993: 203–226.

4. Poskanzer DC, Schwab RS. Cohort analysis of Parkinson's syndrome. Evidence for a single etiology related to subclinical infection about 1920. J Chronic Dis 1963; 16: 961–973.

5. Mjones H. Paralysis agitans: a clinical and genetic study. Acta Psychiatr Neurol 1949; Suppl 54: 1–195.

6. Allen W. Inheritance of the shaking palsy. Arch Intern Med 1937; 60: 424–436.

7. Langston JW, Ballard PA, Tetrud JW, Irwin I. Chronic parkinsonism in humans due to a product of meperidine analog synthesis. Science 1983; 219: 979–980.

8. Ward CD, Duvoisin RC, Ince SE, Nutt JG, Eldridge R, Calne DB. Parkinson's disease in 65 pairs of twins and in a set of quadruplets. Neurol 1983; 335: 815–824.

9. Tanner CM. Marsden CD, Fahn S, eds, Movement Disorders 3. Oxford: Butterworth Heinemann, 1994: 124–146.

10. Duvoisin RC. Research on the genetics of Parkinson's disease: will it lead to the cause and a cure? In, Stern MB, ed, Beyond the Decade of the Brain. Tunbridge Wells: Wells Medical Ltd. 1994: 95–108.

11. Golbe LI, Di Torio G, Bonavita V, Miller DC, Duvoisin RC. A large kindred with autosomal dominant Parkinson's disease. Ann Neurol 1990; 26: 276–282.

12. Golbe LI, Di Torio G, Sanges G, Lazzarini AM, La Sala S, Bonavita V, Duvoisin RC. Clinical genetic analysis of Parkinson's disease in the Contursi kindred. Ann Neurol 1996; 40: 767–775.

13. Polymeropoulos MH, Higgins JJ, Golbe LI, Johnson WG, Ide SE, Di Torio G, Sanges G, Stenros ES, Pho LT, Schaffer AA, et al. Mapping of a gene for Parkinson's disease to chromosome 4q21–q23. Science 1996; 274: 1197–1199.

14. Polymeropoulos MH, Lavedan C, Leroy E, et al. Mutation in the α–synuclein gene identified in families with Parkinson's disease. Science 1997; 276: 2045–2047.

15. Chan P, Tanner CM, Jiang, X, Langston JW. Failure to find the α–synuclein gene missense mutation (G209A) in 100 patients with younger onset Parkinson's disease. Neurol 1998; 50: 513–514.

16. Langston JW, Widner H, Goetz CG, Brooks DJ, Fahn S, Freeman TB, Watts RL. Core assessment program for intracerebral transplantations (CAPIT). Mov Disord 1992; 7: 2–13.

17. Chan P, Jiang, X, Forno LS, DiMonte DA, Tanner CM, Langston JW. Absence of mutation in the coding region of the alpha–synuclein gene in pathologically–proven Parkinson's disease. Neurol 1998; in press.

18. Spellman GG. Report of familial cases of parkinsonism. Evidence of a dominant trait in a patient's family. J Am Med Assoc 1962; 179: 160–162.

19. Muenter MD, Forno LS, Hornykiewicz O, et al. Hereditary form of parkinsonism–dementia. Ann Neurol 1998, in press.

20. Farrer M, Wavrant–DeVrieze F, Crook R, et al. Low frequency of alpha–synuclein with familial Parkinson's disease. Ann Neurol 1998; 43: 394–397.

21. Hrubec Z, Neel JV, Nance WE, eds, Twin Research, Part B: Biology and Epidemiology. New York: Alan R. Liss, 1978: 153–172.

22. Tanner CM, Ottman R, Ellenberg JH, *et al.* Parkinson's disease (PD) concordance in elderly male monozygotic (MZ) and dizygotic (DZ) twins. Neurol 1997; 48: A333.

23. Irwin I, Langston JW, Harvey AL, eds, Natural and Synthetic Neurotoxins. London: Academic Press Limited, 1993: 225–256.

24. Heikkila RE, Youngster SK, Panek DU, Giovanni A, Sonsalla PK. Studies with the neurotoxicant 1–methyl–4–phenyl–1,2,3,6–tetrahydropyridine (MPTP) and several of its analogs. Toxicol 1988; 49: 493–501.

25. Hughes AJ, Daniel SE, Kilford L, Lees AJ. Accuracy of clinical diagnosis of idiopathic Parkinson's disease: A clinico-pathological study of 100 cases. J Neurol Neurosurg Psychiatry 1992; 55: 181–184.

26. Koller WC, Lang AE. Age of onset of Parkinson's disease. Can J Neurol Sci 1987; 14: 179–180.

27. Fall PA, Axelson O, Fredriksson M, Hansson G, Lindvall B, Olsson JE, Granerus AK. Age–standardized incidence and prevalence of Parkinson's disease in a Swedish community. J Clin Epidemiol 1996; 49: 637–641.

28. Mutch WJ, Dingwall–Fordyce I, Downie AW, Paterson JG, Roy SK. Parkinson's disease in a Scottish city. Br Med J 1986; 292: 534–536.

29. Carlsson A, Finch CE, Potter DE, Kenny AD, eds, Parkinson's Disease – II: Aging and Neuroendocrine Relations. New York: Plenum Press, 1978: 1–13.

30. Langston JW, Irwin I, Forno LS, *et al.* In, Fahn S, Marsden CD, Goldstein M, Calne DB, eds, Recent Developments in Parkinson's Disease. Florham Park, New Jersey: Macmillan Healthcare Information, 1987: 59–74.

31. Daly AK, Leathart JBS, London SJ, Idle JR. An inactive cytochrome P450 CYP2D6 allele containing a deletion and a base substitution. Hum Genetics 1995; 95: 337–341.

32. Landi MT, Ceroni M, Martignoni E, Bertazzi PA, Caporaso NE, Nappi G. Gene–environment interaction in Parkinson's disease – the case of CYP2D6 gene polymorphisms. Adv Neurol 1996; 69: 61–72.

33. Agundez JAG, Jimeniz–Jimeniz FJ, Luengo A, Bernal ML, Molina JA, Ayuso L, Vazques A, Parra J, Duarte J, Coria F, *et al.* Association between the oxidative polymorphism and early onset of Parkinson's disease. Clin Pharmacol Ther 1995; 57: 291–298.

34. Ray–Chaudhuri K, Smith C, Gough AC, Novak N, Chamoun V, Wolf CR, Leigh PN. Debrisoquine hydroxylase gene polymorphism in Parkinson's disease and amyotrophic lateral sclerosis. J Neurol Neurosurg Psychiatry 1995; 58: 109.

35. Gasser T, Muller–Myhsok B, Supala A, Zimmer E, Wieditz G, Wszolek ZK, Vieregge P, Bonifati V, Oertel WH. The CYP2D6B allele is not over–represented in a population of German patients with idiopathic Parkinson's disease. J Neurol Neurosurg Psychiatry 1996; 61: 518–520.

36. Diederich N, Hilger C, Goetz CG, Keipes M, Hentges F, Vieregge P, Metz H. Genetic variability of the CYP2D6 gene is not a risk factor for sporadic Parkinson's disease. Ann Neurol 1996; 40: 463–465.

37. McCann SJ, Pond SM, James DG, LeCouteur DG. The association between polymorphisms in the cytochrome P–450 2D6 gene and Parkinson's disease: a case–control study and meta–analysis. J Neurol Sci 1997; 153: 50–53.

38. Chan P, Tanner CM, Langston JW. Genetically determined differences in xenobiotic metabolism as a risk factor in Parkinson's disease. Fund Appl Toxicol 1996; 30 (Suppl.):89.

39. Mannervik B, Danielson UH. Glutathione transferase: structure and catalytic activity. CRC Crit Rev Biochem 1988; 23: 283–337.

40. Tanner CM, Goldman SM. Epidemiology of Parkinson's disease. Neuroepidemiol 1996; 14: 317–335.

41. Seidler A, Hellenbrand W, Robra BP, Vieregge P, Nischan P, Joerg J, Oertel WH, Ulm G, Schneider E. Possible environmental, occupational, and other etiologic factors for Parkinson's disease: A case–control study in Germany. Neurol 1996; 46: 1275–1284.

42. Fleming L, Mann JB, Bean J, Briggle T, Sanchez–Ramos JR. Parkinson's disease and brain levels of organochlorine pesticides. Ann Neurol 1994; 36: 100–103.

43. Semchuk KM, Love EJ, Lee RG. Parkinson's disease and exposure to rural environmental factors: A population based case–control study. Can J Neurol Sci 1991; 18: 279–286.

44. Corsini GU, Pintus S, Chiueh CC, et al. 1–Methyl–4–phenyl–1,2,3,6–tetrahydro pyridine (MPTP) neurotoxicity in mice is enhanced by pretreatment with diethyldithiocarbamate. Eur J Pharmacol 1985; 119: 127–128.

45. Irwin I, Di Monte DA, Thiruchelvam M, et al. Diethyldithiocarbamate (DDC): A promoter of dopaminergic toxicity. Fund Appl Toxicol 1996; 30 (suppl): 263.

46. Tanner CM, Kurland LT, Stern MB, Koller WC, eds, Parkinsonian Syndromes. New York: Marcel Dekker, Inc. 1993: 279–294.

47. Garruto RM, Younghars R, Gajdusek DC. Disappearance of high–incidence amyotrophic lateral sclerosis and parkinsonism–dementia on Guam. Neurol 1985; 35: 193–198.

48. Zhang Z, Anderson DW, Lavine L, Mantel N. Patterns of acquiring parkinsonism–dementia complex on Guam: 1944 through 1985. Arch Neurol 1990; 47: 1019–1024.

49. Garruto RM, Gajdusek DC, Chen KM. Amyotrophic lateral sclerosis among Chamorro migrants from Guam. Ann Neurol 1980; 8: 612–619.

50. Morens DM, Grandinetti A, Reed D, White LR, Ross GW. Cigarette smoking and protection from Parkinson's disease: false association or etiologic clue? Neurol 1995; 45: 1041–1051.

51. Sullivan JP, Tipton KF. Interactions of the neurotoxin MPTP and its demethylated derivative (PTP) with monoamine oxidase–B. Neurochem Res 1992; 17: 791–796.

52. Tetrud JW, Langston JW. The effect of deprenyl (selegiline) on the natural history of Parkinson's disease. Science 1989; 245: 519–522.

53. Parkinson Study Group. Effect of deprenyl on the progression of disability in early Parkinson's disease. N Engl J Med 1989; 321: 1364–1371.

DISCUSSION

Gash: Is it possible that the environmental causes for parkinsonism are ubiquitous around the world and it is the protective factors that vary? In other words, could we be looking in the wrong direction?

Langston: I certainly think that could be the case. In fact, I would go even further. There may also be exacerbating factors in the environment as well. Dithiocarbamates seem to make a number of dopaminergic toxins more toxic, and we have evidence that a non-toxic dose of MPTP can become toxic when combined with dithiocarbamates. It could be that the combination of both protective and exacerbating factors determine whether or not an individual gets the disease. This is a new area in which very little research has been done. Perhaps we are looking at things backwards and should not be asking why some people get PD, but rather why the majority do not. It is important to ask why not everybody develops PD if a universal factor in the environment causes it.

Mizuno: You reported ubiquitin-positive inclusions in cortical areas in an autopsy study of an affected patient from the Contursi kindred. Were these Lewy bodies on H & E staining?

Langston: Yes, there were a few Lewy bodies but there were not many in the substantia nigra. There were more in the locus coeruleus and other areas. There were not a lot of them but several classical Lewy bodies were present. We have not done ubiquitin staining on them yet. The ubiquitinated material that I showed was composed of neurites in the temporal cortex and hypothalamus. We have not yet examined the Lewy bodies to see if they are ubiquitinated

Mizuno: Your patient had dementia, so would you say that the patient had Lewy body disease or Parkinson's disease with dementia?

Langston: I do not know what to call this patient. She began with mild parkinsonism, but did not receive more than 300 mg of levodopa daily during her entire illness. She responded fairly well and it was not until the third or fourth year that she began to develop fairly severe mental problems. From a clinical standpoint, I would have been tempted to make a diagnosis of diffuse Lewy body disease, but neuropathological examination failed to show cortical Lewy bodies. I think that all we can say from a diagnostic point of view is that she was a member of the Contursi kindred. It is interesting that the clinical and pathological changes are similar to those of another family with dominantly inherited disease where four affected members have been studied pathologically.

Mizuno: I would like to make a comment about the etiology of PD. At present we are studying many genetic polymorphisms of PD and, the more we study, the more I believe that genetic factors are also important in the etiology of sporadic PD. Western people and oriental people have almost the same proteins and the same genes, yet we look so different, and this is true even among Western people. We simply do not know very much about how genetic make-up leads to different countenances, characters, ways of thinking, and of course, the risk of developing PD.

Langston: My point is that, at least based on our data from the twin studies we have performed based on the WWII twin veteran registry, there does not appear to be any genetic component in patients with typical PD, at least in those with disease onset over the age of 50 years.

Mizuno: Perhaps introns are involved as we have no idea what they are doing. There may be modification of introns during certain points of development that determine the expression of specific genes.

De Yebenes Justo: There is some difficulty in interpreting data from epidemiological studies based on clinical records. Compare the data you quoted on the prevalence of PD in southern Europe with door-to-door studies. Studies performed by Walter Rocca in Italy and by José Costa in Spain suggest that the real prevalence in door-to-door studies is 300 cases per 100,000 population, which is three times higher than the 80–100 cases per 100,000 reported in most epidemiologic studies. A tremendous number of individuals are never diagnosed with PD, yet may still have it.

Langston: Yes, I think that is an excellent point and I would take it a step further. We are talking about prevalence. The incidence studies are even tougher.

Poewe: Environmental factors such as smoking might also have a genetic basis. I believe there are animal studies on mutants lacking the dopamine transporter gene which show that such animals are not prone to development of addictive behavior and who are protected against cocaine and nicotine abuse. Thus, even an environmental factor might be associated with a genetic component.

Langston: It is an interesting point, but I think you can cut it both ways. If we are to accept the data presented earlier in this conference, the latency of PD may not be as long as we originally thought, certainly not 20 or 30 years. If that is the case, this could be taken as an argument against the hypothesis that the decision not to smoke early in life is simply a result of preclinical disease, which has adversely affected the desire to smoke cigarettes.

Poewe: You miss my point. The same gene that determines whether or not you smoke when you are young may determine whether or not you are at risk for developing PD when you are older.

Koller: One argument often used against the environmental hypothesis is the lack of clusters of PD. Is that really true, and how damaging is that to the environmental hypothesis?

Langston: That is a difficult question to answer. It may be that there is a complexity of exposure factors necessary to induce PD but that it does not occur after a single exposure and that is why clusters are not more evident. I should mention, however, that there is evidence of familial clustering where PD seems to occur at about the same chronological point in time, affecting individuals of differing ages across generations. This could be consistent with an environmental agent. But the classic cluster where there is a toxic spill and everybody gets the disease, we just do not see. It could be that there is a long latency to onset of disease after exposure, but I think that is a genuine criticism and I do not have a good answer for it.

Wood: It is set down in tablets of stone that degeneration on Guam is environmental. And yet, Guam is only ten miles long and five miles wide, at its widest point. There are two towns at the southernmost tip. In Umatac, about half of the Chamorro population have ALS/PDC, but next door in Merizo it is much less frequent despite the similarity in geography and diet. It may not be a single gene, but there must be a strong genetic contribution to that disorder.

Langston: It was originally considered to be genetic in origin. However, the disease is rapidly disappearing, and this seems to correlate well with Westernization of the diet. It seems to me that this does argue for an environmental cause. Genetic drift would not be expected to act nearly as quickly. During WWII, the natives were heavily dependent on the cycad seed as a food source, but since the war this is no longer the case. There may have been a difference in consumption of cycad between these villages. But the disappearance of the disease is the strongest argument that something has changed in the environment, diet being a leading factor.

Olanow: One of things that has changed in the environment of Guam is Dan Perl, who has visited there quite often. Would you like to comment?

Perl: Pure ALS is now extremely rare on the island although it is still seen, but parkinsonism–dementia is still as common as it was. We are currently following 240 cases in this population and one major change has been the age of onset. For both the ALS form and the parkinsonism–dementia form, the age of onset has risen by 10 years in the last 25 years. It is unusual with genetically-based diseases for a change of this magnitude to occur over such a short period of time. More importantly, we now have an epidemic of the same disease, neuropathologically confirmed, among the Filipino migrants who have lived on the island now for 20–25 years. This underscores the likelihood of an environmental etiology for a disease that first was expressed as ALS and now as cases of parkinsonism–dementia. Finally, we have seen two cases of ALS among Caucasian migrants to the island, who show rare but identifiable tangles in their cortex, typical of Guam neurodegeneration but a very unusual finding for ALS. The cases in the Key peninsula were originally described both clinically and pathologically almost 20 years ago but now, not only is ALS still present in this very isolated community but parkinsonism–dementia is also appearing. Environmental factors seem to be the most likely explanation, but underlying genetic susceptibility factors could certainly be playing a role as well. Another point is that over 1,000 autopsies have been performed on Guam natives suffering from neurologic disease over the last 35 years. These have been carefully reviewed and only one single case of Lewy body idiopathic PD has been found in this population, whereas one would have anticipated about 15–20 cases. In other words, these natives do not develop typical PD. Also, there are no cases with incidental Lewy bodies, which is unusual. Are there any other populations in which this disease does not occur? If so, that would be a very important clue. Moreover, this is a disease of man, and has never been described as naturally-occurring in another animal species.

Olanow: We think of PD as a disease of man because we have primarily looked in man. I think that one of the problems with diseases such as occur in Guam is that people go there to study what they already know. As we develop broader and different interests in the disease, its diversion and generalizability to neurodegeneration has become increasingly more evident. Dr. Kordower has a colony of elderly monkeys, many of whom have nigral degeneration and even tremor, which suggests that they may be developing PD. It may be that if we begin to study elderly primates, we will see some of the age-related neurodegenerative diseases of man such as AD, PD, and even the neurodegeneration that occurs on Guam.

Gash: I have a colony of aged Rhesus monkeys and we are also seeing problems that could be spontaneously developing PD, so you are right – PD may occur in other animals.

Olanow: With regard to the multiplicity of toxic events, in the laboratory there are increasing examples of situations where one incident alone does not induce degenerative or neuronal death and parkinsonism, but combinations do. One example is the SOD mutant mouse, which develops an ALS phenotype but also has mild nigral degeneration. If a small dose of MPTP is given to the wild-type littermate, it upregulates striatal dopamine slightly and is perfectly fine. In contrast, striatal dopamine levels in the mutant animals fall by 80% after MPTP administration and they develop parkinsonism. We have seen similar effects with glutathione which by itself has no effect on dopamine neurons but makes the animals vulnerable to 6-OHDA toxicity. These examples illustrate the difficulty of defining either an environmental or genetic cause of PD because so many factors may be involved and they may be different in different individuals.

Melamed: What about conjugal parkinsonism? It is quite rare to see PD in a husband and wife at the same time, and one might expect to see more cases if it was due to an environmental factor.

Langston: We started to collect conjugal cases but never followed this up. The answer to your question may be that, even though a husband and wife share the home environment, they typically spend substantial parts of their lives apart, particularly if one or both are at work. Also, if there really is a 20–30 year latency, then the insult may have occurred before they met.

Schapira: With regard to α-synuclein, we have looked at 70 UK idiopathic parkinsonian patients and not found any of the described mutations. We have not looked for other mutations, so there does appear to be a difference between those families with the mutation and those with the idiopathic disease.

Langston: Yet in both conditions, Lewy bodies are present. At the very least, we have an important model of the neuropathology of PD, and PD itself may be many diseases of which the Contursi kindred has one.

Brooks: In your series of twin pairs, have you identified any common environmental factor that might explain their concordance?

Langston: We have an extensive environmental questionnaire, which is the second part of this study. Most of these data have been collected and we are just starting to analyse them. We are using some very modern techniques for eliciting exposures and surrogates for exposures. Hopefully, with continued support from NIH, we may have some data that will be very useful when fully analyzed.

CHAPTER SIX

Genetics of Parkinson's Disease

THOMAS GASSER

Department of Neurology, Klinikum Großhadern, Munich, Germany

Parkinson's disease (PD) is unlikely to have a single cause. Nigral degeneration with Lewy body formation and the resulting clinical picture of PD is probably a common final pathway of a multifactorial disease process. The identification of a mutation in the gene for α-synuclein in several families with autosomal-dominantly inherited PD was a major recent breakthrough that has provided information on one cause of PD and shown that genetic alterations can be the dominant factor in some cases.

EVIDENCE FOR A GENETIC CONTRIBUTION TO THE ETIOLOGY OF PD

The assumption of a genetic contribution to the etiology of PD is based on epidemiologic surveys, twin studies, and the analysis of families with dominant inheritance of a phenotype that approximates typical Lewy body PD.

Case-control studies

PD appears to be more frequent among relatives of index patients with PD, compared to a matched control population.[1-5] Between 6% and 30% of index patients had other affected first or second degree relatives and, where spouses or age-matched community members were used as controls, there was a 2–14-fold increase in relative risk. The proportion of probands with a positive family history can be as high as 40%, if complete information on all first and second degree family members is available.[6] The study showing the lowest familial rates was population-based,[5] but all other study populations were drawn from movement disorders clinics and may therefore be biased by a disproportionate presence of a positive family history. Interestingly, the risk to relatives appears to increase with the number of individuals already affected in a pedigree, a feature indicative of a multifactorial etiology (either polygenic or genetic plus environmental) with an inheritable component in a subset of families.[6] Even a conservative estimate places the relative risk in first degree relatives of probands with PD (λ_s) in the range of 2–3, which approximates that found in Alzheimer's disease (AD).[7]

Twin studies

Most twin studies have showed low concordance rates,[8–11] in principle arguing against a genetic etiology for PD. However, PET scanning has identified subclinical dysfunction of the nigrostriatal dopaminergic system in clinically asymptomatic individuals and has revealed much higher concordance rates in twins than was appreciated by clinical examination alone.[12] If genetic factors are responsible for the bulk of PD cases, then a significant difference in concordance rates in monozygous *versus* dizygous twins should be expected. This has been observed in a sample of more than 30 twin pairs (D. Brooks, personal communication). The same group demonstrated a high incidence of nigral dysfunction on fluorodopa PET scanning in clinically asymptomatic relatives of patients in families with multiple cases of PD, again arguing that the disease process itself may be much more frequent than clinically overt PD, and that the inherited nature of the disorder may be masked by the low clinical penetrance of the mutation.[13]

Studies of multicase families

Some families show a phenotype within the spectrum of idiopathic PD with a pattern of apparent autosomal dominant inheritance. Several cases of so-called familial parkinsonism show clinical and/or pathologic signs incompatible with the diagnosis of typical Lewy body PD by accepted criteria.[14–19] These have been termed more precisely 'familial parkinsonism-plus' syndromes.[20] In two examples, Japanese autosomal-recessively inherited juvenile parkinsonism and pontopallidal degeneration, gene loci have been assigned.[18,21] Determination of the genetic defect in these families may still be valuable in understanding the molecular pathogenesis of nigral neuronal degeneration, since differences in clinical and pathological appearance do not exclude shared mechanisms in pathogenesis. Those families that more closely resemble idiopathic PD clinically[22] and pathologically[23–25] will presumably be most likely to provide important clues to the understanding of the etiology and mechanism of cell death that occurs in patients with the sporadic disease.

CHROMOSOMES 4-LINKED PD (PARK1)

In one large family with dominantly-inherited PD, the disease has been linked to polymorphic DNA markers on chromosome 4q21.[26] The clinical phenotype is relatively typical of PD but has a relatively early age of onset (mean 46 years *versus* 59.7 years in sporadic PD[27]), a relatively rapid course from onset to death and a high proportion of affecteds with dementia.[23] Neuronal degeneration is present in the substantia nigra with Lewy body formation in the brain stem nuclei.[28] Shortly after identification of linkage to chromosome 4, a mutation was discovered in the gene for α-synuclein cosegregating with the disease in this family and in several Greek kindreds with dominantly-inherited early-onset parkinsonism. The mutation leads to an amino acid exchange in the α-synuclein protein (Ala53Thr).[29] It is unclear whether the mutation is present on the same genetic background in all of these families, but close historical ties between southern Italy and western Greece suggest that a common mutation or founder effect is possible.

Linkage analysis with polymorphic markers spanning the PD1 locus has been performed in 13 multicase families with autosomal dominantly inherited parkinsonism.[30] Strongly negative lod scores excluded linkage to the PD1-region in all but two families, who showed slightly positive lod scores (Figure 1). Subsequent sequence analysis of the α-synuclein gene in all families failed to show a mutation in the coding region (see below). Using a slightly different approach, no evidence for linkage in a population of 94 affected sib and relative pairs with familial PD has been found.[31]

Sequence Analysis of the α-Synuclein Gene in PD

Identification of a putative disease-causing mutation in the chromosome 4-linked families has enabled analysis of these families for this or other alterations in the coding region of the gene. Two hundred and thirty index patients with 'familial' PD (*i.e.* at least one other affected relative with PD, but excluding the multicase families with clear Mendelian inheritance described above), have been examined for the Ala53Thr mutation. Probands were derived from different European populations and selected using rigorous diagnostic criteria. In these cases, the mean age at onset was similar to patients with sporadic PD and in no case was the Ala53Thr mutation identified.[35] Similar observations have been made among 70 cases of sporadic PD from the movement disorders outpatient unit at the University of Munich (unpublished results). The entire coding region of the α-synuclein gene was sequenced in 27 index cases from multicase families,[22,25,32–34] and again no mutation was detected.[36]

In summary, a mutation in the α-synuclein gene, or any other gene in this region, appears to be a very rare cause of familial PD and may be restricted to a few early-onset families. However, direct involvement of α-synuclein in the pathogenesis of PD seems likely, from the present genetic evidence and from the fact that α-synuclein is a major constituent of Lewy bodies in both familial and sporadic PD regardless of whether or not they had a gene mutation.[37] This assumption is further supported by the recent demonstration of an independent α-synuclein mutation cosegregating with Parkinson's disease in a German family.[38] These findings provide an opportunity for future studies that might shed light on this important issue.

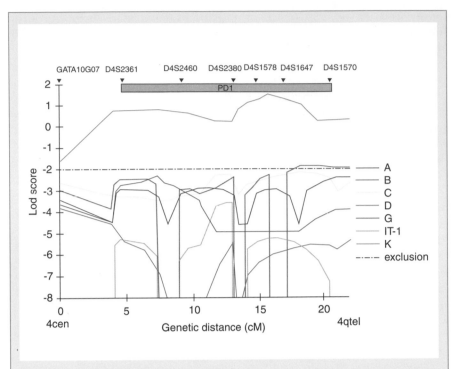

Figure 1: Multipoint linkage analysis of the PD1-region on chromosome 4q21-q23 in 7 families with familial parkinsonism. Polymorphic DNA-fragments were amplified by PCR using published primer sequences and a standard protocol. Multipoint analysis was done using an autosomal dominant mode of inheritance. Unaffecteds were treated as previously described.[26] Reproduced with permission from Gasser *et al.*[30]

CHROMOSOME 2-LINKED PD (PARK3)

Recently, a second locus for autosomal-dominant familial parkinsonism with Lewy-body pathology has been described (PARK3), located on chromosome 2p13.[39] Clinical features closely resembled those of sporadic PD, including a similar mean age of onset (59 years in these families). The maximum multipoint lod score for all 6 families in this study was 3.96, considering affected members only. The penetrance of the mutation was estimated to be 40% in these families, suggesting that it might also play a role in apparently sporadic cases.

IDENTIFICATION OF FURTHER PD GENES

Several strategies could identify other genes which may lead to Lewy body nigral degeneration and parkinsonism – (1) 'classic' linkage analysis in large dominant families, (2) non-parametric linkage following the affected sib-pair approach, or (3) association studies of candidate genes.

The most straightforward approach is total genome screening following the 'classic' linkage analysis lod score method in a single large family sufficiently powerful to demonstrate linkage unequivocally. Thus, the problem of genetic heterogeneity in PD is circumvented, the assumed mode of inheritance is likely to be correct (autosomal dominant), and the problem of unknown penetrance can be tackled by analyzing affected pedigree members only. However, at present, there is no family with a typical PD phenotype large enough to assure a successful linkage analysis. It will therefore be necessary to pool several families. Heterogeneity will have to be minimized by selecting families with a very similar clinical picture, a similar age at onset, and a common region of origin although this does not provide assurance that any abnormality in these families will necessarily be the same. This markedly complicates the problem and makes detection of a gene mutation with PD more difficult.

The relevance of any mutation in a large dominant pedigree to the etiology of sporadic PD, or PD with familial clustering, is unknown. Studies are underway to identify gene loci in large samples of affected sib-pairs or affected pedigree members, using non-parametric linkage analysis, a well-established method in the analysis of genetically complex diseases.[40] This is based on the fact that two siblings share either none, one, or two of their parental alleles at any given chromosomal locus, the prior probability being 0.25 for none, 0.5 for one, and 0.25 for two shared alleles (Figure 2). If, in a subset of affected

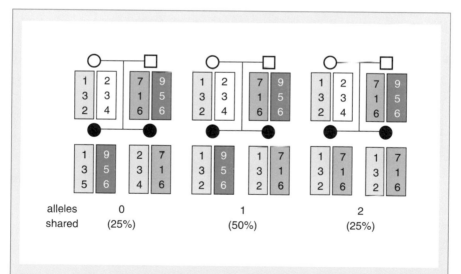

| alleles shared | 0 (25%) | 1 (50%) | 2 (25%) |

Figure 2: Allele-sharing in nuclear families: two siblings share either none, one or two parental alleles at any given chromosomal locus. If a subset of affected sibs inherit the same disease susceptibility gene from either one of their parents, there should be a deviation from this ratio to higher numbers for alleles in close proximity to the incriminated locus.

sib pairs, both sibs inherit the same disease susceptibility gene from either parent, there should be a deviation from this ratio to higher numbers for alleles in close proximity to the incriminated locus. As a number of different loci may each play a role only in a minority of cases, large co-operative studies are necessary to ascertain a sufficient number of affected sibling-pairs to obtain statistically significant results.

Finally, genetic factors may also contribute to the development of apparently sporadic cases of a disease. This has been shown clearly for the ApoE4 allele in sporadic AD.[41] Association studies in PD for a number of polymorphic candidate genes will be discussed in detail elsewhere.[42]

SUMMARY

- There is convincing evidence that genetic factors play an important role in the etiology of PD, at least in some cases. This has been demonstrated by familial aggregation of the disease in case-control and twin-studies, and by the description of large multigenerational families, in whom clinically and pathologically typical PD is inherited in an autosomal dominant fashion.

- A mutation in the α-synuclein gene on chromosome 4 has been described in some families with a clinical and pathological picture consistent with PD.

- Analysis of the mechanism whereby mutated α-synuclein leads to cell death will, in all likelihood, provide important insights into the molecular pathogenesis of nigral degeneration and Lewy body formation.

- Additional genes are now beginning to be identified that are associated with the development of PD. It is likely that many other genes will be discovered that are associated with familial and even apparently sporadic form of PD.

REFERENCES

1. Payami H, Larsen K, Bernard S, Nutt J. Increased risk of Parkinson's disease in parents and siblings of patients. Ann Neurol 1994; 36: 659–661.

2. Vieregge P, Heberlein I. Increased risk of Parkinson's disease in relatives of patients. Ann Neurol 1995; 37: 685.

3. Bonifati V, Fabrizio E, Vanacore N, De Mari M, Meco G. Familial Parkinson's disease: a clinical genetic analysis. Can J Neurol Sci 1995; 22: 272–279.

4. De Michele G, Filla A, Volpe G, et al. Environmental and genetic risk factors in Parkinson's disease: a case-control study in southern Italy. Mov Disord 1996; 11: 17–23.

5. Marder K, Tang MX, Mejia H, et al. Risk of Parkinson's disease among first-degree relatives: A community-based study. Neurol 1996; 47: 155–160.

6. Lazzarini AM, Myers RH, Zimmerman TR, Jr., et al. A clinical genetic study of Parkinson's disease: evidence for dominant transmission. Neurol 1994; 44: 499–506.

7. Farrer LA, O'Sullivan DM, Cupples LA, Growdon JH, Myers RH. Assessment of genetic risk for Alzheimer's disease among first-degree relatives. Ann Neurol 1989; 25: 485–493.

8. Ward CD, Duvoisin RC, Ince SE, et al. Parkinson's disease in twins. Adv Neurol 1984; 40: 341–344.

9. Vieregge P, Schiffke KA, Friedrich HJ, Muller B, Ludin HP. Parkinson's disease in twins. Neurol 1992; 42: 1453–1461.

10. Marttila RJ, Kaprio J, Koskenvuo M, Rinne UK. Parkinson's disease in a nationwide twin cohort. Neurol 1988; 38: 1217–1219.

11. Bharucha NE, Stokes L, Schoenberg BS, et al. A case-control study of twin pairs discordant for Parkinson's disease: a search for environmental risk factors. Neurol 1986; 36: 284–288.

12. Burn DJ, Mark MH, Playford ED, et al. Parkinson's disease in twins studied with ^{18}F-dopa and positron emission tomography. Neurol 1992; 42: 1894–1900.

13. Piccini P, Morrish PK, Turjanski N, et al. Dopaminergic function in familial Parkinson's disease: a clinical and 18F-dopa positron emission tomography study. Ann Neurol 1997; 41: 222–229.

14. Perry TL, Wright JM, Berry K, Hansen S, Perry TL, Jr. Dominantly inherited apathy, central hypoventilation, and Parkinson's syndrome: clinical, biochemical, and neuropathologic studies of 2 new cases. Neurol 1990; 40: 1882–1887.

15. Purdy A, Hahn A, Barnett HJ, et al. Familial fatal Parkinsonism with alveolar hypoventilation and mental depression. Ann Neurol 1979; 6: 523–531.

16. Perry TL, Bratty PJ, Hansen S, Kennedy J, Urquhart N, Dolman CL. Hereditary mental depression and Parkinsonism with taurine deficiency. Arch Neurol 1975; 32: 108–113.

17. Bhatia KP, Daniel SE, Marsden CD. Familial parkinsonism with depression: a clinicopathological study. Ann Neurol 1993; 34: 842–847.

18. Matsumine H, Saito M, Shimoda Matsubayashi S, et al. Localization of a gene for an autosomal recessive form of juvenile Parkinsonism to chromosome 6q25.2-27. Am J Hum Genet 1997; 60: 588–596.

19. Wszolek ZK, Pfeiffer RF, Bhatt MH, et al. Rapidly progressive autosomal dominant parkinsonism and dementia with pallido-ponto-nigral degeneration. Ann Neurol 1992; 32: 312–320.

20. Wilhelmsen KC, Wszolek ZK. Is there a genetic susceptibility to idiopathic parkinsonism? Parkinsonism Relat Disord 1995; 1: 73–84.

21. Wijker M, Wszolek ZK, Wolters EC, et al. Localization of the gene for rapidly progressive autosomal dominant

parkinsonism and dementia with pallido-ponto-nigral degeneration to chromosome 17q21. Hum Mol Genet 1996; 5: 151–154.

22. Wszolek ZK, Cordes M, Calne DB, Munter MD, Cordes I, Pfeifer RF. Hereditary Parkinson disease: report of 3 families with dominant autosomal inheritance. Nervenarzt 1993; 64: 331–335.

23. Golbe LI, Di Iorio G, Sanges G, et al. Clinical genetic analysis of Parkinson's disease in the Contursi kindred. Ann Neurol 1996; 40: 767–775.

24. Markopoulou K, Wszolek ZK, Pfeiffer RF. A Greek-American kindred with autosomal dominant, levodopa-responsive parkinsonism and anticipation. Ann Neurol 1995; 38: 373–378.

25. Wszolek ZK, Pfeiffer B, Fulgham JR, et al. Western Nebraska family (family D) with autosomal dominant parkinsonism. Neurol 1995; 45: 502–505.

26. Polymeropoulos MH, Higgins JJ, Golbe LI, et al. Mapping of a gene for Parkinson's disease to chromosome 4q21-q23. Science 1996; 274: 1197–1199.

27. Di Rocco A, Molinari SP, Kollmeier B, Yahr MD. Parkinson's disease: progression and mortality in the L-dopa era. Adv Neurol 1996; 69: 3–11.

28. Golbe LI, Di Iorio G, Bonavita V, Miller DC, Duvoisin RC. A large kindred with autosomal dominant Parkinson's disease. Ann Neurol 1990; 27: 276–282.

29. Polymeropoulos M, this volume.

30. Gasser T, Müller-Myhsok B, Wszolek Z, et al. Genetic complexity and Parkinson's disease. Science 1997; 277: 388–389.

31. Scott WK, Stajich JM, Yamaoka L, et al. Genetic complexity in Parkinson's disease. Science 1997; 277: 387–388.

32. Mazzetti P, Le Guern E, Bonnet AM, Vidailhet M, Brice A, Agid Y. Familial Parkinson's disease and polymorphism at the CYP2D6 locus [letter]. J Neurol Neurosurg Psychiatr 1994; 57: 871–872.

33. Denson MA, Wszolek ZK. Familial parkinsonism: our experience and a review of the literature. Parkinsonism Relat Disord 1995; 1: 1–8.

34. Bonifati V, Fabrizio E, Vanacore N, Gasparini M, Meco G. A large Italian family with dominantly inherited levodopa-responsive parkinsonism and isolated tremors. Mov Disord 1996; 11(Suppl 1): 86.

35. Vaughan JR, Durr A, Gasser T, et al. The α-synuclein Ala53Thr mutation is not a common cause of familial Parkinson's disease in 230 European cases. Neurol 1998, in press.

36. Vaughan JR, Farrer M, Wszolek ZK, Gasser T, et al. Sequencing of the alpha-synuclein gene in a large series of families with familial Parkinson's disease fails to reveal any further mutations. Hum Mol Genet 1998; 7: 751–753.

37. Spillantini MG, Schmidt ML, Lee VM, Trojanowski JQ, Jakes R, Goedert M. Alpha-synuclein in Lewy bodies. Nature 1997; 388: 839–840.

38. Krüger R, Kuhn W, Müller T, et al. Ala39Pro mutation in the gene encoding a-synuclein in Parkinson's disease. Nat Genet 1998; 18: 106–108.

39. Gasser T, Müller-Myhsok B, Wszolek ZK, et al. A susceptibility locus for Parkinson's disease maps to chromosome 2p13. Nat Genet 1998; 18: 262265.

40. Lander ES, Schork NJ. Genetic dissection of complex traits. Science 1994; 265: 2037–2048.

41. Strittmatter WJ, Saunders AM, Schmechel D, et al. Apolipoprotein E: high-avidity binding to beta-amyloid and increased frequency of type 4 allele in late-onset familial Alzheimer disease. Proc Natl Acad Sci USA 1993; 90: 1977–1981.

42. Wood N, this volume.

DISCUSSION

Mizuno: We are studying autosomal dominant and recessive forms of familial parkinsonism and have found a mutation in the manganese SOD gene which showed complete segregation with the disease. Initially we thought this was the disease gene, but it was instead only a linkage and the actual disease gene appears to be present in a location very close to the manganese SOD gene. A similar possibility exists for the α-synuclein gene mutation. So far I believe that a mutation in the α-synuclein gene is the cause of autosomal–dominant PD in these specific families. But, there is a small possibility that what we see is a very close linkage and that PD in these cases is due to another gene which is very close to the α-synuclein gene. How many microsatellite markers have you studied in your European families? Is there a possibility in any one of your families of linkage to chromosome 4, but that the cause is not a mutation in the α-synuclein gene but rather that the α-synuclein gene is very close to the responsible gene locus?

Gasser: There is a possibility that one family with a slightly positive lod score is, in fact, linked to chromosome 4 and that they do not have an α-synuclein mutation but a mutation in another gene in that region. The family is too small to answer this question. We would have to look for this other gene and we do not really have enough evidence to embark on such an endeavour in this particular family at the present time. We do not have a dominant family that is definitely linked to chromosome 4. A German colleague has unpublished data on another α-synuclein mutation in a patient with familial PD which is distinct from that described by Dr. Polymeropoulos. All the other affected family members have died so it cannot be demonstrated if this mutation is cosegregating with the disease. It appears to be a functionally relevant mutation that leads to an amino acid exchange in the terminal proline group. I think that this is what everybody is looking for, namely a mutation in a different region and in a different population. We do not know if the mutations in the Contursi kindred and the three Greek kindreds are from individuals with the same genetic background. At the moment we are actively looking for mutation in patients with familial PD with a different genetic background or with a different mutation in the α-synuclein gene.

Olanow: What would be the significance of finding no other mutations in α-synuclein? If this is a gain-of-function mutation resulting in a toxic effect, might one not expect to find multiple mutations?

Gasser: The idiopathic torsion dystonia phenotype is apparently caused by a single mutation. If however no other mutation is identified, it will be difficult to prove that it is a disease-causing mutation and not, as Dr. Mizuno said, a polymorphism that cosegregates with a true mutation.

Olanow: The dystonia gene defect is a deletion and the same genetic pattern could be seen with one of two mutations. If an animal model carrying that mutation was created it would be extremely helpful. If it developed a dystonia phenotype it would demonstrate that this was a specific gene defect that resulted in the disorder. Further, such a model would be extremely useful for studying the pathophysiology and pathogenesis of dystonia. The same is true with respect to the α-synuclein mutation. It would be very important indeed to develop α-synuclein transgenic and knock-out and knock-in animal models although this may be difficult because α-synuclein is so widespread. In addition to providing clues as to the mechanism responsible for cell death, such models might be very useful for testing putative neuroprotective drugs.

Jenner: How is one to develop such a model if some normal animals carry the mutant gene? It will be important to test this in animals that do not have the mutant protein as their natural form of α-synuclein.

Olanow: We might still end up with a valuable model of PD if the mutant α-synuclein gene causes cell death by way of a toxic product or a dominant negative effect.

Jenner: Another way to create a model expressing mutant α-synuclein might be through the use of a viral vector. This could be used in tissue culture or animal models.

CHAPTER SEVEN

Genetic risk factors in Parkinson's disease

NICHOLAS W. WOOD

University Department of Clinical Neurology,
Institute of Neurology, London, UK

NATURE *VERSUS* NURTURE

Evidence for the role of genetic factors in the pathogenesis of Parkinson's disease (PD) comes from four sources – twins,[1] large pedigrees and positional cloning,[2,3] candidate studies (this chapter), and epidemiological studies on a range of risk factors.

The twin data to date are rather unsatisfactory,[1,4–6] but molecular genetic studies have already contributed to our understanding of the pathogenesis of PD and will continue to do so. This is illustrated by the identification of the first pathogenic mutation in a gene causing autosomal dominant PD.[2,7,8] The debate continues over the extent of the roles of genetics and environmental factors in the pathology of PD.

PD is clearly a disease with an age-dependent prevalence and this may be the single biggest determinant of developing the disorder. The presence of a family history is also a significant factor. An increased odds ratio for another family member with PD is found in almost all large epidemiological studies.[10–13] While this may be a factor in only the minority of PD patients, genetic risk factors are a clear lead in trying to define the pathophysiologic basis of cell death in PD. Other factors associated with an increased risk of developing PD include rural living, pesticides, and drinking well water (reviewed elsewhere in this book). Smoking tobacco seems to protect the substantia nigra, although the mechanism behind this effect is unclear and appears to be independent of its other life-shortening properties.

LINKAGE AND ASSOCIATION

Linkage[2,3] and association studies can be used to identify genetic factors. The success of linkage and subsequent positional cloning is undoubted and improvement in our understanding of α-synuclein will assist in the search for other genes and environmental triggers.[7] α-Synuclein will, however, only account for a very small proportion of familial PD cases[14] and there is as yet no evidence for its involvement in 'sporadic' PD (Vaughan, personal communication). It is nevertheless clear evidence and is analogous to Alzheimer's disease (AD) where the first identified mutation in amyloid precursor protein demonstrated the importance of amyloid protein in the pathology of the disorder.

Since PD is a disease predominantly of older age, the absence of parents is a problem for genetic researchers. Gene mapping is not straightforward in a disease where large families with multiple affected members are rare, penetrance of the gene or genes is likely to be low, onset is late, the mode of inheritance is not known, and genetic heterogeneity is now certain. A combination of approaches is therefore necessary. The rare autosomal dominant pedigrees[15-17] will continue to be mapped and the genes cloned. The most appropriate strategy for mapping complex disease traits is the study of affected relative pairs using highly informative DNA polymorphisms spanning the genome to detect genetic linkage using non-parametric methods.[3]

These methods are based on a random genome screening approach which is time-consuming and laborious. A potentially quicker approach is to use knowledge of the pathology of PD as a guide towards putative candidate genes. With the tremendous technological strides of the past few years, the array of possible candidates is no longer too onerous to contemplate investigating. The method of analysis should, however, be considered. Linkage detects co-segregation of a particular marker (allele) with a defined phenotype (disease state). It is robust but relatively weak when using small pedigrees. The non-parametric sib-pair method has the additional disadvantage of poor localisation capacity. A useful solution is association studies, which give much greater weight to which allele is co-segregating with the disease. They are extremely powerful, since they involve tens of thousands of meioses. The cost of such power is the reduced genetic distances over which such 'linkage' can exist. This can be circumvented by using selected markers/polymorphisms that are extremely close to, or involve, the gene itself. A second and sometimes neglected corollary is that the marker/polymorphism should have a functional consequence, and that the causative mutation is postulated to be the same in the vast majority of patients (*i.e.* linkage disequilibrium). A third difficulty is that populations, though mixed in many countries, are still stratified, meaning that nearly all association studies are open to bias. The 'gold standard' of association studies is to define the allele frequencies in the patients from within the population at risk, thereby negating these confounding variables. One extremely useful method is to ascertain the parental genotype and consider which allele is transmitted or not transmitted. This is extremely difficult with a late-onset disease such as PD where most of the parents are deceased. This effect can be lessened by the use of other siblings to extrapolate the parental genotype and by using highly informative markers. A second and perhaps better method is to define allele frequencies within a population from which a number of people will develop a given disease. Since the frequencies have been defined from the same population, any difference in allele frequency must be important to disease susceptibility or protection.

A potential problem with any genetic study is the clarity and uniformity of a given diagnosis. The clinical neurologist's approach is to ascertain a population with as clearly defined PD as possible. In doing this, they must look for findings incompatible with the diagnosis of idiopathic PD. These include early dementia or postural instability, a supranuclear gaze palsy, cerebellar or pyramidal signs, and evidence of autonomic failure. Supportive clinical features are a classical rest tremor, a unilateral onset, and a significant response to levodopa treatment. To the neuropathologist, there must be depigmentation of the substantia nigra with cell loss in the zona compacta and the presence of Lewy bodies in remaining nerve cells. Thus, PD can be defined by a clinical syndrome, with exclusion criteria, and a distinctive pathological picture. This does not necessarily mean that there is a single cause for PD, in the same way that there is no single cause for AD. Using the above schema, the misdiagnosis rate in life is likely to be between 10–15%.[18] A solution is to use only case material from pathologically proven cases although this has its own limitations.

CANDIDATE STUDIES TO DATE

The different approaches used in candidate gene research include linkage analyses (pedigrees permitting), direct sequencing and allelic association in small families or sporadic cases. The data are rather confusing and contradictory,[19–32] largely due to the methodological problems listed above. The linkage data are derived from a relatively small number of families and consequently the findings of absence of linkage can only be interpreted in this limited fashion.

The allelic association findings are even more confusing and negative studies are only as good as the power to detect association in the cohort sizes used. The major determinant of the power is the contribution of a given factor to the disease state, which in these cases is unknown, so negative studies can again only be a relative weighting of the evidence rather than an absolute indication of a lack of association. In contrast, positive findings excite more interest and debrisoquine 4-hydroxylase has attracted the most attention. One study found an increased frequency of a mutant allele (CYP2D6B) but failed to find an increased number of poor metabolizers,[19] i.e. the increased risk appeared to be due to allelic association rather than the functional consequences, whereas a second study (using greater numbers of patients) described an increased frequency of poor metabolizers but not an excess of the mutant allele.[31] Some studies have supported these data[32] while others have failed to find an association.[20,22,23]

An association between the presence of slow acetylator phenotypes and the presence of PD has been identified in 100 pathologically proven cases of PD from the UK Parkinson's Disease Brain Bank and in 100 index cases of familial PD.[20] The slow acetylator phenotype (defined from the genotype) was more common in the familial PD group (69%) than in the controls (37%), giving an odds ratio of 3.79 (95% CI 2.08–6.9). The odds ratio for the sporadic PD patients compared with controls was 2.45 (95% CI 1.37–4.38). Moreover, there was a highly significant trend for slow acetylator phenotype from controls through sporadics to familial cases ($p=0.000002$), indicating that the genetic loading for this factor is highest in familial PD. The study clearly needs validating and if it passes this test then the search will be on for the 'naturally occurring' substrate. Most detoxifying enzymes are defined by their ability to handle drugs, but they existed long before man-made chemicals. The demonstration of an association between a detoxifying enzyme and PD could give a direct lead in the search for environmental triggers.

SUMMARY

- There is overwhelming evidence for a role of genetic factors in the etiology of PD.
- Candidate gene studies are a useful and powerful adjunct to the armamentarium of the researcher but robustness of the data is difficult to achieve. This is illustrated by the fact that despite the large literature on this subject only a relatively small proportion of studies have been reproduced.
- Difficulties and possible solutions to some of the inherent biases in most of the studies have been discussed.
- A recent study suggests a relationship between slow acetylator phenotype and PD.

ACKNOWLEDGMENTS

The support of the UK Parkinson's Disease Society and its Brain Bank, the Biomed II project (Contract No. PL950664), the Doris Hillier award of the British Medical Association, and the Brain Research Trust is gratefully acknowledged.

REFERENCES

1. Johnson WG, Hodge SE, Duvoisin R. Twin studies and the genetics of Parkinson's disease—a reappraisal. Mov Disord 1990; 5: 187–194.

2. Polymeropoulos MH, this volume.

3. Gasser T, this volume.

4. Marsden CD. Parkinson's disease in twins [letter]. J Neurol Neurosurg Psychiatry 1987; 50: 105–106.

5. Ward CD, Duvoisin RC, Ince SE, Nutt JD, Eldridge R, Calne DB. Parkinson's disease in 65 pairs of twins and in a set of quadruplets. Neurol 1983; 33: 815–824.

6. Vieregge P, Schiffke KA, Friedrich HJ, Muller B, Ludin HP. Parkinson's disease in twins. Neurol 1992; 42: 1453–1461.

7. Polymeropoulos MH, Lavedan C, Leroy E, Ide SE, Dehejia A, Dutra A, Pike B, Root H, Rubenstein J, Boyer R, Stenroos ES, Chandrasekharappa S, Athanassiadou A, Papapetropoulos T, Johnson WG, Lazzarini AM, Duvoisin RC, Di Iorio G, Golbe LI, Nussbaum RL. Mutation in the alpha-synuclein gene identified in families with Parkinson's disease. Science 1997; 276: 2045–2047.

8. Polymeropoulos MH, Higgins JJ, Golbe LI, Johnson WG, Ide SE, Di Iorio G, Sanges G, Stenroos ES, Pho LT, Schaffer AA, Lazzarini AM, Nussbaum RL, Duvoisin RC. Mapping of a gene for Parkinson's disease to chromosome 4q21–q23. Science 1996; 274: 1197–1199.

9. Langston JW, this volume.

10. De Michele G, Filla A, Volpe G, De Marco V, Gogliettino A, Ambrosio G, Marconi R, Castellano AE, Campanella G. Environmental and genetic risk factors in Parkinson's disease: a case-control study in southern Italy. Mov Disord 1996; 11: 17–23.

11. Marder K, Tang MX, Mejia H, Alfaro B, Cote L, Louis E, Groves J, Mayeux R. Risk of Parkinson's disease among first-degree relatives: A community-based study. Neurol 1996; 47: 155–160.

12. Seidler A, Hellenbrand W, Robra BP, Vieregge P, Nischan P, Joerg J, Oertel WH, Ulm G, Schneider E. Possible environmental, occupational, and other etiologic factors for Parkinson's disease: a case-control study in Germany. Neurol 1996; 46: 1275–1284.

13. Payami H, Larsen K, Bernard S, Nutt J. Increased risk of Parkinson's disease in parents and siblings of patients. Ann Neurol 1994; 36: 659–661.

14. Gasser T, Muller Myhsok B, Wszolek ZK, Durr A, Vaughan JR, Bonifati V, Meco G, Bereznai B, Oehlmann R, Agid Y, Brice A, Wood NW. Genetic heterogeneity in familial parkinsonism: no linkage to the PD-1 locus on chromosome 4q in 11 of 13 families. Science 1997; 277: 388–389.

15. Waters CH, Miller CA. Autosomal dominant Lewy body parkinsonism in a four-generation family. Ann Neurol 1994; 35: 59–64.

16. Wszolek ZK, Pfeiffer B, Fulgham JR, Parisi JE, Thompson BM, Uitti RJ, Calne DB, Pfeiffer RF. Western Nebraska family (family D) with autosomal dominant parkinsonism. Neurol 1995; 45: 502–505.

17. Markopoulou K, Wszolek ZK, Pfeiffer RF. A Greek-American kindred with autosomal dominant, levodopa-responsive parkinsonism and anticipation. Ann Neurol 1995; 38: 373–378.

18. Hughes A, Daniel SE, Kilford L, Lees AJ. Accuracy of clinical diagnosis of idiopathic Parkinson's disease: a clinicopathological study. J Neurol Neurosurg Psychiatry 1992; 55: 181–184.

19. Armstrong M, Daly AK, Cholerton S, Bateman DN, Idle JR. Mutant debrisoquine hydroxylation genes in Parkinson's disease. Lancet 1992; 339: 1017–1018.

20. Bandmann O, Vaughan J, Holmans P, Marsden CD, Wood NW. Association of slow acetylator genotype for N-acetyl-transferase 2 with familial Parkinson's disease. Lancet 1997; 350: 1136–1139.

21. Bordet R, Broly F, Destee A, Libersa C. Genetic polymorphism of cytochrome P450 2D6 in idiopathic Parkinson disease and diffuse Lewy body disease. Clin Neuropharmacol 1994; 17: 484–488.

22. Diederich N, Hilger C, Goetz CG, Keipes M, Hentges F, Vieregge P, Metz H. Genetic variability of the CYP 2D6 gene is not a risk factor for sporadic Parkinson's disease. Ann Neurol 1996; 40: 463–465.

23. Gasser T, Muller Myhsok B, Supala A, Zimmer E, Wieditz G, Wszolek ZK, Vieregge P, Bonifati V, Oertel WH. The CYP2D6B allele is not over represented in a population of German patients with idiopathic Parkinson's disease. J Neurol Neurosurg Psychiatry 1996; 61: 518–520.

24. Kosel S, Lucking CB, Egensperger R, Mehraein P, Graeber MB. Mitochondrial NADH dehydrogenase and CYP2D6 genotypes in Lewy-body parkinsonism. J Neurosci Res 1996; 44: 174–183.

25. Kurth MC, Kurth JH. Variant cytochrome P450 CYP2D6 allelic frequencies in Parkinson's disease. Am J Med Genet 1993; 48: 166–168.

26. Landi MT, Ceroni M, Martignoni E, Bertazzi PA, Caporaso NE, Nappi G. Gene–environment interaction in Parkinson's disease. The case of CYP2D6 gene polymorphism. Adv Neurol 1996; 69: 61–72.

27. Plante Bordeneuve V, Davis MB, Maraganore DM, Marsden CD, Harding AE. Debrisoquine hydroxylase gene polymorphism in familial Parkinson's disease. J Neurol Neurosurg Psychiatry 1994; 57: 911–913.

28. Ray Chaudhuri K, Smith C, Gough AC, Novak N, Chamoun V, Wolf CR, Leigh PN. Debrisoquine hydroxylase gene polymorphism in Parkinson's disease and amyotrophic lateral sclerosis. J Neurol Neurosurg Psychiatry 1995; 58: 109.

29. Saitoh T, Xia Y, Chen X, Masliah E, Galasko D, Shults C, Thal LJ, Hansen LA, Katzman R. The CYP2D6B mutant allele is overrepresented in the Lewy body variant of Alzheimer's disease. Ann Neurol 1995; 37: 110–112.

30. Sandy MS, Armstrong M, Tanner CM, Daly AK, Di Monte DA, Langston JW, Idle JR. CYP2D6 allelic frequencies in young-onset Parkinson's disease. Neurol 1996; 47: 225–230.

31. Smith CA, Gough AC, Leigh PN, Summers BA, Harding AE, Maraganore DM, Sturman SG, Schapira AH, Williams AC, et al. Debrisoquine hydroxylase gene polymorphism and susceptibility to Parkinson's disease. Lancet 1992; 339: 1375–1377 [erratum Lancet 1992; 340: 64].

32. Tsuneoka Y, Matsuo Y, Iwahashi K, Takeuchi H, Ichikawa Y. A novel cytochrome P-450IID6 mutant gene associated with Parkinson's disease. J Biochem Tokyo 1993; 114: 263–266.

CHAPTER EIGHT

Autosomal dominant Parkinson's disease and α-synuclein

MIHAEL H. POLYMEROPOULOS

Laboratory of Genetic Disease Research, National Human Genome Research
Institute, National Institutes of Health, Bethesda, Maryland, USA

Parkinson's disease (PD) is the second most common neurodegenerative disorder after Alzheimer's disease (AD).[1] The primary diagnostic signs of the illness include tremor, bradykinesia, muscular rigidity and postural instability. Responsiveness to levodopa constitutes additional evidence for the accuracy of the diagnosis. The pathologic hallmark in the brains of PD patients is the Lewy body,[2] an intracytoplasmic eosinophilic inclusion found in a number of brain regions in PD patients, which include the substantia nigra, the hypothalamus, the hippocampus, the cerebral cortex, the nucleus basalis of Meynert, the locus ceruleus and in the gastrointestinal tract. Lewy bodies have also been described in diffuse Lewy body dementia, which is characterized by parkinsonism and dementia.[4]

Determination of the genetic factors in PD has been hampered by the same factors that impede genetic discoveries in any late-onset complex disorders. More than one gene abnormality could be responsible, leading to genetic heterogeneity even within the same family. Association studies have been attempted for a number of candidate genes, but none has led to conclusive results.[4-8] In a large Italian kindred, a highly penetrant autosomal dominant PD locus was recently identified on 4q21–q23.[9] The Italian family, known as the Contursi pedigree, segregates for the autosomal dominant form of the illness, which includes typical PD symptoms and the presence of Lewy bodies.[10] Onset of PD in this family occurred at an early average age of 46 years. All but one of the affected individuals examined carried a common haplotype. The affected individual was related to the kindred through his unaffected mother, but his father is unrelated to the family and also carries the diagnosis of PD. This finding is characteristic of the genetic complexities of common diseases, where phenocopies of the disorder are expected to be found in large families, and can frequently obscure the presence of a segregating locus.

The gene for the α-synuclein protein was known to reside in the area of linkage in this family. Mutation analysis in the coding region of the gene in the Contursi pedigree revealed a missense mutation in the third exon.[11] The mutation G209A results in the substitution of one amino acid, Ala53Thr, and the introduction of a new restriction site Tsp45I. The Ala53Thr substitution was not found in 314 control chromosomes, which included 200 control individuals from the areas surrounding Contursi. The mutation has since been shown in five unrelated Greek families which also share the characteristic of early onset PD phenotype. The Greek families came primarily from the north-west Peloponnese and the Ionian regions. Haplotype analysis in these families fails to exclude a shared region immediately surrounding the gene, although the genetic markers used were not very informative. This suggests that there is a possibility for a common founder PD chromosome in the lower Mediterranean basin.

The lack of linkage in the 4q21–q23 region in two recent reports of 13 and 93 PD families suggests that the Ala53Thr mutation will only account for a small portion of families with PD. Although of low frequency, the mutation in α-synuclein offers unique insights into the pathophysiology of the disorder. α-Synuclein was first identified in the Pacific electric ray, *Torpedo californica*, and subsequently in the rat brain.[12,13] It belongs to a gene family, two members of which are highly homologous in humans.[14] It is a small protein of 140 amino acids in length, characterized by repeats with the consensus amino acid motif KTKEGV. α-Synuclein is abundant in the brain, particularly in the olfactory bulb and tract, the hypothalamus and substantia nigra. Its presence in the olfactory neurons is intriguing given the high frequency of anosmia in PD patients. The human protein was first isolated as the precursor of a partial peptide from AD plaques.[15] Its physicochemical properties suggest that it is a natively unfolded molecule that can self-aggregate and form amyloid fibrils *in vitro*.[16] Very little is known about the function of the protein, although its ortholog in the canary, the synelfin gene, has been implicated in song learning.[17]

The missense mutation in the α-synuclein gene in PD families and the natural properties of the protein suggest that the mutation may alter the structure of the molecule, predisposing it to self-aggregation and therefore rendering it less readily degradable. α-Synuclein is an abundant component of the Lewy body,[18] and positive staining was also seen in engorged neurons of the substantia nigra, structures known as Lewy neurites. Since these observations are made in PD patients with and without the mutation in the α-synuclein gene, it appears that α-synuclein may play a central role in the pathophysiology of PD. Environmental factors such as increased oxidative stress and toxins could also contribute to the misfolding of the molecule leading to its increased aggregation. Alternatively, alterations in the ubiquitin pathway for protein degradation by the 26S proteasome could promote the accumulation of polyubiquitinated protein aggregates inside the cell, eventually leading to cell death.

Summary

- Multiple factors have been considered to be contributory and or causative for PD.

- Hereditary factors have recently emerged as a focus of PD research.

- The study of a large Italian family with PD led to linkage at chromosome 4q21–q23.

- Mutation analysis led to mapping of a mutation in the gene that encodes for α-synuclein

- Several unrelated PD families have also been detected to have a missense mutation in this gene.

- α-Synuclein is an abundant presynaptic protein of unknown function. It is possible that the mutation identified in the PD families may result in self aggregation of the α-synuclein protein leading to the development of intracytoplasmic inclusion bodies and eventually to neuronal cell death.

- The discovery of a mutation in the α-synuclein gene may provide insights in the pathways that lead to neuronal degeneration.

REFERENCES

1. Schapira AHV. Nuclear and mitochondrial genetics in Parkinson's disease. J Med Genet 1995; 32: 411–414.

2. Lewy F. Zur pathologischen Anatomie der Paralysis agitans. Dtsch Z Nervenheikd 1913; 50: 50–55.

3. Katzman R, Galasko D, Saitoh T, Thal LJ, Hansen L. Genetic evidence that the Lewy body variant is indeed a phenotypic variant of Alzheimer's disease. Brain Cogn 1995; 28: 259–265.

4. Takakubo F, Yamamoto M, Ogawa N, Yamashita Y, Mizuno Y, Kondo I. Genetic association between cytochrome P450IA1 gene and susceptibility to Parkinson's disease. J Neural Transm Gen Sect 1996; 103: 843–849.

5. Sandy MS, Armstrong M, Tanner CM, Daly AK, Di Monte DA, Langston JW, Idle JR. CYP2D6 allelic frequencies in young-onset Parkinson's disease. Neurol 1996; 47: 225–230.

6. Plante-Bordeneuve V, Davis MB, Maraganore DM, Marsen CD, Harding AE. Debrisoquine hydroxylase gene polymorphism in familial Parkinson's disease. J Neurol Neurosurg Psychiatr 1994; 57: 911–913.

7. Hotamisligil GS, Girmen AS, Fink JS, Tivol E, Shalish C, Trfatter J, Baenziger J, Diamond S, Markham C, Sullivan J. Hereditary variations in monoamine oxidase as a risk factor for Parkinson's disease. Mov Disord 1994; 9: 305–310.

8. Whitehead AS, Bertrandy S, Finnan F, Butler A, Smith GD, Ben-Shlomo Y. Frequency of the apolipoprotein E epsilon 4 allele in a case-control study of early onset Parkinson's disease. J Neurol Neurosurg Psychiatr 1996; 61: 347–351.

9. Polymeropoulos MH, Higgins JJ, Golbe LI, Johnson WG, Ide SE, Di Iorio G, Sanges G, Stenroos ES, Pho LT, Schaffer AA, Lazzarini AM, Nussbaum RL, Duvoisin RC. Mapping of a gene for Parkinson's disease to chromosome 4q21–q23. Science 1996; 274: 1197–1199.

10. Golbe LI, Di Iorio G, Sanges G, Lazzarini AM, La Sala S, Bonavita V, Duvoisin RC. Clinical genetic analysis of Parkinson's disease in the Contursi kindred. Ann Neurol 1996: 40: 767–775.

11. Polymeropoulos MH, Lavedan C, Leroy E, Ide SE, Dehejia A, Dutra A, Pike B, Root H, Rubenstein J, Boyer R, Stenroos ES, Chandrasekharappa S, Athanassiadou A, Papapetropoulos T, Johnson WG, Lazzarini AM, Duvoisin RC, Di Iorio G, Golbe LI, Nussbaum RL. Mutation in the α-Synuclein gene identified in families with Parkinson's disease. Science 1997; 276: 2045–2047.

12. Maroteaux L, Campanelli JT, Scheller RH. Synuclein: a neuron-specific protein localized to the nucleus and presynaptic nerve terminal. J Neurosci 1988; 8: 2804–2815.

13. Maroteaux L, Scheller RH. The rat brain synucleins; family of proteins transiently associated with neuronal membrane. Brain Res Mol Brain Res 1991; 11: 335–343.

14. Jakes R, Spillantini MG, Goedert M. Identification of two distinct synucleins from human brain. FEBS Lett 1994; 345: 27–32.

15. Ueda K, Fukushima H, Masliah E, Xia Y, Iwai A, Yoshimoto M, Otero DA, Kondo J, Ihara Y, Saitoh T. Molecular cloning of cDNA encoding an unrecognized component of amyloid in Alzheimer disease. Proc Natl Acad Sci USA 1993; 90: 11282–11286.

16. Weinreb PH, Zhen W, Poon AW, Conway KA, Lansbury PT. NACP, a protein implicated in Alzheimer's disease and learning, is naturally unfolded. Biochem 1996; 35: 13709–13715.

17. George JM, Jin H, Woods WS, Clayton DP. Characterization of a novel protein regulated during the critical period for song learning in the zebra finch. Neuron 1995; 15: 361–372.

18. Spillantini MG, Schmidt ML, Lee VM, Trojanowski JQ, Jakes R, Goedert M. α-synuclein in Lewy bodies. Nature 1997; 388: 839–840.

DISCUSSION

Mizuno: Congratulations on your excellent study and your exciting findings. You showed immunoreactive α-synuclein in the axons of patients with PD. Did you see similar immunoreactive α-synuclein in axons of individuals with normal brains?

Polymeropoulos: We did not see any aggregates in normal brains. Small speckles of immunoreactivity were found everywhere, in all brains. We looked at diffuse Lewy body dementia brains and Lewy bodies in the cortex were heavily stained in a manner identical to the Lewy bodies in the substantia nigra in PD patients. In Alzheimer's disease, the plaques stain only very weakly. We saw no staining in Pick's disease suggesting that increased staining may be a specific process.

Olanow: It appeared that most of the staining for α-synuclein was around the periphery of the Lewy body rather than in the core. Since the periphery is comprised of different neurofilaments than those in the center of the Lewy body, do you think that this may bear on α-synuclein accumulation?

Polymeropoulos: I do not think so. We do not know how epitopes react, whether they were covered or more exposed. It is too early to say.

Hirsch: Is α-synuclein really ubiquitinated and do you have direct evidence of that? If not, would it be possible to check using Western blot analysis to see if there is a band which is co-stained by anti-ubiquitin and anti-α-synuclein antibodies?

Polymeropoulos: It is not known whether α-synuclein goes through a ubiquitin degradation process. However, most of the cellular proteins go through the ubiquitination process, and the KTKEGV motif could be a signal for ubiquitination. Immunocytochemistry studies indicate that α-synuclein and ubiquitin co-localize. The experiment you suggested we are doing now, but slightly differently. We are transfecting α-synuclein clones in 293 kidney cells and then inhibiting the proteasome which could lead to an accumulation of polyubiquitinated material.

Morrison: Have you done any co-precipitation studies to see if it is complexing with any of the proteins known to be in Lewy bodies?

Polymeropoulos: No. We know that there are a lot of proteins in Lewy bodies, and neurofilaments are very abundant. Virtually every protein gets caught in there so we have not done any co-precipitation.

Morrison: With regard to the question of localization in the normal brain, you mentioned a few specific regions, the olfactory bulb, the amygdala and the hippocampus. Are you implying that those regions are uniquely well-labeled or do you find labeling throughout the brain?

Polymeropoulos: These are not my experiments and they are mRNA *in situ* studies.

Langston: Can you speculate on how α-synuclein missense mutation leads to cell loss in the substantia nigra?

Polymeropoulos: There is evidence in the literature that introduction of β-amyloid in to PC12 cells leads to apoptosis. Whether this death occurs via apoptosis is debatable. I have a feeling that the Lewy body is going to be central in the PD process and not merely a by-product of a dead neuron. If the hypothesis is correct that PD is a disorder of proteasome input or output, then proteasome regulation is very important, as is removal of toxic proteins from the cell. Cells are very sophisticated and there is a very fine balance for regulation through the degradation of protein products. There could be many ways in which cells could become sick if proteasomes were defective. Proteasomes are also found in the nucleus, so I would like to speculate that polyglutamine tract disorders could represent intranuclear proteasome bound protein aggregates.

Shoulson: What do we know about α-synuclein in its wild-type or mutated form, or its distribution within the brain, that might account for the regional vulnerability seen in PD, at least within the nigrostriatal system in the basal ganglia?

Polymeropoulos: α-Synuclein is an abundant protein in the brain. The only area in which it is not found much is the corpus callosum. The substantia nigra is a tissue with very large degrees of oxidation, due to the fact that it produces dopamine. Some metabolites of dopamine are very harmful substances known as quinones. A recent publication in the *EMBO Journal* suggests that a specific glutathione reductase enzyme is expressed in the substantia nigra to accommodate these quinone sub-products. The patterns of oxidation in the substantia nigra are very important and are not found in any other cells in the brain. Glutathione is a very reactive substance, as is ubiquitin. Ubiquitin attaches itself to proteins through a thiol ester between the terminal glycine and the epsilon amino group of lysine. We also know also that glutathione incorrectly attaches to ubiquitin by virtue of the activated thiol ester bond. So glutathione and ubiquitination are not very far apart. In fact, the disattachment of glutathione from ubiquitin is well-regulated inside the cell because addition of 5 nM amounts of glutathione would immediately deplete ubiquitin. There is also literature to suggest that manganese, a known poison, can, in fact, alter the structure of proteins from an α-helical formation to the β-sheet.

Olanow: But systemically administered manganese does this in a different location, so what is special about the substantia nigra that causes it to be preferentially affected in PD? Is there any evidence that α-synuclein preferentially accumulates there?

Polymeropoulos: It is widely distributed and quantitative studies of distribution have not yet been performed.

Jenner: In our studies on oxidative damage in the brain, we find increased levels of protein carbonyls all over the brain in PD, not just in the nigra. One wonders whether there is a very general process occurring but, for some reason, the nigra is extremely sensitive to this process.

Quinn: Do you see any staining in the glia or only in neurons?

Polymeropoulos: We found no staining in the glia.

Marsden: You showed immunostaining for α-synuclein in neurites in the substantia nigra. There is general agreement that there is much greater loss of terminal dopamine content than there is of nigral cells themselves. In the striatum of PD patients, do you see immunostaining for α-synuclein in dopaminergic terminals?

Polymeropoulos: As we move out of the zona compacta, the lack of staining parallels the lack of Lewy bodies.

Melamed: With regard to the theory that oxidative stress is the cause of the original localization of the changes, we should remember that in PD Lewy bodies are present in cholinergic neurons, serotoninergic neurons, monoaminergic neurons, as well as in dopaminergic neurons. They are also present not only in the central nervous system but also in the periphery. Thus, they occur in areas where there is no evident oxidant stress.

Olanow: One could hypothesize that there is a defect in the clearance of proteins in PD. This could be due to mutation of the protein as in your genetic cases. Alternatively there could be a defect in proteasomes, impaired ubiquitination, or oxidative damage severe enough to damage proteins and/or proteasomes and prevent their clearance. As Dr Riederer has pointed out, these protein deposits can generate free radicals, but it is still not clear how a protein aggregate might lead to cell death.

Polymeropoulos: I am uncertain whether anyone has shown a defect in the process of ubiquitination or in the capacity of proteasomes to degrade proteins *per se*. On the other hand, why is there not a proteasome defect in every cell? We know that there are subunit differences between tissues. Some tissues specifically express a set of subunits and the assembly of the proteasome is very dynamic. Every five days, proteasomes are recycled and if cells are treated with IFN-γ they substitute a set of subunits for others.

Marsden: You are linking the protein aggregates related to α-synuclein to similar aggregates in Alzheimer's disease and prion disease. Why is the substantia nigra relatively spared in Alzheimer's disease and prion disease?

Polymeropoulos: Alzheimer's disease is different because the accumulation is extracellular and in prion disorders the deleterious protein is a self-propagating prion protein. I do not know why the substantia nigra is spared. Moreover, an abnormal structure can induce a bad conformation in an otherwise normal protein. Native α-synuclein is unfolded so if the mutated form assumes a rigid conformation, it could force the normal counterpart into an equally rigid structure.

CHAPTER NINE

Structure function in neuroprotection and apoptosis

KATHERINE L.B. BORDEN

Departments of Neurology and Physiology and Biophysics,
Mount Sinai School of Medicine,
New York, New York, USA

STRUCTURE–FUNCTION RELATIONSHIPS IN NEUROPROTECTION

α-Synuclein

The importance of α-synuclein in neurodegenerative disease became apparent when a 35-residue fragment was found in the non-amyloid component (NAC) of Alzheimer's disease (AD) plaques.[1] mRNA for α-synuclein, the precursor protein to NAC, is expressed in high levels in the brain where it is concentrated in presynaptic terminals.[1–3]

α-Synuclein is comprised of three separate domains – the amphipathic repeat region (residues 1–60), the NAC region (residues 61–89), and the acidic region (residues 100–130). It belongs to a highly conserved family of proteins including rat synucleins,[4] rat and bovine phosphoneuroprotein (PNP-14),[1,5,6] canary synelfin[3] and human β-synuclein.[7] The NAC region found in α-synuclein is partly conserved in β-synuclein and PNP-14. Sequence similarities also exist between the NAC region (66–73), Alzheimer β protein (Aβ) (36–42) and prion protein (PrP117–124).[8] The breast cancer susceptibility gene 1 (BCSG1) protein is the newest member of this family and is, interestingly, the only non-neuronally based protein reported thus far. BCGS1 is undetectable in normal or benign breast lesions but partial expression has been observed in ductal carcinoma and high level expression in advanced infiltrating breast cancer.[9]

α-Synuclein has several associated activities. Both α- and β-synuclein are known to bind the Aβ protein, this activity being associated with the first 56 residues of the protein as well as the NAC region, and α-synuclein can increase the rate of Aβ aggregation.[10] The NAC region is a substrate for transglutaminase activity.[11] A molecular function for the synuclein family remains elusive. The songbird homologue, synelfin, is upregulated in the song control circuit during a critical period for song learning, suggesting a role in synaptic plasticity.[3] α-Synuclein is elevated in the brains of mild AD patients in whom there appears to be no difference in expression levels between severe cases and age matched controls.[13]

Mutations in α-synuclein have been found in one family of patients with a hereditary form of Parkinson's disease (PD). A single point mutation (Ala53Thr) has been detected[13] although, intriguingly, non-human forms of the synucleins have Thr at this position normally. The BCSG1 protein is the only human protein known which normally has a Thr at position 53.

α-Synuclein is a natively unfolded protein

α-Synuclein has been shown using hydrodynamic techniques to be elongated, not globular.[14] The Stokes radius of the protein, 34 Å, is much larger than that observed for globular proteins of similar molecular weights. Sedimentation analysis indicated that α-synuclein is monomeric in solution. Hallmarks of stably folded proteins include a regular secondary structure and hydrophobic cores, within which non-polar amino acids pack tightly to avoid contact with aqueous solution, thus stabilizing the folded protein. No hydrophobic core has been found in α-synuclein. It is mainly a random coil with little α-helix or β-sheet present. Neither the secondary structure content nor the lack of hydrophobic core changed in the presence of certain chemicals, extremes of temperature and pH, confirming that there was initially little nascent structure. α-Synuclein can best be described as an extended non-compact mixture of disordered conformers. In the presence of certain alcohols, α-synuclein becomes more helical, suggesting it can undergo conformational transitions. These solvents do not, however, reflect biological environments. Under physiological conditions, α-synuclein has large exposed patches of hydrophobic residues which would normally exclude themselves from aqueous environments by folding into a tightly packed hydrophobic core. However, without this core, the hydrophobic patches aggregate with one another, forming large insoluble intermolecular aggregates.

Conformational effects of the PD mutation on α-synuclein

The mutation within the amphipathic region of α-synuclein in some PD patients may effect the 'stickiness' of α-synuclein. Proteins which normally contain Thr at position 53, including synelfin, tend to be less soluble than wild-type α-synuclein. The mutation could cause α-synuclein to favor a 'stickier' extended conformation than the wild-type. These aggregates may form the basis or contribute to the formation of Lewy bodies, which contain α-synuclein.[15]

Examples of structure function involved in amyloid deposition

In autosomal dominant hereditary amyloidosis, mutations in the lysozyme gene are present. The non-conservative amino acid substitutions are either Ile56Thr or Asp67His, and the mutant proteins have essentially identical structures to the wild-type protein.[16,17] In contrast, the mutant proteins are markedly less stable than normal lysozyme.[18] They aggregate upon heat denaturation whereas the wild-type protein does not. The Asp67His mutant has a predominance of β-sheet and loss of α-helical content compared to the wild-type under conditions in which fibrils form. For both mutations, 85% of the water-extracted fibrils ran in reduced SDS-PAGE similarly to monomeric wild-type lysozyme, and the remainder as oligomeric lysozyme aggregates. Solubilized amyloid fibrils produced monomeric lysozyme which was enzymatically active. However, these proteins have a greater tendency to reaggregate.

Mutant lysozymes, but not the wild type, form a molten globule during folding. This is a metastable non-native conformation with no compact hydrophobic core but a significant secondary structure. Mutant proteins under native conditions bound 1-anilino-naphthalenesulphonic acid, suggesting the presence of exposed hydrophobic residues uncharacteristic of the wild-type protein under these conditions. Dynamic studies indicated that the mutant and wild-type proteins were in equilibrium between folded, partially folded and completely unfolded conformations. The partly-folded forms would be prone to aggregation, thereby driving the equilibrium to produce more partly unfolded forms. These could aggregate through the β-strands, forming a large β-sheet structure and eventually fibrils.

Transition from α-helix to β-sheet

In amyloid fibril formation of Aβ and prion protein, proteins undergo conformational transitions, usually from α-helix to β-sheet. The chameleon sequence[19] is an example of protein folding and design which elucidates how these transitions may occur. The same amino acid sequence was inserted into different parts of the immunoglobulin G (IgG) protein using recombinant DNA technology. These sequences were carefully designed to fulfil structural requirements for both α-helix and β-sheet. The sequence was inserted in the only helical region of IgG, and into one of the β-strands that comprise the single β-sheet of the protein. Both resultant proteins adopted conformations identical to those observed for the parent IgG domain, indicating that tertiary interactions played a dominant role in determination of the secondary structure a given sequence might adopt. Some sequences may be inherently more helical or sheet-like than others. In some instances, however, the preferences may not be very strong, in which case single mutations could lead to an alteration in the equilibrium between forms. In such cases, the transition from α-helix to β-sheet is more easily visualized. Recent structure design experiments have indicated that two proteins could have as high as 50% sequence identity and not have any structural homology.[20]

STRUCTURE–FUNCTION RELATIONSHIPS IN PROTEINS INVOLVED IN APOPTOSIS

PML: A loss in pro-apoptotic activity results from a loss of tertiary structure

The promyelocytic leukemia protein (PML) is known to form large multiprotein complexes in the nuclei of most cells studied. These complexes are compromised in viral infection and oncogenic transformation.[21] Recent data indicate that PML plays a role in apoptosis.[22] It contains three cysteine-rich zinc-binding domains known as RING, B1 B-box and B2 B-box, and mutation in any of these metal binding regions disrupts formation of PML nuclear bodies resulting in a nuclear diffuse pattern.[23,24] Mutation also disrupts the growth and transformation suppression activities of PML.[25]

The pro-apoptotic activity of PML appears to be restricted to cells which have been serum withdrawn and show a 50% increase in cell death over controls.[22] To define the relevant region of PML, various mutant forms were designed using the 3D structures previously determined for the RING and B-box domains.[23,24] In one case, these mutations replaced two of the metal binding cysteine residues with alanine so that the RING could no longer bind zinc. The RING domain is only folded in the presence of zinc[23] so this mutant produced an unfolded RING domain within the PML protein. Transient transfection studies with the RING mutant revealed a complete loss of pro-apoptotic activity, whereas mutation in other key domains of PML resulted in outcomes similar to that observed for the wild-type protein. In the case of the PML protein, a structured RING finger domain is needed to produce nuclear bodies and to retain the pro-apoptotic activity of PML. Thus, in some cases, folded proteins are necessary for formation of large macromolecular aggregates in the cell.

GAPDH: a model for structure function studies

Glyceraldehyde 3-phosphate dehydrogenase (GAPDH) has been shown to possess several activities unrelated to its glycolytic function – uracil DNA glycosylase activity, microtubule and RNA binding activity,[26] specifically AU-rich RNA,[27,28] and tRNA transport.[29] Furthermore, GAPDH has been detected in the nucleus as well as the cytoplasm.[29] It is involved in apoptosis in cerebellar and cerebrocortical cells.[30] Both protein and mRNA levels of GAPDH increase during serum starvation and age-induced apoptosis. Antisense oligonucleotide treatment rescued these cells during various treatments.[30] GAPDH is a tetramer which exists in equilibrium between tetramers, dimers and monomers,[31] strongly favoring the tetrameric form. There are no significant differences in crystal structures of GAPDH between species, so the protein is conserved in both its amino acid sequence and tertiary structure. The active site for glycolysis is located in the Rossmann fold[32–34] to which NAD binds during glycolysis. The ability of GAPDH to bind RNA is abolished in the presence of NAD indicating that these activities occur at the same site.[27]

The molecular charge switch

Analysis of crystal structures indicates no significant structural changes before and after addition of NAD to GAPDH.[33,34] Furthermore, the cleft where RNA most likely binds is still present when NAD is added and certain nucleic acid binding residues (Arg and Lys) still protrude from the site, suggesting that they should still be able to make favorable contacts with RNA. GAPDH and RNA binding should not impede each other, but electrostatic potential calculations of the surface of GAPDH show that the normally very positive charge of the cleft is substantially decreased by the presence of the two phosphate groups of NAD, and this subsequently decreases the attraction for RNA. The ability of GAPDH to bind RNA is therefore modulated through a molecular charge switch mechanism and not conformational alterations.

Summary

- The three-dimensional conformation of proteins influences their potential to function correctly within the cell. Protein conformational issues are particularly important in neurodegeneration as has been shown by misfolded protein existing in the plaques in AD, and prion diseases.

- This review has focused on the structure function relationships of proteins involved in fibril formation and apoptosis, specifically α-synuclein, PML and GAPDH.

- Changes in conformation can cause amyloid fibril formation in several different contexts. Furthermore, the stability of the protein as well as its structure play a role in fibril formation.

- Destroying structure often means a loss in biological activity, but subtle changes such as alteration in charge, even though not accompanied by changes in conformation, can alter biological activity.

REFERENCES

1. Ueda K, Fukushima H, Masliah E, Xia Y, Iwai A, Yoshimoto M, Otero DAC, Kondo J, Ihara Y, Saitoh T. Molecular cloning of cDNA encoding an unrecognized component of amyloid in Alzheimer disease. Proc Natl Acad Sci 1993; 90: 11282–11286.

2. Irizarry MC, Kim T-W, McNamara M, Tanzi RE, George JM, Clayton DF, Hyman BT. Characterization of the precursor protein of the non-Ab component of senile plaques (NACP) in the human central nervous system. J Neuropath Exp Neurol 1996; 55: 889–895.

3. George JM, Jin H, Woods WS, Clayton DF. Characterization of a novel protein regulated during the critical period for song learning in the zebra finch. Neuron 1995; 15: 361.

4. Marteaux L, Scheller RH. The rat brain synucleins: family of proteins transiently associated with neuronal membrane. Mol Brain Res 1991; 11: 335–343.

5. Tobe T, Nakajo S, Tanaka A, Mitoya A, Omata K, Nakaya K, Tomita M, Nakamura, Y. Cloning and characterization of the cDNA encoding a novel brain specific 14 kDa protein. J Neurochem 1992; 59: 1624–1629.

6. Shibayama-Imazu T, Okahashi I, Omata K, Nakajo S, Ochiai H, Nakai Y, Hama T, Nakamura Y, Nakaya K. Cell and tissue distribution and developmental change of neuron specific 14 kDa phosphoneuroprotein. Brain Res 1993; 622: 17–25.

7. Jakes R, Spillantini MG, Goedert M. Identification of two distinct synucleins from human brain. FEBS Lett 1994; 345: 27–32.

8. Han H, Weinreb PH, Lansbury PT. The core of Alzheimer's peptide NAC forms amyloid fibrils which seed and are seeded by beta-amyloid – is NAC a common trigger or target in neurodegenerative disease? Chem Biol 1995; 2: 163–169.

9. Ji H, Liu Y, Jia T, Wang M, Liu J, Xiao G, Joseph BK, Rosen C, Shi YE. Identification of a breast cancer specific gene, BCSG1, by direct differential cDNA sequencing. Cancer Res 1997; 759–764.

10. Jensen PH, Hojrup P, Hager H, Nielsne MS, Jacobsen L, Olesen OF, Gliemann J, Jakes R. Binding of Aβ to α and β synucleins: identification of segments of α-synuclein/NAC precursor that bind Aβ and NAC. Biochem J 1997; 323: 539–546.

11. Jensen PH, Sorensen ES, Petersen TE, Gliemann J, Rasmussen LK. Residues in the synuclein consensus motif of the α-synuclein fragment, NAC, participate in transglutaminase catalyses cross-linking to Alzheimer disease amyloid βA4 peptide. Biochem J 1995; 316: 91–94.

12. Iwai A, Masliah E, Yoshimoto M, Ge N, Flanagan L, Rohan de Silva HA, Kittel A, Saitoh T. The precursor protein of non-Aβ component of Alzheimer's disease amyloid is a presynaptic protein of the central nervous system. Neuron 1995; 14: 467–475.

13. Polymeropoulos MH, Lavedan C, Leroy E, Ide SE, Dehejia A, Dutra A, Pike B, Root H, Rubenstein J, Boyer R, Stenroos ES, Chandrasekharappa S, Athanassiadou A, Papeptropoulos T, Johnson WG, Lazzarini AM, Duvoisin RC, Di Iorio G, Golbe LI, Nussbaum RL. Mutation in the α-synuclein family gene identified in families with Parkinson's disease. Science 1997; 276: 2045–2047.

14. Weinreb PH, Zhen W, Poon AW, Conway KA, Lansbury PT. NACP, a protein implicated in Alzheimer's disease and learning is natively unfolded. Biochemistry 1996; 35: 13709–13715.

15. Spillantini MG, Schmidt ML, Lee VM-Y, Trojanowski JQ, Jakes R, Goedert M. α-Synuclein in Lewy bodies. Nature 1997; 388: 839–840.

16. Artymiuk PJ, Blake CCF. Refinement of human lysozyme at 1.5Å resolution analysis of non-bonded and hydrogen bond interactions. J Mol Biol 1981; 152: 737–762.

17. Funahashi J, Takano K, Ogasahara K, Yamagata Y, Yutani K. The structure, stability and folding process of amyloidogenic mutant lysozyme. J Biochem. 1996; 120: 1216–1223.

18. Booth DR, Sunde M, Bellotti V, Robinson CV, Hutchinson WL, Fraser PE, Hawkins PN, Dobson CM, Radford SE, Blake CC, Pepys MB. Instability, unfolding and aggregation of human lysozyme variants underlying amyloid fibrillogenesis. Nature 1997; 385: 787–793.

19. Minor DL, Kim PS. Context dependent secondary structure formation of a designed protein sequence. Nature 1996; 380: 730–734.

20. Dalal S, Balasubramanian S, Regan L. Protein alchemy: changing β-sheet into α-helix. Nature Structural Biology 1997; 4: 548–552.

21. Borden KLB, Campbell-Dwyer EJ, Salvato MS. The promyeocytic leukemia protein nuclear body function: new insights from lymphocytic choriomeningits virus infection. J Virol 1998; 72: 758–766.

22. Borden KLB, Campbell-Dwyer EJ, Salvato MS. The promyelocytic leukemia protein PML has a pro-apoptotic activity mediated through its RING. Febs Lett 1997; 418: 30–34.

23. Borden KLB, Boddy MN, Lally J, O'Reilly NJ, Martin S, Howe K, Solomon E, Freemont PS. The solution structure of the RING finger domain from the acute promyelocytic leukaemia proto-oncoprotein, pml. EMBO J 1995; 14: 1532–1541.

24. Borden KLB, Lally JM, Martin S R, O'Reilly N J, Reddy BA, Etkin LD, Freemont PS. Novel topology of a zinc-binding domain involved in regulating early *Xenopus* development. EMBO J 1995; 14: 5947–5956.

25. Le XF, Yang P, Chang KS. Analysis of the growth and transformation suppressor domains of the promyelocytic leukemia gene PML. J Biol Chem 1996; 271: 130–135.

26. Sirover MA. Role of the glycolytic protein, glyceraldehyde 3-phosphate dehydrogenase, in normal cell function and in cell pathology. J Cellular Biochem 1997; 66: 133–140.

27. Nagy E, Rigby WFC. Glyceraldehyde 3-phosphate dehydrogenase selectively binds AU-rich RNA in the NAD+-binding region (Rossmann Fold). J Biol Chem 1995; 270: 2755–2763.

28. Schultz DE, Hardin CC, Lemon SM. Specific interaction of glyceraldehyde 3-phosphate dehydrogenase with the 5'-nontranslated RNA of hepatitis A virus. J Biol Chem 1996; 271: 14134–14142.

29. Singh R, Green MR. Sequence specific binding of transfer RNA by glyceraldehyde 3-phosphate dehydrogenase. Science 1993; 259: 365–368.

30. Ishitani R, Chuang D-M. Glyceraldehyde 3-phosphate dehydrogenase antisense oligodeoxynucleotides protect against cytosine arabinonucleoside-induced apoptosis in cultured cerebellar neurons. Proc Natl Acad. Sci 1996; 93: 9937–9941.

31. Minton AP, Wilf J. Effect of macromolecular crowding upon the structure and function of an enzyme: glyceraldehyde 3-phosphate dehydrogenase. Biochem 1981; 20: 4821–4826.

32. Kim H, Feil IK, Verlinde CLMJ, Petra PH, Hol WGJ. Crystal structure of glycosomal glyceraldehyde 3-phosphate dehydrogenase from *Leishmania mexicana*: Implications for structure based drug design and a new position for the inorganic phosphate binding site. Biochem 1995; 34: 14975–14986.

33. Skarzynski T, Wonacott AJ. Coenzyme induced conformational changes in glyceraldehyde 3-phosphate dehydrogenase from *Bacillus stearothermophilus*. J Mol Biol 1988; 203: 1097–1118.

34. Leslie AGW, Wonacott AJ. Structural evidence for ligand induced sequential conformational changes in glyceraldehyde 3-phosphate dehydrogenase. J Mol Biol 1984; 178: 743–772.

DISCUSSION

Olanow: The authors originally proposed in their paper that the α-synuclein mutation was a single point mutation which could allow for a switch from an α-helix to a β-sheet. What is the significance of this conversion and how might this lead to neurodegeneration?

Borden: Making a single point mutation even in a stable protein such as a lysozyme results in a familial form of apoptosis, due to instability in the protein. If this is a normal lysozyme in a partly unfolded form with a high helical content and a couple of β strands, then exposure of these β-sheets will lead to aggregation of the hydrophobic regions of the protein, which can in turn form, as in this case, amyloid fibrils. The β-sheets stack up in a direction perpendicular to the fibril. Precisely how this leads to cell death is at this time unknown but it may be important as β-sheets are seen in many neurodegenerative disorders.

Olanow: And presumably agents such as nicotine might prevent either the abnormal folding or the proteins from becoming sticky?

Borden: Yes, nicotine somehow stabilizes the helical state. All proteins, even well-folded ones, contain a certain unfolded proportion and some of these mutations may tip the equilibrium, resulting in more unfolded protein being present. Nicotine may prevent that.

Olanow: Does this bear some resemblance to prion disease, where there is little apparent change in the structure of the molecule, but abnormal folding seems to be responsible for neurodegeneration?

Borden: I think it is exactly the same. Some proteins or amino acid sequences favor either an α-helix or a β-sheet form, but the majority of the sequences will actually be determined by contact with the whole molecule. Slight tips in the balance, such as a single point mutation, can then stabilize the molecule in another form thereby potentially disrupting the local environment and leading to cell degeneration.

Marsden: This is very new material for the clinician to deal with. When these proteins unfold and aggregate in some way to produce fibrils, is the nature of the fibril determined by the basic protein itself or from constituents within the cell?

Borden: The fibrils normally form from constituents of the cell itself. Certain conformations, or half-folded conformations, will be favored over others. The nature of the fibril will be selected on the basis of the folded, or half-folded, state of the protein.

Marsden: Can you predict what we should be looking for, in terms of the type of fibrils that might occur in the cells and what is the effect of a mutation in α-synuclein and whether or not the protein is in an unfolded state?

Borden: Not really. If the synuclein sequence was put through a standard sequence prediction package, the conclusion would be that it should behave as an α-helix. But synuclein is, in fact, slightly different and firm biochemical data were required to indicate that there was no α-helix or β-sheet. Our knowledge of protein structure does not yet allow us to make predictions, especially with respect to disease, but I think this is something we must work towards.

W. Tatton: The normal songbird synuclein is the same as the mutated synuclein in parkinsonian patients. Why is the mutated form of synuclein stable in the songbird? Are you saying that the songbird protein has a stable region, because of the presence of threonine?

Borden: The songbird, the rat, and the cow all contain threonine, so the mechanism here is unclear. Interestingly, the songbird synuclein actually aggregates more readily than the normal human α-synuclein protein. Unfolded proteins are mixtures of conformations, but perhaps it may be stabilizing an unfolded protein that happens to be stickier than the others. This whole family of natively unfolded proteins is very functional. There are also other natively unfolded proteins, *e.g.* microtubule binding proteins such as tau. It has been suggested that they are proteins which mediate non-specific cellular protein–protein interaction.

Olanow: It is fascinating that the songbird synuclein is the same as the mutated synuclein in PD patients and that what is a normal constituent of the songbird induces a disease in humans.

Borden: It is important to consider that while these molecules are similar, they exist in different environments. So, the synuclein in the songbird and the mutated synuclein in humans, while they have similarities, may not be the same from a functional point of view.

Melamed: Can you explain why, if a mutation occurs in a certain protein, the clinical expression of the neurodegenerative processes begins much later in life?

Borden: Animals do not have the same lifespan as humans so we may not see the same kind of neurodegeneration take place. We could speculate that alanine in α–synuclein may have been selected on the basis of a tendency for slower formation of these large aggregates. Aggregate formation occurs over a long period of time so clearly other processes are going on. It is possible that changes in the environment that occur with aging may promote these conformational changes.

Wood: This is true for almost all dominant disorders. They often develop in adulthood although the gene defect has been present for their entire life and we do not understand why this is. Is α-synuclein the gene that causes PD in the patients with this mutation? I think it is, but it is worth considering that the mutated form is a normal constituent in some animals as you have mentioned. Moreover, the Greek families described are apparently on a trade route with the Italian family, supporting Dr. Mizuno's point that it may be a founder phenomenon. It is interesting, however, that α-synuclein is also found in the Lewy bodies of PD patients who do not have the mutation.

Mizuno: GAPDH is extremely sensitive to oxidative damage, therefore it would be interesting to know the behavior of this enzyme in PD. Has anyone measured GAPDH in patients with PD?

W. Tatton: To the best of my knowledge there are no differences in the protein level in PD patients. The work that Dr. Borden has done with Dr. Carlile and myself suggests that the location of the enzyme matters more than the absolute level. Several groups have shown that GAPDH causes cell death by relocating from its RNA binding site to the nucleus. Oxidative radicals may act to displace GAPDH from its binding site in the Rossmann fold so that it can migrate to the nucleus and promote apoptosis rather than by inducing oxidative damage.

Schapira: Both Dr. Beal's group and ourselves have found that in Huntington's disease GAPDH activity is normal, even in the presence of oxidative stress and damage, and decreased aconitase activity which is a better marker of oxidative stress. So the glycolytic activity of GAPDH, at least, appears to be normal but we cannot say if this is true for its other activities.

W. Tatton: The apoptotic function of GAPDH is unrelated to its glycolytic function, so measuring glycolytic function will not provide any information on its role in cell death.

Schapira: Indeed. The decrease in GAPDH activity was used as a means of determining the reason for a metabolic defect in Huntington's disease and is obviously a red herring, at least in this respect.

Pathogenesis

CHAPTER TEN

Understanding cell death in Parkinson's disease

PETER JENNER[1] AND C. WARREN OLANOW[2]

[1]Neurodegenerative Disease Research Centre, Pharmacology Group, King's College, London, UK, and [2]Department of Neurology, Mount Sinai School of Medicine, New York, New York, USA

No current therapeutic approach to the treatment of Parkinson's disease (PD) prevents the destruction of dopaminergic neurons in the zona compacta of the substantia nigra (SNc). Both genetic and environmental factors are believed to contribute to the initiation of PD. The recent detection of mutations in the α-synuclein gene resulting in Ala53Thr and Ala30Pro substitutions in the protein[1,2] and the finding of abundant α-synuclein staining in Lewy bodies in patients with either sporadic or familial PD[3] suggest that alterations in the folding or clearance of proteins such as α-synuclein may be involved in the pathogenesis of PD. It is likely, however, that multiple gene defects or a complex interaction between gene mutations and environmental toxins account for the majority of cases of PD. While susceptibility genes are suspected, to date few mutations in potential candidates have been identified.[4] Even where an association has been demonstrated, the nature of its involvement in nigral cell death remains unknown.

Similarly, attempts to identify specific environmental factors which initiate PD have not been particularly successful.[5,6] The environmental insults that initiate PD in susceptible individuals may be numerous. The selective nigral toxin 1-methyl-4-phenyl-1,2,3,6-tetrahydropyridine (MPTP) can initiate a PD-like syndrome and provides a model for studying cell death in PD,[7] but no MPTP-like substance has been discovered to explain the bulk of cases of PD. Certain endogenous toxins such as tetrahydroisoquinoline and β-carboline derivatives can exert neurotoxicity through mechanisms similar to MPTP, but this has not led to identification of any specific cause or treatment for PD.

The failure to identify a reason for nigral cell degeneration in PD has hindered the development of neuroprotective approaches to treatment based on blocking etiologic factors. Consequently, interest has focussed on the pathogenic processes which may contribute to nigral neuronal degeneration. One area which has received considerable attention is oxidative stress.[8-10] This chapter reviews the evidence that suggests oxidative stress is a key event in cell death in PD and explores how it may contribute to the progression of nigral degeneration.

OXIDATIVE STRESS IN PD

The metabolism of dopamine, by chemical or enzymatic means, can generate free radicals and other reactive oxygen species (ROS).[11,12] The autoxidation of dopamine leads to the formation of neuromelanin and can generate quinone and semi-quinone species and other ROS. The enzymatic oxidation of dopamine by monoamine oxidase (MAO) leads to the formation of hydrogen peroxide (H_2O_2) which can react with iron and form the highly reactive and cytotoxic hydroxyl radical (OH·) by way of the Fenton reaction. A variety of critical biomolecules, including lipids, proteins, and DNA, can be damaged by free radicals, thereby potentially leading to neurodegeneration.[13,14] ROS have also been shown to promote excitotoxicity and a rise in intracellular calcium, and to initiate signaling pathways for the initiation of apoptosis.[15-17]

The discovery of the selective nigral toxicity of MPTP has provided some indication of how nigral cell degeneration might occur in PD. MPTP is oxidized by MAO-B to the active moiety 1-methyl-4-phenylpyridinium ion (MPP+), which subsequently accumulates in mitochondria of dopaminergic neurons[18] and inhibits both complex I of the respiratory chain and α-ketoglutarate dehydrogenase (α-KGDH), a key enzyme in the Krebs cycle.[19,20] Together these could induce both a bioenergetic defect and free radical formation, thereby leading to nerve cell degeneration. In addition, a complex I defect could cause decreased proton pumping and a drop in the mitochondrial membrane potential which has been shown to be an early event in apoptotic cell death.[21,22] The detection of complex I and α-KGDH defects in PD suggests that the mechanism of nigral cell death following MPTP administration may be relevant to PD. Extensive post-mortem studies support the concept that oxidative stress is occurring in the SNc. Key findings are elevated iron levels, inhibition of mitochondrial function, alterations in antioxidant defenses, and oxidative damage to a variety of critical molecules.[8-10]

Iron

Via its conversion from the ferrous (Fe^{2+}) to the ferric (Fe^{3+}) state,[23,24] iron can catalyze the formation of ROS from the oxidation of dopamine or levodopa.

A variety of imaging and bio-analytic techniques show that levels of iron are elevated in the SNc in PD,[25–27] and these increases are located primarily within neuromelanin granules of dopaminergic neurons.[28,29] It is unclear, however, whether the excess iron is reactive. Levels of the iron-binding protein ferritin have been reported to be increased, decreased or unchanged[30–32] depending on the technology, so the extent to which excess iron in the PD nigra is rendered less reactive by binding to ferritin remains unknown. The origin of the excess iron found in the PD nigra is also unknown. It may be redistributed from its normal storage sites in the globus pallidus or the zona reticulata of the substantia nigra (SNr), or it may also result from gliosis secondary to the local damage that occurs in PD or from a breakdown of the blood–brain barrier, perhaps as the result of an inflammatory response. An increased density of lactoferrin receptors has been described on neurons in the substantia nigra and in the surrounding vasculature[33,34] which may partially explain the regional increase of iron in PD. The decrease in transferrin binding sites on SNc neurons[35] in PD may reflect a compensatory change to the increased iron in these nerve cells.

Alterations in iron levels are not specific to PD and have been described in other neurodegenerative disorders within basal ganglia and elsewhere in the central nervous system.[24,36,37] Further, iron levels are increased in the substantia nigra of 6-hydroxydopamine (6-OHDA)-lesioned rats and MPTP-treated monkeys,[38–40] suggesting that iron accumulation can be secondary to neuronal degeneration irrespective of the cause. This is supported by the failure to detect a change in iron concentration in incidental Lewy body disease (ILBD) which is thought to represent pre-symptomatic PD.[41] Nevertheless, a secondary accumulation of iron may still contribute to the progression of PD. Iron from any cause could promote oxidant stress and facilitate lipid peroxidation.[23] Infusion of iron into the substantia nigra of rats leads to a concentration-related decrease in the numbers of nigral neurons and striatal dopamine content.[42–44]

Clinical trials testing the ability of an iron-chelating drug to decrease the rate of disease progression in PD patients have yet to be performed. Such drugs would ideally remove excess iron selectively in the SNc without affecting iron essential for normal functioning of the nervous system. In rats, the iron-chelating drug CP 94 induced a reduction in both striatal dopamine and serotonin levels, presumably by removing iron essential for the activity of tyrosine and tryptophan hydroxylase.[45] Neurologic deficits in humans have also been reported when the iron chelator desferrioxamine was administered in conjunction with neuroleptics which break the blood–brain barrier for iron.[46] Thus, trials of iron chelators must be carried out judiciously.

Mitochondrial complex I deficiency

A key post-mortem observation in PD is the 30–40% decrease in activity of complex I in the SNc.[47,48] This specific defect does not affect the other components of the mitochondrial respiratory chain and does not occur in other brain areas or in other neurodegenerative diseases.[49] The cause of the complex I inhibition in PD is not clear since no structural abnormalities, or specific disease-related alterations in any of the genes encoding complex I, have been detected,[50,51] neither has any toxin which might be responsible for an impairment of complex I activity or for damage to the mitochondrial genome been found to date.[52] However, the persistence of the complex I defect in cybrids containing mitochondrial DNA derived from platelets of patients with PD[53] indicates that a defect in the mitochondrial genome due to either toxic or genetic causes is likely responsible for the complex I deficiency. It is not certain how a defect in complex I leads to neurodegeneration. Reduced complex I activity could lead to decreased ATP production and 'weak excitotoxicity'.[54] However, the level of reduction in complex I activity may be insufficient to cause a fall in ATP production because of compensatory mechanisms.[55] A defect in both complexes I and II would be of greater significance[56] and could be sufficient to lead to a bioenergetic defect.

More recently, mitochondria have been implicated in apoptotic cell death.[21,22] Increasing evidence indicates that apoptosis is associated with a fall in the mitochondrial membrane potential, opening of a mitochondrial permeability transition pore (PTP), and release of small proteins that signal for the initiation of apoptosis (apoptosis initiating factors).[21,22] A fall in mitochondrial membrane potential is one of the earliest events in the apoptotic process and could occur as a result of the fall in complex I.[57] The number of apoptotic nuclei in the SNc of PD patients is significantly increased in comparison to age-matched controls,[58-60] and mitochondria derived from fibroblasts of PD patients have a reduced mitochondrial membrane potential compared to controls (Redman R, Tatton WG, Olanow CW, unpublished data). The defect in complex I in PD may be fundamental, causing PD by rendering nigral neurons vulnerable to apoptosis and susceptible to toxins that would otherwise be harmless.

Diminished anti-oxidant defenses (GSH)

Further evidence that the SNc is in a state of oxidant stress in PD is alteration in anti-oxidant defenses. Perhaps most significant is the decrease in the level of GSH, which clears H_2O_2 and prevents its reaction with iron to form the highly reactive OH· radical. GSH levels were recently reported to be decreased in the SNc of PD patients and the extent of the GSH loss correlated with the degree of disease severity.[61] A decrease in GSH levels of approximately 30–40% has been detected in PD but there was no corresponding increase in the level of GSSG.[62,63] The importance of this finding lies in its specificity. GSH levels are not reduced in other areas of the PD brain or in other neurodegenerative diseases. GSH levels are reduced to an almost equivalent degree in the SNc of patients with ILBD who are thought to have pre-clinical PD,[41] and this is one of the earliest biochemical markers of nigral degeneration so far uncovered. While remaining dopamine neurons in PD show GSH depletion, much of the GSH loss in the PD nigra presumably occurs from non-neuronal elements such as glia.[64–69] The important questions raised by the loss of GSH relate to the consequences for nigral cell survival and the cause of the GSH depletion.

The effect of GSH depletion on neuronal integrity can be determined using buthionine R,S-sulphoximine (BSO), a specific inhibitor of γ-glutamylcysteine synthetase, the rate limiting enzyme for GSH formation.[70] GSH depletion of approximately 80% was required to induced degeneration of dopaminergic neurons.[71] Interestingly, BSO did not induce cell death in pure neuronal cultures suggesting that depletion of GSH in glia is a critical event that leads to toxicity, possibly through the formation of nitric oxide (NO) or cytokines (Mytilineou C, unpublished observations). GSH depletion to levels seen in PD did not produce toxicity.

Similarly, chronic depletion of GSH in the rat did not lead to a decrease in the number of dopaminergic cells in SNc or to a fall in specific ^{3}H-mazindol binding to dopamine terminals in the striatum,[72] suggesting that GSH depletion alone does not alter the integrity of the nigrostriatal pathway. However, BSO selectively depletes cytosolic GSH while mitochondrial content is maintained[70] and this may differ from what occurs in PD. Alternatively, depletion of GSH may increase the sensitivity of the nigrostriatal pathway to other toxins. In peripheral tissues, BSO-induced GSH depletion has been shown to damage mitochondria in muscle cells and render them sensitive to toxins to which they are normally immune[73] although there are reports that BSO-induced GSH depletion did not render rodents sensitive to the toxic effects of systemic MPTP.[74,75]

The cause of GSH depletion in PD is not obvious. The lack of a corresponding increase in GSSG suggests that it may not be due to oxidative stress. However, the ratio of GSH:GSSG does change in favor of GSSG as would be expected in oxidative stress. There does not seem to be any failure of GSH synthesis since the activity of γ-glutamylcysteine synthetase in the substantia nigra is normal in PD.[76] Similarly, there is no apparent alteration in the activity of glutathione peroxidase or glutathione transferase. There is however an increase in the activity of γ-glutamyltranspeptidase,[76] which appears to be involved in cellular translocation and degradation of the component peptides which constitute GSH. This increase does not occur in any other brain region and is not found in any other neurodegenerative disease.

Consideration must also be given to the role of mitochondria in the depletion of GSH and the effect that GSH depletion may have on mitochondrial function. Inhibition of mitochondrial function results in efflux of GSH[77] so, potentially, GSH depletion in PD could be a consequence of complex I inhibition and the decrease of GSH found in ILBD might reflect an early change in mitochondrial function.

Finally, it is possible that decreased GSH levels in PD may be due to levodopa therapy rather than to the disease process itself. *In vitro*, levodopa induces an increase in GSSG levels[78] although this has not been observed in normal rats treated chronically with levodopa.[79] In primary mesencephalic cultures, levodopa can increase GSH levels.[80] Alternatively, GSH depletion may result from reaction with semiquinone radicals formed from dopamine or levodopa following attack by superoxide.[81]

ROLE OF GLIAL CELLS

There is increasing interest in the possibility that glial cells may be a major contributor to oxidative stress and to the pathogenesis of neuronal death in PD.[82–84] Activated microglia have been detected in the SNc,[85] particularly in regions of maximal neurodegeneration. Activation of glial cells can lead to the production and release of cytokines, ROS, and nitric oxide (NO) that can induce or contribute to cell degeneration.[86] NO is generated by the conversion of arginine to citrulline by calcium activation of NO synthase (NOS), and can react with superoxide radical to form the oxidizing agents peroxynitrite ($ONOO^-$) and $OH\cdot$.[87] Considerable evidence indicates that cell damage associated with excitotoxicity is mediated by NO formation.[15] Increased staining for 3-nitrotyrosine has been observed in PD[88] which implies increased NO formation. Sustained exposure to NO in the presence of diminished GSH levels can damage the neuronal mitochondrial respiratory chain.[89]

Glia have also been implicated in the reduced levels of GSH found in PD. Much of GSH is present in glial cells,[64–69,90,91] and the magnitude of change seen in PD cannot be readily explained by the loss of nigral neurons, suggesting that glia may bear the initial brunt of damage in PD. Importantly perhaps, glial cells which surround neurons in substantia nigra which are most vulnerable to degeneration contain more glutathione peroxidase than surrounding neurons which are resistant to the pathological process.[92] Glial cells might also be involved in the formation and export of toxins that lead to neurodegeneration. Unlike neurons, glial cells are not dependent on glycolysis for their survival and are thus not affected by MPP+ which may interfere with mitochondrial ATP production or signaling for apoptosis.

Glial cells may also be protective and play a role in the survival of nigral dopaminergic neurons,[93] and loss of such a function might contribute to nerve cell death. Glial cells have been shown to produce neurotrophic factors essential for neuronal survival and to protect dopaminergic neurons from levodopa- or 6-OHDA-induced toxicity.[94,95] These benefits are associated with up-regulation of antioxidant defenses, such as GSH, which are already highly-expressed in astrocytes. Failure of one or more of these protective mechanisms may contribute to nerve cell degeneration. Assessment of the potential role of glia in the pathogenesis of dopamine neuronal death may require differentiation between loss of their normal physiological role in maintaining neuronal integrity and their ability, under pathological conditions, to induce neuronal destruction.

EVIDENCE OF OXIDATIVE DAMAGE IN PD

There is evidence for oxidative damage to lipids, proteins and DNA in post-mortem PD tissues. Levels of lipid hydroperoxides were increased by ten fold in the SNc in PD.[96] Further investigations have been few, but supportive evidence of lipid peroxidation comes from the finding of increased immunoreactivity for 4–4-hydroxynonenal-linked proteins in the SNc in PD.[97]

Assessments of DNA damage indicate that only deoxy guanine levels are increased.[98] Selective damage to guanine suggests a relationship to singlet oxygen or peroxyl radicals, but more recent studies indicate that there may be no overall change in the degree of free radical attack on guanine in PD, since levels of another product of radical damage, Fapy-guanine, are correspondingly decreased. Alterations in the deoxyguanine/Fapy-guanine ratio may be due to the more oxidizing environment in the SNc of PD patients compared to controls, supporting the occurrence of oxidative stress.

There is also evidence of increased protein carbonyls in the SNc in PD consistent with increased protein oxidation due to the occurrence of oxidative stress.[99] However, increased levels of protein carbonyls were also found in every other brain area examined. These data support the involvement of free radical-mediated mechanisms contributing to the pathology seen in PD but suggest that it may be a more widespread process than has been previously envisaged.

ALTERED PROTEIN HANDLING AND OXIDANT STRESS

Recent evidence links alterations in protein handling and oxidative stress to the etiology of PD. Mutant α-synuclein is associated with the development of PD in some families[1,2] and α-synuclein accumulates in Lewy bodies even in PD patients without the mutation.[3] The biological function of α-synuclein and its role in nigral degeneration is unknown, but it is widespread in the brain and is present in areas which do not degenerate in PD.[88] So, it is necessary to find a reason why formation of this mutant protein should lead to the relatively selective degeneration of dopaminergic nerve cells.

Protein products are normally ubiquitinated and degraded by proteasomes. This is an essential process as protein accumulation can be toxic to normal cell function. During mild oxidative stress, oxidized proteins are formed but are rapidly processed and degraded by proteasomes.[100] However, when oxidative stress becomes severe, proteasomal function can be impaired either by direct oxidative damage, or because proteins are so severely altered that they are no longer recognized as substrates. Furthermore, the accumulation of oxidized proteins may exceed the capacity of proteasomes to clear them.[100] Oxidant species known to oxidize proteins and to alter proteolysis include superoxide radical, peroxynitrite, and 4-hydroxynonenal, all of which appear to be increased in PD.[101] Mutant α-synuclein may accumulate in PD because it tends to self-aggregate and is not readily processed by proteasomes. Alternatively, oxidative damage or an alteration in proteasome function may impair proteolytic degradation of non-mutated α-synuclein and other modified proteins in sporadic PD.

Interestingly, Lewy bodies in PD patients contain α-synuclein,[3] which may be highly relevant since those areas of the brain which normally contain the highest levels of α-synuclein are those associated with Lewy body formation in PD.[1] In addition, Lewy bodies also show both ubiquitin and abnormal nitrated proteins resulting from peroxynitrite attack.[88] This raises the question as to whether Lewy bodies result from impaired handling of oxidized proteins and whether they represent a cellular mechanism for protecting neurons from the toxicity of protein deposition.

NIGRAL CELL DEGENERATION IN PD: AN HYPOTHESIS BASED ON ALTERED HANDLING OF PROTEINS

On the evidence currently available, it is possible to devise an hypothesis to explain how nigral cell degeneration might occur in both familial and sporadic PD, based on oxidative stress and alterations in protein handling. The key steps might be as follows:

1. A variety of toxic insults (*e.g.* oxidative stress, inflammatory processes, glial-derived mediators etc.) or genetic defects lead to the production of altered proteins particularly in areas that are under oxidant stress such as the SNc.[101]

2. The SNc is a region of the brain which has a high basal level of oxidative stress compared to other brain regions. This is reflected by the finding of a two-fold higher protein carbonyl content in the SNc compared to other areas in normal brains.[102] In PD, the level of oxidative stress is further increased.[8,9]

[152]

3.   Protein degradation is preceded by attachment to ubiquitin. Under conditions of oxidative stress, particularly where GSH levels are reduced, there is a reduction in ubiquitination due to covalent thiolation of the enzymes involved.[103] This may be particularly relevant to PD where GSH levels appear to decline very early in the disease pathology. Consequently, abnormal or oxidized proteins may accumulate to pathological levels as a result of alterations in cellular redox status.

4.   The occurrence of continuous oxidative stress leads to inhibition of proteolysis due to the extent of protein damage and the failure of proteasomes to recognize damaged or mutant proteins as substrates and to clear them. In addition, oxidative stress and damaged proteins may themselves inhibit proteasomal function.[100]

5.   The occurrence of lipid peroxidation in the oxidatively stressed SNc generates 4-hydroxynonenal[97] which itself can react with protein carbonyl groups to further modify their structure. Such processes induce cross linking with protein aggregation and precipitation. Cross linked proteins and those modified by glycation or by products of lipid peroxidation are resistant to proteolysis and can inhibit the ability of proteases to degrade other oxidized proteins.[104]

6.   The degradation of damaged proteins is an essential component of secondary anti-oxidant defenses.[105] Oxidized proteins can generate free radicals and are toxic to cells. Indeed, it has been shown that selective inhibition of proteasome function with consequent failure to clear proteins, leads to apoptotic cell death.[106]

Such a progression of events could help explain how a range of different factors including oxidant stress and protein accumulation could lead to cell death in PD.

SUMMARY

- Current concepts of the cause of PD suggest a role for both genetic and environmental influences.

- Common to a variety of potential causes of nigral cell degeneration in PD is the involvement of oxidative stress. Post-mortem analysis shows increased levels of iron, decreased complex I activity, a reduction in reduced GSH levels, and oxidative damage to a variety of molecules.

- The fall in GSH levels may be particularly important since it occurs in the pre-symptomatic stage of PD.

- There is evidence to suggest that the primary problem may originate in glial cells rather than neurons and alterations in glial function may be an important contributor to the pathological process occurring in PD.

- The inability of the substantia nigra to handle damaged or mutant (*e.g.* α-synuclein) proteins may lead to their aggregation and deposition and to the formation of Lewy bodies.

- Current evidence allows us to hypothesize that a failure to process structurally modified proteins in regions of the brain exhibiting oxidative stress may be a critical factor in cell death in patients with both familial and sporadic PD.

ACKNOWLEDGMENTS

This study was supported by the National Parkinson Foundation, USA and the Parkinson Disease Society, UK.

REFERENCES

1. Polymeropoulos MH, Lavedan C, Leroy E, *et al.* Mutation in the α-synuclein gene identified in families with Parkinson's disease. Science 1997; 276: 2045–2047.

2. Krüger R, Kuhn W, Müller T, Woitalla D, Graeber M, Kösel S, *et al.* Ala30Pro mutation in the gene encoding α–synuclein in Parkinson's disease. Nat Genet 1998; 18: 106–108.

3. Spillantini MG, Schmidt ML, Lee VM-Y, *et al.* α-Synuclein in Lewy bodies. Nature 1997; 388: 839–840.

4. Gasser T, Wszolek ZK, Trofatter J, *et al.* Genetic studies in autosomal dominant parkinsonism: evaluation of seven candidate genes. Ann Neurol 1994; 36: 387–396.

5. Tanner CM, Langston JW. Do environmental toxins cause Parkinson's disease? A critical review. Neurol 1990; 40: 17–30.

6. Koller W, Vetere–Overfield B, Gray C, *et al.* Environmental risk factors in Parkinson's disease. Neurol 1991; 40: 1218–1221.

7. Langston JW, Ballard PA, Tetrud JW, Irwin I. Chronic parkinsonism in humans due to a product of meperidine analog synthesis. Science 1983; 219: 979–980.

8. Jenner P, Olanow CW. Pathological evidence for oxidative stress in Parkinson's disease and related degenerative disorders. In, Olanow CW, Jenner P, Youdim M, eds, Neurodegeneration and Neuroprotection in Parkinson's Disease. London: Academic Press, 1996: 24–45.

9. Jenner P, Olanow CW. Oxidative stress and the pathogenesis of Parkinson's disease. Neurol 1996; 47(Suppl 3): S161–S170.

10. Olanow, CW. A radical hypothesis for neurodegeneration. TINS 1993; 16: 439–444.

11. Halliwell B, Gutteridge J. Oxygen radicals and the nervous system. Trends Neurosci 1985; 8: 22–29.

12. Olanow CW. Oxidation reactions in Parkinson's disease. Neurol 1990; 40: 32–37.

13. Wolff SP, Garner A, Dean RT. Free radicals, lipids and protein degradation. Trends Biol Sci 1986; 11: 27–31.

14. Richter C, Park JW, Arnes BN. Normal oxidative damage to mitochondrial and nuclear DNA is extensive. Proc Natl Acad Sci USA 1988; 85: 6465–6467.

15. Dawson VL, Dawson TM, London ED, *et al.* Nitric oxide mediates glutamate neurotoxicity in primary cortical cultures. Proc Natl Acad Sci USA 1991; 88: 6368–6371.

16. Orrenius S, Burkitt MJ, Kass GE, Dypbukt JM, Nicotera P. Calcium ions and oxidative cell injury. Ann Neurol 1992; 32: 33–42.

17. Ratan RR, Murphy TH, Baraban JM. Oxidative stress induces apoptosis in embryonic cortical neurons. J Neurochem 1994; 62: 376–379.

18. Singer TP, Castagnoli N Jr, Ramsay RR, Trevor AJ. Biochemical events in the development of parkinsonism induced by 1–methyl–4–phenyl–1,2,3,6–tetrahydropyridine. J Neurochem 1987; 49: 1–8.

19. Nicklas WJ, Vyas I, Heikkila RE. Inhibition of NADH–linked oxidation in brain mitochondria by 1–methyl–4–phenyl–pyridine, a metabolite of the neurotoxin 1–methyl–4–phenyl–1,2,5,6 tetrahydropyridine. Life Sci 1985; 36: 2503–2508.

20. Mizuno Y, Saitoh T, Sone N. Inhibition of mitochondrial alpha–ketoglutarate dehydrogenase by 1–methyl–4–phenyl-pyridinium ion. Biochem Biophys Res Commun 1987; 143: 971–976.

21. Kroemer G, Petit P, Xamzami N, *et al.* The biochemistry of programmed cell death. FASEB 1995; 9: 1277–1287.

22. Susin SA, Zamzami N, Kroemer G. The cell biology of apoptosis: evidence for the implication of mitochondria. Apoptosis 1996; 1: 231–242.

23. Gutteridge JMC, Halliwell B, Treffry A, *et al.* Effect of ferritin containing fractions with different iron loading on lipid peroxidation. J Biochem 1983; 209: 557–560.

24. Olanow CW, Youdim MHB. Iron and Neurodegeneration: Prospects for neuroprotection. In, Olanow CW, Jenner P, Youdim M, eds, Neuro-degeneration and Neuroprotection in Parkinson's Disease. London: Academic Press, 1996: 55–67.

25. Olanow CW. Magnetic resonance imaging in parkinsonism. Neurological Clinics of North America. 1992: 405–420.

26. Dexter DT, Wells FR, Lees AJ, *et al.* Increased nigral iron content and alterations in other metal ions occurring in brain in Parkinson's disease. J Neurochem 1989; 52: 1830–1836.

27. Sofic E, Paulus W, Jellinger K, *et al.* Selective increase of iron in substantia nigra zona compacta of parkinsonian brains. J Neurochem 1991; 56: 978–982.

28. Good PF, Olanow CW, Perl DP. Neuromelanin–containing neurons of the substantia nigra accumulate iron and aluminum in Parkinson's disease: a LAMMA study. Brain Res 1992; 593: 343–346.

29. Hirsch EC, Brandel J–P, Galle P, *et al.* Iron and aluminum increase in the substantia nigra of patients with Parkinson's disease: An X–ray micro-analysis. J Neurochem 1991; 56: 446–451.

30. Riederer P, Sofic E, Rausch W–D, *et al.* Transition metals, ferritin, glutathione, and ascorbic acid in parkinsonian brains. J Neurochem 1989; 52: 515–520.

31. Dexter DT, Carayon A, Vidailhet M, *et al.* Decreased ferritin levels in brain in Parkinson's disease. J Neurochem 1990; 55: 16–20.

32. Mann VM, Cooper JM, Daniel SE, *et al.* Complex I, iron, and ferritin in Parkinson's disease substantia nigra. Ann Neurol 1994; 36: 876–881.

33. Faucheux B, Nillesse N, Damier P, *et al.* Expression of lactoferrin receptors is increased in the mesencephalon of patients with Parkinson's disease. Proc Natl Acad Sci USA 1995; 92: 9603–9607.

34. Faucheux BA, Hirsch EC, Villares J, *et al.* Distribution of 125I–ferrotransferrin binding sites in the mesencephalon of control subjects and patients with Parkinson's disease. J Neurochem 1993; 60: 2338–2341.

35. Faucheux BA, Hauw JJ, Agid Y, Hirsch EC. The density of 125I–transferrin binding sites on perikara of melanized neurons of the substantia nigra is decreased in Parkinson's disease. Brain Res 1997; 749: 170–174.

36. Connor JR, Menzies SL, St. Martin SM, Mufson EJ. A Histochemical study of iron, transferrin, and ferritin in Alzheimer's diseased brains. J Neurosci Res 1992; 31: 75–83.

37. Valberg LS, Flanagan PR, Kertesz A, Ebers GC. Abnormalities in iron metabolism in multiple sclerosis. Can J Neurol Sci 1989; 16: 184–186.

38. Temlett JA, Landsberg JP, Watt F, Grime GW. Increased iron in the sub-stantia nigra compacta of the MPTP–lesioned hemiparkinsonian African green monkey: Evidence from proton microprobe elemental microanalysis. J Neurochem 1994; 62: 134–146.

39. Oestreicher E, Sengstock GJ, Riederer P, *et al.* Degeneration of nigrostriatal dopaminergic neurons increases iron within the substantia nigra: a histo-chemical and neurochemical study. Brain Res 1994; 660: 8–18.

40. He Y, Thong PSP, Lee T, *et al.* Increased iron in the substantia nigra of

6–OHDA induced parkinsonian rats: a nuclear microscopy study. Brain Res 1996; 735: 149–153.

41. Dexter DT, Sian J, Rose S, et al. Indices of oxidative stress and mitochondrial function in individuals with incidental Lewy body disease. Ann Neurol 1994; 35: 38–44.

42. Sengstock G, Olanow CW, Dunn AJ, Arendash GW. Iron induces degeneration of nigrostriatal neurons. Brain Res Bull 1992; 28: 645–649.

43. Sengstock GJ, Olanow CW, Menzies RA, et al. Infusion of iron into the rat substantia nigra: nigral pathology and dose–dependent loss of striatal dopaminergic markers. J Neurosci Res 1993; 35: 67–82.

44. Ben–Schachar D, Youdim MBH. Intranigral iron injection induces behavioral and biochemical "Parkinsonism" in rats. J Neurochem 1991; 57: 2133–2135.

45. Ward RJ, Dexter DT, Florence A, et al. Brain iron in the ferrocene–loaded rat: its chelation and influence on dopamine metabolism. Biochem Pharmacol 1995; 49: 1821–1826.

46. Blake DR, Winyard P, Lonec J, et al. Cerebral and ocular toxicity induced by desferrioxamine. Q J Med 1985; 219: 345–355.

47. Schapira AHV, Cooper JM, Dexter D, et al. Mitochondrial complex I deficiency in Parkinson's disease. J Neurochem 1990; 54: 823–827.

48. Mizuno Y, Ohta S, Tanaka M, et al. Deficiencies in complex I subunits of the respiratory chain in Parkinson's disease. Biochem Biophys Res Commun 1989; 163: 1450–1455.

49. Schapira AHV, Mann VM, Cooper JM, et al. Anatomic and disease specificity of NADH CoQ1 reductase (Complex I) deficiency in Parkinson's disease. J Neurochem 1990; 55: 2142–2145.

50. Ikebe S, Tanaka M, Ohno K, et al. Increase of deleted mitochondrial DNA in the striatum in Parkinson's disease

and senescence. Biochem Biophys Res Commun 1990; 170: 1044–1048.

51. Ikebe S, Tanaka M, Ozawa T. Point mutations of mitochondrial genome in Parkinson's disease. Mol Brain Res 1995; 28: 281–295.

52. Ikeda H, Markey CJ, Markey SP. Search for neurotoxins structurally related to 1–methyl–4–phenylpyridine (MPP+) in the pathogenesis of Parkinson's disease. Brain Res 1992; 575: 282–298.

53. Swerdlow RH, Parks JK, Miller SW, et al. Origin and functional consequences of the complex I defect in Parkinson's disease. Ann Neurol 1996; 40: 663–671.

54. Beal MF. Does impairment of energy metabolism result in excitotoxic neuronal death in neurodegenerative illnesses? Ann Neurol 1992; 31: 119–130.

55. Davey GP, Clark JB. 1996. Threshold effects and control of oxidative phosphorylation in non–synaptic rat brain mitochondria. J Neurochem 66: 1617–1624.

56. Mizuno Y, Ikebe S, Hattori N, et al. Role of mitochondria in the etiology and pathogenesis of Parkinson's disease. Biochem Biophys Acta 1995; 1271: 265–274.

57. Wadia JS, Chalmers–Redman RME, Ju WJH, et al. Mitochondrial membrane potential and nuclear changes in apoptosis caused by trophic withdrawal: time course and modification by (–) deprenyl. J Neurosci 1998; 18: 932–947.

58. Tatton NA, Maclean–Fraser A, Tatton WG, Perl DP, Olanow CW, this volume.

59. Anglade P, Vyas S, Javoy–Agid F, et al. Apoptosis and autophagie in nigral neurons of patients with Parkinson's disease. Histol Histopath 1997; 12: 25–31.

60. Mochizuki H, Goto K, Mori H, Mizuno Y. Histochemical detection of apoptosis in Parkinson's disease. J Neurol Sci 1996; 131: 120–123.

61. Riederer P, Sofic E, Rausch W–D. Transition metals, ferritin, glutathione, and ascorbic acid in parkinsonian brains. J Neurochem 1989; 52: 515–520.

62. Sian J, Dexter DT, Lees AJ, et al. Alterations in glutathione levels in Parkinson's disease and other neuro-degenerative disorders affecting basal ganglia. Ann Neurol 1994; 36: 348–355.

63. Sofic E. Lange KW, Jellinger K, Riederer P. Reduced and oxidized glutathione in the substantia nigra of patients with Parkinson's disease. Neurosci Lett 1992; 142: 128–130.

64. Pearce RKB, Owen A, Daniel S, et al. Alterations in the distribution of glutathione in the substantia nigra of Parkinson's disease. J Neural Transm 1997; 104: 661–677.

65. Philbert MA, Beiswanger CM, Waters DK, et al. Cellular and regional distribution of reduced glutathione in the nervous system of the rat: Histochemical localisation by mercury orange and o–phthaldialdehyde–induced histofluorescence. Toxicol Appl Pharmacol 1991; 107: 215–227.

66. Asghar K, Reddy BG, Krishan G. Histochemical localisation of glutathione in tissues. J Histochem Cytochem 1975; 23: 774–779.

67. Hjelle OP, Chaudhry FA, Ottersen OP. Antisera to glutathione: Characterisation and immunocytochemical application to the rat cerebellum. Eur J Neurosci 1994; 6: 793–804.

68. Raps SP, Lai JCK, Hertz L, Cooper AJL. Glutathione is present in high concentrations in cultured astrocytes but not in cultured neurons. Brain Res 1989; 493: 398–401.

69. Slivka A, Mytilineou C, Cohen G. Histochemical evaluation of glutathione in brain. Brain Res 1987; 409: 275–284.

70. Meister A. Glutathione deficiency produced by inhibition of its synthesis, and its reversal; applications in research therapy. Pharm Ther 1991; 51: 155–194.

71. Mytilineou C, Leonardi EK, Radcliffe P, et al. Deprenyl and desmethylselegiline protect mesencephalic neurons from toxicity induced by glutathione depletion. J Pharm Exp Ther 1998; 284: 700–706.

72. Toffa S, Kunikowska GM, Zeng B–Y, et al. Glutathione depletion in rat brain does not cause nigrostriatal pathway degeneration. J Neural Transm 1997; 104: 67–75.

73. Martensson J, Meister A. Mitochondrial damage in muscle occurs after marked depletion of glutathione and is prevented by giving glutathione monoester. Proc Natl Acad Sci USA 1989; 86: 471–475.

74. Perry TL, Yong VW, Jones K, Wright JM. Manipulation of glutathione contents fails to alter dopaminergic nigrostriatal neurotoxicity of 1–methyl–4–phenyl–1,2,3,6–tetrahydr opyridine (MPTP) in the mouse. Neurosci Lett 1986; 70: 261–265.

75. Kunikowska G, Owen A, Rose S, et al. BSO–induced GSH depletion does not sensitize rats to the toxic actions of systemic MPTP administration. J Neural Transm 1998, in press.

76. Sian J, Dexter DT, Lees AJ, et al. Glutathione–related enzymes in brain in Parkinson's disease. Ann Neurol 1994; 36: 356–361.

77. Mithöfer K, Sandy M Smith MT, Di Monte D. Mitochondrial poisons cause depletion of reduced glutathione in isolated hepatocytes. Arch Biochem Biophys 1992; 295: 132–136.

78. Spina MB, Cohen G. Exposure of striatal synaptosomes to l–dopa elevates levels of oxidized glutathione. J Pharmacol Exp Ther. 1988; 247: 502–507.

79. Loeffler DA, DeMaggio AJ, Juneau PL, *et al.* Effects of enhanced striatal dopamine turnover in vivo on glutathione oxidation. Clin Neuropharmacol 1994; 17: 370–379.

80. Mytilineou C, Han S–K, Cohen G. Toxic and protective effects of L–DOPA on mesencephalic cell cultures. J Neurochem 1993; 61: 1470–1478.

81. Spencer JPE, Jenner P, Halliwell B. Superoxide–dependent depletion of reduced glutathione by L–DOPA and dopamine. Relevance to Parkinson's disease. NeuroReport 1995; 6: 1480–1484.

82. Kuhn W, Muller T. Neuroimmune mechanisms in Parkinson's disease. J Neural Transm (Suppl) 1995; 46: 229–233.

83. Hirsch EC, Hunot S, Damier P, Faucheux B, this volume.

84. Olanow CW, Jenner P, Tatton N, Tatton WG. Neurodegeneration in Parkinson's disease. In, Jankovic J, Tolosa E, eds, Parkinson's Disease and Movement Disorders, 3rd edition, in press.

85. McGeer PL, Itagaki S, Boyes BE, McGeer EG. Reactive microglia are positive for HLA–DR in the substantia nigra of Parkinson and Alzheimer disease brains. Neurol 1988; 38: 1285–1291.

86. Benveniste EN. Inflammatory cytokines within the central nervous system: sources, function, and mechanism of action. Am J Physiol 1992; 263: 1–16.

87. Beckman JS, Beckman TW, Chen J, *et al.* Apparent hydroxyl radical production by peroxynitrite: implications for endothelial injury from nitric oxide and superoxide. Proc Natl Acad Sci USA 1990; 87: 1620–1624.

88. Good PF, Hsu A, Werner P, Perl DP, Olanow CW. Protein nitration in Parkinson's disease. J Neuropath Exp Neurol, in press.

89. Bolanos JP, Heales SJR, Peuchen S, *et al.* Nitric oxide–mediated mitochondrial damage: A potential neuroprotective role for glutathione. Free Rad Biol Med 1996; 21: 995–1001.

90. Langeveld CH, Schepens E, Jongenelen CAM, *et al.* Presence of glutathione immunoreactivity in cultured neurones and astrocytes. NeuroReport 1996; 7: 1833–1836.

91. Pileblad E, Eriksson PS, Hansson E. The presence of glutathione in primary neuronal and astroglial cultures from rat cerebral cortex and brain stem. J Neural Transm [Gen Sect] 1991; 86: 43–49.

92. Damier P, Hirsch EC, Zhang P, *et al.* Glutathione peroxidase, glial cells and Parkinson's disease. Neurosci 1993; 52: 1–6.

93. Makar TK, Nedergaard M, Preuss A, *et al.* Vitamin E, ascorbate, glutathione, glutathione disulfide, and enzymes of glutathione metabolism in cultures of chick astrocytes and neurones: Evidence that astrocytes play an important role in antioxidative processes in the brain. J Neurochem 1994; 62: 45–53.

94. Mena MA, Casarejos MJ, Carazo A, *et al.* Glia protect fetal midbrain dopamine neurons in culture from L–DOPA toxicity through multiple mechanisms. J Neural Transm 1997; 104: 317–328.

95. Hou J–GG, Cohen G, Mytilineou C. Basic fibroblast growth factor stimulation of glial cells protects dopamine neurons from 6–hydroxydopamine toxicity: Involvment of the glutathione system. J Neurochem 1997; 69: 76–83.

96. Dexter DT, Holley AE, Flitter WD, *et al.* Increased levels of lipid hydroperoxides in the parkinsonian substantia nigra: An HPLC and ESR study. Mov Disord 1994; 9: 92–97.

97. Yoritaka A, Hattori N, Uchida K, *et al.* Immunohistochemical detection of 4–hydroxynonenal protein adducts in Parkinson disease. Proc Natl Acad Sci USA 1996; 93: 2696–2701.

98. Alam ZI, Jenner A, Daniel SE, *et al.* Oxidative DNA damage in the

parkinsonian brain: An apparent selective increase in 8–hydroxyguanine levels in substantia nigra. J Neurochem 1997; 69: 1195–1203.

99. Alam ZI, Daniel SE, Lees AJ, *et al.* A generalised increase in protein carbonyls in the brain in Parkinson's but not incidental Lewy body disease. J Neurochem 1997; 69: 1326–1329.

100. Grune T, Reinheckel T, Joshi M, Davies KJA. Proteolysis in cultured liver epithelial cells during oxidative stress. Role of multicatalytic proteinase complex proteasome. J Biol Chem 1995; 270: 2344–2351.

101. Berlett BS, Stadtman ER. Protein oxidation in aging, disease, and oxidative stress. J Biol Chem 1997; 272: 20313–20316.

102. Floor E, Wetzel MG. Increased protein oxidation in human substantia nigra pars compacta in comparison with basal ganglia and prefrontal cortex measured with an improved dinitrophenylhydrazine assay. J Neurochem 1998; 70: 268–275.

103. Jahngen–Hodge J, Obin MS, Gong X, *et al.* Regulation of ubiquitinconjugating enzymes by glutathione following oxidative stress. J Biol Chem 1997; 272: 28218–28226.

104. Friquet B, Szweda LI. Inhibition of the multicatalytic proteinase (proteasome) by the 4–hydroxy–2–nonenal cross–linked protein. FEBS Lett 1997; 405: 21–25.

105. Grune T, Davies KJA. Breakdown of oxidised proteins as a part of secondary antioxidant defenses in mammalian cells. BioFactors 1997; 6: 165–172.

106. Lopes UG, Erhardt P, Yao R, Cooper GM. p53–dependent induction of apoptosis by proteasome inhibitors. J Biol Chem 1997; 272: 12893–12896.

DISCUSSION

Olanow: How much of the ratio between reduced versus oxidized glutathione can be a post-mortem artefact and what steps do you take to prevent that from occurring?

Jenner: Oxidation of glutathione does not occur quickly. We have carried out mock post-mortem experiments to examine the rate at which reduced glutathione is lost and oxidized glutathione appears. The changes are not dramatic. In the post-mortem studies, we have demonstrated 98–99% reduced glutathione and about 1% oxidized glutathione, so the results are probably not artifactual.

Youdim: The concept of using glutathione derivatives for treatment is appealing, but the blood–brain barrier is a problem. People have used N-acetylcysteine with some success to treat oxidative stress associated with glutathione deficiency in peripheral tissues such as the liver. This situation is very much like what we see in PD and suggests that if we could get glutathione or a glutathione precursor into the brain, it might be a useful treatment.

Jenner: Absolutely. We could not effectively get pro-drugs of glutathione into the brain so as to replenish reduced levels of glutathione in BSO-depleted animals. We have tried one or two precursors of glutathione and had very little success in restoring brain glutathione content. Glutamylcysteine has, I think, been used with some success in restoring glutathione content, at least in cells. We have also tried thioctic acid which acts as another redox couple, like reduced and oxidized glutathione, but that will not take over the function of glutathione.

Youdim: We have been doing the same thing, but we may be doing the wrong experiment. We have, in fact, been trying to induce enzymes to synthesize more glutathione in the brain, without success.

Shoulson: In the normal state, reduced glutathione accounts for 98–99% of the total glutathione level in the brain. We are assuming that in PD there has to be a substantial decrease in the amount of reduced glutathione in order for there to be enhanced vulnerability to toxins. Are you, therefore, trying to increase the reduced glutathione from a very low level in specific brain regions (the only low level presumably being in the nigra), or are you trying to increase total brain glutathione which is already at about 98%?

Jenner: The only way forward, initially, would be to attempt to increase the total glutathione content of the brain with the expectation that it would permit a critical level to accumulate in the substantia nigra. The problem is that we have an approximate loss of glutathione of only 30–40% in PD, but we do not know anything specific about where the loss is occurring at a cellular or a sub-cellular level. If the entire loss of glutathione were in the mitochondrial compartment of neurons, that would be very important. Most glutathione is in glial cells and my suspicion is that glial cells are very important in the pathogenesis of PD. I believe that we have to start examining the role of glutathione in the glia, as well as the role that the glia plays in toxic mechanisms in PD. Also, what does this level of reduction in glutathione mean? In studies from Dr. Olanow's group, glutathione had to be depleted by 80% in order for dopamine neuronal cell death to occur. On the other hand, a reduction in glutathione of even a modest degree could mean that there is an increased susceptibility to toxins.

Borden: Do you believe that the increased prevalence of disulfide bonds in the cell, and in the Lewy bodies in particular, is relevant to the formation of large aggregates as a result of the reduction in glutathione levels? Additionally, glutathione is known to chelate divalent metal ions, so do you believe this could be a major role for glutathione in the mitochondria?

Jenner: Your first question is extremely interesting but I do not know the answer. Secondly, we think about glutathione as an anti-oxidant molecule in the glutathione cycle. But, as you are saying, it has other actions and does chelate divalent metal ions. Glutathione acts as a carrier for peroxynitrite, so how does glutathione depletion affect the role of nitric oxide in PD? There is some evidence that glutathione can be released from neurons in the same way that transmitters are released. There is a glutathione binding site on the NMDA receptor and we know that glutathione, both reduced and oxidized, can also influence glutamate function. There are indeed many ways in which alterations or reductions in glutathione might contribute to the pathology of PD.

Melamed: We are also involved in trying to synthesize precursors of glutathione, or glutathione compounds, that could cross the blood–brain barrier and are having major difficulties in doing so. We think we may have a few compounds that might cross the blood–brain barrier and we are looking at them now. But are we on the right track? If glutathione, or a thiol-containing compound, crosses the blood–brain barrier, could it be neuroprotective in PD and other neurodegenerative disorders? This has yet to be shown. Another point is that levodopa toxicity may also be mediated by depletion of glutathione, as levodopa forms an adduct with glutathione. On the other hand, if cells are exposed to sub-lethal doses of levodopa, there is a dramatic increase in glutathione content. This may be another lesson for us with regard to the properties of glutathione. Moreover, glial cells are extremely resistant to levodopa and dopamine toxicity, which may be due to their having a higher content of glutathione.

Olanow: The cells which survived in experiments in which toxins were administered to cultured dopamine cells after exposure to sub-lethal doses of levodopa, were not TH-positive cells. Further, BSO, which inhibits glutathione formation, does not interfere with this effect. It appears to be an entirely injury-related phenomenon, because if ascorbate is added to block the levodopa-related injury, the effect is lost. This same effect is seen following sub-lethal injury with other toxins. Therefore I think it is a non-specific transcriptional response with upregulation of a variety of protective molecules in response to a minor injury.

Jenner: We talk about how oxidative stress kills neurons, but why are the glial cells not killed, if oxidative stress is also going on in the glia? Glial cells may have more defense mechanisms and contain larger concentrations of glutathione. In addition, as I understand it, there are metabolic differences between glial cells and neuron where for example interference with glycolysis in glial cells does not have the same effect on their integrity as it does in neurons.

Youdim: Your comments on glial cells are very important, because we see large changes in reduced glutathione which cannot be attributed solely to neuronal loss. We calculate that neurons constitute 5–10% of the total cells in the nigra. We need more specific methods to differentiate glutathione in neurons *versus* glia. A second point is that there is a relationship between iron metabolism and glutathione. Every neurotoxin or cytotoxin that has been reported to cause release of iron with toxicity, depletes glutathione. The same occurs in the brain. I think we have to consider this if we are going to develop new therapies. We know that iron is increased in the substantia nigra, in PD, but simply increasing glutathione might not protect against this. We should also think about removing the iron.

Jenner: In incidental Lewy body disease, there is certainly a loss of glutathione but no global increase of iron. The difficulty with handling pieces of tissue is, of course, that we do not know what is happening at the cellular level in terms of subtle changes in glutathione and iron, or indeed in complex I activity. Drs. Smith and Di Monte have shown that, in hepatocytes, if mitochondrial activity is impaired in a variety of ways, the first event is an efflux of reduced glutathione from the cells with no change in the level of oxidized glutathione. So one could in fact argue that, in incidental Lewy body disease, the early change in glutathione could be a reflection of mitochondrial defects which can not be detected biochemically.

Olanow: Did you look for any evidence of increased cytokines in your incidental Lewy body cases?

Jenner: Not so far. The incidental Lewy body cases that we had were from source, which is now completely depleted. As a group, we need to examine a very large number of controls and define another series of incidental Lewy body disease brains, because some very important biochemical studies need to be done on that material.

Olanow: We have some preliminary data indicating that pure neuronal cultures depleted of glutathione by BSO are unaffected. Glutathione depletion only seems to cause degeneration in dopaminergic neurons in mixed cultures, raising the possibility that neuronal degeneration occurs as a result of glutathione depletion in glia which in turn induces glial activation with release of toxic products such as cytokines or nitric oxide that kill the neurons.

Jenner: We seem to be returning repeatedly to the role of the glial cells in PD. We keep asking what's wrong with the neurons in PD. Perhaps we should be asking what's wrong with the glia in PD.

Hirsch: The glial cells may play a protective role. Dr. Damier has analyzed glutathione peroxidase by immunohistochemistry in the human brain post-mortem, and it was found mostly in the glial cells. This is also the site of production of large amounts of oxygen free radicals. MAO-B is also present in the glial cells, so they are definitely a key factor.

Jenner: We know that certain drugs used in the treatment of PD, – deprenyl, for example, and pergolide and other dopamine agonists – if administered repeatedly to animals, cause an up-regulation of some of these protective enzymes, such as glutathione peroxidase.

Beal: We have studied the glutathione system, and looked at the glutathione prodrug developed a few years ago by Meister for evidence of any neuroprotective effects. We were unable to see anything, despite a previous report in the literature on some protective effects against MPTP toxicity. The issue about glutathione peroxidase is interesting. We have been looking at some glutathione peroxidase knockout mice and they are more susceptible to some mitochondrial toxins, but not nearly as much as might be expected. This indicates the likelihood of significant compensation in the nervous system for the knockout of glutathione peroxidase, which is rather surprising.

Jenner: Dr. Halliwell believes that when one of the antioxidant systems is knocked out, then the other antioxidant systems will often compensate for that loss. Consequently, we must look for compensation which might explain why we see relatively little toxicity in knockout mice. In our experience, we cannot increase brain glutathione content by using glutathione precursors, even after depletion, nor do we see any neuroprotection. We need to tackle the question of what glutathione is doing in the brain and if modifying glutathione content is of any value.

W. Tatton: Dr. Green and others have looked at glutamylcysteine and its effect in reducing cell damage and death, and have shown that its action is unrelated to its conversion to glutathione. If this conversion is blocked, glutamylcysteine is still effective at concentrations down to 10^{-11} M and it acts by turning on gene transcription. This underscores the fact that sometimes we assume an obvious mechanism, when a completely different action of the molecule may be responsible for its effects.

Olanow: This is also the case with levodopa. Upregulation of glutathione occurs with mild toxicity but is unnecessary for the protective effect which is seen with low dose levodopa administration in tissue culture. Protection is probably due to induction of transcriptional changes with upregulation of numerous protective molecules of which glutathione is just one. Have you or anyone else looked at the effect in this type of model of blocking transcription?

W. Tatton: Blocking transcription does removes this effect. This has been done with cycloheximide and also with actinomycin and topotecin. The work with cycloheximide now is suspect because it acts on a number of proteases, so other agents have to be used to prove a transcriptional or a translational dependency.

De Yebenes Justo: I was interested in the fact that there are derivatives of cysteine and glutathione that could be potentially toxic. One of my colleagues in Madrid has been using NMR spectroscopy to study dogs which were injected into the striatum with MPP+, and has found an acute increase in lactate in dogs treated with high doses of glutathione, of the order of 400 μM. In this model, therefore, glutathione seems to increase lactate.

Jenner: I was speculating that potentiating flux through those pathways, whether by levodopa, dopamine, glutathione or cysteine, gives rise to products of metabolism which are extremely toxic. No-one has yet looked for these products in human post-mortem brains but I would very much like to know if any of them are actually present in the brain.

Melamed: We have been experimenting with BCL-2 deficient mice and found a dramatic increase in glutathione peroxidase in their brains. However, cortical neurons and other neurons from these animals are still very sensitive to MPP+, dopamine and levodopa. Therefore, regardless of the fact that there are probably compensatory increases in this enzyme, they are probably inadequate and the neurons remain vulnerable to toxicity.

Jenner: In the last available tissue from the series of patients with incidental Lewy bodies, we measured levels of BCL-2 in tissue homogenates. Although the numbers are unfortunately smaller than we would have liked, there seemed to be an increase in BCL-2 in these incidental Lewy body disease cases. Unfortunately, we have no further tissue for localization studies. As a group, we need to examine a very large number of controls and define another series of incidental Lewy body disease brains, because some very important biochemical studies need to be done on that material.

CHAPTER ELEVEN

Advanced Glycation Endproducts in neurodegeneration – more than early markers of oxidative stress?

G. MÜNCH[2], M. GERLACH[1], J. SIAN[1],
A. WONG[2] AND P. RIEDERER[1]

[1]Department of Clinical Neurochemistry, University School of Medicine, and
[2]Department of Physiological Chemistry I, Biocenter, University of Würzburg,
Würzburg, Germany

OXIDATIVE STRESS AND ABNORMAL PROTEIN CROSSLINKING IN NEURODEGENERATIVE DISEASES

Oxidative stress results from excess production of reactive oxygen species which cannot be contained by cellular protective systems.[1] Mild oxidative stress usually induces a compensatory elevation in the production of antioxidants, but during severe oxidative stress protective defense mechanisms are overwhelmed by increased oxygen radical formation and cell death results. Oxidative stress has been associated with neurodegenerative diseases and chronic inflammatory disease. A more chronic form of oxidative stress is believed to occur in Parkinson's disease (PD).

During the occurrence of oxidative stress, the formation of peroxides and other related reactive oxygen species may occur. Peroxides are generated during normal metabolic reactions, when insufficient oxygen supply results in the formation of oxygen free radicals.[2] Reactive oxygen species or free radicals are highly unstable by virtue of their unpaired electron(s).[3] These reactive species can be produced by the loss or gain of a single electron from a non-radical entity, subsequently leading to neuronal death. Although the role of oxidative stress remains undefined, it may be a cause of neuronal cell death and a manifestation of cell destruction.

Current theories of the pathogenesis of neurodegenerative diseases including PD focus on the formation of oxygen free radicals which may in turn elicit neuronal damage. Post-mortem studies have shown alterations in brain iron content, impaired mitochondrial function, changes in the ratio of activities of superoxide dismutase to catalase and reduction of reduced glutathione, all of which may play a role in PD.[4-6] PD is characterized by the presence of intracellular neuronal inclusions such as Lewy bodies which accumulate very early in the course of the disease. The protein deposits are crosslinked by 'advanced glycation endproducts' (AGEs).[7] AGE formation starts with the reaction of the amino groups of proteins, particularly the side chains of lysine, arginine and histidine, with reducing sugars, including glucose, fructose, hexose-phosphates, trioses and triose-phosphates. This reaction leads ultimately to protein-bound Amadori products, and subsequent rearrangements, dehydrations and oxidations produce a heterogeneous group of fluorescent compounds and brown pigments, the AGEs, with concomitant release of superoxide anions. AGE formation is irreversible and causes protease-resistant cross-linking of peptides and proteins, leading to protein deposition and amyloidosis.[8-10]

In PD and Lewy body dementia, Lewy bodies contain biochemically altered neurofilament proteins. Immunoreactivity to pentosidine and pyrraline, two specific AGEs, was seen in the substantia nigra of PD and the neocortex of diffuse Lewy body disease. Immunolocalization of AGEs as a marker of oxidative stress provides evidence that glycoxidation and oxidative stress may be an important pathogenic factor in diseases characterized by Lewy body formation, and supports the evidence that formation of inclusions from cytoskeletal proteins is linked to oxidative stress.[7]

AGEs as Early Markers of Redox–Active Transition Metals and Oxidative Stress

AGEs can be formed by oxidative reaction pathways, which are significantly accelerated by transition metals such as copper and iron. In this glycoxidation reaction, protein-bound AGEs, highly reactive dicarbonyl products and oxygen free radicals are formed. Transition metals can also oxidize monosaccharides in solution to form dicarbonyl products, which subsequently crosslink proteins through 'auto-oxidative glycosylation'. The oxidation steps in both pathways can be inhibited by metal chelators, emphasizing the significance of transition metals for AGE-formation.[11] Since levels of iron are increased in the substantia nigra of PD patients, transition metal catalyzed oxidation of glycated proteins, glucose and other reactive intracellular sugars can actively lead to the cross-linking of intracellular proteins to form Lewy bodies.

AGE formation and protein cross-linking can be inhibited by thiol antioxidants such as thioctic acid and N-acetylcysteine (Münch, unpublished results). Since GSH is the major intracellular thiol antioxidant, its depletion, which occurs in the early stages of PD,[12] might be the decisive factor triggering the formation of Lewy bodies in presymptomatic cases of PD.

AGEs Cause Oxidative Stress

The involvement of AGEs in the formation of abnormal protein deposits in the brains of individuals with neurodegenerative disorders has been clarified, but their interaction with cell surface receptors and intracellular signal transduction is a new direction of research which might solve certain aspects of the etiopathogenesis of PD. AGEs were once regarded as static by-products of the disease rather than dynamic participants in neuronal death, but they are now recognized to exert multiple detrimental effects on cells.

Glycated proteins produce radicals through oxidation reactions

Glycated proteins produce nearly 50-fold more oxygen free radicals than non-glycated proteins.[13] This process commences with the production of superoxide radicals by the transition metal-catalyzed autoxidation of protein-bound Amadori products, followed by the dismutation of superoxide to hydrogen peroxide, and the generation of hydroxyl radicals. This results in a site-specific attack on proteins, with consequent protein damage and lipid peroxidation, as well as damage to DNA.[9] This may be relevant to PD where increased markers of lipid peroxidation, carbonyl proteins and DNA oxidation products have been detected.

AGEs activate microglia and induce cytokine production and release of oxygen free radicals

Interaction of AGEs with cells increases oxidative stress. It is not yet clear whether this occurs simply by the binding of AGEs to the cell surface and subsequent diffusion of chemically-produced free radicals across the membrane, or by a receptor-mediated oxidative signalling pathway. In addition to the recently described AGE-receptor, RAGE,[14] other receptors with AGE binding properties have been described. These AGE-mediated effects can be blocked by antioxidants and by antibodies to the AGE-receptor. In cell culture experiments, NFT-tau isolated from post-mortem tissue and recombinant AGE-tau each generate oxygen free radicals with subsequent activation of the transcription via NFκB (up-regulated in PD[15]), leading to the up-regulation of NFκB-regulated gene products including interleukin-1β and interleukin-6, TGF, and TNF-α,[16,17] all of which are increased in brains and CSF of PD patients.[18,19] However, this inflammatory process accompanied or caused by the elevated level of AGEs is not a unique feature of PD, but is also present in a further neurodegenerative disorder, Alzheimer's disease.[20]

AGEs Create Positive Feedback Loops Leading to Vicious Circles of Neurodegeneration

Neurodegeneration involves positive feedback loops of cellular damage and compensatory mechanisms which keep the cell in a metastable condition of damage and repair. The 'error catastrophy theory of aging' proposes that noxious influences accumulate during the aging process of cells, whereas repair and defense mechanisms weaken. When the accumulated damage cannot be compensated, the cell leaves this metastable condition and begins the irreversible journey characterized by loss of function and finally cell death.

Promotors of feedback loops have to cause a condition in which their own formation is favored. AGEs might be one of these factors and could thus be dynamic participants in neuronal death. Thus, positive feedback loops involving oxidative stress may be an important pathogenic factor in diseases such as PD characterized by formation of intracellular cytoskeletal protein deposits with impairment of axonal transport and subsequent cellular dysfunction and death.

SUMMARY

- Oxidative stress has been implicated in the pathogenesis of cell death in PD and other neurodegenerative disorders.
- Advanced glycation end products (AGEs) are a marker of oxidative stress and their formation is promoted by transition metals.
- AGEs promote crosslinking of protein deposits and are present in Lewy bodies in PD.
- AGEs contribute to the formation of free radicals and oxidant stress and they may play a role in the continuum of the neurodegenerative process.

REFERENCES

1. Simonian NA, Coyle JT. Oxidative stress in neurodegenerative diseases. Ann Rev Pharmacol Toxicol 1997; 36: 83–106.

2. Meister A. Glutathione deficiency produced by inhibition of its synthesis and its reversal; applications in research and therapy. Pharm Ther 1991; 51: 155–194.

3. Halliwell B. Free radicals, antioxidants and human disease: curiosity, cause or consequence? Lancet 1994; 344: 721–724.

4. Gerlach M, Riederer P, Youdim MBH. Molecular mechanisms for neuro-degeneration: Synergism between reactive oxygen species, calcium and exictotoxic amino acids. In, Battistin L, Scarlato G, Caraceni T, Ruggieri S, eds, Adv Neurol. Philadelphia: Lippincott-Raven 1996; 69: 177–194.

5. Jenner P, Olanow CW. Oxidative stress and the pathogenesis of Parkinson's disease. Neurol 1996; 47: S161–S170.

6. Owen AD, Schapira AHV, Jenner P, Marsden CD. Indices of oxidative stress in Parkinson's disease, Alzheimers-disease and dementia with Lewy bodies. J Neural Transm 1997; 51: S167–S173.

7. Castellani R, Smith MA, Richey PL, Perry G. Glycoxidation and oxidative stress in Parkinson disease and diffuse Lewy body disease. Brain Res 1996; 737: 195–200.

8. Smith MA, Taneda S, Richey PL, Miyata S, Yan SD, Stern D, Sayre LM, Monnier VM, Perry G. Advanced Maillard reaction end products are associated with Alzheimer's disease pathology. Proc Natl Acad Sci USA 1994; 91: 5710–5714.

9. Smith MA, Sayre LM, Monnier VM, Perry G. Radical AGEing in Alzheimer's disease. Trends Neurosci 1995; 18: 172–176.

10. Vitek MP, Bhattacharya K, Glendening JM, Stopa E, Vlassara H, Bucala R, Manogue K, Cerami A. Advanced glycation end products contribute to amyloidosis in Alzheimer disease. Proc Natl Acad Sci USA 1994; 91: 4766–4770.

11. Wells-Knecht MC, Thorpe SR, Baynes JW. Pathways of formation of glycoxidation products during glycation of collagen. Biochem 1995; 34: 15134–15141.

12. Sian J, Gerlach M, Riederer P. The role of altered glutathione status in the development of Parkinson's disease. In, Shaw CA, ed, Glutathione in the central nervous system. Bristol: Taylor & Francis, 1998: 287–304.

13. Mullarkey CJ, Edelstein D, Brownlee M. Free radical generation by early glycation products: a mechanism for accelerated atherogenesis in diabetes. Biochem Biophys Res Commun 1990; 173: 932–939.

14. Schmidt AM, Hori O, Cao R, Yan SD, Brett J, Wautier JL, Ogaea S, Kuwabara K, Matsumoto M, Stern D. RAGE, a novel cellular receptor for advanced glycation endproducts. Diabetes 1996; 45: 77–80.

15. Hunot S, Brugg B, Ricard D, Michel PP, Muriel MP, Ruberg M, Faucheux BA, Agid Y, Hirsch EC. Nuclear translocation of NFkB is increased in dopaminergic neurons of patients with Parkinsons disease. Proc Natl Acad Sci USA 1997; 94: 7531–7536.

16. Yan SD, Chen X, Schmidt AM, Brett J, Godman G, Zou YS, Scott CW, Caputo C, Frappier T, Smith MA, Perry G, Yen SH, Stern D. Glycated tau protein in Alzheimer disease: a mechanism for induction of oxidant stress. Proc Natl Acad Sci USA 1994; 91: 7787–7791.

17. Yan SD, Yan SF, Chen X, Fu J, Chen M, Kuppusamy P, Smith MA, Perry G, Godman GC, Nawroth P, Stern D. Non-enzymatically glycated tau in Alzheimer's disease induces neuronal oxidant stress resulting in cytokine gene expression and release of amyloid beta-peptide. Nat Med 1995; 1: 693–699.

18. Mogi M, Harada M, Kondo T, Riederer P, Inagi H, Minami M, Nagatsu T. Interleukin -1ß, interleukin-6, epidermal growth factor and transforming growth factor-a are elevated in the brain of Parkinsonian patients. Neurosci Lett 1994; 180: 147–150.

19. Blum-Degen D, Müller T, Kuhn W, Gerlach M, Przuntek H, Riederer P. Interleukin 1ß and intrerleukin 6 are elevated in the cerebrospinal fluid of Alzheimer's and *de novo* Parkinson's disease patients. Neurosci Lett 1996; 202: 17–20.

20. Münch G, Thome J, Foley P, Schinzel R, Riederer P. Advanced glycation endproducts in ageing and Alzheimer's disease. Brain Res Rev 1997; 23: 134–143.

DISCUSSION

Gash: You focused on nigrostriatal striatal projections, primarily to the putamen. Nigral projections to the globus pallidus, and also connections between the pars compacta of the nigra and the pars reticulata, are also very important in controlling motor functions. Did you see any differences in the pathology in these areas, compared to the nigrostriatal sections?

Riederer: We have studied that a great deal, and there are changes in the glutamate receptor function. There is some decrease in the glutamate binding sites in the globus pallidus internus while in the putamen there is some increase. There are also some subtle changes with regard to NMDA receptors in these areas that are in line with the principal pathobiochemical mechanism concerning the motor loop in PD. These changes were not as dramatic as predicted by animal experiments, probably due to the fact that in humans with PD neurodegeneration is not so dramatic as has been constructed in animal models. Excitotoxicity is certainly occurring in PD, but we do not know whether this is a very early or late event.

Olanow: How much of the evidence for oxidative damage in the nigra is firm? For instance, there is some controversy over the measures of lipid peroxidation. Measures of lipid peroxidation that do not control for increased iron may not be reliable. Oxidative damage to proteins and DNA is widely disseminated and affects many areas other than the substantia nigra and thus may be relatively non-specific. Does anything point to clear and unequivocal oxidative events taking place specifically in the substantia nigra pars compacta?

Riederer: There are several answers to that question. There is general agreement that oxidative stress does occur. I am not sure whether we can achieve homogenous groups of PD for studies in the laboratory. Atypical forms of PD might have been included in such assays. Oxidative stress seems to play a role, and this is certainly substantiated by hard data on the advanced glycation end-products, which can be demonstrated in Lewy bodies and which implicate the occurrence of oxidative stress. As such, oxidative stress is found at all locations in which Lewy bodies can be demonstrated and therefore is not specific to the substantia nigra and may represent a secondary event.

Koller: One of the crucial issues seems to be determination of the primary event in the pathological cascade. Can you speculate on which of the many changes you mentioned might be primary pathogenic events?

Riederer: If we can demonstrate oxidative stress in very early patients, even in incidental Lewy body disease, then it must already play a role at a very early stage in the development of PD. Biochemists, neurobiologists, and molecular

[173]

biologists must find a screening method for these early subtle changes. Dr. Jenner has looked for oxidative stress parameters in incidental Lewy bodies but has not found any increase in iron, or any changes in complex I activity, but these measures might be too insensitive for the very subtle changes that are occurring. However, GSH levels were significantly reduced in cases with incidental Lewy body disease, indication that it is an early event. Therefore, I think oxidative stress could be one of the primary events leading to cell degeneration, together with some genetic predisposition in such patients.

Mizuno: Regarding Dr. Olanow's comments on the specificity of oxidative stress in the substantia nigra, we did an immunohistochemical study to detect oxidative stress in the substantia nigra in patients with PD. During the process of oxidative stress, hydroxynonenal, an unsaturated aldehyde, is released from arachidonic acid and reacts with proteins. We used antibodies to detect hydroxynonenal-modified proteins in the substantia nigra of a patient with PD and found a strongly positive immunohistochemical reaction in many nigral neurons but not in other areas. Interestingly, patients with multiple system degeneration also showed positive immunological staining for the presence of hydroxynonenal-modified proteins. Therefore it is not specific for PD but a substance in the nigra appears to undergo oxidative stress more intensely compared to other structures.

Schapira: You had quite a large group of early PD cases that did not show any pathology. Was there a statistically significant difference in the GSH values between those and your matched controls?

Riederer: No, because there were only three cases which showed a very subtle decrease. There was a tendency towards overall decrease with time.

Youdim: We have seen biochemical changes not only in the substantia nigra but also in the compacta. We need much more sensitive methods for the indication of oxidative stress. Lipid peroxidation is not very good. The methods that have been used are neither sensitive nor specific. Your data would suggest that PD may be an inflammatory disease because of the substantial increases in various cytokines that are being measured. Could this be a cytokine-induced inflammatory process which leads to the formation of radicals which give rise to oxidative stress? That could be the cascade of events.

Riederer: I do not think there is inflammation in PD. The data would fit instead with the concept of so-called acute phase reaction. Inflammation cannot be shown by neuropathological methods but acute phase reaction may be a possible explanation for that finding. If interleukins or other cytokines are released, or if microglial cells are involved, oxidative stress could be generated.

Youdim: There is a tremendous proliferation of reactive microglia in and around the substantia nigra, which could be the result of an inflammatory process.

Riederer: It could be but there is no sign of inflammation. Leukocytes are not seen, neither are any other neuropathological signs of inflammation, so I think it is an acute phase reaction perhaps to local injury from any cause.

W. Tatton: What role you think NFκB might be playing in PD, based on your data? It is such a powerful transcriptional modulator at the AP1 site and I wondered if you had any comments about that aspect.

Riederer: It probably plays a role in other neurodegenerative disorders but the NFκB cascade also fits very well into the PD pathology, in terms of oxidative stress, cytokines, chemokine alterations and acute phase reactions. It is non-specific, but certainly has a role in the advanced glycation end-product cascade. We are currently looking at the AP1 issue.

Hirsch: We have shown that activation of the sphingomyelin transduction pathway, which involves NFκB, can result in the death of dopaminergic neurons *in vitro*. In PD patients we see translocation of NFκB from the cytoplasm to the nucleus, so this pathway may be involved in the degenerative process, but probably more as a secondary event than a primary cause of the disease.

CHAPTER TWELVE

Mitochondria in the etiology and pathogenesis of Parkinson's disease

A.H.V. Schapira[1,2], M. Gu[1], J-W. Taanman[1],
S.J. Tabrizi[1], T. Seaton[1], M. Cleeter[1]
and J.M. Cooper[1]

[1]University Department of Clinical Neurosciences, Royal Free Hospital School of Medicine, and [2]University Department of Clinical Neurology, Institute of Neurology, London, UK.

The clinical features of Parkinson's disease (PD) overlap with other neurodegenerative disorders, especially those included in the multiple system atrophies. The neuropathology of PD is characterized by severe degeneration of the dopaminergic nerve cells of the substantia nigra pars compacta and their projections to the striatum, and the presence of Lewy bodies in the cytoplasm of a proportion of surviving neurons. A PD-like syndrome is known to be induced by 1-methyl-4-phenyl-1,2,3,6-tetrahydropyridine (MPTP) toxicity[1–3] and an α-synuclein mutation[4]. That two such widely different etiological factors can produce similar clinical and pathological outcomes strongly supports the contention that idiopathic PD may well have multiple etiologies. It seems inevitable that both genetic and environmental factors are likely to be involved in PD. Against this background, the contribution of mitochondria and mitochondrial dysfunction to both the etiology and pathogenesis of PD is considered in this chapter.

MITOCHONDRIA: MOLECULAR BIOLOGY AND BIOENERGETICS

Mitochondria are ubiquitous and are pivotal in cellular metabolism. Cellular mitochondrial density reflects metabolic activity. Thus neurons, and skeletal and myocardial muscles have high mitochondrial mass. Mitochondrial components are generated by both nuclear and mitochondrial DNA (mtDNA). Mt DNA is a circular double stranded molecule encoding a full complement of 22 transfer RNAs (tRNAs) and 12S and 16S ribosomal RNAs in addition to 13 proteins, all of which are part of the respiratory chain and oxidative phosphorylation (OXPHOS) system.

The OXPHOS system is located on the mitochondrial inner membrane and comprises five multimeric proteins, complexes I–V. Seventy of the 83 subunits of the OXPHOS system are encoded by nuclear DNA, the remainder by mtDNA. Numerous mutations of mtDNA have now been associated with human disease. As mtDNA is exclusively inherited through the maternal line, mtDNA related defects would be expected to exhibit maternal inheritance. This is indeed seen, although only in a minority of cases. Patients with mtDNA deletions appear as sporadic cases. For example, even 40% of patients with the 11778bp Leber's hereditary optic neuropathy mutation have no family history.[5] Thus, whilst maternal inheritance may alert the physician to a mtDNA defect, it is not a requisite for a disease related to a mitochondrial mutation, and such a pattern will not necessarily be apparent in the majority of those with mtDNA mutations.

MITOCHONDRIAL FUNCTION IN PD

Analysis of OXPHOS activity in PD post-mortem brain has demonstrated an approximate mean decrease of 37% in complex I activity in the substantia nigra pars compacta although not all PD patients exhibit this complex I defect.[6–9] This defect exactly mimics the biochemical lesion induced by MPTP,[10] providing a direct parallel between the toxin model of PD and the idiopathic disease. Similar assays of other brain areas in PD have not identified any deficiency of OXPHOS,[8,9,11–13] neither have OXPHOS defects been identified in the brains of patients with multiple system atrophy who have degeneration of dopamine neurons in the substantia nigra.[14] Thus, the OXPHOS abnormality in PD appears to be selective for the substantia nigra, and complex I deficiency is not simply the result of neuronal degeneration.

In vivo and *in vitro* analyses of skeletal muscle in PD have given conflicting information on OXPHOS function.[15–17] In contrast, analysis of complex I activity in PD platelets shows more consistency. Whilst platelet homogenates in PD show no deficiency,[18] purified platelet mitochondria show a complex I defect with or without a less severe deficiency of the other complexes.[17,19] A systemically expressed mitochondrial abnormality in PD would imply either a genetic or toxic cause. There are several confounding factors for a genetic etiology. Firstly, whilst some PD families with autosomal dominant or maternal inheritance[20] have been described, most patients with idiopathic PD appear as sporadic cases. This however is compatible with a mtDNA defect, autosomal dominant inheritance with low penetrance, or genetic (nuclear or mitochondrial) environmental interaction. Secondly, the complex I defect could be caused by a mutation of nuclear or mtDNA encoded subunits. Lastly, the apparent variability of tissue expression of a systemically distributed mutation may be the result of (a) differential expression of a nuclear encoded protein, (b) variations in load of a mtDNA mutation, or (c) sampling error.

[178]

Mitochondrial studies *in vivo* are limited by which tissues are readily available for analysis. Platelets have been selected because they are easily obtainable and have consistently revealed a complex I deficiency in PD. In 25 PD patients, we showed a mean defect of 16% specific for complex I in platelet OXPHOS activity,[21] but there was significant overlap between the PD patients and controls such that the assay was insufficiently sensitive to be a diagnostic test. We hypothesised that the PD patients with the lowest platelet complex I activity are those most likely to carry any putative mtDNA mutation. Among eight idiopathic PD patients with low platelet complex I activities, four had three serial complex I measurements, each one month apart, to assess the consistency of the defect with time,[22] and activity consistently fell more than one standard deviation below the control mean thus demonstrating the consistency and reliability of the assay.

THE GENETIC BASIS OF COMPLEX I DEFICIENCY IN PD

The cell cybrid system for the investigation of mtDNA mutations[23] uses $\rho 0$ (mtDNA-less) cells developed from a parent cell line by exposure to ethidium bromide through serial passage. The $\rho 0$ cells can survive and grow in medium enriched with pyruvate and uridine. They serve as recipients for donor mtDNA, thereby placing the donor mtDNA in a novel nuclear environment which allows the structural and functional consequences of a mtDNA mutation to be investigated without the compounding effects of its own nuclear influence.[24-26] This system has been used to investigate the origins of the complex I defect in PD[22]. Platelets from PD patients with low complex I activity were fused with $\rho 0$ cells. If the complex I defect is still expressed in the resulting cybrids, the only cause could be the PD mtDNA derived from the platelets with the complex I deficiency. If the complex I function is normalised, then the original platelet defect must have been either determined by a nuclear defect in the PD patients or an endogenous toxin circulating in the blood or sequestered in the bone marrow from which the platelets were derived. OXPHOS analysis in the cybrids produced two intriguing results. Firstly, the PD cybrids had a specific 25% ($p=0.007$) complex I deficiency, which had therefore been transferred with the mitochondria and maintained through multiple passages through which the mtDNA was the only remnant of the donor mitochondria. The donor PD mtDNA must therefore determine the complex I defect in both the platelets and the cybrids. Secondly, there was a high correlation ($r=0.86$, $p<0.001$) between the complex I activity in a PD patient's platelets and that in his/her fusion cybrids. The combination of platelet and cybrid complex I activities discriminates more specifically between PD patients and controls. These results also imply that the mitochondrially encoded subunits of complex I are important in determining the activity of the enzyme.

Cultured A549 cells were used as $\rho 0$ cells in the PD studies. To address whether the complex I deficiency was influenced by the nuclear background of the $\rho 0$ cells, a similar study was conducted on patients with sporadic focal dystonia,[27] who had a complex I defect in platelets of the same order of magnitude as that seen in PD patients.[28] Following fusion with A549 ρ0 cells and both mixed and clonal cybrid growth, OXPHOS function was normal in the dystonia derived cells. This indicates that the complex I defect in dystonia is not caused by a defect in mtDNA. These cells serve as an important disease control for the PD studies and demonstrate that the results from the PD study using the A549 cells were not due to any influence of the host ρ0 cell nucleus.

We undertook investigations to determine whether the implicated mtDNA mutation in PD was heteroplasmic (mutant and wild-type molecules co-existing in the same cell and probably the same mitochondrion) using expanded clonal analysis of the cybrids from one of the PD patients with platelet complex I deficiency.[22] OXPHOS assays showed a range of complex I and complex IV activities, the mean of all PD clones revealing significant reductions of 25% ($p<0.005$) and 20% ($p<0.005$) respectively for complex I and IV activities compared to controls. Similar studies on dystonia cybrids showed no difference from control clones. These results support the platelet fusion results in implicating mtDNA in the cause of the OXPHOS defect in PD, and the hypothesis that a heteroplasmic mtDNA mutation is present in the PD clones. Furthermore, the combination of complex I and IV deficiency is typical of a mtDNA-tRNA mutation, which might be responsible for the OXPHOS defect. Taken together, these studies implicate mtDNA in the dopamine neuronal degeneration that occurs in some PD patients. They do not permit a determination as to whether this defect is due to an inherited or somatic mutation. Furthermore, not all PD patients have a complex I defect, and it is possible that dopamine cell death occurs through other mechanisms. For example, the PD that occurs in association with a mutation in the α-synuclein gene might occur as a result of different mechanisms, or alternatively α-synuclein may induce a mitochondrial defect through a presently unexplained mechanism.

MITOCHONDRIA IN THE PATHOGENESIS OF PD

There is a complex I defect in the substantia nigra and platelets in at least a proportion of PD patients. Other factors operating at the level of the nigra might selectively enhance or even produce a complex I deficiency and in such cases platelet complex I function may be normal. For instance, levodopa causes a complex I defect in rat substantia nigra[29] and auto-oxidation of dopamine results in free radical generation which may also impair complex I function.[30] Complex I may also be the target of exogenous as well as endogenous toxins.

MPTP

It is increasingly clear that MPTP, *via* its active metabolite 1-methyl-4-phenylpyridinium (MPP+), is not only an inhibitor of complex I, but also a cause of increased free radical generation. MPP+ induces more severe and irreversible inhibition of complex I if complex IV is inhibited.[31] Complex I inhibition results in increased free radical generation from the respiratory chain and so the MPP+ model suggests that a self-amplifying cycle of complex I deficiency and damage may result in progressive cell damage. This fits well with the progressive striatal lesion in MPTP exposed patients as determined by [18]fluorodopa PET.[32] In addition, the nitric oxide (NO) synthase inhibitor, 7-nitroindazole, can protect against MPTP toxicity in primates[33] and rats[34] implicating NO· production in the mediation of MPTP toxicity.[35] NO· has been shown to inhibit directly complex I, II and III.[36] The striatum and substantia nigra contain NO· synthase positive neurons[37,38] and so the elements for NO· involvement in MPTP toxicity are in place.

Complex I inhibitors and apoptosis

The demonstration that MPTP could induce parkinsonism has focused attention on a possible role for more common environmental agents in the etiology of PD. Structurally related compounds, isoquinolines, have been shown to inhibit complex I and α-ketoglutarate dehydrogenase,[39–41] cause free radical generation[42,43] and induce parkinsonism in primates[44] and rats.[45] The complex I inhibitors rotenone, MPP+, isoquinoline and tetrahydroisoquinoline (TIQ) all reduced cell survival in PC12 cells,[46] which appears to be directly related to the reduction in ATP synthesis by these compounds. As little as a 20% decrease in ATP synthesis by TIQ caused marked cell death, which was proven to be by apoptosis. Interestingly apoptotic cell death induced in both PC12 and SKNMC cells by these toxins was reduced by 20–79% by a variety of antioxidants including N-acetylcysteine, dihydrolipoic acid and pyrrolidine dithiocarbamate. This implicates the involvement of free radicals and decreased ATP production in mediating the pro-apoptotic action of these complex I inhibitors.

Mitochondria and apoptosis

The inner mitochondrial membrane potential is produced and maintained by the activity of the respiratory chain and the pumping of protons out of the mitochondrial matrix. ρ0 cells can still maintain membrane potential,[47] but lose it in response to agents that stimulate apoptosis. The loss of membrane potential precedes nuclear fragmentation and results in the opening of permeability transition pores (megachannels).[48] Permeability transition and membrane potential collapse allow the escape of molecules from the inner mitochondria which can induce apoptotic changes in isolated nuclei.[49] It is thus possible that a mitochondrial defect in complex I as is seen in PD could lead to a decrease in proton pumping with a fall in mitchondrial membrane potential and consequent apoptotic cell death.

Summary

- Mitochondrial defects due to inborn or toxic abnormalities could induce dopaminergic cell death in PD.

- In cybrid systems, the transfer of a complex I deficiency from mtDNA derived from platelets of PD patients clearly implicates mtDNA mutations as the cause of the defect. Death may be due to a fall in membrane potential with apoptosis.

- Additional factors, *e.g.* exogenous toxins, including levodopa, may enhance the complex I deficiency, cause a further fall in membrane potential and precipitate cell death. A similar scenario could explain the potential contribution of other factors such as endogenous toxins, *e.g.* dopamine, NO and free radicals.

- Thus, the etiology and the pathogenesis of dopaminergic cell death in PD may be multifactorial, and the processes outlined above may be relevant to only a proportion of PD patients. The mechanisms by which a mutation in the α-synuclein gene might cause neuronal death are unknown, and may involve entirely different pathways. Alternatively, the α-synuclein mutation may also affect energy or free radical metabolism and follow similar pathways to cell death as a mtDNA defect.

- Identification of the mtDNA genotype responsible for PD may allow the testing of neuroprotective strategies in appropriate patients.

Acknowledgments

This work was supported by The Medical Research Council (UK), The Parkinson's Disease Society (UK), The Thorn Trust, The Wellcome Trust and The Parkinson's Disease Society Brain Bank.

References

1. Langston JW, Ballard P, Tetrud JW, Irwin I. Chronic parkinsonism in humans due to a product of meperidine analog synthesis. Science 1983; 219: 979–980.

2. Langston JW, Forno LS, Robert CS, Irwin I. MPTP causes selective damage to the zona compacta of the substantia nigra in the squirrel monkey. Brain Res 1984; 292: 390–394.

3. Forno LS, Langston JW, DeLanney LE, Irwin I. An electron microscopic study of MPTP–induced inclusion bodies in an old monkey. Brain Res 1988; 448: 150–157.

4. Polymeropoulos MH, Lavedan C, Leroy E, et al. Mutation in the α–synuclein gene identified in families with Parkinson's disease. Science 1997; 276: 2045–2047.

5. Harding AE, Sweeney MG, Govan GG, Riordan–Eva P. Pedigree analysis in Leber hereditary optic neuropathy families with a pathogenic mtDNA mutation. Am J Hum Genet 1995; 57: 77–86.

6. Schapira AHV, Cooper JM, Dexter D, Jenner P, Clark JB, Marsden CD. Mitochondrial complex I deficiency in Parkinson's disease. Lancet 1989; 1: 1269.

7. Schapira AHV, Cooper JM, Dexter D, Clark JB, Jenner P, Marsden CD. Mitochondrial complex I deficiency in Parkinson's disease. J Neurochem 1990; 54: 823–827.

8. Janetzky B, Hauck S, Youdim MBH, et al. Unaltered aconitase activity but decreased complex I activity in substantia nigra pars compacta of patients with Parkinson's disease. Neurosci Lett 1994; 169: 126–128.

9. Gu M, Owen AD, Toffa SEK, et al. Mitochondrial function, GSH and iron in neurodegeneration and Lewy body diseases. J Neurol Sci 1998; 158: 24–29.

10. Nicklas WJ, Vyas I, Heikkila RE. Inhibition of NADH–linked oxidation in brain mitochondria by MPP^+, a metabolite of the neurotoxin MPTP. Life Sci 1985; 36: 2503–2508.

11. Schapira AHV, Mann VM, Cooper JM, et al. Anatomic and disease specificity of NADH CoQ_1 reductase (complex I) deficiency in Parkinson's disease. J Neurochem 1990; 55: 2142–2145.

12. Mann VM, Cooper JM, Daniel SE, Jenner P, Marsden CD, Schapira AHV. Complex I, iron and ferritin in Parkinson's disease substantia nigra. Ann Neurol 1994; 36: 876–881.

13. Cooper JM, Daniel SE, Marsden CD, Schapira AHV. L–dihydroxyphenylalanine and complex I deficiency in Parkinson's disease brain. Mov Disord 1995; 10: 295–297.

14. Gu M, Gash MT, Cooper JM, et al. Mitochondrial respiratory chain function in multiple system atrophy. Mov Disord 1997; 12; 418–422.

15. Taylor DJ, Krige D, Barnes PRJ, et al. A ^{31}P magnetic resonance spectroscopy study of mitochondrial function in skeletal muscle of patients with Parkinson's disease. J Neurol Sci 1994; 125: 77–81.

16. Penn AMW, Roberts T, Hodder J, Allen PS, Zhu G, Martin WRW. Generalized mitochondrial dysfunction in Parkinson's disease detected by magnetic resonance spectroscopy of muscle. Neurol 1995; 45: 2097–2099.

17. Schapira AHV. Evidence for mitochondrial dysfunction in Parkinson's disease: a critical appraisal. Mov Disord 1994; 9: 125–138.

18. Mann VM, Cooper JM, Krige D, Daniel SE, Schapira AHV, Marsden CD. Brain, skeletal muscle and platelet homogenate mitochondrial function in Parkinson's disease. Brain 1992; 115: 333–342.

19. Haas RH, Nasirian F, Nakano K, et al. Low platelet mitochondrial complex I and complex II/III activity in early untreated Parkinson's disease. Ann Neurol 1995; 37: 714–722.

20. Wooten GF, Currie LJ, Bennett JP, Harrison MB, Trugman JM, Parker WD. Maternal inheritance in Parkinson's disease. Ann Neurol 1997; 41: 265–268.

21. Krige D, Carroll MT, Cooper JM, Marsden CD, Schapira AHV. Platelet mitochondrial function in Parkinson's disease. Ann Neurol 1992; 32: 782–788.

22. Gu M, Cooper JM, Taanman JW, Schapira AHV. Mitochondrial DNA transmission of the mitochondrial defect in Parkinson's disease. Ann Neurol 1998, in press.

23. King MP, Attardi G. Human cells lacking mtDNA: Repopulation with exogenous mitochondria by complementation. Science 1989; 246: 500–503.

24. Chomyn A, Martinuzzi A, Yoneda M, et al. MELAS mutation in mtDNA binding site for transcription termination factor causes defects in protein synthesis and in respiration but no change in levels of upstream and downstream mature transcripts. Proc Natl Acad Sci USA 1992; 89: 4221–4225.

25. Chomyn A, Lai ST, Shake R, Bresolin N, Scarlato G, Attardi G. Platelet–mediated transformation of mtDNA–less human cells: analysis of phenotypic variability among clones from normal individuals – and complementation behaviour of the tRNA^{Lys} mutation causing myoclonic epilepsy and ragged red fibers. Am J Hum Genet 1994; 34: 966–974.

26. Dunbar DR, Moonie PA, Zeviani M, Holt IJ. Complex I deficiency is associated with 3243G:C mitochondrial DNA in osteosarcoma cell cybrids. Hum Mol Genet 1996; 5: 123–129.

27. Tabrizi SJ, Cooper JM, Schapira AHV. Mitochondrial DNA in focal dystonia: a cybrid analysis. Ann Neurol 1998, in press.

28. Schapira AHV, Warner T, Gash MT, Cleeter MJW, Marinho CFM, Cooper JM. Complex I function in familial and sporadic dystonia. Ann Neurol 1997; 41: 556–559.

29. Przedborski S, Jackson–Lewis V, Muthane U, et al. Chronic levodopa administration alters cerebral mitochondrial respiratory chain activity. Ann Neurol 1993; 34: 715–723.

30. Zhang Y, Marcillat O, Giulivi C, Ernster I, Davies KJ. The oxidative inactivaton of mitochondrial electron transport chain components and ATP. J Biol Chem 1990; 265: 16330–16336.

31. Cleeter MJW, Cooper JM, Schapira AHV. Irreversible inhibition of mitochondrial complex I by 1–methyl–4–phenylpyridinium: evidence for free radical involvement. J Neurochem 1992; 58: 786–789.

32. Vingerhoets FJG, Snow BJ, Tetrud JJ, Langston JW, Schulzer M, Calne DB. Positron emission tomographic evidence for progression of human MPTP–induced dopaminergic lesions. Ann Neurol 1994; 36: 765–770.

33. Hantraye P, Brouillet E, Ferrante R, et al. Inhibition of neuronal nitric oxide synthase prevents MPTP–induced parkinsonism in baboons. Nature Med 1996; 2: 1017–1021.

34. Przedborski S, Donaldson D, Murphy PL, et al. Role of neuronal nitric oxide in 1–methyl–4–phenyl 1,2,3,6 tetrahydropyridine (MPTP)–induced dopaminergic neurotoxicity. Proc Natl Acad Sci USA 1996; 93: 4565–4571.

35. Di Monte DA, Royland JE, Anderson A, et al. Inhibition of monoamine oxidase contributes to the protective effect of 7–nitroindazole against MPTP neurotoxicity. J Neurochem 1997; 69: 1771–1773.

36. Bolaños JP, Almeida A, Stewart V, et al. Nitric oxide–mediated mitochondrial damage in the brain: mechanisms and implications for neurodegenerative diseases. J Neurochem 1997; 68: 2227–2240.

37. Bredt DS, Glatt CE, Hwang PM, Fotuhi M, Dawson TM, Snyder SH. Nitric oxide synthase protein and messenger RNA are discretely localised in neuronal populations of the mammalian CNS together with NAPDH and diaphorase. Neuron 1991; 7: 615–624.

[184]

38. McGeer PL, Itagaki S, Akiyama H, McGeer EG. Rate of cell death in parkinsonism indicates active neuropathological process. Ann Neurol 1988; 24: 574–576.

39. McNaught KStP, Thull U, Carrupt PA, et al. Inhibition of complex I by isoquinoline derivatives structurally related to 1–methyl–4–phenyl–1,2,3,6– tetrahydropyridine (MPTP). Biochem Pharmacol 1995; 50: 1903–1911.

40. McNaught KStP, Altomare C, Cellamare S, et al. Inhibition of α–ketoglutarate dehydrogenase by isoquinoline derivatives structurally related to 1–methyl–4–phenyl–1,2,3,6–tetrahydro pyridine (MPTP). Neuroreport 1995; 6: 1105–1108.

41. Suzuki K, Mizuno Y, Yoshida M. Inhibition of mitochondrial NADH–ubiquinone oxidoreductase activity and ATP synthesis by tetrahydroisoquinoline. Neurosci Lett 1988; 86: 105–108.

42. Maruyama W, Dosert W, Naoi M. Dopamine–derived 1–methyl–6,7–dihydroxyisoquinoline as hydroxyl promotors and scavengers: in vivo and in vitro studies. J Neurochem 1995; 64: 2635–2643.

43. Maruyama W, Dosert W, Matsubara K, Naoi M. N–methy(R)salsolinol produces hydroxyl radicals: Involvement to neurotoxicity. Free Rad Biol Med 1995; 19: 67–75.

44. Nagatsu T, Yoshida, M. An endogenous substance of the brain, tetrahydro-isoquinoline, produces parkinsonism in primates with decreased dopamine, tyrosine hydroxylase and biopterin in the nigrostriatal regions. Neurosci Lett 1988; 87: 178–182.

45. Naoi M, Maruyama W, Dosert P, et al. Dopamine–derived endogenous 1(R),2(N)–dimethyl–6,7–dihydroxy–1, 2,3,4–tetrahydroisoquinoline, N–methyl–(R)salsolinol, induced parkinsonism in rat: biochemical, pathological and behavioural studies. Brain Res 1966; 709: 285–295.

46. Seaton TA, Cooper JM, Schapira AHV. Free radical scavengers protect dopaminergic cell lines from apoptosis induced by complex I inhibitors. Brain Res 1997; 777: 110–118.

47. Marchetti P, Susin SA, Decaudin D, et al. Apoptosis–associated derangement of mitochondrial function in cells lacking mitochondrial DNA. Cancer Res 1996; 56: 2033–2038.

48. Bernardi P, Broeckemeier KM, Pfeiffer DR. Recent progress on regulation of the mitochondrial permeability transition pore: a cyclosporin–sensitive pore in the inner mitochondrial membrane. J Bioenerg Biomembr 1994, 26: 509–517.

49. Zamzami N, Susin SA, Marchetti P, et al. Mitochondrial control of nuclear apoptosis. J Exp Med 1996; 83: 1533–1544.

[185]

DISCUSSION

Mizuno: I think the cybrid is a very nice model with which to study the etiology and pathogenesis of PD. As you indicated, cybrids constructed from the mitochondrial DNA of PD platelets show a decrease in the activity of complex I. You interpret this as evidence that mitochondrial DNA is abnormal in PD. This could be the result of an inherited mutation in mitochondrial DNA. Alternatively, mitochondrial DNA in platelets of PD patients might have undergone toxic injury with consequent damage to the mitochondrial genome. Therefore, the finding of an abnormality in complex I in cybrids derived from platelets of PD patients may not necessarily mean that there is a primary defect in mitochondrial DNA. Would you comment on this issue?

Schapira: When the mitochondrial DNA from the source is put into the cybrids, it is removed from many other factors which could contribute to its malfunction, such as a defect in repair mechanisms, which are encoded by the nucleus. If there were a putative defect in nuclear encoded subunits or mitochondrial DNA repair mechanisms, it would not appear in the cybrid system because it has a new nucleus which will produce normal levels of subunits and repair enzymes. It is unlikely that a deletion in the parkinsonian platelets would be propagated in the cybrid systems because deletions in particular are eradicated in culture. What we are seeing then in the cybrid system, particularly in the clonal analysis, is a mitochondrial defect that can be retained in perpetuity and can only be due to a primary base change. We can not say whether this change occurred as a result of an inherited or toxic event although I would favor the former. In addition, this may not be the specific cause of PD, but rather a vulnerability factor.

Jenner: Dr. Schapira, is the α-ketoglutarate dehydrogenase change seen in the substantia nigra neurons also found in platelets of PD patients, and what is your view on how it might contribute to the overall mitochondrial defects that are found in PD?

Schapira: We have not looked at the level of α-ketoglutarate dehydrogenase in PD platelets, and I am unaware of anyone who has. The deficiency is found in the substantia nigra and it is interesting that it is also seen with MPTP toxicity. α-Ketoglutarate dehydrogenase is, of course, an important metabolic enzyme in its own right in that it plays a role in Krebs cycle function. Any enzyme deficiency in a neurodegenerative disorder has to be interpreted in the light of changes in other enzymes too, as well as in the light of any changes in mitochondrial mass. We have always been careful to correct any change in mitochondrial complex I activity for the total mass of mitochondria present. This is more difficult with α-ketoglutarate dehydrogenase because we would have to utilize another mitochondrial enzyme or, alternatively, a mitochondrial protein such as porin. In answer to your question, I think the observation of a reduction in α-ketoglutarate dehydrogenase is certainly interesting, and in combination with a defect in complex I, could well contribute to an energy defect.

Olanow: Have you looked at it the other way round by generating ρ0 cells from PD patients and adding normal mitochondria to determine if there are any nuclear defects that might account for the complex I deficiency?

Schapira: No, but we now have ρ0 lines from PD patients. The important thing about generating these lines is that they have to be transformed first into cells that can continue to grow, because any primary cell line has a limited lifespan. In order to generate clonal lines a number of passages is required to produce sufficient cell numbers to study their biochemistry. Inevitably, the results have to be interpreted in the light of any change the transformation system may have brought about. This is an important factor in interpreting the cybrid studies, because the transformation of these cells may itself have actually generated the complex I defect. We have used another disease control, that is, cells and platelets from patients with dystonia who also have a significant decrease in complex I activity in their platelets. We have fused these with the same cells and did not see the same picture as in the PD patients. This is an important control factor.

Tatton: How important do you think impairment in ATP production is in the initiation of apoptosis due to mitochondrial defects? One study of isolated mitochondria demonstrated that a reduction of up to 40% in complex I activity was not associated with any reduction in ATP production. In our own work, we have shown that a fall in mitochondrial membrane potential is one of the earliest events in nerve cell apoptosis and that this could be caused by impaired proton pumping rather than impaired ATP synthesis. As a complex I defect could result in impaired proton pumping, we believe that this is the major risk associated with the fall in complex I activity seen in PD.

Schapira: It is certainly possible that this mechanism is operative in PD. In our own studies, we do show that ATP production is reduced when complex I activity is impaired to the degree that it is in PD and we do not feel that this mechanism can be ignored. Furthermore, we have shown that complex I inhibitors induce apoptosis in a dose-dependent manner which correlates with a drop in ATP synthesis. This may be inhibited by cyclosporin, clearly implicating the membrane permeability transition pore in these events.

Jenner: Based on these concepts of neurodegeneration, what agents do you think might be neuroprotective?

Schapira: I would suggest that bioenergetic agents such as coenzyme Q might be helpful. One could anticipate that such an agent might facilitate electron transfer across the respiratory chain from complexes I and II and might help to compensate for any ATP deficiency. Some benefits have been shown with this drug in mitochondrial myopathies and it would be reasonable to test it in PD.

Beal: We have been very interested in this area and indeed have shown that CoQ10 can be neuroprotective in models of Huntington's disease. In addition we have shown that it has anti-oxidant effects. Based on these preliminary results, we are beginning a clinical trial in PD. Another agent that we have been interested in is creatinine which also has the potential to enhance energy metabolism.

Olanow: Another promising area for the future clinical research is with agents that block the mitochondrial megapore and help to preserve the mitochondrial membrane potential. Several anti-apoptotic molecules have been described to act in this manner such as BCL-2. If the mitochondrial defect is a primary problem in PD, and dopamine cells are vulnerable because they have low mitochondrial membrane potential and go into apoptosis in response to a small and transient rise in calcium, this type of approach might be very fruitful.

CHAPTER THIRTEEN

Mitochondrial dysfunction in Parkinson's disease

YOSHIKUNI MIZUNO, HIROYO YOSHINO, SHIN-ICHIRO IKEBE, NOBUTAKA HATTORI, TOMONORI KOBAYASHI, SATOE SHIMODA-MATSUBAYASHI, HIROTO MATSUMINE AND TOMOYOSHI KONDO

Department of Neurology, Juntendo University School of Medicine, Tokyo, Japan

More than 90% of oxygen entering the body is used for oxidative phosphorylation within mitochondria. If electron transport is compromised, oxygen free radicals form in the electron transfer chain and can spill over to the matrix space and induce damage.[1] The electron transfer chain consists of five protein–enzyme complexes of which complex I is the most complicated.[2,3] Since the discovery of the reduction in complex I activity in Parkinson's disease (PD) and the inhibition of complex I by the neurotoxin MPP+,[4–7] mitochondria have become a focus of research on the pathogenesis of PD.

MITOCHONDRIAL DYSFUNCTION IN PD

The decrease in the amount and activity of complex I of the mitochondrial respiratory chain in the PD nigrostriatal system is well established,[7–11] but the primary cause is unknown. If the deficiency is systemic, it may be either genetically determined or secondary to neurotoxicity, or both. If complex I deficiency is localized to the nigrostriatal system, then one must consider how genetic factors or toxins could account for such a selective effect. Alternatively, one must consider the role of oxidative stress secondary to dopamine metabolism or local endogenous neurotoxins produced within the nigra, or both, as the cause of mitochondrial damage.

In skeletal muscle, both reduced activity[12–16] and normal activity[17–20] have been reported for complex I in PD. [31]P magnetic resonance spectroscopy of resting muscle showed a significant difference between PD patients and controls, indicating mild impairment in energy metabolism in the skeletal muscle of PD patients.[21] Likewise, in platelets and lymphocytes, both reduced and normal activity have been reported.[22–29] The discrepancies are perhaps due to methodological factors or post-mortem changes.[30] Additional reports suggest a systemic abnormality in complex I in PD.[31,32] In general, loss of complex I in systemic organs was mild compared with the loss in the substantia nigra, suggesting that local influence may also be contributing to complex I deficiency in the nigrostriatal system in PD. The question is whether this defect is due to genetic predisposition and/or neurotoxins and whether it plays a role in initiation of the neurodegenerative process in the substantia nigra.

PRIMARY CAUSE OF MITOCHONDRIAL DYSFUNCTION IN PD

Mitochondrial dysfunction is unlikely to be merely secondary to neuronal degeneration because other electron transfer complexes and Krebs cycle enzymes, except α-ketoglutarate dehydrogenase complex,[33] are not reduced in PD. This situation is unlikely to occur in the presence of oxidative stress alone. A genetic component for mitochondrial dysfunction in PD has therefore been sought.

Mitochondrial DNA in PD

Each mitochondrion has several copies of circular mitochondrial DNA (mtDNA).[34] Multiple deletions and eight mutations resulting in amino acid substitutions have been found in mtDNA of two PD patients,[35] and 134 different types of deletions were found in the brain of a patient who died of PD.[36] The mechanism for multiple mtDNA deletion is not well elucidated, but oxidative stress within mitochondria may render mtDNA susceptible to deletions. Age-related oxidative damage to mtDNA is enormous[37] and the presence of oxidative damage in the substantia nigra is well established in PD.[38] Although a mutation specific for PD has not been found, many point mutations rare in control subjects have been found in PD.[39] These replacements had significant effects on the hydropathy plot and/or the protein secondary structure.

A higher frequency of A to G mutation in tRNA(Gln) has been reported in PD compared to controls,[40] and an elevated frequency of alterations in the tRNA(Thr) gene was recently described.[41] A heteroplasmic mutation from G to A affecting the ND2 subunit of complex I has been found not only in the substantia nigra but also in many other brain regions in PD.[42] This mutation does not therefore appear to constitute a genetic risk factor for PD.

Complex I can be divided into three distinct fractions – flavoprotein, iron-sulfur protein, and hydrophobic fractions.[43] Polymorphism of the gene for the 24-kDa subunit of the flavoprotein fraction has been of interest, since this is one of the most important subunits of complex I.[44] The human subunit is encoded by a single gene (NDUFV2) located on chromosome 18 and consisting of eight exons.[45,46] When the exons were screened for mutations in PD patients, a new polymorphic mutation was found in the signal peptide.[47] The frequency of the mutant allele was similar in PD patients and controls (p=0.16), but the allotype distribution was significantly different (p=0.015). The frequency of the mutant homozygote was significantly higher in PD patients (p< 0.01), and the risk of developing PD was calculated as 2.40 (95% CI, 1.18–4.88). The alanine residue at this polymorphic site is highly conserved, suggesting functional importance. The Ala29Val mutation changes the secondary structure of the 24-kDa subunit from an α-helix conformation to a β-sheet structure and may affect the cleavage process of the signal peptide, influencing the level of the mature form of 24-kDa subunit of complex I within mitochondria.

α-Ketoglutarate dehydrogenase genes in PD

MPP+ inhibits not only complex I but also α-ketoglutarate dehydrogenase complex (KGDHC).[48] KGDHC is a key enzyme of the Krebs cycle[49] and dual loss of complex I may deleteriously affect mitochondrial respiration to a greater extent than either group alone. KGDHC consists of three enzymes, E1, E2 and E3. The genomic sequence for E2 has been determined and the locus for E2 mapped to chromosome 14.[50,51] Genomic DNA from PD patients was found to contain a diallelic polymorphism in the E2 gene,[52] which was due to a single nucleotide substitution. This substitution does not, however, cause an amino acid sequence change. The genetic polymorphisms of either the E2 gene or a closely-linked locus may constitute a risk factor for PD.

Manganese SOD gene in PD

Manganese (Mn) SOD (SOD-2) is pivotal to the interaction of mitochondrial dysfunction and oxidative stress, and its activity is increased in sporadic PD.[53] cDNA for *sod-2* from 20 PD patients was sequenced and compared with published sequences[54,55] and a new polymorphic mutation in the mitochondrial targeting sequence was found.[56] The wild type signal peptide constitutes a β-sheet stretch near the amino terminal of the signal peptide, but the mutated form is an α-helix structure,[57] which is important for efficient mitochondrial transport of precursor peptides.[58] Therefore, patients homozygous for this mutation might be expected to have higher

SOD-2 activity. Allele frequency for the mutated gene was significantly higher among PD patients,[56] so this may also be a genetic risk factor for PD.

Familial parkinsonism linked to SOD 2

A family of autosomal recessive parkinsonism shows complete segregation with the mutation in *sod-2*.[59] The *sod-2* locus has been mapped to the long arm of chromosome 6.[60] Linkage analysis revealed that the coding region for mature Mn SOD did not contain specific mutations,[59] so the disease gene for this familial form does not appear to be *sod-2* itself, but a nearby gene perhaps closely linked to *sod-2*. A patient with homozygosity of Ala16 was found on autopsy to have significantly higher Mn SOD activity in the frontal cortex, putamen and substantia nigra than sporadic PD patients and control subjects.[61] Thus, 16Ala homozygosity may be associated with higher expression of Mn SOD within mitochondria but whether this mutation influences the risk of developing oxidative damage remains unanswered. Recently, we identified the disease gene for this type of autosomal recessive familial parkinsonism.[62]

EXOGENOUS MITOCHONDRIAL TOXINS

MPTP-like substances have been screened extensively for their ability to inhibit complex I. Tetrahydroisoquinolines (TIQs)[63–67] and β-carbolines[68] inhibit complex I to varying degrees, and TIQs with a phenyl ring close to the C1 position were more potent inhibitors than those without. When the catechol hydroxyl groups are methylated, inhibitory potency is augmented. PD could be induced by such compounds in susceptible persons, but proof of their accumulation in the substantia nigra of PD patients is lacking.

ENDOGENOUS NEUROTOXINS IN PD

If complex I deficiency is restricted to the substantia nigra, it may be caused by neurotoxins endogenous to the nigrostriatal region. Enzymes which synthesize R-salsolinol from dopamine and methylate the amino-residue of salsolinol have been found,[62,69] and N-methylsalsolinol is very toxic to the substantia nigra in experimental animals.[70] Accumulation of N-methyl-(R)-salsolinol in the nigrostriatal system of the human brain and in the CSF from PD patients has been reported.[71,72] Differences in these enzyme levels may reflect gene polymorphisms.

OXIDATIVE STRESS AS A CAUSE OF MITOCHONDRIAL DYSFUNCTION

Complex I deficiency in PD could be secondary to oxidative stress in the substantia nigra.[73–76] Hydroxynonenal generated from lipid peroxidation reacts with cysteine, histidine or lysine residues to induce conformational changes and functional disturbance of proteins,[77] and is an important mediator of free radical tissue damage. Immunoreactive hydroxynonenal-modified proteins were significantly increased in the cytoplasm of PD nigral neurons.[76] Since more than 90% of the body's oxygen is used within mitochondria, they may be the site of initiation of oxidative stress in PD and complex I may therefore be injured at an early stage in the disease.

If oxidative stress is the initial event in PD, what then is its primary cause? Accumulation of iron may be a contributing factor[75] but this is not restricted to PD. The increase in SOD activity reported in PD[53,78] is unlikely to be a cause of oxidative stress. The reduced form of glutathione (GSH) is low in PD,[79] but reduction in GSH in experimental animals did not cause complex I deficiency.[80] Our present knowledge suggests instead that mitochondrial respiratory failure occurs first, followed by oxidative stress within mitochondria.

Summary

- By reviewing the published data on the etiology and pathogenesis of PD, it seems unlikely that a single common etiology is responsible for nigral cell death in every case of sporadic PD.

- Mitochondrial respiratory defects and oxidative stress are two potential contributors to nigral neuronal death in PD. Complex I deficiency has been reported and there is evidence of oxidative stress and oxidant damage.

- Complex I deficiency appears to be systemic. The primary cause may be a combination of genetic background and exogenous or endogenous neurotoxins.

- An autosomal recessive form of juvenile parkinsonism was mapped to the long arm of chromosome 6 near the Mn SOD gene locus. Information obtained in these familial cases will contribute to research on sporadic PD.

Acknowledgments

This study was in part supported by a Grant-in-Aid for Scientific Research on Priority Areas and by a Grant-in-Aid for Neuroscience Research from Ministry of Education, Science and Culture, Japan, and by a Center of Excellence Grant from the National Parkinson Foundation, Miami, USA.

REFERENCES

1. Boveris A. Mitochondrial production of superoxide radical and hydrogen peroxide. Adv Exp Biol Med 1977; 10: 161–169.

2. Walker JE. The NADH:ubiquinone oxidoreductase of respiratory chains. Quart Rev Biophys 1992; 25: 253–324.

3. Walker JE, Arimendi JM, Dupuis A, Fearnley IM, Finel M, Medd SM, Pilkington SJ, Runswick MJ, Skehel JM. Sequences of 20 subunits of NADH:-ubiquinone oxidoreductase from bovine heart mitochondria: application of a novel strategy for sequencing proteins using the polymerase chain reaction. J Mol Biol 1992; 226: 1051–1072.

4. Nicklas WJ, Vyas I, Heikkila RE. Inhibition of NADH–linked oxidation in brain mitochondria by 1–methyl–4–phenyl–pyridine, a metabolite of the neurotoxin, 1–methyl–4–phenyl–1,2,5,6–tetrahydropyridine. Life Sci 1985; 36: 2503–2508.

5. Ramsay RR, Salach JI, Dadgar J, Singer TP. Inhibition of mitochondrial NADH dehydrogenase by pyridine derivatives and its possible relation to experimental and idiopathic parkinsonism. Biochem Biophys Res Commun 1986; 135: 269–275.

6. Mizuno Y, Saitoh T, Sone N. Inhibition of mitochondrial NADH–ubiquinone oxidoreductase activity by 1–methyl–4–phenylpyridinium ion. Biochem Biophys Res Commun 1987; 143: 294–299.

7. Schapira AHV, Cooper JM, Dexter D, Jenner P, Clark JB, Marsden CD. Mitochondrial complex I deficiency in Parkinson's disease. Lancet 1989; 1: 1269.

8. Schapira AHV, Cooper JM, Dexter D, Clark JB, Jenner P, Marsden CD. Mitochondrial Complex I deficiency in Parkinson's disease. J Neurochem 1990; 54: 823–827.

9. Mizuno Y, Ohta S, Tanaka M, Takamiya S, Suzuki K, Sato T, Oya H, Ozawa T, Kagawa Y. Deficiencies in Complex I subunits of the respiratory chain in Parkinson's disease. Biochem Biophys Res Commun 1989; 163: 1450–1455.

10. Hattori N, Tanaka M, Ozawa T, Mizuno Y. Immunohistochemical studies on Complex I, II, III, and IV of mito-chondria in Parkinson's disease. Ann Neurol 1991; 30: 563–571.

11. Janetzky B, Hauck S, Youdim MBH, Riederer P, Jellinger K, Pantrucek F, Zöehling R, Boissl KW, Reichmann H. Unaltered aconitase activity, but decreased complex I activity in substantia nigra pars compacta of patients with Parkinson's disease. Neurosci Lett 1994; 126–128.

12. Bindoff LA, Birch–Machin M, Cartlidge NEF, Parker WD Jr, Turnbull DM. Mitochondrial function in Parkinson's disease. Lancet 1989; 2: 49,1989.

13. Shoffner JM, Watts RL, Juncos JL, Torroni A, Wallace DC. Mitochondrial oxidative phosphorylation defects in Parkinson's disease. Ann Neurol 1991; 30: 332–339.

14. Nakagawa–Hattori Y, Yoshino H, Kondo T, Mizuno Y, Horai S. Is Parkinson's disease a mitochondrial disorder? J Neurol Sci 1992; 107: 29–33.

15. Cardellach F, Martí MJ, Fernández–Solá J, Martín C, Hoek JB, Tolosa E, Urbano–Márquez A. Mitochondrial respiratory chain activity in skeletal muscle from patients with Parkinson's disease. Neurol 1993; 43: 2258–2262.

16. Blin O, Desnuelle C, Rascol O, Borg O, Borg M, Paul HPS, Azulay JP, Billé, Figarella D, Coulom F, Pellissier JF, Montastruc JL, Chatel M, Serrantrice G. Mitochondrial respiratory failure in skeletal muscle from patients with Parkinson's disease and multiple system atrophy. J Neurol Sci 1994; 125: 95–101.

17. Mann VM, Cooper JM, Krige D, Daniel SE, Schapira AH, Marsden CD. Brain, skeletal muscle and platelet homogenate mitochondrial function in Parkinson's disease. Brain 1992; 115: 333–342.

18. Anderson JJ, Ferrari R, Davis TL, Baronti F, Chase TN, Dagani F. No evidence for altered muscle mitochondrial function in Parkinson's disease. J Neurol Neurosurg Psychiatry 1993; 56; 477–480.

19. Didonato S, Zeviani M, Giovannini P, Savarese N, Rimoldi M, Mariotti C, Girotti F and Caraceni T. Respiratory chain and mitochondrial DNA in muscle and brain in Parkinson's disease patients. Neurol 1993; 43: 2262–2268.

20. Reichmann H, Janetzky B, Bischof F, Seibel P, Schöls L, Kuhn W, Przuntek H. Unaltered respiratory chain enzyme activity and mitochondrial DNA in skeletal muscle from patients with idiopathic Parkinson's syndrome. Eur Neurol 1994; 34: 263–267.

21. Penn AMW, Roberts T, Hodder J, Allen PS, Shu G, Martin WRW. Generalized mitochondrial dysfunction in Parkinson's disease detected by magnetic resonance spectroscopy of muscle. Neurol 1995; 45: 2097–2099.

22. Parker WD Jr, Boyson SJ, Parks JK. Abnormalities of the electron transport chain in idiopathic Parkinson's disease. Ann Neurol 1989; 26: 719–723.

23. Yoshino H, Nakagawa–Hattori Y, Kondo T, Mizuno Y. Mitochondrial complex I and II activities of lymphocytes and platelets in Parkinson's disease. J Neural Transm 1992; 4: 27–34.

24. Benecke R, Strümper P, Weiss H. Electron transfer complexes I and IV of platelets are abnormal in Parkinson's disease but normal in Parkinson-plus syndromes. Brain 1993; 116: 1451–1463.

25. Haas RH, Nasirian F, Nakano K, Ward D, Pay M, Hill R, Shults CW. Low platelet mitochondrial complex I and complex II/III activity in early untreated Parkinson's disease. Ann Neurol 1995; 37: 714–722.

26. Krige D, Carroll MT, Cooper JM, Marsden CD, Schapira AHV. Platelet mitochondrial function in Parkinson's disease. Ann Neurol 1992; 32: 782–788.

27. Blake CT, Spitz E, Leehey M, Hoffer BJ, Boyson SJ. Platelet mitochondrial respiratory chain function in Parkinson's disease. Mov Disord 1997; 12: 3–8.

28. Barroso N, Campos Y, Huertas R, Esteban J, Molina JA, Alonso A, Gutierrez–Rivas E, Arenas J. Respiratory chain enzyme activities in lymphocytes from untreated patients with Parkinson's disease. Clin Chim 1993; 39: 667–669.

29. Martin MA, Molina JA, Jimenez–Jimenez FJ, Benite–Leon J, Orti–Pareja M, Campos Y. Arenas J. Respiratory–chain enzyme activities in isolated mitochondria of lymphocytes from untreated Parkinson's disease patients. Neurol 1996; 46: 1343–1346.

30. Singer TP, Ramsay RR, Ackrell BA. Deficiencies of NADH and succinate dehydrogenases in degenerative disease and myopathies. Biochim Biophys Acta 1995; 1271: 211–219.

31. Mytilineou C, Werner P, Molinari S, Di–Rocco A, Cohen G, Yahr MD. Impaired oxidative decarboxylation of pyruvate in fibroblasts from patients with Parkinson's disease. J Neural Transm [PD section] 1994; 8: 223–228.

32. Sheehan JP, Swerdlow RH, Parkier WD, Miller SW, Davis RE, Tuttle JB. Altered calcium homeostasis in cells transformed by mitochondrial from individuals with Parkinson's disease. J Neurochem 1997; 68: 1221–1233.

33. Mizuno Y, Matuda S, Yoshino H, Mori H, Hattori N, Ikebe S. An immuno-histochemical study on α–ketoglutarate dehydrogenase complex in Parkinson's disease. Ann Neurol 1994; 35: 204–210.

34. Anderson S, Bankier AT, Barrell BG, de Bruijn MHL, Coulson AR, Drouin J, Eperon IC, Nierlich DD, Roe BA, Sanger F, Schreier PH, Smith AJH, Staden R, Young IG. Sequence and organization of the human mito-

chondrial genome. Nature 1981; 90: 457–465.

35. Kapsa RM, Jeean–Francois MJ, Lertrit P, Weng S, Siregar N, Ojaimi J, Donnan G, Masters C, Byrne E. Mitochondrial DNA polymorphism in substantia nigra. J Neurol Sci 1996; 144: 204–211.

36. Ozawa T, Hayakawa M, Katsumata K, Yoneda M, Ikebe S, Mizuno Y. Fragile mitochondrial DNA: the missing link in the apoptotic neuronal cell death. Biochem Biophys Res Commun 1997; 235: 158–161.

37. Hayakawa M, Hattori K, Sugiyama S, Ozawa T (1992) Age–associated oxygen damage and mutations in mitochondrial DNA in human hearts. Biochem Biophys Res Commun 1992; 189: 979–985.

38. Jenner P, Schapira AH, Marsden CD. New insights into the cause of Parkinson's disease. Neurol 1992; 42: 2241–2250.

39. Ikebe S, Tanaka M, Ozawa T. Point mutations of mitochondrial genome in Parkinson's disease. Mol Brain Res 1995; 28: 281–295.

40. Shoffner JM, Brown MD, Torroni A, Lott MT, Cabell MF, Mirra SS, Beal MF, Yang CC, Gearing M, Salvo R, Watts RL, Juncos JL, Hansen LA, Crain BJ, Fayad M, Reckord CL, Wallace DC. Mitochondrial DNA variants observed in Alzheimer disease and Parkinson disease patients. Genomics 1993; 17: 171–184.

41. Mayr–Wohlfart U, Rodel G, Hennesberg A. Mitochondrial tRNA(Gln) and tRNA(Thr) gene variants in Parkinson's disease. Eur J Med Res 1997; 2: 111–113.

42. Schnopp NM, Kösel S, Egensperger R, Graeber MB. Regional heterogeneity of mtDNA heteroplasmy in parkinsonian brain. Clin Neuropathol 1996; 15: 348–352.

43. Hatefi Y. The mitochondrial electron transport and oxidative phosphorylation system. Ann Rev Biochem 1985; 54: 1015–1069.

44. Ohnishi T, Ragan CI, Hatefi Y. EPR studies of iron–sulfur clusters in isolated subunits and subtractions NADH–ubiquinone oxidoreductase. J Biol Chem 1985; 260: 2782–2788.

45. de Coo R, Buddiger P, Smeets H, van Kessel AG, Morgan–Hughes J, Weghuis DO, Overhauser J, van Oost B. Molecular cloning and characterization of the active human mitochondrial NADH:-ubiquinone oxidoreductase 24–kDa gene (NDUFV2) and its pseudogene. Genomics 1995; 26: 461–466.

46. Hattori N, Suzuki H, Wang Y, Minoshima S, Shimizu N, Yoshino H, Kurashima R, Ozawa T, Mizuno Y. Structural organization and chromosomal localization of the human nuclear gene (NDUFV2) for the 24–kDa iron–sulfur subunit of complex I in mitochondrial respiratory chain. Biochem Biophys Res Commun 1995; 216: 771–777.

47. Hattori N, Yoshino H, Tanaka M, Suzuki H, Mizuno Y. Allele in the 24–kDa subunit gene (NDUFV2) of mitochondrial complex I and susceptibility to Parkinson's disease. Genomics 1998, in press.

48. Mizuno Y, Saitoh T, Sone N. Inhibition of mitochondrial alpha–ketoglutarate dehydrogenase by 1–methyl–4–phenylpyridinium ion. Biochem Biophys Res Commun 1987; 143: 971–976.

49. Lai JCK, Cooper AJL. Brain α–ketoglutarate dehydrogenase complex: kinetic properties, regional distribution, and effects of inhibitors. J Neurochem 1986; 47: 1376–1386.

50. Nakano K, Takase C, Sakamoto T, Ohta S, Nakagawa S, Ariyama T, Inazawa J, Abe T, Matuda S. An unspliced cDNA for human dihydrolipoamide succinyl-transferase: characterization and mapping of the gene to chromosome 14q24.2–q24.3. Biochem Biophys Res Commun 1993; 196: 527–533.

51. Nakano K, Matuda S, Sakamoto T, Takase C, Nakagawa S, Ohta S, Ariyama T, Inazawa J, Abe T, Miyata T. Human dihydrolipoamide succinyltransferase:

cDNA cloning and localization on chromosome 14q24.2–q24.3. Biochim Biophys Acta 1993; 1216: 360–368.

52. Kobayashi T, Matsumine H, Matsubayashi S, Matuda S, Mizuno Y. Polymorphism of the gene encoding dihydrolipoamide succinyltransferase, a subunit of α–ketoglutarate dehydrogenase complex, is associated with the susceptibility to Parkinson disease: a population based study. Ann Neurol 1998; 43: 120–123.

53. Saggu H, Cooksey J, Dexter D, Wells FR, Lees A, Jenner P, Marsden CD. A selective increase in particulate superoxide dismutase activity in parkinsonian substantia nigra. J Neurochem 1989; 53: 692–697.

54. Beck Y, Oren G, Amit B, Levanon A, Gorecki, Hartman JR. Human Mn superoxide dismutase cDNA sequence. Nucleic Acids Res 1987; 15: 9076.

55. Heckl K. Isolation of cDNAs encoding human manganese superoxide dismutase. Nucleic Acids Res 1988; 16: 6224.

56. Shimoda–Matsubayashi S, Matsumine H, Kobayashi T, Nakagawa–Hattori Y, Shimizu Y, Mizuno Y. Structural dimorphism in the mitochondrial targeting sequence in the human Mn SOD gene. A predictive evidence for conformational change to influence mitochondrial transport and a study of allelic association in Parkinson's disease. Biochem Biophys Res Commun 1996; 226: 561–565.

57. Chou PY, Fasman GD. Prediction of protein conformation. Biochem 1974; 13: 222–245.

58. Roise D, Horvath SJ, Tomich JM, Richards J, Schatz G. A chemically synthesized pre–sequence of an imported mitochondrial protein can form an amphiphilic helix and perturb natural and artificial phospholipid bilayers. EMBO J 1986; 5: 1327–1334.

59. Matsumine H, Saito M, Shimoda–Matsubayashi S, Tanaka H, Ishikawa A, Nakagawa–Hattori Y, Yokochi M, Kobayashi T, Igarashi S, Takano H, Sanpei K, Koike R, Mori H,

Kondo T, Mizutani Y, Schaffer AA, Yamamura Y, Nakamura S, Kuzuhara S, Tsuji S, Mizuno Y. Localization of a gene for autosomal recessive form of juvenile parkinsonism (AR–JP) to chromosome 6q25.2–27. Am J Hum Genet 1997; 60: 588–596.

60. Church SL, Grant JW, Meese EU, Trent JM. Sublocalization of the gene encoding manganese superoxide dismutase (Mn SOD/sod 2) to 6q25 by fluorescence in situ hybridization and somatic cell hybrid mapping. Genomics 1992; 14: 823–825.

61. Shimoda–Matsubayashi S, Hattori T, Matsumine H, Shinohara A, Yoritaka Y, Mori H, Kondo T, Chiba M, Mizuno Y. Mn SOD activity and protein in a patient with chromosome 6–linked autosomal recessive parkinsonism in comparison with Parkinson's disease and control. Neurol 1997; 49: 1257–1262.

62. Kitada T, Asakawa S, Hattori N, Matsumine H, Yamamura Y, Minoshima S, Yokochi M, Mizuno Y, Shimizu N. Deletion mutation in a novel protein 'Parkin' gene causes autosomal recessive juvenile parkinsonism (AR–JP). Nature, in press.

63. Naoi M, Maruyama W, Dostert P, Kohda K, Kaiya T. A novel enzyme enantio–selectively synthesize (R) salsolinol, a precursor of a dopaminergic neurotoxin, N–methyl (R) salsolinol. Neurosci Lett 1996; 212: 183–186.

64. Suzuki K, Mizuno Y, Yoshida M. Inhibition of mitochondrial NADH–ubiquinone oxidoreductase activity and ATP synthesis by tetrahydroisoquinoline. Neurosci Lett 1988; 86: 105–108.

65. McNaught KSP, Thull U, Carrupt PA, Altomare C, Cellamare S, Carotti A, Testa B, Jenner P, Marsden D. Inhibition of complex I by isoquinoline derivatives structurally related to 1–methyl–4–phenyl–1,2,3,6–tetrahydropyridine (MPTP). Biochem Pharmacol 1995; 50: 1903–1911.

66. McNaught KSP, Thull U, Carrupt PA, Altomare C, Cellamare S, Carotti A, Testa B, Jenner P, Marsden D. Effects of

isoquinoline derivatives structurally related to 1–methyl–4–phenyl–1,2,3,6–tetrahydropyridine (MPTP) on mitochondrial respiration. Biochem Pharmacol 1996; 51: 1503–1511.

67. Morikawa N, Nakagawa–Hattori Y, Mizuno Y. Effect of dopamine, dimethoxyphenylethylamine, papaverine, and related compounds on mitochondrial respiration and complex I activity. J Neurochem 1996; 66: 1174–1181.

68. Morikawa N, Naoi M Maruyama W, Ohta S, Kotake Y, Kawa I H, Niwa T, Dostert P, Mizuno Y. Effects of various tetrahydroisoquinoline derivatives on mitochondrial respiration and the electron transfer complexes. J Neural Transm 1998, in press.

69. Albores R, Heafsey EJ, Drucker G, Fields JZ, Collins MA. Mitochondrial respiratory inhibition by N–methylated beta–carboline derivatives structurally resembling N–methyl–4–phenylpyridine. Proc Natl Acad Sci USA 1990; 87: 9368–9372.

70. Naoi M, Matsuura S, Takahashi T, Nagatsu T. A N–methyltransferase in human brain catalyzes N–methylation of 1,2,3,4–tetrahydroisoquinoline into N–methyl–1,2,3,4–tetrahydroisoquinoline, a precursor of a dopaminergic neurotoxin N–methylisoquinolinium ion. Biochem Biophys Res Commun 1989; 161: 1213–1219.

71. Naoi M, Maruyama W, Dostert P, Hashizume Y, Nakahara D, Takahashi T, Ota M. Dopamine–derived endogenous 1(R),2(N)–dimethyl–6,7–dihydroxy–1,2,3,4–tetrahydroisoquinoline, N–methyl–(R)–salsolinol, induced parkinsonism in rat: biochemical, pathological and behavioral studies. Brain Res 1996; 709: 285–295.

72. Maruyama W, Sobue G, Matsubara K, Hashizume Y, Dostert P, Naoi M. A dopaminergic neurotoxin, 1(R), 2(N)–dimethyl–6,7–dihydoxy–1,2,3,4–t etrahydroisoquinoline, N–methyl(R) salsolinol, and its oxidation product, 1,2(N)–dimethyl–6,7–dihydro-xyisoquinolinium ion, accumulate in the nigrostriatal system of the human brain.

Neurosci Lett 1997; 223; 61–64.

73. Maruyama W, Abe, T, Tohgi H, Dostert P, Naoi M. A dopaminergic neurotoxin, (R)–N–methylsalsolinol, increases in Parkinsonian cerebrospinal fluid. Ann Neurol 1996; 40: 119–122.

74. Dexter DT, Carter CJ, Wells FR, Javoy–Agid F, Agid Y, Lees A, Jenner P, Marsden CD. Basal lipid peroxidation in substantia nigra is increased in Parkinson's disease. J Neurochem 1989; 52: 381–389.

75. Jenner P, Dexter DT, Sian J, Schapira AHV, Marsden CG. Oxidative stress as a cause of nigral cell death in Parkinson's disease and incidental Lewy body disease. Ann Neurol 1992; 32: S82–S87.

76. Youdim MBH, Ben–Shachar, Riederer P. Review: The possible role of iron in the ethiopathogenesis of Parkinson's disease. Mov Disord 1993; 8: 1–12.

77. Yoritaka A, Hattori N, Uchida K, Tanaka M, Stadtman ER, Mizuno Y. Immunohistochemical detection of 4–hydroxynonenal protein adducts in Parkinson's disease. Proc Natl Acad Sci USA 1996; 93: 2696–2701.

78. Uchida K, Stadtman ER. Modification of histidine residues in proteins by reaction with 4–hydroxynonenal. Proc Natl Acad Sci USA 1992; 89: 4544–4548.

79. Mochizuki H, Imai H, Endo K, Yokomizo K, Murata Y, Hattori N, Mizuno Y. Iron accumulation in the substantia nigra of 1–methyl–4–phenyl–1,2,3,6–tetrahydropyridine (MPTP)–induced hemiparkinsonian monkeys. Neurosci Lett 1994; 168: 251–253.

80. Sian J, Dexter DT, Lees AJ, Daniel S, Agid Y, Javoy Agid F, Jenner P, Marsden CD. Alterations in glutathione levels in Parkinson's disease and other neurodegenerative disorders affecting basal ganglia. Ann Neurol 1994; 36: 348–355.

81. Seaton TA, Jenner P, Marsden CD. Mitochondrial respiratory enzyme function and superoxide dismutase activity following brain glutathione depletion in the rat. Biochem Pharmacol 1996; 52: 1657–1663

[198]

DISCUSSION

Jenner: I have always been interested in the fact that inhibition of α-ketoglutarate dehydrogenase and complex I occurs with both MPTP and PD. What is the functional consequence of having inhibition of both? Is it greater than inhibition of complex I alone?

Mizuno: Yes it is. There are two pathways for electron transfer in the respiratory chain at complex I and complex II. At complex I, NADH is the electron donor. For the electron transfer through complex II, you need succinate as an electron donor, and the succinate is provided by the α-ketoglutarate dehydrogenase complex. When you have loss of complex I alone, electron transfer is still possible through complex II. But if you knock out both complex I and α-ketoglutarate dehydrogenase then the electron transfer through complex I, as well as through complex II, will be compromised leading to a marked decrease in ATP synthesis.

Marsden: It is fascinating that you have connected chromosome 6 linkage to autosomal–recessive juvenile parkinsonism, of which you have considerable experience in Japan. To assess the relevance of this for parkinsonism worldwide, can you remind us of the current Japanese view of the neuropathology of autosomal–recessive juvenile parkinsonism?

Mizuno: We have one autopsy case. Our autosomal recessive patient showed marked degeneration of the substantia nigra as well as the locus coeruleus but other regions were entirely normal. There were no Lewy bodies in our patient. The substantia nigra showed atrophy. The first implication of our case is that nigral degeneration can occur without Lewy body formation. The second implication is that a protein which is necessary for Lewy bodies may be missing in our patient, although this is still too speculative. We call our patients early onset autosomal recessive familial parkinsonians. We do not call them familial parkinsonians, as the presence of Lewy bodies is considered necessary for a diagnosis of PD by most neuropathologists. Clinically, however, our patients are essentially similar to other young onset PD patients. They respond to levodopa very nicely, develop motor fluctuations and dyskinesias, but more easily than usual young onset patients.

Wood: I think that you are correct in saying that mitochondrial DNA mutates a lot and that there are a lot of polymorphisms. However, we have looked at our DNA database from our frozen PD brains and not found any of the reported polymorphisms so far. We have looked again and it is still not there. I think this emphasizes the point that you must have a good resource, and you must know what you are looking for, in terms of the brains and the controls, to exclude and have the power of exclusion. It is equally important to have decent negatives as positive findings, as mitochondrial DNA is very polymorphic. My question for you is as follows. You have this juvenile parkinsonism linked to chromosome 6-Q. Is it just chance, then, that you found an associated polymorphism in SOD-2 in generalised PD patients, or is this just linkage disequilibrium because the gene for juvenile parkinsonism is quite common? What is the explanation? I do not understand how you can have PD and juvenile parkinsonism linked or associated to the same small chromosomal location.

Mizuno: Yes, mitochondrial DNAs are very polymorphic. We found polymorphic mutations in the brains of PD patients but the same mutations were also found in some control subjects. So far, we have not found a mtDNA mutation which is specific to PD. Talking about the Mn-SOD gene on chromosome 6, linkage of our families is to the long arm of chromosome 6 near the Mn-SOD gene locus, but the Mn-SOD gene itself was not the disease gene. We have not found the specific gene as yet. Genetic association studies on sporadic patients with PD using this Mn-SOD polymorphic mutation is a part of our systematic association studies in PD. Mutation from valine to alanine was a genetic risk factor for sporadic PD although it did not appear to be a strong risk factor. This mutation was found in only one family of our initial 13 families with early onset parkinsonism studied for the linkage. Therefore, the role of Mn-SOD in our familial cases is still an open question although it did give us a clue for the genetic linkage analysis.

Leenders: The pathology and biochemical features are, of course, most evident in the substantia nigra. Other systems may be involved to a lesser or different extent, but similar reactions in other brain regions may give a better clue than looking only at events taking place in the substantia nigra.

Mizuno: You may be right. But we believe that nigral neurons are one of the most vulnerable neurons to oxidative damage because of the presence of dopamine and monoamine oxidase. The locus coeruleus may be as well. I believe that this is the reason for selective degeneration of the pigmented neurons in PD. Therefore, I believe that the nigrostriatal system is still the best target to study to try and elucidate the mechanisms of neuronal death. Another important target may be the autonomic nervous system.

Beal: A recent report suggests that in sporadic ALS there may be mutations in the promoter region to Mn-SOD. This was not seen in any of the controls, and it may block the normal up-regulation of SOD in response to an oxidative stress. It might be worthwhile to re-examine the promoter region as well as the coding region in the Mn-SOD gene. We have looked at transgenic mice that over-express the human gene to a small degree, 30%, and achieved good neuroprotection against MPTP and other toxins. With regard to the screening of the mitochondrial DNA genome, there is the problem of heteroplasmy, which raises the issue of how many clones or molecules you actually examined when you searched for the DNA mutations. If the frequency of mutation is low, it could be missed. When you looked for the DNA mutations in the mitochondrial genome, I presume that was from post-mortem human tissue?

Mizuno: Thank you for the suggestion of looking at the promotor region of the Mn-SOD gene. We will look at it. Regarding mtDNA mutations, we looked at both brain specimens and peripheral blood DNA in patients with PD and found many polymorphic mutations in both PD patients and control subjects, but were unable to find a mtDNA mutation which is specific for PD. Accumulation of such mutations however, including deletion mutations, may be important in some patients. Studies on the quantitative aspects of mtDNA mutation are still limited.

Wood: Mitochondrial heteroplasmy is crucial and it is important to look at frozen brains from brain banks. The PD brain bank in London is extremely useful for this purpose, because any functional mitochondrial mutations should be present in the substantia nigra or somewhere in the basal ganglia, even if they are not found in blood, muscle or other tissues. The sensitivity of detecting mitochondrial diseases with PCR sequencing is about 5% and we know from other mitochondrial diseases that considerably more than 5% mutation in mitochondrial DNA is required to be pathogenic. Therefore, even when heteroplasmy is taken into account in terms of tissue distribution and amount, I think it is sensitive enough to exclude any relationship to PD.

Quinn: With regard to focusing on nigral tissue or the locus coeruleus, has anyone looked specifically at areas which contain Lewy bodies that cannot be attributed to dopamine turnover, such as the nucleus basalis? If so, what biochemical markers are found?

Mizuno: In our familial patient who died, we looked at non-catecholaminergic areas where Lewy bodies are found in sporadic PD, such as the nucleus basalis and the dorsal motor nucleus. We did not find any pathologic changes nor any Lewy bodies. We have not done biochemical studies on these structures.

De Yebenes Justo: Do you have any data on the activity of Mn-SOD in individuals with the polymorphism valine for alanine?

Mizuno: Yes, we have. We measured mitochondrial Mn-SOD activity in our familial patient with homozygous valine-to-alanine mutation in the signal peptide of Mn-SOD precursor protein and compared the activity with those of sporadic PD patients and control subjects. The Mn-SOD activity in this patient was well beyond two standard deviations higher than the means of the sporadic PD patients as well as control subjects in the frontal cortex, putamen and the substantia nigra. Therefore this signal peptide mutation may have an influence on the amount of mature Mn-SOD protein expressed within mitochondria. As we have only one patient having this homozygous mutation, statistical analysis could not be performed. In addition, there was no difference in the activity of Mn-SOD between sporadic parkinsonian patients and control subjects.

CHAPTER FOURTEEN

Iron-chelating, antioxidant and cytoprotective properties of the dopamine receptor agonist apomorphine

MOUSSA B.H. YOUDIM, AVIVA GROSS, AND MICHAEL GASSEN

Department of Pharmacology, Eve Topf and National
Parkinson's Foundation Centers, Bruce Rappaport Family
Research Institute, Faculty of Medicine, Haifa, Israel

Abnormal iron metabolism, uptake and storage are prominent biochemical features of neurodegeneration. Iron metabolism in the brain is closely associated with the blood–brain barrier (BBB) which tightly regulates the access of iron from the serum into the brain.[1] The BBB allows iron to enter the brain during infancy but closes when the brain reaches maturity, preventing further access of serum iron to the brain. Thus, brain iron metabolism is conservative and all iron present in the brain is conserved throughout life.

Neurodegenerative diseases such as Parkinson's disease (PD), Alzheimer's disease (AD) and Huntington's disease are generally typified by highly specific patterns of cell death in characteristic regions of the brain, leading to the clinically distinguishing features. Evidence supports the importance of free radicals, iron, catecholamine oxidation, and neuromelanin for the nigrostriatal neurodegeneration which characterizes PD.[2-5] Specifically, iron has the capacity to promote oxidation reactions and the formation of cytotoxic free radicals.[1] Increased levels of iron may therefore represent a state of oxidative stress and a risk factor for cell death. One of the main pathological features of PD is the appearance of abundant deposition of iron at the site of neurodegeneration but the basis of the increased iron levels remains unclear.[6] The neurotoxins 6-hydroxydopamine (6-OHDA) and 1-methyl-4-phenyl-1,2,3,6-tetrahydropyridine (MPTP) can also release iron from its binding site on ferritin. This suggests that in the course of neurodegeneration in PD, some factor may be responsible for releasing iron, which then can participate in the process of oxidative stress.[7] Iron-deficient rats are protected from the neurotoxic actions of 6-OHDA and kainate, suggesting the involvement of iron in the mechanism of action of 6-OHDA.[8,9]

The identification of endogenous 6-OHDA formed through iron-catalyzed oxidation of dopamine in the presence of hydrogen peroxide supports the concept of iron-induced oxidative stress as a key factor in neurodegeneration of dopamine neurons in PD.[7,10,11] This raises serious questions about the long-term effects of treatment of PD with levodopa. In contrast, the mixed dopamine D_1/D_2-receptor agonist apomorphine is one of the most potent iron chelators and radical scavengers with highly potent cytoprotective properties. It may therefore have a protective effect on the course of PD.[12,13]

PD AND REACTIVE OXYGEN SPECIES

Free oxygen radicals and other reactive oxygen species (ROS) are normally rapidly deactivated by highly efficient scavenging systems before they can cause any damage. Pathological conditions or tissue aging lead to increased formation of ROS and decreased scavenging capacity in the cell. ROS can cause widespread structural damage to unsaturated membrane lipids, proteins or DNA, leading to cell death. In addition, the reaction between ROS and polyunsaturated fatty acids generates aldehydic breakdown products, many of which are themselves toxic. These species have a much longer half-life than ROS, so can diffuse and exert their effects remote from the site of primary radical damage.[14,15]

Iron, like other transition metals, can form reactive hydroxyl radicals (OH·) from hydrogen peroxide (H_2O_2) and superoxide (O_2-). A marked increase in the concentration of iron in affected brain areas has been confirmed for PD, Huntington's disease, progressive supranuclear palsy, multiple system atrophy (MSA) and AD.[4] The late stage of PD is characterized by accumulation of iron in the substantia nigra (pars compacta) of the affected brains,[16] which parallels disease progression since, in the early phases, iron content and distribution in parkinsonian brains is normal.[17]

CATECHOLAMINE TOXICITY: FREE RADICAL AND MITOCHONDRIAL MECHANISMS

Catecholamines may interfere with the cellular oxygen metabolism at several points: (1) catecholamine metabolism by monoamine oxidases leads to the formation of H_2O_2, which can be converted into the more reactive hydroxyl radicals through the interaction with ferrous iron (Fe^{2+}); (2) catecholamines can be auto-oxidized in the presence of iron to generate O_2-, H_2O_2, and reactive quinones and semiquinone radicals as intermediates with neuromelanin as the end product (3); catecholamines and their catechol metabolites, as well as neuromelanin, are excellent iron chelators which can form stable complexes, especially with ferric iron (Fe^{3+}). Thus, they can contribute to maintain the low molecular weight iron pool that can participate in redox chemistry at a low and safe level. On the other hand, neuromelanin selectively binds Fe^{3+} and reduces it, releasing reactive Fe^{2+} back into the cytosol.[18]

The reaction between H_2O_2, iron and dopamine[10] may be a source of endogenous 6-OHDA formation. This risk is increased in PD where the relatively high concentrations of iron in the striatum are even higher.[19] Iron-dependent mechanisms and ROS may also contribute to the toxicity of 6-OHDA, which liberates iron from ferritin[20] and increases the availability of Fe^{2+}. This could explain the finding that the iron chelator desferrioxamine provides protection against brain lesions induced by 6-OHDA injections in rats.[21]

Some catecholamines such as dopamine[22] and 6-OHDA[23] are also potent reversible inhibitors of complexes I and IV of the mitochondrial respiratory chain. This interaction does not seem to be free radical-dependent. However, the interference of catecholamines with cellular respiration may be an additional free radical-forming process.

ANTIOXIDANT AND IRON CHELATING PROPERTIES OF APOMORPHINE

Apomorphine has been used in the therapy of late stage PD.[24] The gastrointestinal side effects of apomorphine can be controlled by co-administration of the peripherally-acting dopamine receptor antagonist domperidone.[25] The discovery that catecholamines can be cytotoxic has raised the question of the long-term effects of the treatment of PD with levodopa or apomorphine. Catecholamines can be both pro- and antioxidants. The radical-scavenging potency of catechols is dopamine = norepinephrine > dihydroxyphenylacetic acid > homovanillic acid.[26] Apomorphine in particular has been shown to have anti-oxidant effects.

Free radical biochemistry can be easily studied in isolated mitochondria. Incubation of rat brain mitochondria with ascorbic acid and ferrous sulphate leads to a rapid increase of thiobarbituric acid reactive substances (TBARS) formation and this effect can be almost completely abolished by addition of apomorphine.[12] The concentration of apomorphine required for an effective protection depends on the Fe^{2+} concentration. Auto-oxidation of apomorphine is slow in the presence of ascorbic acid, but markedly accelerated in the presence of mitochondria, reflecting the protection of mitochondrial lipids. There was however a negative correlation between apomorphine oxidation and TBARS formation. The former occurred initially at a high rate, completely suppressing TBARS formation. When apomorphine oxidation later decelerated, increasing amounts of TBARS were generated in the system. Dopamine also shows antioxidant properties in rat brain mitochondrial system, although it was not quite as effective as apomorphine, which provides complete inhibition at concentrations much lower than the observed Fe^{2+}-concentration. Apomorphine also protects against oxidation of proteins.[27] Iron chelation by dopamine is likely to be a major contributor to the observed inhibition of TBARS, but apomorphine appears to have both iron chelating and antioxidant activities, and iron chelation may not play a major role in scavenging.[12,13]

PROTECTION OF PHEOCHROMOCYTOMA (PC12) CELLS AGAINST H$_2$O$_2$– AND 6–OHDA–INDUCED CYTOTOXICITY BY APOMORPHINE AND OTHER DOPAMINE RECEPTOR AGONISTS

A key question concerns the balance between catecholamine toxicity and beneficial neuroprotective effects due to antioxidation. PC12 cell culture is a well-established system to study apoptotic and necrotic cell death,[28] in which oxidative stress can be induced by H$_2$O$_2$, organic hydroperoxides or 6-OHDA. Although the maximum cell death is not observed until 24 hours, only two hours' exposure to the toxic agent is sufficient to induce the full damaging effects. Concentrations of 400 mM H$_2$O$_2$ and 150 mM 6-OHDA were required to kill 50% of the cultured cells. Dopamine and apomorphine were tested for their ability to protect PC12 cells from the oxidative insults, and toxicity was monitored to obtain information about the therapeutic window of the agents. Apomorphine was far more efficient as an antioxidant, but the toxicity of apomorphine was much higher than that of dopamine which, unlike 6-OHDA, does not lead to any significant cell degeneration at concentrations below 250 mM. Any protection against H$_2$O$_2$ by apomorphine was dependent on the presence of the drug during the insult. Preincubation with apomorphine and washout prior to H$_2$O$_2$ addition or addition of H$_2$O$_2$ one hour after administration of the toxin did not improve the cell survival. Apomorphine but not dopamine protected against 6-OHDA. This is the first example of a catecholamine attenuating the toxicity of 6-OHDA in cell culture.[13] The antioxidant and cytoprotective actions of lisuride, bromocriptine, pergolide and flurpitine have also been examined, but none showed the antioxidant potency of apomorphine against hydrogen peroxide and 6-OHDA cytotoxicity using PC12 cells as the neuronal model.[13] As dopamine and apomorphine are widely used in the treatment of PD, it is of considerable interest to further investigate the influence of these agents on the biochemical processes involved in the progression of neurodegeneration.

SUMMARY

- Iron is a pro-oxidant that can promote oxidative reactions and the formation of cytoxic free radicals.

- Catecholamines can be both pro-oxidant depending on concentration and model system tested.

- Apomorphine is a catecholamine that has been employed in patients with advanced PD. The major problem with apomorphine has been its rapid metabolism and side effect profile.

- Apomorphine has pronounced antioxidant effects, although problems might arise due to its small therapeutic window. This finding is an incentive for the design of novel, less toxic catecholaminergic dopamine receptor agonists with antioxdant properties. We are presently examining the neuroprotective properties of apomorphine in the MPTP and 6-OHDA models of PD.

ACKNOWLEDGMENTS

The authors acknowledge the support of the Goldings Parkinson Fund (Technion, Haifa, Israel), the National Parkinson Foundation (USA), the Minerva Foundation (Heidelberg, Germany) for postdoctoral fellowship of MG, and Bilha Pinchasi for experimental support.

References

1. Youdim MBH, Ben-Shachar D, Riederer P. The possible role of iron in the etiopathology of Parkinson's disease. Mov Disord 1993; 8: 1–12.

2. Youdim MBH. Neuropharmacological and neurochemical aspects of iron deficiency. In, Dobbing J, ed, Brain, Behaviour and Iron in the Infant Brain. Berlin: Springer Verlag, 1990: 83–132.

3. Youdim MBH, Ben-Shachar D, Riederer P. Iron-melanin interaction and Parkinson's disease. NIPS 1993; 8: 45–49.

4. Gerlach M, Ben Shachar D, Riederer P, Youdim MB. Altered brain metabolism of iron as a cause of neurodegenerative diseases? J Neurochem 1994; 63:-793–807.

5. Youdim MBH, Riederer P. Understanding Parkinson's disease. Sci Am 1997; 267: 52–59.

6. Riederer P, Sofic E, Rausch WD, Jellinger K, Youdim MBH. Transition metals, ferritin, glutathione and ascorbic acid in parkinsonian brains. J Neurochem 1989; 52: 515–520.

7. Linert W, Herlinger E, Jameson RF, Keizl E, Jellinger K, Youdim MBH. Dopamine, 6-hydroxydopamine, iron and dioxygen, their mutal interaction and possible implications in the development of Parkinson's disease. Biochim Biophys Acta 1996; 131: 160–168.

8. Shoham S, Glinka Y, Tenne Z, Youdim MBH. Brain iron: function and dysfunction in relation to cognitive processes. In, Hallberg L, Asp NG, eds, Iron Nutrition in Health and Disease. London: John Libbey, 1996: 205–218.

9. Glinka Y, Gassen M, Youdim MBH. Mechanism of 6-hydroxydopamine neurotoxicity. J Neural Transm 1997; 50 (Suppl): 55–66

10. Jellinger K, Linert L, Kienzl E, Herlinger E, Youdim MB, Ben Shachar D, Riederer P. Chemical evidence for 6-hydroxydop-amine to be an endogenous toxic factor in the pathogenesis of Parkinson's disease. J Neural Transm 1991: 57 (Suppl): 1609–1614.

11. Andrew R, Watson DG, Best SA, Midgley JM, Wenlong H, Petty RK. The determination of hydroxydopamines and other trace amines in the urine of parkinsonian patients and normal controls. Neurochem Res 1993; 18: 1175–1177.

12. Gassen M, Glinka Y, Pinchasi B, Youdim MB. Apomorphine is a highly potent free radical scavenger in rat brain mitochondrial fraction. Eur J Pharmacol 1996; 308: 219–225.

13. Gassen M, Gross A, Youdim MBH. Apomorphine enantiomers protect pheochromocytoma (PC12) cells from oxidative stress induced by hydrogen peroxide and 6-hydroxydopamine. Mov Disord 1998, in press.

14. Stadtman ER. Oxidation of free amino acids and amino acid residues in proteins by radiolysis and by metal-catalyzed reactions. Ann Rev Biochem 1993; 62: 797–821.

15. Yoritaka A, Hattori N, Uchida K, Tanaka M, Stadtman ER, Mizuno Y. Immunohistochemical detection of 4-hydroxynonenal protein adducts in Parkinson disease. Proc Natl Acad Sci USA 1996; 93: 2696–2701.

16. Esterbauer H. Aldehydes of lipid peroxidation. In, McBrien DCH, Slater TF, eds, Free radicals, peroxidation, and cancer. London: Academic Press, 1980: 101–122.

17. Sofic E, Paulus W, Jellinger K, Riederer P, Youdim MB. Selective increase of iron in substantia nigra zona compacta of parkinsonian brains, J Neurochem 1991; 56: 978–982.

18. Riederer P, Dirr A, Goetz M, Sofic E, Jellinger K, Youdim MB. Distribution of iron in different brain regions and subcellular compartments in Parkinson's

disease. Ann Neurol 1992; 32 (Suppl): S101–S104.

19. Ben Shachar D, Riederer P, Youdim MB. Iron-melanin interaction and lipid peroxidation: implications for Parkinson's disease. J Neurochem 1991; 57: 1609–1614.

20. Dexter DT, Jenner P, Schapira AHV, Marsden CD. Alterations in levels of iron, ferritin, and other trace metals in neurodegenerative diseases affecting the basal ganglia. The Royal Kings and Queens Parkinson's Disease Research Group. Ann Neurol 1992; 32 (Suppl.): S94–S100.

21. Monteiro HP, Winterbourn CC, Mytilineou C, Danias P. 6-Hydroxydopamine releases iron from ferritin and promotes ferritin-dependent lipid peroxidation. 6-Hydroxydopamine toxicity to dopamine neurons in culture: potentiation by the addition of superoxide dismutase and N-acetylcysteine. Biochem Pharmacol 1989; 38: 1872–1875.

22. Ben Shachar D, Eshel G, Finberg JP, Youdim MB. The iron chelator desferrioxamine (Desferal) retards 6-hydroxydopamine-induced degeneration of nigrostriatal dopamine neurons. J Neurochem 1991; 56: 1441–1444.

23. Ben Shachar D, Zuk R, Glinka Y. Dopamine neurotoxicity: inhibition of mitochondrial respiration. J Neurochem 1995; 64: 718–723.

24. Glinka Y, Tipton KF, Youdim MB. Nature of inhibition of mitochondrial respiratory complex I by 6-hydroxydopamine. J Neurochem 1996; 66: 2004–2010.

25. Gancher ST, Nutt JG, Woodward WR. Apomorphine infusional therapy in Parkinson's disease: clinical utility and lack of tolerance. Mov Disord 1995; 10: 37–43.

26. Lees AJ. Dopamine agonists in Parkinson's disease: a look at apomorphine. Fundam Clin Pharmacol 1993; 7: 121–128.

27. Liu J, Mori A. Monoamine metabolism provides an antioxidant defense in the brain against oxidant- and free radical-induced damage. Arch Biochem Biophys 1993; 302: 118–127.

28. Vimard F, Nouvelot A, Duval D. Cytotoxic effects of an oxidative stress on neuronal-like pheochromocytoma cells (PC12). Biochem Pharmacol 1996; 51: 1389–1395.

[209]

DISCUSSION

Gash: The finding that there are normally high levels of iron in the reticulata area of the nigra is fascinating. There is, of course a tremendous release of dopamine in this region from the dendrites of dopaminergic neurons. The dendritic innervation is phenomenal. We are using *in vivo* microdialysis to study the release of dopamine in the reticulata in response to various stimuli. Dr. Olanow, do you think we need to have high levels of iron in the compacta for dopaminergic cell damage to occur or would the iron levels in the reticulata be sufficient to combine with the high levels of dopamine present to cause neurotoxicity?

Olanow: I do not know the answer to that. Iron levels are normally very high in the substantia nigra pars reticularis, the same as it is in the globus pallidus pars interna. This was first described by Hallgren in the 1950s. However, it is not known in what form the iron is stored. If it is present in the ferrous or free form, then it could be toxic and promote cell death in either the reticularis or compacta. More likely, it is stored as ferric iron bound to ferritin and in this form it is relatively safe and does not participate in the Fenton reaction. The body has developed this way of storing iron so that it is not toxic to neighboring tissues. In experiments in which we try to induce cell death, we infuse iron as ferrous citrate. In PD, iron appears to be primarily increased in the pars compacta, and there is some suggestion that it may be in the reactive form based on a lack of upregulation of the storage protein ferritin. It harder to say whether iron is increased in the reticularis where iron concentrations are normally high and storage capacity can probably deal with a modest rise.

Youdim: My own bet is that the iron in the SNc is free since ferritin is increased and transferrin receptors are downregulated in PD. This is what is seen in iron overload in the liver. In fact, on several occasions we have suggested that PD may effectively be siderosis of the substantia nigra. At a recent meeting on neurodegenerative diseases there were reports that in AD, ALS, Huntington's chorea, and even multiple sclerosis and Hallervorden-Spatz disease there is accumulation of iron in the neurodegenerative sites and significant evidence for oxidative disease was provided in these disorders. Similarly to PD, radical scavenging therapy is being envisaged. In publications appearing shortly, aspirin and salicylate show neuroprotection in MPTP and 6-OHDA models of PD. We also know that the turnover of iron in the brain is about one-fifth of the turnover rate in the liver, and that the iron that accumulates in the brain remains there for the rest of an individual's life. At birth, most of the iron in the rat is in the cortex which is the site of the transferrin receptors. As the animal ages, the iron disappears from the cortex and accumulates in the nigra and in the pallidum. We believe this is a very exciting finding and shows the capacity for axonal transfer whereby iron is transported from one brain site to another. This may account for the rise in SNc iron in PD, since serum iron has no access to the brain because of the blood–brain barrier. We have measured iron uptake to the brain using PET scan and examined 25 parkinsonian and 20 control subjects. Approximately half of the parkinsonian patients showed increased iron uptake into the brain.

Leenders: The positron-emitting iron citrate tracer is very difficult to measure in the brain. We administer iron ^{52}citrate which is immediately bound to transferrin in the blood, so we have an *in vivo* marker of iron transferrin. Normally, it is taken up by the brain at an extremely slow rate. In those diseases where there is a disorder of iron transport such as Hallervorden–Spatz syndrome or Wilson's disease, we see a remarkable increase in the iron signal in the brain with global distribution. In PD it is more difficult to say what is going on, because some patients show increased iron uptake while others do not. I suspect that the time-window in which we can measure the uptake is only two hours, which is too small to be certain that in PD patients there is a change in the rate of iron-transferrin uptake into the brain. If there is, it also appears to be a global effect. This would raise the possibility that uptake of iron- transferrin is increased everywhere in the brain, but accumulates and causes damage only in selected regions for reasons that are presently not known.

Youdim: Do you think the blood–brain barrier may be broken down at that site?

Leenders: Changed perhaps, but not broken down.

Langston: Dr. Olanow, you described changes in the nigra of the SOD mutant mouse which normally has an ALS phenotype. I think this is a very interesting model. You indicated that dopamine levels are decreased, but are cell bodies also decreased?

Olanow: Przedborski and colleagues reported an approximate 18–20% reduction in dopaminergic nigral nerve cells in the SOD mutant mouse developed by Mark Gurney. We used the model developed by Dr. Jon Gordon. However, preliminary data show that when a small dose of MPTP is administered, the cell numbers in the nigra and the striatal dopamine content fall to a significantly greater degree than is seen in the wild-type mouse. This model illustrates how a combination of a genetic defect and an environmental toxin can lead to a parkinsonian state where neither mechanism alone is sufficient to induce behavioral changes.

Youdim: We have a model with over-expression of SOD and monoamine oxidase B. They seem to be more sensitive to kainic acid than the wild type but not to MPTP toxicity.

Olanow: There is also a serious question as to whether the increase in iron in the SNc found in PD is primary or secondary. We have shown that iron can increase dramatically in the rodent SNc after a 6-OHDA lesion of the median forebrain bundle.

Mizuno: There is no question about the accumulation of iron in the parkinsonian substantia nigra. I believe that iron plays an important role in the progression of the disease, but several years ago, we studied MPTP monkeys to see if they had iron accumulation in the nigra. There was accumulation of iron in the substantia nigra and ferritin was normal. Thus, we thought that accumulation of iron could be secondary to degeneration of the substantia nigra and that sick neurons are unable to handle or remove iron from the substantia nigra. It is not clear where this iron comes from. Iron in the blood does not cross the blood–brain barrier, so it must come from some other source.

Youdim: This problem has baffled us for the last ten years. The observation that MPTP and 6-OHDA cause secondary accumulation of iron in the substantia nigra pars compacta is identical to the observations of many others including Drs. Riederer and Olanow, and consistent with the findings of Dr. Jellinger in human PD brains. Last year a paper appeared in the *Journal of Neurochemistry* which showed that the iron chelator desferrioxamine prevents MPTP toxicity in mice, which is similar to what we found in 1991 with 6-OHDA neurotoxicity. My question is whether even a secondary accumulation of iron may contribute to disease progression. Both Drs. Olanow and Riederer have reported that a low dose of intranigral iron can cause progressive degeneration of dopamine neurons in rats. Iron has a very slow turnover in the brain and it is possible that its toxic effect persists through to the time of death. We need to learn more about the nature of the effect of iron on disease progression. I believe that iron is a very good candidate to contribute to cell death in PD because free iron can promote oxidative damage and cause inflammatory events with activation of microglia.

Jenner: Iron may be important as an event in cellular degeneration but it is not specific to PD. Increases in iron can be found in MSA, Huntington's chorea, multiple sclerosis, AD, spastic paraplegia and tardive dyskinesia.

Olanow: Those findings have to be taken with a grain of salt because we do not know what form the iron is in and whether or not it is in a free form capable of promoting oxidative stress.

Youdim: The fact that there is an increase in iron in all of these disorders suggests that these diseases may have a common denominator and perhaps we can use just one drug to treat them. For example, antioxidants are neuroprotective in both MPTP and 6-OHDA models of PD.

Riederer: I agree that increases in iron are not very selective for PD but, on the other hand, there is a selective increase in specific regions which undergo degeneration in each of these disorders. A study we performed with Dr. Olanow in which we injected 6-OHDA into the median forebrain bundle showed that not only was iron secondarily increased in the substantia nigra, but there was also an increase in protein. This led us to assume that the iron increase is probably coming from a breakdown in the blood–brain barrier.

Youdim: Dr. Jenner, when you used ferrocene loading of the brain did you see any neurotoxicity, because chronic treatment with ferrous sulphate for up to 6 months does not alter brain iron while liver iron increases by up to 20-fold?

Jenner: We saw some changes in dopamine turnover but no cell loss. Ferrocene is an iron complex that is lipophilic and may cross the blood–brain barrier. Our studies were performed in young rodents so it is possible that the blood–brain barrier was not fully mature.

Langston: When you got secondary iron accumulation in the nigra, what was the cellular location?

Olanow: We did not study that and obviously it should be done. Connor and colleagues have shown that iron is normally primarily stored in oligodendroglial cells. In PD and AD patients the increase was largely in astrocytes. With Dan Perl, we have shown that there is also an increase in neuromelanin granules in the SNc of PD patients.

Youdim: In PD, I agree, the increase is largely in the microglia oligodendrites and in some astrocytes. Obviously this needs to be looked at in the MPTP and 6-OHDA models.

Marsden: Switching to the apomorphine data, the concentration required to achieve protection is around 0.5 µM in PC12 cells?

Youdim: The IC_{50} was, depending on the iron concentration used, about 2.5 µM.

Marsden: The plasma levels achieved with constant apomorphine infusions are around 200 ng/ml. What synaptic concentration of apomorphine might that produce?

Youdim: We should be looking at this. We believe that plasma levels could be sufficient to provide protection. Dr. Corsini has also shown that apomorphine in these doses could, by signal transduction, induce up-regulation of dopamine D_2 receptor activity at almost exactly the same concentration at which we see protection.

Stocchi: You showed a dose-related effect for pergolide in terms of protection but the effects of lisuride and bromocriptine seemed to decrease with increasing dosage.

Youdim: This is exactly what we saw with apomorphine. There was protection with low doses but at high doses, apomorphine appeared to promote cell degeneration. It can therefore be a pro-oxidant as well as an anti-oxidant. There is a window of antioxidant activity that we have to get right.

Stocchi: So why does pergolide not seem to show it?

Youdim: It is most likely due to the structure of apomorphine.

Olanow: With Dr. Catherine Mytilineou, we have done similar studies with pergolide and our findings are the same as what Dr. Youdim described; a U-shaped curve where at high doses the drug begins to lose its protective activity and may actually promote cell death. Some recent studies now show that dopamine agonists can both protect against and induce apoptosis depending on concentration.

Youdim: This is one of the contradictions regarding vitamin C which can, in fact, become a pro-oxidant and can actually have a toxic effect as well as being an antioxidant.

Shoulson: You mentioned that S-apomorphine was not a dopamine agonist, so could one presume that it would not induce emesis at all, and could therefore be taken without restriction?

Youdim: I think the dopamine agonist activity is unrelated to radical scavenging activity, and this is also true for pergolide. S-apomorphine has very similar antioxidant and protective effects as the R form, and it is not a dopamine D_1 or D_2 agonist. I am not sure whether S-apomorphine can be taken without restriction but it is a thought.

Olanow: In these discussions about the protective capacity of apomorphine, it should be mentioned that similar results have been seen with other dopamine agonists including bromocriptine, pergolide, ropinirole, and pramipexole. It is therefore reasonable to consider that this may be a class effect and not specific to any one particular agonist. The basis of this effect is not known but may involve D_2 receptor stimulation and post synaptic signaling events as these effects can be prevented by a D_2 receptor antagonist and are not seen with pure D_1 receptor agonists.

CHAPTER FIFTEEN

Excitotoxicity and nitric oxide in Parkinson's disease pathogenesis

M. Flint Beal

Neurochemistry Laboratory, Neurology Service, Massachusetts General Hospital
and Harvard Medical School, Boston, Maryland, USA

A role for excitotoxicity in Parkinson's disease (PD) is supported by the recent observations of systemic defects in complex I activity of the electron transport chain in cybrid cell lines and PD patients.[1] Initial studies demonstrated that complex I defects could be transferred from platelets of PD patients into mitochondrial deficient cell lines,[2] and that this transfer was followed by increased free radical production. These cell lines became more susceptible to toxicity mediated by 1-methyl-phenylpyridinium ions (MPP[+]), providing further evidence for an interaction between a potential environmental factor and a genetic defect. The cell death induced by MPP[+] was apoptotic in nature, and these cell lines also showed markedly impaired calcium buffering to a variety of stimuli. This is consistent with other observations indicating that mitochondrial defects are associated with impaired intracellular calcium buffering.

Impaired energy metabolism due to a mitochondrial defect in PD raises the possibility that slow or weak excitotoxicity may contribute to the ensuing neuronal degeneration. That impaired energy metabolism could result in excitotoxicity was demonstrated by the finding that inhibitors of either oxidative phosphorylation or of the sodium potassium ATPase increased the neurotoxicity of glutamate[3] presumably via a reduction in ATP, which is crucial for maintaining the normal resting potential of the cell membrane. When the cell membrane is depolarized from -90 mV to between -60 and -30 mV, the voltage-dependent magnesium blockade of the N-methyl-D-aspartate (NMDA) receptor is relieved, leading to persistent receptor activation. In cultured chick retina, partial neuronal depolarization induced by inhibitors of either glycolysis or oxidative phosphorylation resulted in NMDA receptor activation and cell death in the absence of any increase in extracellular glutamate concentrations.[4] Titration of membrane potential with potassium mimicked the toxicity produced by graded metabolic inhibition.[5] Similar mechanisms could occur in the pathogenesis of PD. The substantia nigra neurons in man contain NMDA receptors which could be activated by such a mechanism, and interestingly, glutamate receptors are depleted in PD.[6]

Intracellular calcium levels are known to predict excitotoxic neuronal death,[7] and the increased levels following activation of NMDA receptors are buffered by mitochondria. Accumulation of calcium within mitochondria followed by mitochondrial depolarization are critical features of excitotoxic cell death[8,9] and are associated with increased free radical production[10] and activation of nitric oxide (NO) synthase. The increased generation of superoxide as well as NO radicals can lead to the production of peroxynitrite[11] via chemical interaction of superoxide with NO. Peroxynitrite appears to be a critical mediator of cell death in both *in vitro* and *in vivo* models of excitotoxicity.

The role of NO in excitotoxicity was demonstrated by the exposure of cultured cortical neurons to NMDA, and the subsequent attenuation of neurotoxicity by inhibitors of NO synthase (NOS), calmodulin antagonists, and reduced hemoglobin which scavenges nitric oxide.[12] Removal of L-arginine from the medium, a substrate necessary for the formation of NO, also blocked toxicity. Similarly, NOS inhibitors also block glutamate neurotoxicity in cultured striatal and hippocampal neurons. Pretreatment with quisqualate, which preferentially kills NOS neurons, blocked glutamate neurotoxicity in cultured cortical and striatal neurons.[13]

In the human and non-human primate models of PD, MPTP is used to produce clinical, biochemical and neuropathologic changes which resemble those occurring in idiopathic PD.[14] The pathogenesis involves the conversion of MPTP to an active metabolite, MPP+, by monoamine oxidase B (MAO-B).[15] MPP+ is selectively taken up by the dopamine transporter which is subsequently accumulated within mitochondria where it disrupts oxidative phosphorylation by binding to or near the rotenone binding site on complex I. This can result in increased intracellular calcium, followed by increased free radical production and activation of neuronal NOS. This in turn can lead to increased production of NO which reacts with superoxide to produce peroxynitrite and consequent cell damage.

Direct evidence for excitotoxicity following administration of MPTP toxicity has been controversial. MK-801 does not protect mesencephalic dopaminergic neurons from MPP+ *in vitro*, but these cells may be less dependent on oxidative phosphorylation than those *in vivo*.[16,17] The neurotoxic effects of intranigral MPP+ *in vivo* can be almost completely prevented by either systemic or intranigral administration of a variety of NMDA antagonists including CPP and MK-801.[18] Subsequent studies using a similar dosing regimen in rodents have failed to confirm these results[19] and MK-801 did not protect against MPTP-induced dopamine depletion in mice,[20] although it produced partial but significant attenuation.[21] The glutamate release inhibitors lamotrigine and riluzole are also neuroprotective against experimental neurotoxicity in rodents.[22–24]

In a study in primates, repeated low doses of MK-801 partially attenuated MPTP-induced dopamine depletions and protected against neuronal loss in the substantia nigra.[25] Similarly, CPP, a competitive NMDA antagonist, can significantly protect against depletion of substantia nigra dopaminergic neurons and striatal dopamine depletions.[26] Systemic administration of riluzole also showed some neuroprotection against MPTP toxicity in primates.[27]

The selective neuronal NOS inhibitor 7-nitroindazole (7-NI) dose-dependently protected against MPTP-induced dopamine depletion in mice with two differing degrees of dopamine depletion.[28] At 50 mg/kg, 7-NI produced almost complete protection at both levels of depletion. Following administration of MPTP, there was also a significant increase in 3-nitrotyrosine levels, which was blocked by 7-NI. These observations have been confirmed.[29] Furthermore, 7-NI also protected against depletion of tyrosine hydroxylase-positive neurons or an increase in silver stained neurons in the substantia nigra. Mice deficient in neuronal NOS were resistant to MPTP neurotoxicity, and 7-NI had no effect on MPP^+ levels following administration of MPTP.[29] Another relatively selective neuronal NOS inhibitor, S-methyl-thiocitrulline, acts on a different site on the enzyme, and also produced significant neuroprotection against MPTP-induced dopamine depletions,[30] albeit less marked than observed with 7-NI. L-nitroarginine, a nonspecific NOS inhibitor, protected against MPP^+-induced increases in hydroxyl radical generation, and partially protected against MPTP induced dopamine depletions.[31]

In baboons, an acute dosing regimen of MPTP results in a 94–98% depletion of dopamine in the putamen and caudate nucleus. 7-NI alone had no effect on dopamine levels, but when co-administered with MPTP at 25 mg/kg *bid*, 7-NI completely protected against MPTP-induced dopamine depletion.[32] There was also significant protection against the loss of tyrosine hydroxylase-positive neurons in the substantia nigra. Furthermore, the administration of 7-NI protected against motor and cognitive deficits.

A recent study has suggested that 7-NI also inhibits MAO-B and that this is central to its capacity to provide neuroprotection against MPTP neurotoxicity.[33] 7-NI was found to almost completely block dopamine depletion produced by a single subcutaneous injection of MPTP at 20 mg/kg, but there was a significant reduction in striatal levels of MPP^+. The MPP^+ levels produced by MPTP at 40 mg/kg in the presence of 7-NI were similar to those produced by MPTP alone at 20 mg/kg. The authors noted that with comparable MPP^+ levels 7-NI produced 20% protection against dopamine depletion. In these studies, 7-NI was administered intraperitoneally rather than subcutaneously, which would have resulted in rapid absorption. 7-NI at 50 mg/kg can significantly reduce cerebral blood flow, so some of the effect on MPP^+ levels may have been due to impaired uptake of MPTP into the brain.

Studies have been carried out to examine the effects of neuronal NOS (nNOS) inhibition on MPP^+-induced substantia nigra degeneration[34] in mutant mice lacking either the nNOS or the endothelial NOS (eNOS) genes.

The substantia nigra degeneration is due to retrograde transport of MPP[+] to the substantia nigra, since comparably-sized excitotoxic lesions of the striatum do not result in a depletion of substantia nigra neurons. Degeneration was significantly attenuated in the nNOS deficient mice, but not in the eNOS deficient mice, which parallels findings in experimental stroke models and in malonate-induced neuronal degeneration in the striatum.[35] Furthermore, MPP[+] caused increased striatal 3-nitrotyrosine concentrations in controls and in eNOS deficient mice. 3-Nitrotyrosine is thought to be a relatively specific neurochemical marker for peroxynitrite-mediated nitration,[36] which suggests that peroxynitrite can generate hydroxyl radicals directly through an activated transition state.

The ability of 7-NI to block MPP[+]-induced substantia nigra degeneration in rats was examined by administration of 50 mg/kg, prior to MPP[+] injections and then at approximately 12 h intervals for up to 48 h after MPP[+]. 7-NI significantly attenuated MPP[+]-induced degeneration of the substantia nigra of rats,[34] providing almost complete protection against the ensuing cell loss. This observation provides further evidence that the effects of 7-NI on MPTP neurotoxicity are unlikely to be the result of a nonspecific effect on MPTP metabolism by MAO-B or MPP[+] uptake, and concurs with the results in the nNOS deficient mice.

The source of NO in the substantia nigra is unclear. One potential source could be inducible NOS (iNOS) in either microglia or astrocytes.[37,38] Neuronal injury leads to the expression of iNOS in astrocytes[39] and of nNOS in neurons. Immunohistochemical evidence suggests that a small population of nNOS-positive interneurons is distributed throughout the substantia nigra, and show direct apposition of nNOS processes with substantia nigra tyrosine hydroxylase-positive neurons.[34] Taken together, these observations provide strong evidence implicating NO and peroxynitrite in the pathogenesis of MPP[+]-induced degeneration of substantia nigra neurons.

Summary

- A potential role of excitotoxicity in PD has been strengthened by the discovery of a mitochondrial encoded defect in complex I activity of the electron transport chain in a cybrid system using mitochondia derived from PD platelets.

- A mitochondrial defect could lead to loss of the ATP-dependent magnesium blockade of NMDA receptors and activation of amino acid receptors by physiologic concentrations of glutamate.

- Studies on MPTP neurotoxicity in both mice and primates have shown that inhibition of neuronal NOS exerts neuroprotective effects. Excitatory amino acid receptor antagonists have given inconsistent results in mice, but show significant neuroprotective effects in primates.

- These results raise the prospect for a role of excitatory amino acid antagonists as neuronal NOS inhibitors in the treatment of PD.

ACKNOWLEDGMENT

The secretarial assistance of Sharon Melanson is gratefully acknowledged. Supported by NIH grant NS31579 and NS10828.

REFERENCES

1. Schapira AHV, Gu M, Taanman J-W, Tabrizi SJ, Seaton T, Cleeter M, Cooper JM, this volume.

2. Swerdlow RH, Parks JK, Miller SW, Tuttle JB, Trimmer PA, Sheehan JP, Bennett JP, Davis RE, Parker WD. Origin and functional consequences of the complex I defect in Parkinson's disease. Ann Neurol 1996; 40: 663–671.

3. Novelli A, Reilly JA, Lysko PG, Henneberry RC. Glutamate becomes neurotoxic via the N-methyl-D-aspartate receptor when intracellular energy levels are reduced. Brain Res 1988; 451: 205–212.

4. Zeevalk GD, Nicklas WJ. Chemically induced hypoglycemia and anoxia: relationship to glutamate receptor-mediated toxicity in retina. J Pharmacol Exp Ther 1990; 253: 1285–1292.

5. Zeevalk GD, Nicklas WJ. Mechanisms underlying initiation of excitotoxicity associated with metabolic inhibition. J Pharmacol Exp Ther 1991; 257: 870–878.

6. Difazio MC, Hollingsworth Z, Young JB, Penney J. Glutamate receptors in the substantia nigra of Parkinson's disease brains. Neurol 1992; 42: 402–406.

7. Hyrc K, Handran SD, Rothman SM, Goldberg MP. Ionized intracellular calcium concentration predicts excitotoxic neuronal death: observations with low-affinity fluorescent calcium indicators. J Neurosci 1997; 17: 6669–6677.

8. White RJ, Reynolds IJ. Mitochondria and Na^+/Ca^{2+} exchange buffer glutamate-induced calcium loads in cultured cortical neurons. J Neurosci 1995; 15: 1318–1328.

9. Schinder AF, Olson EC, Spitzer NC, Montal M. Mitochondrial dysfunction is a primary event in glutamate neurotoxicity. J Neurosci 1996; 16: 6125–6133.

10. Dykens JA. Isolated cerebral and cerebellar mitochondria produce free radicals when exposed to elevated Ca^+ and Na^+: implications for neurodegeneration. J Neurochem 1994; 63: 584–591.

11. Beckman JS, Crow JP. Pathological implications of nitric oxide superoxide and peroxynitrite formation. Biochem Soc Trans 1993; 21: 330–334.

12. Dawson VL, Dawson TM, London ED, et al. Nitric oxide mediates glutamate neurotoxicity in primary cortical cultures. Proc Natl Acad Sci USA 1991; 88: 6368–6371.

13. Dawson VL, Dawson TM, Bartley DA, et al. Mechanisms of nitric oxide mediated neurotoxicity in primary brain cultures. J Neurosci 1993; 13: 2651–2661.

14. Bloem BR, Irwin I, Buruma OJS, et al. The MPTP model: versatile contributions to the treatment of idiopathic Parkinson's disease. J Neurol Sci 1990; 97: 273–293.

15. Singer TP, Castagnoli N, Ramsay RR, Trevor AJ. Biochemical events in the development of parkinsonism induced by MPTP. J Neurochem 1987; 49: 1–8.

16. Finiels-Markier F, Marini AM, Williams P, et al. The N-methyl-D-aspartate antagonist MK-801 fails to protect dopaminergic neurons from 1-methyl-4-phenylpyridinium toxicity in vitro. J Neurochem 1993; 60: 1968–1971.

17. Michel PP, Agid Y. The glutamate antagonist, MK-801, does not prevent dopaminergic cell death induced by the 1-methyl-phenylpyridinium ion (MPP$^+$) in rat dissociated mesencephalic cultures. Brain Res 1992; 597: 233–240.

18. Turski L, Bressler K, Rettig K-J, et al. Protection of substantia nigra from MPP$^+$ neurotoxicity by N-methyl-D-aspartate antagonists. Nature 1991; 349: 414–418.

19. Sonsalla PK, Zeevalk GD, Manzino L, *et al.* MK-801 fails to protect against the dopaminergic neuropathology produced by systemic 1-methyl-4-phenyl-1,2,3,6-tetrahydropyridine in mice or intranigral 1-methyl-4-phenylpyridinium in rats. J Neurochem 1992; 58: 1979–1982.

20. Kupsch A, Loschmann PA, Sauer H. Do NMDA receptor antagonists protect against MPTP-toxicity. Biochemical and immunocytochemical analyses in black mice. Brain Res 1992; 592: 74–83.

21. Chan P, Langston JW, Di Monte DA. MK-801 temporarily prevents MPTP-induced acute dopamine depletion and MPP^+ elimination in the mouse striatum. J Pharmacol Exp Ther 1993; 267: 1515–1520.

22. Jones-Humble SA, Morgan PF, Cooper BR. The novel anticonvulsant lamotrigine prevents dopamine depletion in C57 black mice in the MPTP animal model of Parkinson's disease. Life Sci 1994; 54: 245–252.

23. Barneoud P, Mazadier M, Miquet J-M, *et al.* Neuroprotective effects of riluzole on a model of Parkinson's disease in the rat. Neurosci 1996; 74: 971–983.

24. Boireau A, Dubedat P, Bordier F, *et al.* Riluzole and experimental parkinsonism: antagonism of MPTP-induced decrease in central dopamine levels in mice. NeuroReport 1994; 5: 2657–2660.

25. Zuddas A, Oberto G, Vaglini F, *et al.* MK-801 prevents 1-methyl-4-phenyl-1,2,3,6-tetrahydropyridinine-induced Parkinsonism in primates. J Neurochem 1992; 59: 733–739.

26. Lange KW, Loschmann P-A, Sofic E, *et al.* The competitive NMDA antagonist CPP protects substantia nigra neurons from MPTP-induced degeneration in primates. Naunyn-Schmiedebergs Arch Pharmacol 1993; 348: 586–592.

27. Benazzouz A, Boraud T, Dubedat P, *et al.* Riluzole prevents MPTP-induced parkinsonism in the rhesus monkey: a pilot study. Eur J Pharmacol 1995; 284: 299–307.

28. Schulz JB, Matthews RT, Muqit MMK, *et al.* Inhibition of neuronal nitric oxide synthase by 7-nitroindazole protects against MPTP-induced neurotoxicity in mice. J Neurochem 1995; 64: 936–939.

29. Przedborski S, Jackon-Lewis V, Yokoyama R, *et al.* Role of neuronal nitric oxide in 1-methyl-4-phenyl-1,2,3,6-tetrahydropyridine (MPTP)-induced dopaminergic neurotoxicity. Proc Natl Acad Sci USA 1996; 93: 4565–4571.

30. Matthews RT, Yang L, Beal MF. S-methylthiocitrulline, a neuronal nitric oxide synthase inhibitor, protects against malonate and MPTP neurotoxicity. Exp Neurol 1997; 143: 282–286.

31. Smith TS, Swerdlow RH, Parker J.W.D, W.D., Bennett J. Reduction of MPP^+-induced hydroxyl radical formation and nigrostriatal MPTP toxicity by inhibiting nitric oxide synthase. NeuroReport 1994; 5: 2598–2600.

32. Hantraye P, Brouillet E, Ferrante R, *et al.* Inhibition of neuronal nitric oxide synthase prevents MPTP-induced parkinsonism in baboons. Nature Med 1996; 2: 1017–1021.

33. Di Monte D, Royland JE, Anderson A, *et al.* Inhibition of monoamine oxidase contributes to the protective effect of 7-nitroindazole against MPTP neurotoxicity. J Neurochem 1997; 69: 1771–1773.

34. Matthews RT, Beal MF, Fallon J, *et al.* MPP^+ induced substantia nigra degeneration is attenuated in nNOS knockout mice. Neurobiol Dis 1997; 4: 114–121.

35. Schulz JB, Huang PL, Matthews RT, *et al.* Striatal malonate lesions are attenuated in neuronal nitric oxide knockout mice. J Neurochem 1996; 67: 430–433.

36. Ischiropoulos H, Zhu L, Chen J, *et al.* Peroxynitrite-mediated tyrosine nitration catalyzed by superoxide dismutase. Arch Biochem Biophys 1992; 298: 431–437.

37. Boje KM, Arora PK. Microglial-produced nitric oxide and reactive nitrogen oxides mediate neuronal cell death. Brain Res 1992; 587: 250–256.

38. Skaper ST, Facci L, Leon A. Inflammatory mediator stimulation of astrocytes and meningeal fibroblasts induces neuronal degeneration via the nitridergic pathway. J Neurochem 1995; 64: 266–276.

39. Wallace MN, Tayebjee MH, Rana FS, *et al.* Pyramidal neurons in pathological human motor cortex express nitric oxide synthase. Neurosci Lett 1996; 212: 187–190.

DISCUSSION

Burke: In your studies with the laser confocal microscope, is it your impression that cells that stain for neuronal NOS and for TH are generally not co-localized in the substantia nigra?

Beal: Correct. NOS and TH staining are not co-localized in the substantia nigra. NOS-positive neurons in the substantia nigra are a small population of intensely stained neurons, as in the striatum and the cortex. They have extensive ramifications and dendritic and axonal arbors, but they do not co-localize with TH in the studies we have performed. It is possible that there is a very small degree of NOS staining in TH-positive neurons that we could not see. After certain forms of injury to cells there is evidence that up-regulation, particularly of NOS, can occur in some neuronal systems and we have not explored the possibility that there might be upregulation of NOS in TH neurons following injury.

Jenner: Likewise, we have been unable to see any NOS-positive cells which are dopaminergic in the substantia nigra. Interestingly, the nigral cells also contain heme-oxygenase-2 which produces carbon monoxide and can bind NO. One wonders therefore whether dopaminergic neurons in the SNc use carbon monoxide as a modulator of heme containing enzymes whereas other cells produce nitric oxide as a modulator.

Melamed: In our hands, phenyl butyl nitrone (PBN), the electron spin trap antioxidant, was very effective in blocking toxicity of dopamine and levodopa, and also MPP+. Do you have any information as to whether it can cross the blood–brain barrier? In our search for antioxidants for use in the treatment of progressive degenerative disorders, could it be one of the candidates? Do you know about any potential toxicity in man?

Beal: I think PBN is better *in vitro* than *in vivo*, but it does have some efficacy *in vivo*. A paper in *Neuroscience* this year showed some *in vivo* efficacy for PBN against MPTP-induced toxicity. There are, however, more potent analogues. We have some other analogues based on an azulenyl backbone that are being synthesized by a chemist at MIT, and they work against MPTP toxicity also. These are being developed for use in man by Centaur Pharmaceuticals and they have analogues based on these molecules that work very well against MPTP toxicity in experimental animals. They are going into phase I studies now. They penetrate into the brain very readily but the mechanism by which they work is debatable. Interestingly, they also down-regulate iNOS. One might expect, stoichiometrically, that the amount in the brain would be insufficient to scavenge radicals on a mass action basis. However, there is some evidence that they may be able to regenerate, so they might even have an SOD-like activity. Another interesting point is that these agents tend to concentrate in mitochondria which might also be beneficial.

Olanow: Are you at liberty to describe the specific manner by which they cross the blood–brain barrier and in which parts of the brain are they are most effective?

Beal: They probably go across by passive diffusion because they are lipophilic.

Olanow: But is there not some preference for what kind of injury they protect against and evidence that protection occurs predominantly in a perivascular distribution?

Beal: There were some protective effects in ischemia models with PBN. It did not seem to penetrate the brain very well and the effects were mostly in a perivascular distribution. The mechanism responsible for this effect is not known. Data on tissue homogenates have demonstrated increases in cellular concentrations in the brain, and at the sub-cellular level this was noted particularly in mitochondria.

Gash: What are the long-term effects of continuously inhibiting nitric oxide in primates or humans?

Beal: No one knows because it has not been examined, even in experimental animals. The longest studies have been in the SOD mutant mouse, the transgenic ALS mouse model, with the Astra compound which is a very selective nNOS inhibitor and which did have some benefits in these animals. There was no major toxicity. In nNOS knockout animals, however, there are marked behavioral effects. The animals become very aggressive sexually and kill their cage-mates so they have to be housed individually. The effects of nNOS inhibition in man remain to be seen.

Langston: We have shown that 7-NI is a fairly potent MAO inhibitor, so one has to interpret the studies you have described with some caution. That would not apply to the MPP+ studies, of course, where MAO inhibition would not be thought to effect toxicity. Also, your studies on cell death over time are interesting. Is one month as far as you have got?

Beal: Yes. We also injected MPP+ into a rat because it was easier. I am aware of the MAO-B effect of 7-NI in your work. A potential complication of your data is that 7-NI will reduce blood flow to the brain, particularly when given intraperitoneally, so you may have had a delivery problem which could account for reduced levels of MPP+ and reduced toxicity. We gave it subcutaneously. Other experiments need to be done to determine whether this is an issue in the *in vivo* situation.

Jenner: We have studied the effects of another NOS inhibitor, L-NAME, on MPTP toxicity in common marmosets but could find no protection. L-NAME is a longer lasting and irreversible inhibitor of NOS compared to the short acting reversible effects of 7-NI. Thus not all NOS inhibitors protect against MPTP toxicity and other mechanisms should still be sought.

[224]

Beal: I appreciate your point. It should be noted that L-NAME is a relatively non-specific NOS inhibitor that affects endothelial NOS, which might alter cerebral blood flow thereby increasing MPTP delivery to the brain. Have you studied it with the MPP+ model which might help to sort out this difference?

Jenner: No, but of course we should.

Schapira: In relation to the potential role of NO in toxicity, we have shown *in vitro* that an NO generator, at concentrations that do not themselves affect complex I activity, increases inhibition of complex I induced by MPP+ by 100%. This suggests that perhaps there is a synergistic effect between NO and MPP+ on complex I protein. Whether they are acting on different sites of the complex I molecule, or through the generation of free radicals as a consequence of increased inhibition of complex I, is not certain. But it is clear that NO can enhance by 100% the MPP+ inhibition of complex I.

Beal: NO also, of course, has the effect of regulating cytochrome oxidase which has been well described by your colleagues in the UK.

Burke: Could you clarify the nature of the progressive loss of neurons in the SNc following intrastriatal injection of MPP+?

Beal: We inject MPP+ into the striatum and see some degree of cell loss in the substantia nigra at seven days. We give no further MPP+ and see a progressive drop-off in SNc cells at day 28. We believe this is due to retrograde transport of MPP+ to the substantia nigra with subsequent cell death.

Burke: When you assess cell death, are you looking at cell phenotype or TH staining, or are you looking at viability as demonstrated by retrograde labeling?

Beal: We do Nissl counts and evaluate all nigral neurons because of the possibility of down-regulation of TH.

W. Tatton: Just to come back to that issue, I have looked at Tao Hagg's results in which striatal terminals were damaged by various methods as well as by just cutting the pathway. They pre-marked the cells and found that there was retrograde death of the nigral cells in the rat after striatal damage. Pre-marking the cells prior to lesioning circumvented the complication of depending upon TH or Nissl counts. I am surprised that you did not find any retrograde death of nigral cells in the rat after that kind of striatal damage.

Beal: There is some evidence for retrograde loss in the reticulata, but no clear evidence for loss in the compacta.

CHAPTER SIXTEEN

Glial cells and inflammation in Parkinson's disease: a role in neurodegeneration?

ETIENNE C. HIRSCH, S. HUNOT,
P. DAMIER, AND B. FAUCHEUX

INSERM U289, Hôpital de la Salpêtrière, Paris, France

Degeneration of dopaminergic neurons during early PD may activate secondary phenomena, aggravating the pathological process and maintaining disease progression. In this context, the glial reaction observed in neurodegenerative disorders may simply be a consequence of nerve cell death, but recent evidence suggests that it may also be involved in the evolution of the disease.

PD IS NOT A GENERALIZED DISEASE OF ALL DOPAMINERGIC NEURONS

Only recently has it become clear that PD is not a disorder of all dopaminergic neurons. The level of dopamine depletion varies from one striatal region to another, being highest in the putamen, slightly less in the caudate nucleus and relatively low in the ventral striatum, which includes the nucleus accumbens.[1] Mesolimbic dopaminergic neurons are assumed to be less severely affected in PD than mesostriatal neurons.[2] Since separate populations of dopaminergic neurons in the mesencephalon give rise to the mesostriatal and mesolimbic pathways, different populations of dopaminergic neurons may not be uniformly affected in the mesencephalon of parkinsonian patients. This has been validated by immunohistochemical methods coupled to image analysis techniques, allowing precise quantification of dopaminergic neurons in PD. The loss of dopaminergic neurons was severe in the substantia nigra pars compacta (76% loss), intermediate in the substantia nigra pars lateralis (34% loss), ventral tegmental area (55% loss) and peri- and retrorubral region (31% loss) and almost nil in the central gray substance (3% loss).[3] Even within the substantia nigra pars compacta, neurons located dorsally seemed to be less severely affected than those located in the ventral portion of the structure.[4] Furthermore, there was a marked heterogeneity in the distribution of the processes of the striatonigral neurons expressing calbindin.[5] Interestingly, most of the dopaminergic neurons were located in the calbindin-poor zones but some were also detectable in the surrounding calbindin-rich matrix. Furthermore, an additional population of dopaminergic neurons was located dorsally to the calbindin-rich neuropil zone, in an area corresponding to the pars γ of the substantia nigra pars compacta according to the classification of Olziewski and Baxter.[6] The loss of dopaminergic neurons in PD was heterogeneous across these different subdivisions, being highest in the calbindin-poor neuropil zones (76–98% loss), less severe in the calbindin-rich neuropil (80% loss), and least severe in the dorsal part of the substantia nigra (57% loss). Neurons may not therefore be sensitized to the pathological process solely by the dopaminergic phenotype. The neurons most susceptible to the disease are particularly sensitive to oxidative stress and increased intracellular calcium concentrations.[7] Glial cells may also account for some of the selective vulnerability of dopaminergic neurons found in PD.

GLIAL CELLS COULD BE INVOLVED IN THE DIFFERENTIAL VULNERABILITY OF DOPAMINERGIC NEURONS IN PD

An inverse relationship exists between the degree of neuronal loss in the dopaminergic cell groups of the mesencephalon and the density of astroglial cells initially present in these groups.[8] Specifically, an inverse relationship has been found within the substantia nigra, the density of astroglial cells also being lowest in the most severely affected group of neurons, located in the zones of low calbindin immunoreactivity.[9] Neurons may therefore be less susceptible to the disease when they are located in an astroglial-rich rather than an astroglial-poor environment. The glial factors protecting dopaminergic neurons in PD are unknown but may involve (1) neurotrophic factors secreted by glial cells and acting on dopaminergic neurons,[10–14] and (2) their capacity to catabolize dopamine and oxygen free radicals. Indeed, dopamine is susceptible to spontaneous oxidation to form neuromelanin,[15] a reaction leading to the formation of harmful oxygen free radicals which is pH-dependent and is more likely to occur at neutral pH in the cytoplasm of the neurons than in synaptic vesicles where low pH prevents the auto-oxidation of dopamine. Thus, since dopamine is largely cytoplasmic in the substantia nigra, its enzymatic catabolism may prevent the production of oxygen free radicals through dopamine auto-oxidation. Interestingly, monoamine oxidase B (MAO-B), which catabolizes dopamine, is present in the glial cells of the substantia nigra and the density of glial cells expressing MAO-B in control subjects is lowest where dopaminergic denervation is highest in the parkinsonian mesencephalon.[16] Dopamine released by the dendrites of dopaminergic neurons in the substantia nigra could be taken up by MAO-B in glial cells, preventing its reuptake in the neurons and its auto-oxidation. The catabolism of dopamine by MAO-B would also produce oxygen free radicals but this would occur within the glial cells where free radical scavenging mechanisms are particularly well-developed.[8] Indeed, glutathione peroxidase, which inhibits the transformation of hydrogen peroxide into the highly toxic hydroxyl radical, is highly expressed by glial cells in the human mesencephalon,[8] and especially in the catecholaminergic cells groups that are least affected in PD. Glial cells which express MAO-B and glutathione peroxidase may therefore protect dopaminergic neurons from the deleterious effects of dopamine auto-oxidation. However, this assumption challenges the use of MAO-B inhibitors as neuroprotective agents in PD. Finally, a subpopulation of glial cells may protect dopaminergic neurons against degeneration in PD.

GLIAL CELLS SECRETING MEDIATORS OF THE INFLAMMATORY REACTION COULD PLAY A DELETERIOUS ROLE IN PD

It is also possible that glial cells could contribute to the neurodegenerative process in PD. Activated microglial cells and/or subpopulations of astroglial cells are involved in inflammation of the adult central nervous system because of their phagocytic function, and their ability to produce neutral proteinases and cytokines.[17] The inflammatory cytokines, interleukin-1 (IL-1), interferon γ (IFN-γ) and tumor necrosis factor α (TNF-α), appear to have a deleterious role but may also be neuroprotective in certain circumstances.

IL-1 can be synthesized directly within the central nervous system[18–20] where it can promote neuronal sprouting, scar formation and neovascularization, which may constitute evidence of a protective role for neurons after brain injury.[21,22] However, an IL-1 receptor antagonist markedly reduces the infarct volume in an animal model of focal ischemia,[23] suggesting that this cytokine could have participated directly in the neuronal degeneration. The deleterious effect of IL-1 does not seem to be observed solely in ischemia since identical results were obtained by a direct activation of NMDA receptors.[23] Mechanisms could include (1) the formation of free radicals by arachidonic acid release,[24] (2) stimulation of nitric oxide production[25] and (3) an increase in intracellular calcium concentrations.[26] Immunohistochemical analysis of human brain post-mortem showed almost no expression of IL-1β in patients without neurological or psychiatric diseases, in agreement with the extremely low IL-1 levels in normal brain.[27,28] In contrast, numerous glial cells displaying IL-1β immunoreactivity were detected in the substantia nigra of patients with PD,[29] suggesting that dopaminergic neurons could be exposed to the possible deleterious effects of this cytokine. Neurons which degenerate in PD are particularly sensitive to oxidative stress and a rise in calcium concentration,[30] which could be partially induced by IL-1 production. Furthermore, IL-1β may account at least in part for the induction of nitric oxide synthase in glial cells of the substantia nigra of PD patients.[31] Nitric oxide in the NO· state can react directly with the superoxide radical to form the extremely toxic ONOO⁻ which may also be increased by the alteration of mitochondrial functions reported in PD.[32]

[229]

Nitric oxide may also alter iron homeostasis, a phenomenon that could also be involved in the degeneration of dopaminergic neurons in PD given the role of iron in generation of hydroxyl radicals.[33] The rise in IL-1β observed in PD may therefore activate a complex cascade of deleterious events involving various toxic molecules.

IFN-γ is produced by activated CD4+ and CD8+ cells in the immune system, and also by natural killer cells.[34] In the central nervous system its major sources are microglial cells, astrocytes and lymphocytes,[35–37] but its role is less well-known than that of IL-1β. IFN-γ may be involved in modulation of both class I and class II major histocompatibility complex expression on a wide variety of cells including glial cells.[38] Increased expression of IFN-γ in the substantia nigra of parkinsonian patients[29] may account for the presence of glial cells expressing the class II major histocompatibility complex antigen HLA-DR.[39] Like IL-1β, IFN-γ can also stimulate the production of nitric oxide and thus activate the same cascade of deleterious events.

In the central nervous system, TNF-α is synthesized by astrocytes[40–42] and microglial cells.[40,43,44] Glial cells of patients with PD express TNF-α in the substantia nigra, although it was almost undetectable in control subjects.[45] TNF-α-positive glial cells were detected in the vicinity of neuromelanized neurons or neuromelanin debris from previously degenerated neurons, suggesting an involvement with neuronal death events. Increased expression of TNF-α has also been reported in the striatum and the cerebrospinal fluid of patients with PD suggesting a more generalized increased production of this cytokine in the disease.[46] A major function of TNF-α is to provoke cytotoxicity in various tumor cell lines, and this effect is mediated by the type 1 receptor[47,48] which is expressed by nigral dopaminergic neurons in humans,[45] so the increased expression of TNF-α in the substantia nigra of PD patients could participate in the neurodegenerative process. In primary cultures of rat mesencephalon, activation of the TNF-α transduction pathway involved a transient production of oxygen free radicals and translocation of the transcription factor NFκB, and these phenomena resulted in an almost complete neuronal degeneration by apoptosis.[49] In PD it is difficult to determine whether the increased production of TNF-α has a similar consequence, but the 70-fold increase in NFκB translocation in the dopaminergic neurons of patients with PD and the presence of cells displaying the characteristic morphological features of apoptosis argue in favor of such an effect.[49]

SUMMARY

- Degeneration of dopaminergic neurons that occurs during PD is limited to subpopulations of these neurons and that glial cells may participate in this selective vulnerability.

- Cytokines may induce an inflammatory reaction which could be involved in the degeneration of dopaminergic neurons by various mechanisms, including nitric oxide production, deregulation of iron and calcium homeostasis, and induction of apoptosis. TNF-α, IL-1β and

IFNγ are increased in the PD substantia nigra and may act synergistically to induce the inflammatory reaction.

- These reactions are not specific to PD as some are also observed in other cases of neuronal degeneration, such as brain injury, ischemia, multiple sclerosis, Down's syndrome and Alzheimer's disease. Thus, the deleterious effects of inflammation probably represent a common event associated with neurodegeneration.

- This finding is potentially of great importance since it may point to targets for possible therapeutic intervention, such as the inhibition of cytokine production, binding to receptors and intracellular signaling pathways.

ACKNOWLEDGMENTS

This research was supported by INSERM, the Association Claude Bernard pour le Développement des Recherches Biologiques et Médicales dans les Hôpitaux de l'Assistance Publique à Paris, the National Parkinson Foundation (Miami, Florida, USA) and the French Ministry of Research and Education.

References

1. Ehringer H, Hornykiewicz O. Vertailung von Noradrenalin und Dopamin (3-hydroxytyramin) im Gehirn des Menschen und ihr Verhalten bei Erkrankungen des extrapyramidalen Systems. Wien Klin Wschr 1960; 38: 1236–1239.

2. Javoy-Agid F, Agid Y. Is the mesocortical dopaminergic system involved in Parkinson's disease? Neurol 1980; 30: 1326–1330.

3. Hirsch EC, Graybiel AM, Agid Y. Melanized dopaminergic neurons are differentially susceptible to degeneration in Parkinson's disease. Nature 1988; 334 (6180): 345–348.

4. Fearnley JM, Lees A. Ageing and Parkinson's disease: substantia nigra regional selectivity. Brain 1991; 114: 2283–2302.

5. Damier P, Hirsch EC, Agid Y, Graybiel AM. Temporospatial progression of the loss on dopaminergic neurons in the substantia nigra in Parkinson's disease. Mov Disord 1997; 12 (Suppl.1): 274.

6. Olszewski J, Baxter D. Cytoarchitecture of the human brainstem. Philadelphia: Lippincott, 1954.

7. Hirsch EC. Parkinsonism and cell vulnerability. In, Rhône-Poulenc Rorer Foundation, Proceedings of the 8th International Round Table on Neurodegenerative Diseases, Annecy, 13–14 May 1993. Academic Press, 1994: 155–167.

8. Damier P, Hirsch EC, Zhang P, et al. Glutathione peroxidase glial cells and Parkinson's disease. Neurosci 1993; 52: 1–6.

9. Damier P, Agid Y, Graybiel AM, Hirsch EC. Role of astroglial environment in selectivity of dopaminergic lesion in Parkinson's disease. Soc Neurosci Abstr 1996; 22: 219.

10. Lin LFH, Doherty DH, Lile JD, et al. GDNF: a glial cell line-derived neurotrophic factor for midbrain dopaminergic neurons. Science 1993; 260: 1130–1132.

11. Beck K, Knüsel B, Hefti F. The nature of the trophic action of brain-derived neurotrophic factor, des (1–3)-insulin-like growth factor-1, and basic fibroblast growth factor on mesencephalic dopaminergic neurons developing in culture. Neurosci 1993; 52: 855–866.

12. Otto D, Unsicker K. Basic FGF-2-mediated protection of cultured mesencephalic dopaminergic neurons against MPTP and MPP+: specificity and impact of culture conditions, non-dopaminergic neurons, and astroglial cells. J Neurosci Res 1993; 34: 382–393.

13. Otto D, Unsicker K. Basic FGF reverses chemical and morphological deficits in the nigrostriatal system of MPTP-treated mice. J Neurosci 1990; 10: 1912–1921.

14. Mayer E, Dunnett SB, Pellitteri R, Fawcett JW. Basic fibroblast growth factor promotes the survival of embryonic ventral mesencephalic dopaminergic neurons. I. Effects in vitro. Neurosci 1993; 56: 379–388.

15. Graham DG. On the origin and significance of neuromelanin. Arch Pathol Lab Med 1979; 103: 359–362.

16. Damier P, Kastner A, Agid Y, Hirsch EC. Does monoamine oxidase type B play a role in dopaminergic nerve cell death in Parkinson's disease? Neurol 1996; 46: 1262–1269.

17. Benveniste EN. Inflammatory cytokines within the central nervous system: sources, function, and mechanism of action. Am J Physiol 1992; 263: 1–16.

18. Hétier E, Ayala J, Denefle P, et al. Brain macrophages synthesize IL-1 and IL-1 mRNAs in vitro. J Neurosci Res 1988; 21: 391–397.

19. Van Dam A, Brouns M, Louisse S, Berkenbosch F. Appearance of IL-1 in

macrophages and in ramified microglia in the brain of endotoxin-treated rats : a pathway for the induction of non-specific symptoms of sickness? Brain Res 1992; 588: 291–296.

20. Sébire G, Emilie D, Wallon C, *et al.* In vitro production of IL-6, IL-1β and tumor necrosis factor-α by human embryonic microglial and neural cells. J Immunol 1993; 150: 1517–1523.

21. Giulian D, Lachman LB. Interleukin-1 stimulation of astroglial proliferation after brain injury. Science 1985; 228: 497–499.

22. Lachman LB, Brown DC, Dinarello CA. Growth promoting effect of recombinant IL-1 and TNF for human astrocyte cell line. J Immunol 1987; 138: 2913–2916.

23. Relton JK, Rothwell NJ. Interleukin-1 receptor antagonist inhibits neuronal damage induced by cerebral ischaemia or NMDA-receptor activation in the rat. Brain Res Bull 1992; 585: 135–160.

24. Dinarello C. Interleukin-1 and interleukin 1 antagonist. Blood 1991; 77: 1627–1652.

25. Beasley D, Schwartz JH, Brenner BM. Interleukin-1 induces prolonged L-arginine-dependent cyclic guanosine monophosphate and nitrite production in rat vascular smooth muscle cells. J Clin Invest 1991; 87: 602–608.

26. Logan A. CNS growth factors. Br J Hosp Med 1990; 43: 428–437.

27. Berkenbosch F, Robakis N, Blum M. Interleukin-1 in the central nervous system: A role in the acute phase response and in brain injury, brain development, and the pathogenesis of Alzheimer's disease. In, Frederickson RCA, McGaugh JL, Felten DL, eds, Peripheral signaling of the brain. Toronto: Hogrefe & Huber, 1991: 131–145.

28. Giulian D, Woodward J, Young D, Krebs JF, Lachman LB. Interleukin-1 injected into mammalian brain stimulates astrogliosis and neovascularization. J Neurosci 1989; 8: 2485–2490.

29. Hunot S, Betard C, Faucheux B, Agid Y, Hirsch EC. Immunohistochemical analysis of interferon-γ and interleukin-1β in the substantia nigra of Parkinsonian patients. Mov Disord 1997; 12 (Suppl.1): 20.

30. Hirsch EC. Does oxidative stress participate in nerve cell death in Parkinson's disease? Eur Neurol 1993; 33: 52–59.

31. Hunot S, Boissière F, Faucheux B, *et al.* Nitric oxide synthase and neuronal vulnerability in Parkinson's disease. Neurosci 1996; 72: 355–363.

32. Schapira AHV, Cooper JM, Dexter D, *et al.* Mitochondrial complex I deficiency in Parkinson's disease. J Neurochem 1990; 54: 823–827.

33. Hirsch EC, Faucheux BA. Iron metabolism and Parkinson's disease. Mov Disord, in press.

34. Ijzermans JNM, Marquet RL. Interferon-gamma: a review. Immunobiol 1989; 179: 456–473.

35. Merrill JE, Chen IS. HIV-1, macrophages, glial cells, and cytokines in AIDS nervous system disease. FASEB J 1991; 5: 2391–2397.

36. Morganti-Kossmann MC, Kossmann T, Wahl SM. Cytokine mediated neuropathology. Trends Pharmacol Sci 1992; 13: 286–291.

37. Frei K, Nadal D, Fontana A. Intracerebral synthesis of tumor necrosis factor α and interleukin-6 in infectious meningitis. Ann NY Acad Sci 1990; 594: 326–335.

38. Cogswell JP, Zelesnik-Le N, Ting JPY. Transcriptional regulation of the HLA-DRA gene. Crit Rev Immunol 1991; 11: 87–112.

39. McGeer PL, Itagaki S, Boyes BE, McGeer EG. Reactive microglia are positive for HLA-DR in the substantia nigra of Parkinson's and Alzheimer's disease brains. Neurol 1988; 38: 1285–1291.

40. Lee S, Liu W, Dickson D, Brosnan C, Berman J. Cytokine production by human foetal microglial and astrocytes. Differential induction by lipopolysaccharides and IL-1β. J Immunol 1993; 150: 2659–2667.

41. Lieberman A, Pitha P, Shin H, Shin M. Production of TNF and other cytokines by astrocytes stimulated with lipopolysaccharide or a neurotropic virus. Proc Natl Acad Sci USA 1989; 86: 6348–6352.

42. Chung I, Benveniste E. TNFα production by astrocytes: induction by lipopolysaccharide, IFN and IL-1β. J Immunol 1989; 144: 2999–3007.

43. Sawada M, Kondo N, Suzumura A, Marunouchi T. Production of TNF-α by microglia and astrocytes in culture. Brain Res 1989; 491: 394–397.

44. Hétier E, Ayala J, Bousseau A, Denefle P, Prochiantz A. Amoeboid microglial cells and not astrocytes synthesize TNF-α in Swiss mouse brain cell cultures. Eur J Neurosci 1990; 2: 762–768.

45. Boka G, Anglade P, Wallach D, et al. Immunocytochemical analysis of tumor necrosis factor and its receptors in Parkinson's disease. Neurosci Lett 1994; 172: 151–154.

46. Mogi M, Harada M, Riederer P, et al. Tumor necrosis factor-alpha (TNF-alpha) increases both in the brain and in the cerebrospinal fluid from parkinsonian patients. Neurosci Lett 1994; 165: 208–210.

47. Tartaglia L, Weber R, Figari I, et al. The two different receptors for TNF mediate distinct cellular responses. Proc Nat Acad Sci USA 1991; 88: 9292–9296.

48. Tartaglia L, Rothe M, Hu YF, Goeddel D. Tumor necrosis factor's cytotoxic activity is signalled by the p55 TNF receptor. Cell 1993; 73: 213–216.

49. Hunot S, Brugg B, Ricard D, et al. Nuclear translocation of NFκB is increased in dopaminergic neurons of patients with Parkinson disease. Proc Natl Acad Sci USA 1997; 94: 7531–7536.

DISCUSSION

W. Tatton: Do you think there are enough neurons to do gel-shift assays on the substantia nigra of parkinsonian patients to look for AP1 binding?

Hirsch: No, there is a major problem using *in vitro* techniques on homogenates. We are dealing only with the remaining dopaminergic neurons and, among these, only a few degenerate. I would not therefore rely on negative results using gel-shift assays.

N. Tatton: You mentioned type 1 and type 2 TNF-α receptors on dopaminergic neurons. A recent *in vitro* study on glial cells demonstrated a differential distribution of these receptor sub-types and suggested that TNF-α excitation of the type 1 receptor would induce cytotoxic cell death and that seemed to be expressed on all the sites. In contrast, type 2 receptor stimulation resulted in increased transcription and the production of what seemed to be neuroprotective cytokines. I wondered if you knew which might be the predominantly active receptor on the dopaminergic neurons?

Hirsch: All I can say at present is that on dopaminergic neurons both receptors are present. I only showed one transduction pathway of TNF-α receptor. There is another pathway which can, by a different mechanism, play a role in activation of apoptosis. We are currently analyzing this and we already know that some mediators of this second pathway are present in the dopaminergic neurons.

Melamed: We have just finished a study in which we have shown that if cells are exposed to dopamine, translocation of NFκB into the nucleus also occurs, and they die. This indicates either that the TNF-α receptor does not need to be involved for translocation of NFκB and apoptosis, or that dopamine activates TNF-α in a way that we still do not understand. Is it mandatory that if NFκB is translocated to the nucleus the cell is destined to die and there is no way back? Secondly, I would like to draw your attention to the situation in multiple sclerosis. In MS patients, many cytokines are found near the demyelinated lesions. Are these responsible for demyelination or are they produced by migratory macrophages in the region?

Hirsch: There is no proof that when NFκB is translocated in the nucleus the neuron is destined to die. Yet, what may be common between your model and ours is that the production of oxygen free radicals also occurs. Perhaps this is the factor that activates the translocation of NFκB and also is responsible for cell death. By using various compounds which inhibit increased production of oxygen free radicals, we can prevent translocation of NFκB.

Melamed: In our model, translocation of NFκB to the nucleus was totally blocked by the addition of N-acetylcysteine to the system.

Hirsch: Exactly. We have to think more generally about oxygen free radicals, not only as compounds that directly attack proteins, DNA, lipids and so on, but also as another type of messenger which may activate some specific genes. Concerning the second part of your question on reversibility, I do not know the answer and we have no proof that translocation of NFκB is directly involved in cell death or the activation of this process. It may be an attempt by the cell to protect itself. There is certainly contradictory data in the literature suggesting that NFκB translocation could either be deleterious or neuroprotective.

Langston: Are there any other cytokines we should be looking for? Secondly, can you think of any way in which apoptotic cell death might produce a Lewy body during the process?

Hirsch: Dr. Riederer discussed other cytokines earlier. The three I mentioned were present in the substantia nigra, but I do not know if other cytokines have been studied in the glial cells in the substantia nigra. We also have to look at the striatum. Secondly, we have tried very hard to find cells with both Lewy bodies and apoptotic features but have never found both in the same cell. I do not know if this means anything and perhaps the two phenomena are completely different.

Polymeropoulos: Do you see NFκB immunoreactivity within the Lewy body?

Hirsch: We have not looked at the Lewy bodies using double-staining techniques but this should be done.

Polymeropoulos: NFκB is very well regulated inside cells and its half-life is very short. How does that fit with your mechanism?

Hirsch: NFκB can activate different genes, so I do not think that it is that short-lived or that its presence within the cytoplasm is regulated in such a rapid manner. However, the translocation of NFκB is probably regulated relatively rapidly, so that it is only present in the nucleus for a few hours. This information comes from studies performed *in vitro*, in which NFκB is present in the nucleus for about 4 hours. We do not know what the situation is *in vivo*.

Youdim: We identified reactive microglia some years ago with the same staining technique. When microglia are co-cultured with dopaminergic neurons they do kill them. You have developed another part of the cascade, a series of events in which perhaps the initial event may be glial-mediated free radical production, which is a good therapeutic target. Dr. McGeer has shown benefits by directing activity against this target with indomethacin and now cyclosporin. More recently, PK 1195, which was developed for binding peripheral benzodiazepine receptors, has been shown to be an effective anti-inflammatory drug with no side effects. Clearly this has clinical potential.

[236]

Schapira: There is now a considerable volume of literature on inflammatory changes in Alzheimer's disease and I wonder if you could compare and contrast the changes that you found in PD?

Hirsch: Dr. Youdim mentioned the work of Dr. McGeer's group who have found similar results in patients with Alzheimer's disease. We have also shown that in the basal forebrain cholinergic column in which there is cell loss in Alzheimer's disease, a few neurons also show translocation of NFκB. These phenomena are not specific for a given disease but appear to be associated with the neurodegenerative process.

Olanow: It is interesting that prospective clinical studies of anti-inflammatory agents in Alzheimer's disease have largely been negative so far.

Hirsch: This points to the difficulty of targeting the drug to the correct places in the brain, as we are dealing with a few neurons within a given structure and they are almost impossible to target specifically.

Caraceni: Do you think this is a reactive process that induces progression of the disease or could it be the primary process that causes the disease?

Hirsch: I have no answer to that question. As far as the number of cells is concerned, I would suggest that it is mostly a very slow process, occurring locally within the substantia nigra. Interestingly, we found clusters of cells displaying NFκB in the nucleus within the substantia nigra in glial cells expressing TNF-α. This would appear to confirm that it is a local process within the substantia nigra. But it does not indicate if it is primary or secondary.

Marsden: The interpretation of all these changes could indicate exposure to either the causative factor of PD which is still ongoing at the time of the patient's death, or to triggering of these events which then continue as a secondary phenomenon. Have you looked at these phenomena in post-encephalitic parkinsonian brains?

Hirsch: Unfortunately we do not have brains of post-encephalitic patients. In this disease, the primary insult is probably no longer present at the time of death, thus what we would be looking for at post-mortem would not be the primary insult. Similarly it would be interesting to look at MPTP-intoxicated humans.

Marsden: Dr. Perl, how much activated microglia do you see in the late stage post-encephalitic cases?

Perl: We have not stained our post-encephalitic specimens for activated microglia, but I would guess that it is likely to be fairly extensive. There is much tissue destruction and evidence of a glial reaction in these cases, even though the insult may have been 70 years ago.

CHAPTER SEVENTEEN

Neuroprotective and neurorestorative properties of GDNF

DON M. GASH[1], ZHIMING ZHANG[1],
AND GREG GERHARDT[2]

[1]Department of Anatomy and Neurobiology and Center for Magnetic Resonance Imaging and Spectroscopy, University of Kentucky College of Medicine, Lexington, Kentucky, USA and [2]Departments of Psychiatry and Pharmacology, University of Colorado Health Sciences Center, Denver, Colorado, USA

Glial cell line-derived neurotrophic factor (GDNF) is the first member of a new family of trophic factors distantly related to the transforming growth factor-β superfamily.[1,2] It is synthesized by many cell types and effects the survival and development of a diverse set of neuronal and non-neuronal cells.[3-6] A related trophic factor, neurturin, has recently been identified and cloned, and shares a 42% homology with mature GDNF.[7]

Dopaminergic trophic factors have long been considered capable of halting or reversing degeneration of the nigrostriatal dopamine system in Parkinson's disease (PD). Dopamine neurons in the substantia nigra of the midbrain are the principal target of the pathophysiological processes underlying parkinsonism. Their injury and subsequent degeneration leads to the profound depletion of basal ganglia dopamine levels which characterizes the pathology underlying the disease.[8,9] A working hypothesis is that GDNF exerts direct trophic effects on dopamine neurons which are neurorestorative and/or neuroprotective. Neuroprotection is defined as the prevention or amelioration of injury to a cell, whereas neurorestoration is the process of recovery that occurs after an injury. It is not easy to separate the two processes. For example, if GDNF is administered shortly before a lesion and increased neuronal survival is found, restoration may still be involved. This would be the case if sufficient GDNF remained *in situ* in GDNF recipients, so that rapid regeneration could ensue following the injury. Likewise, GDNF administration shortly after a lesion does not ensure that only restorative processes are being studied, since under these circumstances GDNF could induce protective responses to the developing lesion. Converging evidence suggests that GDNF has both properties, and different mechanisms of action may be involved in producing the two effects.

NEURORESTORATION

Recovery from nigrostriatal injury in rodents

Injection of 6-hydroxydopamine (6-OHDA) into the nigral region of rats results in some neuronal injury within 24 h. The lesion continues to evolve and appears complete by the fifth day. Thus, if trophic factor administration is delayed for a week or more following nigral infusion of 6-OHDA, the restorative effects of GDNF should be apparent, rather than the protective effects. With a four-week interval between the lesion and trophic factor treatment, a significant decrease in apomorphine-induced rotational behavior was observed by one week after a single injection of 100 µg GDNF into the supranigral region.[10] Dopamine levels in the substantia nigra were three-fold higher five weeks after trophic factor administration.

A number of morphological and functional features of the midbrain dopamine neurons are restored by GDNF. The number of neurons expressing tyrosine hydroxylase (TH, the rate-limiting enzyme in dopamine synthesis), the number of TH+ neurites, and TH activity levels are all significantly increased.[11,12] The effects from a single injection of GDNF last for at least a month, and amphetamine- and potassium/amphetamine-evoked release of dopamine in the substantia nigra is significantly elevated.[13]

GDNF injection into either the lateral ventricles or into the midbrain promoted recovery of nigral dopamine neurons in rats.[12,14] Autoradiographic analysis with ^{125}I-GDNF has shown penetration of many brain areas including the striatum and substantia nigra.[14] In mice with degeneration of nigrostriatal dopamine neurons and processes induced by systemic 1-methyl-4-phenyl-1,2,3,6-tetrahydropyridine (MPTP) treatment, striatal or nigral administration of GDNF begun a week after the lesion promoted recovery of midbrain dopamine levels.[15] Some recovery of striatal dopamine levels was also seen in mice receiving striatal, but not nigral, injections of GDNF.

Some effects from GDNF remain for weeks following a single treatment, but the time course for expression of features induced by GDNF administration is complex. For example, normal young adult rats showed an increase in the distance traveled in an activity box by two days after a single intracerebral GDNF injection.[16] Activity levels remained elevated for another five days and then gradually fell to control levels. While the velocity of the movements was not different from age-matched controls at one week, GDNF recipients were faster at three weeks.[18]

Recovery from nigrostriatal injury in nonhuman primates

Rhesus monkeys have brain organization and function closer to that of humans, and neuronal degeneration of the nigrostriatal dopaminergic system was modeled using MPTP.[18-21] The lesion was produced by infusion of MPTP via the right carotid artery to create a hemiparkinsonian model,[20,21] with a minimum interval of six weeks between the last MPTP treatment and initiation of trophic factor therapy. Regardless of the route of administration of GDNF, behavioral improvement was evident by one week and reached statistical significance by two weeks.[23] This functional recovery could be maintained by monthly injections into the right lateral ventricle. Improvements have been found in three of the cardinal features of PD – bradykinesia, rigidity and postural stability.[23-25] On the less severely lesioned left side, the number of dopamine neurons was increased by 50%, the neurons were 18% larger and more dopaminergic fibers were evident when compared to vehicle recipients. GDNF therefore not only upregulates phenotypic markers in injured primate dopamine neurons but also promotes neuronal growth and elaboration of neurites.

The effects of GDNF on the neurochemistry of primate dopamine neurons injured by MPTP toxicity was evaluated in monkeys three weeks after their third monthly ventricular infusion of trophic factor. Significant increases in dopamine levels were seen only in the severely lesioned right substantia nigra, ventral tegmental area and globus pallidus. The behavioral actions of GDNF in reducing movement dysfunctions in parkinsonian rhesus monkeys may be due to its dopaminergic effects at these sites.

Dose-dependent improvements in movement functions were seen in parkinsonian rhesus monkeys receiving monthly ventricular injections of 100–1000 µg GDNF.[25] After trophic factor treatment was discontinued, the parkinsonian features in most animals began to return to baseline levels within 60 days, but the functional improvements in monkeys receiving 300 µg GDNF/month were maintained over the 120-day washout period.

The primary adverse effect of GDNF treatment has been weight loss, but little is known about the long term effects of trophic factor treatment on the mature nervous system. The only adverse consequence from stopping trophic factor treatment was a loss of benefit and a gradual return towards the pretreatment condition.

The interaction between levodopa and GDNF has been evaluated in parkinsonian rhesus monkeys.[24] At baseline, each animal was tested for its dose-response to levodopa treatment. Levodopa alone produced dose-dependent improvements in parkinsonian features, but at higher levels typical levodopa-induced side effects (dyskinesias and dystonias) were prominent. Following two monthly injections of 300 µg GDNF or vehicle into the right lateral ventricle, GDNF improved motor functions comparably to levodopa, but combined GDNF–levodopa treatment was the most efficacious. Not only were parkinsonian features reduced to their lowest levels with increasing doses of levodopa, but levodopa-induced side effects were significantly ameliorated. In addition, weight loss following GDNF administration was attenuated by levodopa treatment.

The induction of neuroprotective changes in dopamine neurons by GDNF was demonstrated by varying the timing between GDNF infusion into the substantia nigra before a 6-OHDA lesion from 0 to 24 h.[26] Significantly increased survival of nigral dopamine neurons was found in male rats receiving 10 µg of GDNF at either 6, 12 or 24 h before an intranigral 6-OHDA lesion. GDNF pretreatment was most effective at the 6 h time point, with virtually 100% of the neurons surviving the subsequent 6-OHDA lesion. No significant improvement was evident in rats pretreated with GDNF 1 h prior to the lesion, implying that protective mechanisms are operating at the 6–24 h time points. If restoration was involved, it should have depended upon residual GDNF levels after the lesion and survival should have increased with the shortest intervals between GDNF treatment and the 6-OHDA lesion.

Another important difference between the protective and restorative effects of GDNF was seen in the striatum. Striatal dopamine levels and dopaminergic functions were preserved with GDNF pretreatment. The reduction in striatal dopamine release from methamphetamine-induced injury, as measured by potassium-evoked dopamine overflow, can be prevented by GDNF pretreatment 24 h prior to exposure to the toxin.[27] In contrast, where 6-OHDA lesions or axotomy have either severely injured or severed dopamine projections to the rat striatum[10,28–30] GDNF post-treatment has not restored striatal function.

TWO FOR ONE: PROTECTION AND RESTORATION

The ideal antiparkinsonian drug would be both neuroprotective and neurorestorative. A challenge in future studies will be to define dosing protocols and delivery systems for GDNF which optimize both actions. Several studies using novel methods for chronic delivery of GDNF into the nigrostriatal pathway have already been reported in rodents.[30]

Another approach has utilized adenovirus vectors to transfect cells in adult rats to produce GDNF.[31,32] When rats with transfected nigral cells were challenged with an intranigral 6-OHDA injection a week later, 75% of the striatal projecting neurons in the substantia nigra survived, compared to only 25–30% in non-transfected and adenovirus vector controls.[31] When cells in the striatum were transfected via adenoviral vectors and 6-OHDA later injected into the striatum, approximately 60% of TH+ neurons were preserved in the nigra of GDNF-transfected rats *versus* 40% in controls.[32] Survival of nigral dopamine neurons also correlated with reduction in amphetamine-induced rotation behavior.

SUMMARY

- GDNF both protects and promotes recovery of the injured nigrostriatal dopamine system and improves motor functions in both rodent and nonhuman primate models of PD.

- The neurorestorative effects of a single administration of GDNF last for at least one month and can be maintained in rhesus monkeys by monthly injections. Adult midbrain dopamine neurons stimulated by GDNF show increased cell size, neuritic extent and expression of phenotypic markers.

- In parkinsonian nonhuman primates, GDNF treatment improves the cardinal features of PD: bradykinesia, rigidity and postural instability.

- While intracerebral administration is necessary because of the blood–brain barrier, intraventricular, intrastriatal and intranigral routes of administration have also been found to be efficacious in rodents and nonhuman primates.

- GDNF induces neuroprotective changes in dopamine neurons which are active within hours following trophic factor administration.

- The powerful neuroprotective and neurorestorative properties of GDNF seen in preclinical studies suggests trophic factors may play a role in treating PD.

ACKNOWLEDGMENTS

This work was supported by USPHS grants NS09199 (GG), AG06434 (GG), NS35642 (DG) and contracts with Amgen (DG, ZZ, GG).

REFERENCES

1. Lin L-FH, Doherty DH, Lile JD, Bektesh S, Collins F. GDNF: A glial cell line-derived neurotrophic factor for midbrain dopaminergic neurons. Science 1993; 260: 1130–1132.

2. Lin, L.-F.H., Zhang TJ, Collins F, Armes LG. Purification and initial characterization of rat B49 glial cell line-derived neurotrophic factor. J Neurochem 1994; 63: 758–768.

3. Moore MW, Klein RD, Fariñas I, Sauer H, Armanini M, Phillips H., Reichardt LF, Ryan AM, Carver-Moore K, Rosenthal A. Renal and neuronal abnormalities in mice lacking GDNF. Nature 1996; 382: 76–79.

4. Pichel JG, Shen L, Sheng HZ, Granholm A-C, Drago J, Grinberg A, Lee EJ, Huang SP, Saarma M, Hoffer BJ, Sariola H, Westphal H. Defects in enteric innervation and kidney development in mice lacking GDNF. Nature 1996; 382: 73–76.

5. Sánchez MP, Silos-Santiago I, Frisén J, He B, Lira SA, Barbacid M. Renal agenesis and the absence of enteric neurons in mice lacking GDNF. Nature 1996; 382: 70–73.

6. Trupp M, Belluardo N, Funakoshi H, Ibanez C. Complementary and over-lapping expression of glial cell line-derived neurotrophic factor (GDNF), c-ret proto-oncogene, and GDNF receptor α indicates multiple mechanisms of trophic actions in the adult CNS. J Neurosci 1997; 17: 3553–3567.

7. Kotzbauer PT, Lampe PA, Heuckeroth RO, Golden JP, Creedon DJ, Johnson Jr EM, Milbrandt J. Neurturin, a relative of glial cell line-derived neurotrophic factor. Nature 1996; 384: 467–470.

8. Jellinger K. Overview of morphological changes in Parkinson's disease. Adv Neurol 1986; 45: 1–18.

9. Hornykiewicz O. Parkinson's disease and the adaptive capacity of the nigrostriatal dopamine system: possible neuro-chemical mechanisms. Adv Neurol 1993; 60: 140–147.

10. Hoffer BJ, Hoffman A, Bowenkamp K, Huettl P, Hudson J, Martin D, Lin L-F, Gerhardt GA. Glial cell line-derived neurotrophic factor reverses toxin-induced injury to midbrain dopa-minergic neurons *in vivo*. Neurosci Lett 1994; 182: 107–111.

11. Bowenkamp KE, Hoffman AF, Gerhardt GA, Henry MA, Biddle PT, Hoffer BJ, Granholm A-C. Glial cell line-derived neurotrophic factor supports survival of injured midbrain dopaminergic neurons. J Comp Neurol 1995; 355: 479–489.

12. Lapchak PA, Miller PJ, Collins F, Jiao, S. Glial cell line-derived neurotrophic factor attenuates behavioural deficits and regulates nigrostriatal dopaminergic and peptidergic markers in 6-hydroxydopamine-lesioned adult rats: comparison of intraventricular and intranigral delivery. Neurosci 1997; 78: 61–72.

13. Hoffman AF, van Horne CG, Eken S, Hoffer BJ, Gerhardt GA. *In vivo* microdialysis studies of somatodendritic dopamine release in the rat substantia nigra: effects of unilateral 6-OHDA lesions and GDNF. Exp Neurol 1997; 147: 130–141.

14. Lapchak PA, Jiao S, Collins F, Miller PJ. Glial cell line-derived neurotrophic factor: distribution and pharmacology in the rat following a bolus intraventricular injection. Brain Res 1997; 747: 92–102.

15. Tomac A, Lindqvist E, Lin L-FH, Ogren SO, Young D, Hoffer BJ, Olson L. Protection and repair of the nigrostriatal dopaminergic system by GDNF *in vivo*. Nature 1995; 373: 335–339.

16. Hudson J, Granholm A-C, Gerhardt GA, Henry MA, Hoffman A, Biddle P, Leela NS, Mackerlova L, Lile JD, Collins F, Hoffer BJ. Glial cell line-derived neurotrophic factor augments midbrain

dopaminergic circuits *in vivo*. Brain Res Bull 1995; 36: 425–432.

17. Hebert MA, Van Horne CG, Hoffer BJ, Gerhardt GA. Functional effects of GDNF in normal rat striatum: pre-synaptic studies using in vivo electro-chemistry and microdialysis. J Pharmaco Exp Ther 1996; 279: 1181–1190.

18. Langston JW, Ballard P, Tetrud JW, Irwin I. Chronic parkinsonism in humans due to a product of meperidine-analog synthesis. Science 1983; 219: 979–980.

19. Langston JW, Forno LS, Rebert CS, Irwin I. Selective nigral toxicity after systemic administration of 1-methyl-4-phenyl-1,2,5,6-tetrahydropyrine (MPTP) in the squirrel monkey. Brain Res 1984; 292: 390–394.

20. Bankiewicz KS, Oldfield EH, Chiueh CC, Doppman JL, Jacobowitz DM, Kopin, IJ. Hemiparkinsonism in monkeys after unilateral internal carotid artery infusion of 1-methyl-4-phenyl-1,2,3,6-tetrahydropyridine (MPTP). Life Sci 1986; 39: 7-16.

21. Ovadia A, Zhang Z, Gash DM. Increased susceptibility to MPTP toxicity in middle-aged rhesus monkeys. Neurobiol Aging 1995; 16: 931–937.

22. Gash DM, Zhang Z, Cass WA, Ovadia A, Simmerman L, Martin D, Russell D, Collins F, Hoffer BJ, Gerhardt GA. Morphological and functional effects of intranigrally administered GDNF in normal rhesus monkeys. J Comp Neurol 1995; 363: 345–358.

23. Gash DM, Zhang Z, Ovadia A, Cass W, Yi A, Simmerman L, Russell D, Martin D, Lapchak P, Collins F, Hoffer BJ, Gerhardt GA. Functional recovery in parkinsonian monkeys treated with GDNF. Nature 1996; 380: 252–255.

24. Miyoshi Y, Zhang Z, Ovadia A, Lapchak PA, Collins F, Hilt D, Lebel C, Kryscio R, Gash DM. Glial cell line-derived neurotrophic factor-levodopa inter-actions and reduction of side effects in parkinsonian monkeys. Ann Neurol 1997; 42: 208–214.

25. Zhang Z, Miyoshi Y, Lapchak PA, Collins F, Hilt D, Lebel C, Kryscio R, Gash DM. Dose response to intraventricular glial cell line-derived neurotrophic factor administration in parkinsonian monkeys. J Pharmaco Exp Ther 1997; 282: 1396–1401.

26. Kearns CM, Cass WA, Smoot K, Kryscio R, Gash DM. GDNF protection against 6-OHDA: time dependence and requirement for protein synthesis. J Neurosci 1997; 17: 7111–7118.

27. Cass WA. GDNF selectively protects dopamine neurons over serotonin neurons against the neurotoxic effects of methamphetamine. J Neurosci 1996; 16: 8132–8139.

28. Beck KD, Valverde J, Alexi T, Poulson K, Moffat B, Vandlen RA, Rosenthal A, Hefti F. Mesencephalic dopaminergic neurons protected by GDNF from axotomy-induced degeneration in the adult brain. Nature 1995; 373: 339–341.

29. Winkler C, Sauer H, Lee CS, Bjorklund A. Short-term GDNF treatment provides long term rescue of lesioned nigral dopaminergic neurons in a rat model of Parkinson's disease. J Neurosci 1996; 16: 7206–7215.

30. Tseng JL, Baetge EE, Zurn AD, Aebischer P. GDNF reduces drug-induced rotational behavior after medial forebrain bundle transection by a mechanism not involving striatal dopamine. J Neurosci 1997; 17: 325–333.

31. Choi-Lundberg DL, Lin Q, Chang Y-N, Chiang YL, Hay CM, Mohajeri H, Davidson BL, Bohn MC. Dopaminergic neurons protected from degeneration by GDNF gene therapy. Science 1997; 275: 838–841.

32. Bilang-Bleuel A, Revah F, Colin P, Locquet I, Robert J-J, Mallet J, Horellou P. Intrastriatal injection of an adenoviral vector expressing glial cell line-derived neurotrophic factor prevents dopaminergic neuron degeneration and behavioral impairment in a rat model of Parkinson's disease. Proc Natl Acad Sci USA 1997; 94: 8818–8823.

[245]

DISCUSSION

Obeso: To make these results meaningful relative to clinical PD, it will be necessary to use an experimental design in which there is a preceding or ongoing lesion followed by the administration of GDNF. I will be much more enthused if you can show a protective effect with this type of design. What are your thoughts about using such a reverse scenario, and is there any model for a chronic progressive lesion that would permit you to assess the effect of a neuroprotective treatment and its putative mechanism of action?

Gash: That is a very important question. It is also difficult to set up a model of progressive neurodegeneration in Rhesus monkeys so that one could try to assess protection and/or restoration. With a progressive lesion, one also has to consider the time of administration of GDNF. Do we give it early and try to see protection or do we give it late and look for restoration? I think we could do such a study in the MPTP model and preliminary data, as discussed in the presentation, indicate that GDNF has a restorative effect if given late and a protective effect if given before the MPTP in mice. There is some evidence from other groups that GDNF may protect against a progressive lesion. Dr. Björklund's group injected 6-OHDA into the rat striatum, and this led to a progressive loss of dopamine neurons. There was relative preservation of dopamine neurons with GDNF administration. Whether this was a restorative or protective effect is much harder to interpret. If GDNF is to be used clinically in PD, it would obviously be given to patients with a progressive neurodegenerative disease. It will be valuable if it can be shown to either promote restoration or rescue of injured neurons or if it protects against ongoing neuronal degeneration.

Olanow: It is not so clear that 6-OHDA induces a progressive lesion. If anything, striatal dopamine levels and behavioral effects tend to improve over time, probably as a result of compensatory mechanisms.

Leenders: We are currently performing studies in Rhesus monkeys which are implanted on one side with GDNF-producing cells before receiving MPTP systemically. Using fluorodopa PET scans, on the implanted side we see that the fluorodopa uptake in the striatum is better preserved than on the non-protected side. This would be in line with your studies. You mentioned that GDNF protects against MPTP toxicity. In addition, you mention that GDNF administration is associated with a 150–200% increase in the number of TH-positive cells compared to normal. What is the explanation for that?

Gash: In rats that have received GDNF and 6-OHDA, we have consistently been able to count more than 100% of the cells that we would expect to see in normal animals. Our interpretation is that GDNF induces higher levels of TH, the marker we are using, and cells that we might otherwise miss because they have low titers of TH are now detectable because of the GDNF stimulation. We do not believe that we are inducing new cells to produce TH, but rather, because of increased TH expression we are getting a more accurate view of the number of dopamine cells in the nigra.

Leenders: Is there any deficit in endogenous levels of GDNF after the 6-OHDA lesions?

Gash: GDNF levels in the striatum of the normal adult rat are relatively low. Therefore it is difficult to determine if there is a reduction in association with any toxin or with PD itself. There are GDNF receptors in the striatum of the non-human primate, but we do not know whether, other ligands also interact with receptors that have been identified as being GDNF receptors.

De Yebenes Justo: If I remember correctly, in your treated monkeys you found an increase in the size of the arborization of neurons in the substantia nigra, but there was no increase in the number of TH-positive neurons?

Gash: In our 1996 paper in *Nature*, we reported that on the side where the carotid was infused with MPTP, there was a very severe lesion with a marked loss of cells in the nigra. On the severely lesioned side, it was difficult to determine what effect GDNF had on cell numbers because of the variability and the relatively small number of animals that we studied. We had a less severe lesion on the contralateral side. Here, GDNF infusion induced an increase in cell numbers compared to vehicle-treated animals.

De Yebenes Justo: We have obtained the same findings in a more chronic MPTP model. Your data were obtained only four weeks after the treatment. I wonder if you now have new long-term data that show changes in numbers of TH-positive neurons? After intracarotid administration of MPTP, we find that if the animals are maintained for a very long period of time, they will continue to deteriorate after an initial period of recovery. Dr. Leenders has performed sequential striatal fluorodopa PET scans in these animals and found that MPTP-treated animals continue to show a decrease in their striatal fluorodopa uptake. I wonder, therefore, if there is progressive deterioration in the animal after administration of MPTP, both in terms of behavior and striatal fluorodopa uptake. Would prolonged treatment with GDNF lead to any increase in number of TH-positive neurons, even on the more lesioned side, in these animals?

Gash: Behaviorally, we find relative stability for about two years after an MPTP lesion in the hemiparkinsonian model, and find no significant deterioration. You may have different data on that. We had several monkeys in our colony which were four years post MPTP treatment. GDNF infusion produced significant behavioral improvement in these animals. So we can see functional improvement with GDNF even four years after MPTP treatment.

Olanow: Are you able to give us any information about the results of the early clinical trials in PD? Specifically, was there clinical improvement and did they suffer side effects such as the weight loss and flu like symptoms that have been seen in other human and animal trials of trophic factors?

Gash: At this time I do not have any information. I am also very curious as to what will be found.

Marsden: I understand that they have not yet reached the doses of GDNF that might be predicted to have a clinical effect.

Gash: They started with very low doses of GDNF and, given some of the problems with the other trophic factors that have gone into clinical trials for ALS and Alzheimer's disease, they are being extremely cautious about escalating the dose.

Marsden: I think they are also having some problems with vomiting even at small doses.

Shoulson: Can you comment on the delivery of GDNF via the intraventricular route in your non-human primates?

Gash: We are using the same approach that is being used in the clinical trials. That is, we are injecting GDNF into the lateral ventricle. In preliminary studies with iodinated GDNF in the rat, we found that some GDNF does cross the ventricular wall and concentrates in the nigral area. I would like to repeat this with more animals, but the initial studies are encouraging. In the one or two Rhesus monkeys in which we have also done this, we are also seeing accumulation of GDNF in the nigra.

Polymeropoulos: The requirement for protein synthesis to obtain a protective effect with GDNF is intriguing. Do you have any idea what these protein factors are?

Gash: We are looking at this right now in a large collaborative study, but I do not have anything ready for presentation at this time.

Polymeropoulos: Have you looked at the other side of the coin, namely protein degradation? What happens if protein degradation is inhibited and then GDNF is administered?

Gash: We have not looked at that, but it would be an interesting experiment to do.

W. Tatton: Have you used any other agents beside cycloheximide to inhibit protein synthesis, since there is evidence to suggest that cycloheximide may at least partially mediate its effect by acting on apoptotic proteases?

Gash: That too is ongoing.

SECTION IV

Apoptosis

CHAPTER EIGHTEEN

Programmed cell death: does it play a role in Parkinson's disease?

ROBERT E. BURKE AND NIKOLAI G. KHOLODILOV

Department of Neurology, Columbia University, New York, New York, USA

Programmed cell death (PCD) is a form of death in which genetic programs intrinsic to the cell act to bring about its destruction.[1] It is distinguished from passive cell death due to harsh environmental factors. Various lines of evidence now suggest a role for PCD in the pathogenesis of neurodegenerative disorders[2,3]. PCD can certainly occur in the human central nervous system in some pathologic states, such as AIDS encephalopathy.[4] While PCD was first identified as a normal, physiologic event which occurs abundantly in the nervous system during development, it clearly also has a pathologic role in the destruction of mature neurons in the mammalian CNS.[5]

Although the growth of interest in PCD is recent, it has long been known that cells spontaneously degenerate during normal development.[6,7] In the nervous system, this spontaneous cell death has been termed programmed, developmental, or natural cell death. The concept of PCD advanced with the definition of apoptosis as a specific morphologic form of PCD.[8] The essential features of apoptosis include early preservation of intracellular organelles (such as mitochondria), the formation of electron-dense nuclear chromatin masses, preservation of nuclear and cellular membranes, formation of membrane-enclosed apoptotic bodies, and the lack of an inflammatory response. Many, but not all, of the deaths which occur during normal development of the nervous system conform to the morphology of apoptosis.[9]

While developmental neuronal death in the mammalian nervous system is probably not predetermined, it may be mediated by genetic programs intrinsic to the cell. Evidence for this derives from studies in the nematode *C.elegans*.[10] In this organism, precisely 131 cells undergo programmed cell death during development. These deaths are mediated by genes involved in the regulation of the death process, or in the killing, engulfment, or degradation of the cells.[10] One gene, *ced-3*, is homologous to interleukin-1β-converting enzyme (ICE), and to a number of other cysteine proteases (the caspases)[11] which have been implicated in PCD in mammalian cells.[12] Another gene, *ced-9*, is a negative regulator of PCD in *C.elegans* and is homologous to *bcl-2*, a negative regulator of PCD in mammalian cells.[13] Thus, the genetic pathways of PCD in *C.elegans* have been a useful model of pathways in higher organisms. Further evidence that PCD is mediated by intrinsic genetic programs is that drugs which block gene transcription or translation also block neuronal death in some models of PCD induced either by trophic factor withdrawal[14] or by deprivation of target-derived support.[15]

The most definitive morphologic evidence of apoptosis is ultrastructural.[16] It is critically important to identify intranuclear clumping of chromatin.[8] True apoptotic chromatin clumping is extremely and homogeneously electron-dense, has distinct, well-defined edges, and is located either subjacent to the nuclear membrane or within the nuclear space. Another valuable morphologic technique is the demonstration of free 3'-ends generated by endonuclease cleavage of genomic DNA during PCD, by *in situ* terminal deoxynucleotidyl transferase-mediated dUTP nick end labeling (TUNEL)[17] or *in situ* end labeling (ISEL). Since this method labels free 3'-ends generated not only by orderly internucleosomal cleavage but also the random DNA breakage characteristic of necrosis,[18,19] it is critical to visualize apoptotic morphology as well as the positive staining reaction. Apoptotic chromatin clumps can sometimes be visualized by TUNEL alone, but their demonstration with a basophilic dye, such as a thionin Nissl stain, is often required.[20] The simple demonstration of free 3'-ends with a positive TUNEL reaction without visualization of apoptotic morphology does not constitute definitive evidence of apoptosis in particular or PCD in general.

APOPTOSIS OCCURS IN DOPAMINE NEURONS OF THE SUBSTANTIA NIGRA DURING NORMAL DEVELOPMENT, AND IS INDUCIBLE IN MODELS OF DISEASE

The possibility that PCD may occur within dopaminergic neurons was first suggested by the observation that an excitotoxic lesion to the target striatum during development led to a reduced adult number of nigrostriatal dopaminergic neurons,[21,22] in spite of the axon-sparing nature of the lesion and in the absence of any direct injury to the nigra. That the nigrostriatal dopaminergic system may be target-dependent during development was also confirmed by the ability of striatal components to support *in vitro* the viability and differentiation of developing dopaminergic neurons.[23–26] These observations suggested that the dopaminergic nigrostriatal system may develop according to principles of classic neurotrophic theory[27,28] in which a natural cell death event occurs in the substantia nigra pars compacta (SNpc), with morphology typical of apoptosis being demonstrated both by Nissl staining and suppressed silver staining.[29] A double-labeling technique has also been used to identify apoptotic natural cell death in phenotypically-defined dopaminergic neurons.[30] An initial major peak of natural cell death begins on embryonic day 20, and abates by postnatal day (PND) 8. A second minor peak occurs on PND 14. The occurrence of a major cell death event within the first post-natal week is in keeping with a reported decrement in the number of tyrosine hydroxylase (TH)-positive neurons in SN in the first postnatal week.[31]

Natural cell death in SNpc can be regulated during development. Excitotoxic injury to the striatum on PND 7 results in an eight-fold increase in the number of apoptotic profiles in the SN at 24 hours post-lesion.[32] These profiles are morphologically identical to those observed during natural cell death, and meet ultrastructural and 3' end-labeling criteria for apoptosis. Within SNpc, induction of cell death is identified within phenotypically-defined dopaminergic neurons, and during a two-week postnatal developmental window, the level of natural cell death is sensitive to target size.[33]

PCD in Animal Models of Parkinsonism

If early target support is necessary for the viability of dopaminergic neurons, then early developmental destruction of their terminals with the selective neurotoxin 6-hydroxydopamine (6-OHDA) should interfere with attainment of support, and result in induced death. Intrastriatal injection of 6-OHDA in developing animals does result in the induction of apoptotic death in dopamine neurons of the SNpc[34] in a developmentally-dependent manner, with a major effect during the first two postnatal weeks but only a minor effect at later times. Interestingly, intrastriatal 6-OHDA induces two different morphologies of cell death in the SNpc, apoptotic and non-apoptotic.[34] This suggests either that the toxin induces cell death by two different mechanisms, or that the same fundamental mechanism induces an apoptotic morphology in less mature animals, and a non-apoptotic morphology in more mature animals. 6-OHDA itself may induce apoptosis directly, since it has been shown *in vitro* to induce apoptosis in PC12 cells.[35] However, 6-OHDA injected directly into SN in adults does not induce apoptosis.[36]

The 1-methyl-phenylpyridinium ion (MPP$^+$) can induce apoptotic morphology and DNA fragmentation in postnatal cerebellar granule cells in culture.[37] Subsequently, it has been shown to induce apoptosis in embryonic mesencephalon culture,[38] in differentiated[39] and undifferentiated[40] PC12 cells, and in a human neuroblastoma cell line.[41] Apoptotic cell death was not observed in SN *in vivo* following injection of MPTP at 40, 60 or 80 mg/kg given in four separate doses, administered every 2 hours.[42] However, in a chronic model in which MPTP was administered at 30 mg/kg daily for 5 days, apoptosis was observed in phenotypically-defined dopamine neurons.[43]

The weaver mouse is a genetic model of spontaneous degeneration of dopaminergic neurons of the SN, and of cerebellar granule cells. Cell death among cerebellar granule cells in weaver mice is apoptotic by morphologic and end-labeling criteria.[44–47] Apoptotic cell death occurs postnatally with equal magnitude in heterozygote and wild-type littermates[48] and therefore represents a natural cell death event, similar to that observed in rats.[29] Unique to weaver mice is non-apoptotic cell death which occurs later in the postnatal period than the apoptotic cell death event and which does not show positive end-labeling.[48]

PCD in PD – Does it Play a Role in Neuron Death?

There is evidence for apoptotic cell death in the SN in post-mortem Parkinson's disease (PD) brains.[49] Electron-dense intranuclear aggregates were detected, but they did not show clearly the characteristic features of apoptotic chromatin clumps. Another report identified positive TUNEL labeling in the SN of 4/7 patients with typical late-onset PD.[50] While free 3'-end labeling was demonstrated in neurons of the SN, it was not clear that the morphology was apoptotic. In a study of post-mortem brain tissue from patients with Alzheimer's disease (AD), PD and diffuse Lewy body disease (DLBD), some micrographs, particularly of DLBD, clearly showed *in situ* end-labeling with apoptotic morphology in neuromelanin-containing neurons of the SNpc,[51] thus presenting clear evidence for apoptosis in neurons in a degenerative disorder related to PD. There was also evidence for apoptotic bodies in the SNpc of patients with PD and DLBD. However, in another study, definitive apoptotic morphology could not be identified in a single neuron in the brains of 22 pathologically-confirmed cases of PD using *in situ* end-labeling.[52]

Thus, evidence for apoptotic morphology in the brains of patients with PD or related disorders is mixed. Three factors should be considered when reviewing this evidence. Firstly, PD and related disorders are due to neuronal degeneration which takes place over years, whereas in experimental models, apoptotic cell death occurs within a brief period of time. Secondly, ultrastructural studies on human post-mortem material are limited by the quality of tissue preservation. Thirdly, apoptosis is only one of the morphologies of PCD, thus inability to identify its features does not exclude a possible role for PCD. Better biochemical markers for PCD are clearly needed.

There are some interesting parallels between the neurochemical pathology of PD, and the biochemical correlates of PCD. Ubiquitin staining is observed in Lewy bodies,[53] and in degenerating neurites in PD brains.[54] Activation of polyubiquitin gene expression has been identified during developmental cell death.[55] Lewy bodies are composed of aggregates of neurofilaments,[56] they contain neurofilament antigens,[57] and are immunostainable with antibodies to phosphorylated neurofilaments.[58,59] The brain kinase cdk5 is the predominant cyclin-dependent kinase activity in brain,[60] and is likely to catalyze the *in vivo* phosphorylation of neurofilament proteins. Expression of cdk5 has been observed in Lewy bodies,[61,62] and in apoptotic profiles in induced PCD within the SN.[63]

One of the most important recent findings is the discovery that some forms of familial parkinsonism are due to a mutation in α-synuclein.[64] This mutation was identified in a single large Italian family[65] and in three smaller Greek kindreds. These families have a G to A substitution at position 209 within the fourth exon of the α-synuclein gene, resulting in an Ala to Thr substitution at amino acid position 53. Of particular interest is that human α-synuclein was originally identified by analysis of proteolytic fragments derived from senile plaques of AD.[66] Little is known about the neurobiology of the synucleins. The possibility of a relationship between α-synuclein and the processes of PCD is of interest. The model of induced death following striatal target lesion can be induced unilaterally[32] and is therefore ideal for the application of the differential display technique.[67,68] The two sides of the brain are identical in every way except for the induction of cell death on the experimental side, so differentially displayed products should be relevant to the death process. One of the first differentially displayed bands of interest was homologous to human α-synuclein[69] and was part of the 3'-untranslated region of rat synuclein 1. Most of the mRNA signal was localized to the SNpc, and increased expression of synuclein 1 protein was also identified.[70] The functional significance of this correspondence between synuclein 1 expression and induction of apoptotic neuron death in SN will require further exploration.

PCD IN PD – OTHER ISSUES

Even if PCD does not have a direct role in neuron death in PD, it may be relevant to other aspects of pathogenesis and treatment. For example, the likelihood of developing PD may depend on an individual's endowment of dopaminergic neurons in the SN. The mature number of dopaminergic neurons is likely to be regulated during development by target and other factors which control the magnitude of a natural cell death event which occurs among these neurons. Genetic and environmental factors which affect the regulation of this death event may, therefore, influence the likelihood of developing this disease.

A major new approach to the treatment of PD is that of transplantation of fetal mesencephalic dopaminergic neurons.[71–73] Very few transplanted dopaminergic neurons survive,[74] and their death was assumed to be mediated by tissue handling, local trauma, or the lack of a vascular supply. However, it has been shown recently that implanted mesencephalic tissue undergoes apoptotic cell death.[75] If the factors which regulate natural cell death in the SN can be identified, they could be utilized to augment cell survival in transplants.

PCD may also be relevant to the effects of chronic levodopa treatment on the parkinsonian brain. Some clinical evidence suggests that levodopa may aggravate PD.[76] If the metabolism of dopamine leads to oxidative stress, then augmentation of dopamine availability by ingestion of levodopa may worsen the underlying disease process. Dopamine or levodopa can induce apoptosis *in vitro*, and dopamine induces apoptosis in cultured embryonic chick sympathetic neurons.[77] Levodopa, in micromolar concentrations, induces apoptosis in PC12 cells, and this effect is inhibited by antioxidants.[78] As yet, there have been no *in vivo* studies on possible levodopa toxicity, utilizing methods to identify apoptosis.

Summary

- Programmed cell death occurs during development in dopamine neurons of the substantia nigra and has recently been implicated to play a role in the cell death that occurs in PD and other neurodegenerative disorders.

- Most of the evidence for an active role for PCD in these disorders is partial or indirect, and remains an area of active investigation.

- Whatever the role of PCD in the pathogenesis of these disorders, it is clear that developmental cell death and its regulation are major determinants of the mature number of neurons.

- α-Synuclein mutations have been detected in some patients with a familial form of PD. Interestingly α-synuclein has been shown to upregulate early in differential display in some models of apoptosis.

- It is likely that PCD and its regulation will have immediate and direct implications for fetal tissue implantation approaches to these disorders.

REFERENCES

1. Jacobson MD, Weil M, Raff MC. Programmed cell death in animal development. Cell 1997; 88: 347–354.

2. Bredesen DE. Neural apoptosis. Ann Neurol 1995; 38: 839–851.

3. Stefanis L, Burke RE, Greene LA. Apoptosis in neurodegenerative disorders. Curr Opin Neurol 1997; 10: 299–305.

4. Petito CK, Roberts B. Evidence of apoptotic cell death in HIV encephalitis. Am J Path 1995; 146: 1121–1130.

5. Nitatori T, Sato N, Waguri S, et al. Delayed neuronal death in the CA 1 pyramidal cell layer of the gerbil hippocampus following transient ischemia is apoptosis. J Neurosci 1995; 15: 1001–1011.

6. Glucksmann A. Cell deaths in normal vertebrate ontogeny. Biol Rev 1951; 26: 59–86.

7. Hamburger V. History of the discovery of neuronal death in embryos. J Neurobiol 1992; 23: 1116–1123.

8. Kerr JFR, Wyllie AH, Currie AR. Apoptosis: a basic biological phenomenon with wide-ranging implications in tissue kinetics. Br J Cancer 1972; 26: 239–257.

9. Oppenheim RW. Cell death during development of the nervous system. Ann Rev Neurosci 1991; 14: 453–501.

10. Ellis RE, Yuan J, Horvitz HR. Mechanisms and functions of cell death. Ann Rev Cell Biol 1991; 7: 663–698.

11. Alnemri ES, Livingston DJ, Nicholson DW, et al. Human ICE/CED-3 protease nomenclature. Cell 1996; 87: 171.

12. Martin SJ, Green DR. Protease activation during apoptosis: Death by a thousand cuts? Cell 1995; 82: 349–352.

13. Korsmeyer SJ. Regulators of cell death. Trends Genetics 1995; 11: 101–105.

14. Martin DP, Schmidt RE, DiStefano P, Lowry O, Carter J, Johnson E. Inhibitors of protein synthesis and RNA synthesis prevent neuronal death caused by nerve growth factor deprivation. J Cell Biol 1988; 106: 829–844.

15. Oppenheim RW, Prevette D, Tytell M, Homma S. Naturally occurring and induced neuronal death in the chick embryo in vivo requires protein and RNA synthesis: Evidence for the role of cell death genes. Dev Biol 1990; 138: 104–113.

16. Kerr JFR, Gobe GC, Winterford CM, Harmon BV. Anatomical methods in cell death. In, Schwartz LM, Osborne BA, eds, Methods in Cell Biology: Cell Death. New York: Academic Press, 1995: 1–27.

17. Gavrieli Y, Sherman Y, Ben-Sasson SA. Identification of programmed cell death in situ via specific labeling of nuclear DNA fragmentation. J Cell Biol 1992; 119: 493–501.

18. Grasl-Kraupp B, Ruttkay-Ndicky B, Koudelka H, Bukowska K, Bursch W, Schulte-Hermann R. In situ detection of fragmented DNA (TUNEL assay) fails to discriminate among apoptosis, necrosis, and autolytic cell death: A cautionary note. Hepatol 1995; 21: 1465–1468.

19. Ferrer I, Tortosa A, Macaya A, et al. Evidence of nuclear DNA fragmentation following hypoxia-ischemia in the infant rat brain, and transient forebrain ischemia in the adult gerbil. Brain Path 1994; 4: 115–122.

20. Oo TF, Henchcliffe C, Burke RE. Apoptosis in substantia nigra following developmental hypoxic-ischemic injury. Neurosci 1995; 69: 893–901.

21. Burke RE, Macaya A, DeVivo D, Kenyon N, Janec EM. Neonatal hypoxic-ischemic or excitotoxic striatal injury results in a decreased adult number of substantia nigra neurons. Neurosci 1992; 50: 559–569.

22. Macaya A, Burke RE. Effect of striatal lesion with quinolinate on the development of substantia nigra dopaminergic neurons: a quantitative morphological analysis. Dev Neurosci 1992; 14: 362–368.

23. Prochiantz A, di Porzio U, Kato A, Berger B, Glowinski J. *In vitro* maturation of mesencephalic dopaminergic neurons from mouse embryos is enhanced in presence of their striatal target cells. Proc Natl Acad Sci USA 1979; 76: 5387–5391.

24. Hemmendinger LM, Garber BB, Hoffmann PC, Heller A. Target neuron-specific process formation by embryonic mesencephalic dopamine neurons *in vitro*. Proc Nat Acad Sci USA 1981; 78: 1264–1268.

25. Hoffmann PC, Hemmendinger LM, Kotake C, Heller A. Enhanced dopamine cell survival in reaggregates containing target cells. Brain Res 1983; 274: 275–281.

26. Tomozawa Y, Appel SH. Soluble striatal extracts enhance development of mesencephalic dopaminergic neurons *in vitro*. Brain Res 1986; 399: 111–124.

27. Barde YA. Trophic factors and neuronal survival. Neuron 1989; 2: 1525–1534.

28. Clarke PGH. Neuronal death in the development of the vertebrate nervous system. Trends Neurosci 1985; 8: 345–349.

29. Janec E, Burke RE. Naturally occurring cell death during postnatal development of the substantia nigra of the rat. Mol Cell Neurosci 1993; 4: 30–35.

30. Oo TF, Burke RE. The time course of developmental cell death in phenotypically defined dopaminergic neurons of the substantia nigra. Dev Brain Res 1997; 98: 191–196.

31. Tepper JM, Damlama M, Trent F. Postnatal changes in the distribution and morphology of rat substantia nigra dopaminergic neurons. Neurosci 1994; 60: 469–477.

32. Macaya A, Munell F, Gubits RM, Burke RE. Apoptosis in substantia nigra following developmental striatal excitotoxic injury. Proc Natl Acad Sci USA 1994; 91: 8117–8121.

33. Kelly WJ, Burke RE. Apoptotic neuron death in rat substantia nigra induced by striatal excitotoxic injury is developmentally dependent. Neurosci Lett 1996; 220: 85–88.

34. Marti MJ, James CJ, Oo TF, Kelly WJ, Burke RE. Early developmental destruction of terminals in the striatal target induces apoptosis in dopamine neurons of the substantia nigra. J Neurosci 1997; 17: 2030–2039.

35. Walkinshaw G, Waters CM. Neurotoxin induced cell death in neuronal PC12 cells is mediated by induction of apoptosis. Neurosci 1994; 63: 975–987.

36. Jeon BS, Jackson-Lewis V, Burke RE. 6-Hydroxydopamine lesion of the rat substantia nigra: time course and morphology of cell death. Neurodegen 1995; 4: 131–137.

37. Dipasquale B, Marini AM, Youle RJ. Apoptosis and DNA degradation induced by 1-methyl-4-phenylpyridinium in neurons. Biochem Biophys Res Comm 1991; 181: 1442–1448.

38. Mochizuki H, Nakamura N, Nishi K, Mizuno Y. Apoptosis is induced by 1-methyl-4-phenylpyridinium ion (MPP+) in ventral mesencephalic striatal co-culture in rat. Neurosci Lett 1994; 170: 191–194.

39. Mutoh T, Tokuda A, Marini AM, Fujiki N. 1-methyl-4-phenylpyridinium kills differentiated PC12 cells with a concomitant change in protein phosphorylation. Brain Res 1994; 661: 51–55.

40. Hartley A, Stone JM, Heron C, Cooper JM, Schapira AHV. Complex I inhibitors induce dose dependent apoptosis in PC12 cells relevance to Parkinsons Disease. J Neurochem 1994; 63: 1987–1990.

41. Itano Y, Nomura Y. 1-Methyl-4-phenyl-pyridinium ion (MPP(+)) causes DNA

fragmentation and increases the Bcl-2 expression in human neuroblastoma, SH-SY5Y cells, through different mechanisms. Brain Res 1995; 704: 240–245.

42. Jackson-Lewis V, Jakowec M, Burke RE, Przedborski S. Time course and morphology of dopaminergic neuronal death caused by the neurotoxin 1-methyl-4-phenyl-1,2,3,6,-tetrahydro-pyridine. Neurodegen 1995; 4: 257–269.

43. Tatton NA, Kish SJ. *In situ* detection of apoptotic nuclei in the substantia nigra compacta of 1-methyl-4-phenyl-1,2,3,6-tetrahydropyridine-treated mice using terminal deoxynucleotidyl transferase labelling and acridine orange. Neurosci 1997; 77: 1037–1048.

44. Smeyne RJ, Goldowitz D. Development and death of external granular layer cells in the weaver mouse cerebellum: A quantitative study. J Neurosci 1989; 9: 1608–1620.

45. Migheli A, Attanasio A, Lee W-H, Bayer SA, Ghetti B. Detection of apoptosis in weaver cerebellum by electron microscopic *in situ* end-labeling of fragmented DNA. Neurosci Lett 1995; 199: 53–56.

46. Wullner U, Loschmann PA, Weller M, Klockgether T. Apoptotic cell death in the cerebellum of mutant weaver and lurcher mice. Neurosci Lett 1995; 200: 109–112.

47. Harrison SMW, Roffler-Tarlov S. Apoptotic and non-apoptotic cell death in the mouse mutant weaver. Soc Neurosci Abstr 1995; 424: 16.

48. Oo TF, Blazeski R, Harrison SMW, *et al.* Neuron death in the substantia nigra of weaver mouse occurs late in development and is not apoptotic. J Neurosci 1996; 16: 6134–6145.

49. Anglade P, Vyas S, Javoy-Agid F, *et al.* Apoptosis and autophagy in nigral neurons of patients with Parkinson's disease. Histol Histopathol 1997; 12: 25–31.

50. Mochizuki H, Goto K, Mori H, Mizuno Y. Histochemical detection of apoptosis in Parkinsons Disease. J Neurol Sci 1996; 137: 120–123.

51. Tompkins MM, Basgall EJ, Zamrini E, Hill WD. Apoptotic-like changes in Lewy-body-associated disorders and normal aging in substantia nigral neurons. Am J Path 1997; 150: 119–131.

52. Kosel S, Egensperger R, von Eitzen U, Mehraein P, Graeber MB. On the question of apoptosis in the parkinsonian substantia nigra. Acta Neuropath 1997; 93: 105–108.

53. Lowe J, Mayer RJ, Landon M. Ubiquitin in neurodegenerative diseases. Brain Path 1993; 3: 55–65.

54. Gai WP, Blessing WW, Blumbergs PC. Ubiquitin-positive degenerating neurites in the brainstem in Parkinson's disease. Brain 1995; 118: 1447–1459.

55. Schwartz LM, Myer A, Kosz L, Engelstein M, Maier C. Activation of polyubiquitin gene expression during developmentally programmed cell death. Neuron 1990; 5: 411–419.

56. Duffy PE, Tennyson VM. Phase and electron microscopic observations of Lewy bodies and melanin granules in the substantia nigra and locus coeruleus in Parkinson's disease. J Neuropath Exp Neurol 1965; 24: 398–414.

57. Goldman JE, Yen S-H, Chiu F-C, Peress NS. Lewy bodies of Parkinson's disease contain neurofilament antigens. Science 1983; 221: 1082–1084.

58. Forno LS, Sternberger LA, Sternberger NH, Strefling AM, Swanson K, Eng LF. Reaction of Lewy bodies with antibodies to phosphorylated and non-phosphorylated neurofilaments. Neurosci Lett 1986; 64: 253–258.

59. Bancher C, Lassman H, Budka H, *et al.* An antigenic profile of Lewy bodies: Immunocytochemical indication for protein phosphorylation and ubiquitination. J Neuropath Exp Neurol 1989; 48: 81–93.

60. Lew J, Wang JH. Neuronal cdc2-like kinase. Trends Biol Sci 1995; 20: 33–37.

61. Brion J-P, Couck A-M. Cortical and brainstem-type Lewy bodies are immunoreactive for the cyclin-dependent kinase 5. Am J Path 1995; 147: 1465–1476.

62. Nakamura S, Kawamoto Y, Nakano S, Ikemoto A, Akiguchi I, Kimura J. Cyclin-dependent kinase 5 in Lewy body-like inclusions in anterior horn cells of a patient with sporadic amyotrophic lateral sclerosis. Neurol 1997; 48: 267–270.

63. Henchcliffe C, Burke RE. Increased expression of cyclin-dependent kinase 5 in induced apoptotic neuron death in rat substantia nigra. Neurosci Lett 1997; 230: 41–44.

64. Polymeropoulos MH, Lavedan C, Leroy E, et al. Mutation in the α-synuclein gene identified in families with Parkinson's disease. Science 1997; 276: 2045–2047.

65. Golbe LI, Di Iorio G, Bonavita V, Miller DC, Duvoisin RC. Autosomal dominant Parkinson's disease. Ann Neurol 1990; 27: 276–282.

66. Ueda K, Fukushima H, Masliah E, et al. Molecular cloning of cDNA encoding an unrecognized component of amyloid in Alzheimer disease. Proc Nat Acad Sci USA 1993; 90: 11282–11286.

67. Liang P, Pardee AB. Differential display of eukaryotic RNA by means of the polymerase chain reaction. Science 1992; 257: 967–971.

68. Livesey FJ, Hunt SP. Identifying changes in gene expression in the nervous system: mRNA differential display. Trends Neurosci 1996; 19: 84–88.

69. Kholodilov NG, Neystat M, Burke RE. Investigation of apoptotic neuron death in substantia nigra with mRNA differential display. Neurol 1997; 48: A322.

70. Kholodilov NG, Neystat M, Burke RE. mRNAs overexpressed during induced apoptosis in substantia nigra identified by RNA differential display. Soc Neurosci Abstr 1997; 23: 631.

71. Lindvall O, Rehncrona S, Brundin P, et al. Human fetal dopamine neurons grafted into the striatum in two patients with severe Parkinson's disease. Arch Neurol 1989; 46: 615–631.

72. Lindvall O, Brundin P, Widner H, et al. Grafts of fetal dopamine neurons survive and improve motor function in Parkinson's disease. Science 1990; 247: 574–577.

73. Lindvall O, Sawle G, Widner H, et al. Evidence for long-term survival and function of dopaminergic grafts in progressive Parkinson's disease. Ann Neurol 1994; 35: 172–180.

74. Yurek DM, Sladek JR. Dopamine cell replacement: Parkinson's disease. Ann Rev Neurosci 1990; 13: 415–440.

75. Mahalik TJ, Hahn WE, Clayton GH, Owens GP. Programmed cell death in developing grafts of fetal substantia nigra. Exp Neurol 1994; 129: 27–36.

76. Fahn S. Controversies in the therapy of Parkinson's disease. Adv Neurol 1996; 69: 477–486.

77. Ziv I, Melamed E, Nardi N, et al. Dopamine induces apoptosis like cell death in cultured chick sympathetic neurons: A possible novel pathogenetic mechanism in Parkinsons Disease. Neurosci Lett 1994; 170: 136–140.

78. Walkinshaw G, Waters CM. Induction of apoptosis in catecholaminergic PC12 cells by L-dopa. J Clin Invest 1995; 95: 2458–2464.

DISCUSSION

Melamed: The differential display technique is particularly attractive. It enables one to insult or challenge cultured cells and to look for up- or down-regulation of genes that contribute to cell death or survival. We have used this technique in our dopamine exposure model, and have found that post-mitotic neurons show a sudden upregulation of genes involved in cell cycling before they die. When sympathetic neurons are exposed to dopamine they become post-mitotic and forget how to divide, and then two waves of cycline B1 expression take place. We were fascinated to discover that catalytic units of cell cycling message and proteins were found in Lewy bodies in the substantia nigra of patients with PD and also in amyloid plaques of patients with Alzheimer's disease. Is it possible that before the cell dies, the ubiquitination process traps proteins that are abnormally accumulated in these cells which are about to undergo the death process? I wonder whether you could comment on this non-specific expression of several proteins that are dormant but are activated during cell death?

Burke: It is very important to determine the functional significance of up-regulation of a particular message and/or its protein. That is why we have proceeded with studies to determine which proteins and genes are upregulated and what is their functional role. The differential display technique is a very powerful technique for detecting gene changes but false positives are common and problematic. One has to be careful about defining strict controls for the regions of interest. In our studies, we would run four animals at 4 hours and four animals at 24 hours and would only pursue a band that was differentially displayed in at least three animals. A colleague is investigating differential display in parkinsonian brains compared to disease related controls. This is going to be extremely difficult because one has to dissect two areas that are precisely the same in order to control for regional differences. Any differences that may be related to individuality, age, or pre-mortem situation have to be taken into account. Tissue culture is easier to control. Animal models with unilateral lesions are also good models for differential display because you can use the contralateral side as a control. Your results on the relationship between apoptosis and cell cycling have been of great interest, particularly the finding that collapsin is over-expressed on induction of cell death.

Melamed: I had not mentioned collapsin, but since you raised it, we are very interested in this molecule. The use of differential display in tissue culture often shows induction of molecules that you were not aware even existed. Collapsin is an axon guidance molecule that is activated only during the development of the central nervous system and the retina. It kills axons that go astray when they try to find their target. It is dramatically activated after an insult in cell culture under physiological conditions, and when we block collapsin with an antibody we can totally prevent apoptosis. We have now developed an antibody with a fluorescent probe and have begun to look at Alzheimer's disease brains.

W. Tatton: Regarding the timing of the change in α-synuclein expression, if you were going to use the phasic *c-jun* increase as a marker, would this be before or after that marker peak?

Burke: We have done predominantly protein expression studies on *c-fos* and *c-jun* but have not done very much yet at the mRNA level. Protein expression for *c-jun* occurs in the same time frame with a maximum at 24 hours but there is some expression at 12 hours. So *c-jun* and α-synuclein are relatively correlated. If anything, *c-jun* protein expression may occur slightly earlier.

Gash: Is there anything unique about the substantia nigra in this response? If you were to induce damage with quinolinic acid or another excitotoxin in another part of the brain, would you see a similar upregulation in expression of α-synuclein?

Burke: I cannot say that this is specific for the substantia nigra because we do not know. We have not looked at other models of this type of injury such as quinolinic acid or damage to other brain regions. It is entirely possible that a similar response would be seen in other regions that express the α-synuclein message. We have not explored other lesion models yet such as 6-OHDA or MPTP. Obviously, there is still a lot of work to be done to define how broadly α-synuclein is expressed in models of neuronal death, both within and outside of the substantia nigra.

Polymeropoulos: Regarding the difference between the anti-NACP antibody and the nuclear staining, I believe that the former recognizes a much higher molecular weight band in Western blots. Is that correct?

Burke: The Saitoh group has raised two anti-NAC antibodies. The antibody we used was raised by Dr. Iwai and was characterized by him. On Western blots, using that antibody, they see the NAC 35 amino acid peptide as expected. If the peptide is left in aqueous buffer at room temperature for a period of time, it self-aggregates. His antibody recognizes those aggregates as well. Interestingly, this antibody did not recognize the full length 19 kDa, 140 amino acid NACP from human brain homogenates. This epitope therefore behaves somewhat differently, but you are correct in that this anti-NAC antibody recognized only the peptide fragment or aggregates thereof.

Polymeropoulos: Actually, I am worried that it does not recognize α-synuclein at all but in fact recognizes an epitope of some folded protein somewhere else. If I remember, they used PH11 which supposedly will dissolve the aggregates *in vitro* and that band did not get any smaller.

Burke: Yes, a good point. In relation to that, another splice variant in rats is synuclein 2. Synuclein 2 shares this sequence with synuclein 1 so it is conceivable that some of this staining is not synuclein 1 but synuclein 2, as there is a considerable amino acid similarity.

Polymeropoulos: Would you not expect synuclein 2 to be shorter?

Burke: Actually, I think the synuclein 2 is longer.

Polymeropoulos: Synuclein 1 is the full length 140 amino acids. Synuclein 2 is a splice variant so it misses one of the exons. What Scheller and Marito described is synuclein 3. On careful inspection, the sequence is a mistake. They had a frame shift in the sequence which translated longer but actually it is not longer. In fact, it has a stop codon and they read the sequence wrong.

Burke: I will have to speak to Richard Scheller because in their paper synuclein 3 is the shortest form and synuclein 2 is somewhat longer than synuclein 1.

CHAPTER NINETEEN

Mitochondria in neurodegenerative apoptosis: and opportunity for therapy?

WILLIAM G. TATTON AND RUTH M.E. CHALMERS-REDMAN

Department of Neurology, Mount Sinai School of Medicine,
New York, New York, USA

APOPTOSIS IN NEURODEGENERATION – INITIATION BY MULTIPLE FACTORS

Selective nerve cell death, the cardinal feature of neurodegenerative disease, was originally thought to be mediated by necrosis, a process characterized by rapid organelle disruption, cell swelling and plasma membrane rupture. Recent evidence indicates instead that apoptosis mediates much of the nerve cell death in neurodegeneration.[1,2] Apoptosis is a more gradual, multi-step process defined by initiation, effector and degradation phases.

Massive apoptotic death of neurons, initiated by competition for limited obligatory trophic molecules, is part of vertebrate prenatal and postnatal brain development, and was therefore thought to account for apoptosis in neurodegenerative diseases.[3] It may indeed contribute to some forms of neurodegenerative apoptosis, but not all. Neuronal apoptosis can also be initiated by excitotoxins,[4] beta amyloid,[5,6] the presenilins,[7,8] MPTP,[9] cycad flour[10] and mitochondrial complex inhibitors,[11] all of which have been used to model human neurodegenerative diseases.

There is now evidence for apoptotic degradation, as determined by nuclear DNA fragmentation and chromatin condensation in Alzheimer's disease, Parkinson's disease (PD), Huntington's disease and amyotrophic lateral sclerosis.[2] A variety of anti-apoptotic and pro-apoptotic proteins are altered in brain regions affected by neurodegeneration. Changes in pro-apoptotic proteins were found in nerve cells with nuclear DNA fragmentation, indicative of apoptosis, and have included increases in c-JUN,[12] transglutaminase[13] and BAX[14] as well as the appearance of cyclin-dependent kinase inhibitor p16,[15] cyclin B, cyclin E and Cdc2 kinase.[16] BAX was also found to be heavily concentrated in senile plaques and in neurofibrillary tangles.[17] Similarly, FAS antigen was concentrated in senile plaques[18] and increases in p53 were found in astrocytes.[19] The anti-apoptotic oncoprotein, BCL-2, was decreased in neurons with neurofibrillary tangles but was increased or unchanged in nearby unaffected neurons.[20] Increased expression of BCL-2 was revealed in surviving neurons in the substantia nigra of PD brains suggesting that a survival program had been activated.[21] Apoptosis is therefore likely to be an important terminal process in human neurodegeneration.

MITOCHONDRIA ARE VOLTAGE-DEPENDENT POWER CONVERTERS AND APOPTOTIC EFFECTORS

Mitochondria are specialized energy-converting organelles, converting energy into forms that can be used to drive cellular reactions. Each mitochondrion has an outer and an inner membrane. The inner membrane bounds an intramitochondrial matrix space while a narrow intermembraneous space lies between the two membranes. The inner membrane is extremely impermeable due in part to high levels of cardiolipin.

Three mitochondrial complexes, I, III and IV, pump protons out of the mitochondrial matrix across the inner mitochondrial membrane using electron energy provided by the carrier molecules nicotinamide adenine dinucleotide (NADH), ubiquinone and cytochrome C (Cyt C). The outward pumping of protons produces an electron gradient that is reflected biochemically by a pH difference and electrically by a voltage across the inner mitochondrial membrane termed the mitochondrial membrane potential ($\Delta\Psi_M$).[22] $\Delta\Psi_M$ and the pH difference contribute to a proton electromotive force that drives the conversion of ADP to ATP. Since $\Delta\Psi_M$ is by far the greater contributor to the proton electromotive force, it follows that $\Delta\Psi_M$ varies with the ATP/ADP ratio and therefore provides an estimate of the ATP production within individual mitochondria.

Different apoptotic initiation pathways appear to converge upon a common effector step – the opening of the mitochondrial permeability transition pore (PTP)[23] which is believed to be critical in apoptosis and to constitute an irreversible death decision. A decrease in $\Delta\Psi_M$, in the presence of increased intramitochondrial Ca^{2+},[24] induces the opening of the PTP which spans both the inner and outer mitochondrial membranes. The precise structure of the PTP is uncertain.[25] An adenine nucleotide translator appears to be a critical element. The PTP also includes a voltage dependent anion channel (a porin) and a peripheral benzodiazepine binding protein.[25] Those components are closely associated with other molecules that are known to modulate apoptosis. Opening of the PTP allows free exchange of solutes and small proteins (< 1500da) between the mitochondrial matrix and the extramitochondrial cytosol.[26] Glutathione is actively concentrated in the mitochondrial matrix and its release from mitochondria is considered a definitive marker of PTP opening.[27]

[266]

$\Delta\Psi_M$ is reduced very early in the apoptotic process, prior to the onset of nuclear DNA fragmentation and chromatin condensation in a variety of blood, hepatic and immune cell models.[28] In blood cells, early apoptotic decreases in $\Delta\Psi_M$ are associated with PTP opening and the consequent release of heat labile factors can initiate the nuclear degradation of apoptosis.[29]

Decreases in $\Delta\Psi_M$ early in apoptosis can be extended to neuronal models. NGF-differentiated PC12 cells were examined after trophic withdrawal by laser confocal microscopy.[30] $\Delta\Psi_M$ was significantly reduced in a considerable proportion of mitochondria prior to nuclear DNA fragmentation and chromatin condensation. The decreases in $\Delta\Psi_M$ were temporally correlated with increases in intramitochondrial Ca^{2+} but not with increases in cytosolic oxidative radical levels, which increased only after the decreases in $\Delta\Psi_M$ were well established. Since opening of the PTP requires both a decrease in $\Delta\Psi_M$ and an increase in intramitochondrial Ca^{2+}, the changes observed in this model were appropriate for PTP opening.

Mitochondrial factors can effect apoptosis

One mitochondrial apoptosis initiation factor (AIF) has been identified as an interleukin converting enzyme (ICE)-like protease.[31] Mitochondrial AIFs may be released through the PTP or through mitochondrial membranes fractured by swelling due to solute exchange between the matrix and cytosol. BCL-2 has been found to bind to the peripheral benzodiazepine binding component of the mitochondrial PTP[32] and acts to maintain PTP closure. BCL-2 prevents decreases in $\Delta\Psi_M$ and the release of the ICE-like AIF.[29,31,33,34] dATP, when accompanied by holocytochrome C (cyt C), can promote apoptosis in some cell free systems.[35] In some forms of apoptosis, increased levels of Cyt C can be found in the extramitochondrial cytosol in the early stages of apoptosis.[36] Studies in multiple myeloma cells showed that cytosolic Cyt C levels increased in early apoptosis induced by ionizing radiation but not in that induced by dexamethasone or anti-FAS antibody.[37] The former is likely p53-dependent while the latter two methods are p53-independent. Similarly, microinjection of Cyt C induces apoptosis in human kidney 293 cells but not in MCF7 breast carcinoma cells.[38] Different mitochondrial effectors may therefore be released in different apoptosis models. It is not yet known whether the ICE-like protease or Cyt C effect apoptosis in neuronal cells, particularly in neurodegenerative apoptosis.

New protein synthesis is not usually required for apoptosis

Apoptotic neuronal death was thought to depend on intrinsic gene expression requiring new protein synthesis.[39] It is now apparent that apoptosis can occur in the presence of purely constitutive proteins.[40] Undifferentiated or partially-differentiated PC12 cells undergo apoptosis after trophic withdrawal that is unaffected by transcriptional or translational blockade.[41,42] In contrast, fully-differentiated PC12 cells undergo apoptosis after trophic withdrawal requiring new protein synthesis.[43] Apoptosis can be p53-dependent or p53-independent.[44] Transcriptional transactivation by p53 in response to DNA damage, inappropriate oncogene activation, some cytokines and hypoxia induces marked changes in gene expression including p21[WAF1], *bax* and cyclin g. Cells expressing mutant p53 do not undergo apoptosis by mechanisms dependent on decreased $\Delta\Psi_M$ with PTP opening, while those expressing wild type p53 show $\Delta\Psi_M$ dependence. An understanding of the relationship between p53 increases and decreases in $\Delta\Psi_M$ in early apoptosis may offer new avenues for intervention in neurodegenerative apoptosis.

A mitochondrial complex I defect may be responsible for neuronal apoptosis in PD

Measurements of mitochondrial enzyme activity in regional homogenates of the postmortem substantia nigra compacta from control and levodopa treated PD patients revealed decreases of 20 to 40% in complex I (CI) activity without significant decreases for complexes II, III and IV.[45–50] Other brain regions showed normal levels of CI activity, while platelets taken from both levodopa treated[50–52] and untreated[53] PD patients showed decreased CI activity of 16–20% below control levels. Cybrids carrying mitochondrial DNA (mtDNA) from PD patients showed average decreases in CI activity of 20%.[54] Western blots[55,56] and immunocytochemistry[57,58] have suggested a decreased abundance of CI proteins and the α-ketoglutarate complexes of PD postmortem nigral tissue. Finally, impaired oxidative decarboxylation of pyruvate, but not succinate, has been reported in fibroblasts taken from patients with PD.[59] Therefore, nigral cells and some peripheral tissues like fibroblasts or platelets from PD patients have a modest but selective defect in CI.

Whether and how a CI defect contributes to the genesis of PD is uncertain. No differences have been found in mtDNA deletions for tissues from PD patients *versus* age-matched controls.[60–63] Studies in submitochondrial particles indicate that CI is the major contributor to the generation of $\Delta\Psi_M$.[64] We hypothesized that decreased CI activity may induce neuronal death by reducing proton pumping with a consequent decrease in $\Delta\Psi_M$ which would render cells vulnerable to apoptosis effected by PTP opening. Laser confocal microscopic image analysis revealed a loss of mitochondria with high levels of $\Delta\Psi_M$ in the fibroblasts of some PD patients compared with age-matched controls.[30] However, the prevalence of a defect in $\Delta\Psi_M$ in PD fibroblasts is still unclear, as is whether any decrease in $\Delta\Psi_M$ is the result of the previously-described decrease in CI activity found in some PD patients. Lastly, it will be important to determine whether therapeutic factors rather than an intrinsic defect account for any decreases in $\Delta\Psi_M$.

If a decrease in $\Delta\Psi_M$ is an intrinsic defect in PD fibroblasts and the loss of high $\Delta\Psi_M$ mitochondria results from reduced proton pumping caused by decreased CI activity, then a downshift in $\Delta\Psi_M$ could render cells vulnerable to PTP opening in a proportion of their mitochondria and the initiation of apoptosis. Fibroblasts could compensate for an increase in apoptosis by increasing replication while post-mitotic nigral neuron numbers would be reduced since they cannot replicate. If a decrease in $\Delta\Psi_M$ is a feature of PD mitochondria in substantia nigra neurons, it could render the neurons vulnerable to apoptosis if presented with any other insult that further compromises $\Delta\Psi_M$. This would constitute a new 'double hit' theory for PD —neurons with relatively low levels would be particularly vulnerable to exposure to increased ROS levels. Furthermore, metabolic failure caused by hypoxia or hypoglycemia would also decrease NADH levels and reduce proton pumping and $\Delta\Psi_M$.

Possibilities for therapeutic intervention include agents that protect the PTP and prevent the release of AIFs. The primary metabolite of deprenyl, desmethyldeprenyl, selectively alters gene transcription and new protein synthesis.[65] Levels of Bcl-2 and Sod-1 are thus preserved in early apoptosis which in turn results in a maintenance of $\Delta\Psi_M$ and a decrease in apoptosis.[30,65]

SUMMARY

- Apoptotic cell death has been shown to constitute the terminal process in some neurodegenerative diseases, notably PD and Alzheimer's disease.

- A decrease in $\Delta\Psi_M$ causing opening of the PTP in mitochondrial membranes has been implicated as a critical step in the development of apoptosis in a variety of non-neural cells. Opening of the PTP leads to the release of AIFs that induce the degradative events of apoptosis such as nuclear chromatin condensation and DNA fragmentation.

- These findings have been extended to a neuronal model of apoptosis which showed that a decrease in $\Delta\Psi_M$, coupled with an increase in mitochondrial calcium, is an early event occurring before the degradative events of apoptosis.

- A deficiency in mitochondrial CI activity has been demonstrated in the substantia nigra of post-mortem brains and several peripheral tissues from PD patients. Since $\Delta\Psi_M$ is generated in part by the pumping of protons across the inner mitochondrial membrane by CI, we hypothesize that the decrease in complex I activity could result in a decrease in $\Delta\Psi_M$ which would render PD substantia nigra neurons vulnerable to apoptosis.

- In preliminary studies, a decrease has been found in $\Delta\Psi_M$ in PD fibroblasts. If this is an intrinsic defect, it would open new avenues for the reduction of neuronal apoptosis in PD.

References

1. Tatton WG, Chalmers-Redman RME, Ju WYH, Wadia J, Tatton NA. Apoptosis in neurodegenerative disorders: Potential for therapy by modifying gene transcription. J Neural Transm 1997; 245–268.

2. Tatton N, Maclean-Fraser A, Tatton WG, Perl DF, Olanow CW, this volume.

3. Johnson J, Oppenheim R. Neurotrophins. Keeping track of changing neurotrophic theory. Curr Biol 1994; 4: 662–665.

4. Mitchell IJ, Lawson S, Moser B, Laidlaw SM, Cooper AJ, Walkinshaw G, et al. Glutamate-induced apoptosis results in a loss of striatal neurons in the parkinsonian rat. Neurosci 1994; 63: 1–5.

5. Estus S, Tucker HM, vanRooyen C, Wright S, Brigham EF, Wogulis M, et al. Aggregated amyloid-beta protein induces cortical neuronal apoptosis and concomitant 'apoptotic' pattern of gene induction. J Neurosci 1997; 17: 7736–7745.

6. Forloni G, Chiesa R, Smiroldo S, Verga L, Salmona M, Tagliavini F, et al. Apoptosis mediated neurotoxicity induced by chronic application of beta amyloid fragment 25-35. Neuroreport 1993; 4: 523–526.

7. Guo Q, Sopher BL, Furukawa K, Pham DG, Robinson N, Martin GM, et al. Alzheimer's presenilin mutation sensitizes neural cells to apoptosis induced by trophic factor withdrawal and amyloid beta-peptide: Involvement of calcium and oxyradicals. J. Neurosci 1997; 17: 4212–4222.

8. Janicki S, Monteiro MJ. Increased apoptosis arising from increased expression of the Alzheimer's disease-associated presenilin-2 mutation (N141I). J Cell Biol 1997; 139: 485–495.

9. Tatton NA, Kish SJ. In situ detection of apoptotic nuclei in the substantia nigra compacta of 1-methyl-4-phenyl-1,2,3,6-tetrahydropyridine-treated mice using terminal deoxynucleotidyl transferase labelling and acridine orange staining. Neurosci 1997; 77: 1037–1048.

10. Gobe GC. Apoptosis in brain and gut tissue of mice fed a seed preparation of the cycad Lepidozamia peroffskyana. Biochem Biophys Res Comm 1994; 205: 327–333.

11. Hartley A, Stone JM, Heron C, Cooper JM, Schapira AH. Complex I inhibitors induce dose-dependent apoptosis in PC12 cells: relevance to Parkinson's disease. J Neurochem 1994; 63: 1987–1990.

12. Anderson AJ, Su JH, Cotman CW. DNA damage and apoptosis in Alzheimer's disease: colocalization with c-Jun immunoreactivity, relationship to brain area and the effect of postmortem delay. J Neurosci 1996; 16: 1710–1719.

13. Johnson GVW, Cox TM, Lockhart JP, Zinnerman MD, Miller ML, Powers RE. Transglutaminase activity is increased in Alzheimer's disease brain. Brain Res 1997; 751: 323–329.

14. Su JH, Deng GM, Cotman CW. Bax protein expression is increased in Alzheimer's brain: Correlations with DNA damage, Bcl-2 expression, and brain pathology. J Neuropathol Exp Neurol 1997; 56: 86–93.

15. Arendt T, Rodel L, Gartner U, Holzer M. Expression of the cyclin-dependent kinase inhibitor p16 in Alzheimer's disease. Neuroreport 1996; 7: 3047–3049.

16. Nagy Z, Esiri MM, Cato AM, Smith AD. Cell cycle markers in the hippocampus in Alzheimer's disease. Acta Neuropathol 1997; 94: 6–15.

17. MacGibbon GA, Lawlor PA, Sirimanne ES, Walton MR, Connor B, Young D, et al. Bax expression in mammalian neurons undergoing apoptosis, and in

Alzheimer's disease hippocampus. Brain Res 1997; 750: 223–234.

18. Nishimura T, Akiyama H, Yonehara S, Kondo H, Ikeda K, Kato M, et al. Fas antigen expression in brains of patients with Alzheimer-type dementia. Brain Res 1995; 695: 137–145.

19. Kitamura Y, Kosaka T, Shimohama S, Nomura Y, Taniguchi T. Possible involvement of rapamycin-sensitive pathway in Bcl-2 expression in human neuroblastoma SH-SY5Y cells. Jap J Pharmacol 1997; 75: 195–198.

20. Vyas S, JavoyAgid F, Herrero MT, Strada O, Boissiere F, Hibner U, et al. Expression of Bcl-2 in adult human brain regions with special reference to neurodegenerative disorders. J Neurochem 1997; 69: 223–231.

21. Mogi M, Harada M, Kondo T, Mizuno Y, Narabayashi H, Riederer P, et al. Bcl-2 protein is increased in the brain from parkinsonian patients. Neurosci Lett 1996; 215: 137–139.

22. Sherratt HSA. Mitochondria: structure and function. Rev Neurol (Paris) 1991; 147: 417–430.

23. Kroemer G, Zamzami N, Susin SA. Mitochondrial control of apoptosis. Immunol Today 1997; 18: 44–51.

24. Scorrano L, Petronilli V, Bernardi P. On the voltage dependence of the mitochondrial permeability transition pore – A critical appraisal. J Biol Chem 1997; 272: 12295–12299.

25. Zoratti M, Szabo I. The mitochondrial permeability transition. Biochim Biophys Acta Rev Biomem 1995; 1241: 139–176.

26. Bernardi P, Broekemeier KM, Pfeiffer DR. Recent progress on regulation of the mitochondrial permeability transition pore. A cyclosporin-sensitive pore in the inner mitochondrial membrane. J Bioenerget Biomemb 1994; 26, 509–517.

27. Hirsch T, Marzo I, Kroemer G. Role of the mitochondrial permeability transition pore in apoptosis. Biosci Reports 1997; 17: 67–76.

28. Susin SA, Zamzami N, Kroemer G. The cell biology of apoptosis: evidence for the implication of mitochondria. Apoptosis 1996; 1: 231–242.

29. Zamzami N, Marchetti P, Castedo M, Hirsh T, Susin SA, Masse B, et al. Inhibitors of permeability transition interfere with the disruption of mitochondrial transmembrane potential during apoptosis. FEBS Letters, 1996; 384: 53–57.

30. Wadia JS, Chalmers-Redman RME, Ju WJH, Carlile GW, Phillips JL, Tatton WG. Mitochondrial membrane potential and nuclear changes in apoptosis caused by trophic withdrawal: time course and modification by (-)-deprenyl. J Neurosci 1998; 18: 932–947.

31. Susin SA, Zamzami N, Castedo M, Hirsch T, Marchetti P, Macho A, et al. Bcl-2 inhibits the mitochondrial release of an apoptogenic protease. J Exp Med 1996; 184: 1331–1341.

32. Carayon P, Portier M, Dussossoy D, Bord A, Petipretre G, Canat X, et al. Involvement of peripheral benzodiazepine receptors in the protection of hematopoietic cells against oxygen radical damage. Blood 1996; 87: 3170–3178.

33. Marchetti P, Castedo M, Susin SA, Zamzami N, Hirsch T, Macho A, et al. Mitochondrial permeability transition is a central coordinating event of apoptosis. J Exp Med 1996; 184: 1155–1160.

34. Marchetti P, Hirsch T, Zamzami N, Castedo M, Decaudin D, Susin SA, et al. Mitochondrial permeability transition triggers lymphocyte apoptosis. J Immunol 1996; 157: 4830–4836.

35. Liu XS, Kim CN, Yang J, Jemmerson R, Wang XD. Induction of apoptotic program in cell-free extracts: Requirement for dATP and cytochrome c. Cell 1996; 86: 147–157.

36. Yang J, Liu XS, Bhalla K, Kim CN, Ibrado AM, Cai JY, et al. Prevention of apoptosis by Bcl-2: Release of cytochrome c from mitochondria blocked. Science 1997; 275: 1129–1132.

[271]

37. Chauchan D, Pandey P, Ogata A, Teoh G, Krett N, Halgren R, et al. Cytochrome c-dependent and -independent induction of apoptosis in multiple myeloma cells. J Biol Chem 1997; 272: 29995–29997.

38. Li F, Srinivasan A, Wang Y, Armstrong RC, Tomaselli KJ, Fritz LC. Cell specific induction of apoptosis by microinjection of cytochrome c. J Biol Chem 1997; 272: 30299–30305.

39. Oppenheim RW, Prevette D, Tytell M, Homma S. Naturally occurring and induced neuronal death in the chick embryo in vivo requires protein and RNA synthesis: evidence for the role of cell death genes. Dev Biol 1990; 138: 104–113.

40. Eastman A. Apoptosis: a product of programmed and unprogrammed cell death. Toxicol Appl Pharmacol 1993; 121: 160–164.

41. Rukenstein A, Rydel RE, Greene LA. Multiple agents rescue PC12 cells from serum-free cell death by translation- and transcription-independent mechanisms. J Neurosci 1991; 11: 2552–2563.

42. Tatton WG, Ju WY, Holland DP, Tai C, Kwan M. (-)-Deprenyl reduces PC12 cell apoptosis by inducing new protein synthesis. J Neurochem 1994; 63: 1572–1575.

43. Mesner PW, Epting CL, Hegarty JL, Green SH. A timetable of events during programmed cell death induced by trophic factor withdrawal from neuronal PC12 cells. J Neurosci 1995; 15: 7357–7366.

44. Bellamy CO. p53 and apoptosis. Br Med Bull 1997; 53: 522–538.

45. Mann VM, Cooper JM, Daniel SE, Srai K, Jenner P, Marsden CD. Complex I, iron and ferritin in Parkinson's disease substantia nigra. Ann Neurol 1994; 36: 876–881.

46. Mann VM, Cooper JM, Krige D, Daniel SE, Schapira AH, Marsden CD. Brain, skeletal muscle and platelet homogenate mitochondrial function in Parkinson's disease. Brain 1992; 115: 333–342.

47. Parker WD, Boyson SJ, Parks JK. Abnormalities of electron transport in Parkinson's disease. Ann Neurol 1989; 50: 719–723.

48. Reichmann H, Naumann M, Hauck S, Janetzky B. Respiratory chain and mitochondrial deoxyribonucleic acid in blood cells from patients with focal and generalized dystonia. Mov Disord 1994; 9: 597–600.

49. Schapira AH, Cooper JM, Dexter D, Clark JB, Jenner P, Marsden CD. Mitochondrial complex I deficiency in Parkinson's disease. J Neurochem 1990; 54: 823–827.

50. Yoshino H, Nakagawa Hattori Y, Kondo T, Mizuno Y. Mitochondrial complex I and II activities of lymphocytes and platelets in Parkinson's disease. J Neural Transm Park Dis Dement Sect 1992; 4: 27–34.

51. Benecke R, Strumper P, Weiss H. Electron transfer complexes I and IV of platelets are abnormal in Parkinson's disease but normal in Parkinson-plus syndromes. Brain 1993; 116: 1451–1463.

52. Krige D, Carroll MT, Cooper JM, Marsden CD, Schapira AH. Platelet mitochondrial function in Parkinson's disease. Ann Neurol 1992; 32: 782–788.

53. Haas RH, Nasirian F, Nakano K, Ward D, Pay M, Hill R, et al. Low platelet mitochondrial complex I and complex II/III activity in early untreated Parkinson's disease. Ann Neurol 1995; 37: 714–722.

54. Swerdlow RH, Parks JK, Miller SW, Tuttle JB, Trimmer PA, Sheehan JP, et al. Origin and functional consequences of the complex I defect in Parkinson's disease. Ann Neurol 1996; 40: 663–671.

55. Mizuno Y, Ohta S, Tanaka M, Takamiya S, Suzuki K, Sato T, et al. Deficiencies in complex I subunits of the respiratory chain in Parkinson's disease. Biochem Biophys Res Comm 1989; 163: 1450–1455.

56. Schapira AH, Mann VM, Cooper JM, Dexter D, Daniel SE, Jenner P, et al. Anatomic and disease specificity of NADH CoQ1 reductase (complex I) deficiency in Parkinson's disease. J Neurochem 1990; 55: 2142–2145.

57. Hattori N, Tanaka M, Ozawa T, Mizuno Y. Immunohistochemical studies on complexes I, II, III, and IV of mitochondria in Parkinson's disease. Ann Neurol 1991; 30: 563–571.

58. Mizuno Y, Matuda S, Yoshino H, Mori H, Hattori N, Ikebe S. An immuno-histochemical study on alpha-ketoglu-tarate dehydrogenase complex in Parkinson's disease. Ann Neurol 1994; 35: 204–210.

59. Mytilineou C, Werner P, Molinari S, DiRocco A, Cohen G, Yahr MD. Impaired oxidative decarboxylation of pyruvate in fibroblasts from patients with Parkinson's disease. J Neur Transm Park Dis Dement Sect 1994; 8:223–228.

60. Brown MD, Shoffner JM, Kim YL, Jun AS, Graham BH, Cabell MF, et al. Mitochondrial DNA sequence analysis of four Alzheimer's and Parkinson's disease patients. Am J Med Gen 1996; 61: 283–289.

61. Lucking CB, Kosel S, Mehraein P, Graeber MB. Absence of the mitochondrial A7237T mutation in Parkinson's disease. Biochem Biophys Res Commun 1995; 211: 700–704.

62. Mizuno Y, Ikebe S, Hattori N, Nakagawa Hattori Y, Mochizuki H, Tanaka M, et al. Role of mitochondria in the etiology and pathogenesis of Parkinson's disease. Biochim Biophys Acta 1995; 1271: 265–274.

63. Schapira AH. Nuclear and mito-chondrial genetics in Parkinson's disease. J Med Genet 1995; 32: 411–414.

64. Ghelli A, Benelli B, Esposti MD. Measurement of the membrane potential generated by complex I in submitochon-drial particles. J Biochem 1997; 121: 746–755.

65. Tatton WG, Chalmers-Redman RME. Modulation of gene expression rather than monoamine oxidase inhibition: (-)-deprenyl-related compounds in controlling neurodegeneration. Neurol 1996; 47: S171–S183.

DISCUSSION

Langston: I have a question about the effects you saw with desmethyl selegiline. Am I correct in saying that the drug prevented the decrease in membrane potential and of free radical generation but did not prevent calcium accumulation?

W. Tatton: Yes, in other words one would expect that changes in calcium flux should affect the mitochondrial membrane potential. In PC12 cells subjected to trophic withdrawal, the calcium fluxes out of the endoplasmic reticulum and is taken into the mitochondria and leads to a reduction in the mitochondrial membrane potential. Interestingly, when desmethyl selegiline is added, calcium levels within mitochondria do not return to normal, but the mitochondrial membrane potential is preserved and the cells do not go into apoptosis.

Langston: How do you think this happens?

W. Tatton: The permeability of an ion relative to the natural log of its concentration across the membrane indicates how it will contribute to a potential, such as the mitochondrial membrane potential. For example, if you reduce calcium permeability and its ability to enter mitochondria, then its contribution to the mitochondrial membrane potential will be minimized. We know that desmethyl selegiline increases the synthesis of a number of proteins including BCL-2 which is known to protect the mitochondrial membrane potential by maintaining closure of the permeability transition pore. Bredesen has also shown that mitochondria are able to maintain ATP production and sequester very large amounts of calcium in the presence of BCL-2. Thus, we think that upregulation of BCL-2 is the primary basis of the mechanism of action of desmethyl selegiline in preventing apoptosis in the PC12 cell model.

Polymeropoulos: If fibroblasts are transfected with BCL-2, can you change the potential of the membrane?

W. Tatton: Yes you can. Kromer and his group have shown this very nicely.

Polymeropoulos: Why do the PD patients' fibroblasts not enter apoptosis if their mitochondrial membrane potential is reduced?

W. Tatton: It appears that mitochondrial membrane potential has to fall substantially before they release apoptosis initiation factors. From the preliminary data that we have, the PD fibroblast mitochondrial membrane potential has not fallen that far. However, an abnormally low mitochondrial membrane potential might set the stage for the initiation of apoptosis by a second defect that lowers the potential even further thereby inducing apoptosis. An environmental or toxic exposure might be such a second event.

Olanow: Is it possible that PD fibroblasts do undergo apoptosis? Has anyone looked?

W. Tatton: No-one has looked and we do not know that fibroblasts do not enter apoptosis at an abnormal rate.

Shoulson: Would it be possible to measure in circulating platelets the same things that you did in fibroblasts?

W. Tatton: Yes, we are doing that now, as well as in white blood cells.

Shoulson: And might you also be able to image peripheral benzodiazepine receptors? I believe such ligands are available.

W. Tatton: I do not know if we can image them, but we are very interested in agents such as BCL-2 which change the configuration of the peripheral benzodiazepine receptor by covalent bonding thereby forming a configuration that tends to hold the permeability transition pore closed. We could try to mimic this with peripheral benzodiazepine agonists. I have now looked at about 40 of these agents, and so far found two that block apoptosis. I have not yet been able to prove that they do this by binding to the peripheral benzodiazepine receptor on mitochondria and maintaining closure of the pore.

Shoulson: Is it correct to assume that the defects seen in the respiratory chain, i.e. complex I, would therefore be secondary to a more primary defect in terms of the pore?

W. Tatton: No. I believe that the complex I defect is probably a primary defect which reduces proton pumping, thereby reducing mitochondrial membrane potential and leading to an increased risk of the opening of the permeability transition pore. According to this theory, changes in the pore are secondary. Dr. Mizuno has shown that by decreasing pumping permeability at complex I and disabling α-ketoglutarate, the cell cannot maintain its mitochondrial membrane potential. This is a different way of looking at how changes in mitochondria could lead to apoptosis and contribute to the development of neurodegeneration.

Schapira: I would like to extend upon the question Dr. Shoulson asked. We extracted mitochondrial DNA from platelets of PD patients with low complex I activity and constructed cybrids. We then stained these cells with JC-1, a voltage-dependent dye, and showed precisely the same thing as Dr. Tatton has described. In this case, it seems clear that the drop in the mitochondrial membrane potential is a consequence of the alterations in the PD patient's mitochondrial DNA. I emphasize that we looked at a preselected group of parkinson patients, but one can use this technique to screen for a mitochondrial DNA defect. Dr. Tatton, what was the passage number of the parkinsonian fibroblasts that you studied? We found that when looking at myoblasts and fibroblasts of both PD patients and controls, we have to control very carefully for passage number. Actually, the age of the patient does not matter so much as the passage number. In fact, the JC-1 staining decreases with passage number.

W. Tatton: I agree with what you are saying. They may also lose the defect with increasing numbers of passage. I am not sure of the passage number of these cells but I think it was not very high.

Olanow: I am not sure of the passage number, but the control and parkinsonian samples were taken at the same time and had the same number of passages, and yet there was a major difference in the number of mitochondria with a defect between the PD patients and the controls.

Mizuno: In your diagram you show reactive oxygen species attacking the adenine nucleotide translocater from the cytoplasmic side but according to my understanding more than 90% of oxygen is consumed within mitochondria. Therefore I would have thought that reactive oxygen species would have attacked the adenine nucleotide translocater from the inside of the mitochondria?

W. Tatton: I agree with that. It was just cartoon licence on my part that I drew them on the outside. And I also think that you are right that their action on the pore is more likely to be mediated from the inside because the most vulnerable part of the adenine nucleotide translocater is on the inner mitochondrial membrane.

Bonuccelli: Do you have an idea if N-acetylcysteine can modify the permeability transition pore?

W. Tatton: Yes, the preliminary work was done by Dr. Green at Columbia University. He blocked the conversion of N-acetylcysteine to glutathione and showed that it still had the capacity to reduce apoptosis. He then showed that its capacity at low concentrations, i.e. 10^{-9}, 10^{-10} M, was dependent upon new protein synthesis. Most recently, he has found that it increases the synthesis of a number of proteins including BCL-2. We did similar work with deprenyl and desmethyl deprenyl showing that there was also protein synthesis dependency. So this is another example of an agent which we thought worked one way, but has a number of other functions including a transcriptional action.

Shoulson: What is the effect of coenzyme Q10 on this system?

W. Tatton: It acts to facilitate proton pumping and therefore potentially helps to preserve the mitochondrial membrane potential.

Polymeropoulos: If megakaryocytes are treated with phorbol esters, interestingly α-synuclein is extremely upregulated while its homolog β-synuclein is downregulated. It would be interesting to do your experiments in megakaryoctes and to correlate the changes in α-synuclein with alterations in mitochondrial membrane potential.

W. Tatton: Dr Burke pointed out that α-synuclein is upregulated in apoptosis at about the same time as *c-jun*. Changes in *c-jun* is one of the very earliest gene changes that one sees in the cascade of events leading to apoptosis. The fact that α-synuclein is upregulated as early as *c-jun* suggests that it may be directly involved in the mechanism of apoptosis and I agree that further studies in this area are warranted.

CHAPTER TWENTY

A fluorescent double-labeling method to detect and confirm apoptotic nuclei in Parkinson's disease

NADINE A. TATTON[1], A. MACLEAN-FRASER[1], WILLIAM G. TATTON[1], DAN P. PERL[2] AND C. WARREN OLANOW[1]

Departments of [1]Neurology and [2]Pathology, Mount Sinai School of Medicine, New York, New York, USA

New methods are required to determine whether dopaminergic nigral neurons in Parkinson's disease (PD) die *via* apoptosis or necrosis, since new 'anti-apoptotic' compounds may protect neurons from cell death and slow the rate of degeneration. There is no current consensus on whether apoptosis occurs in PD. *In situ* end-labeling (ISEL) marks endonuclease-induced DNA fragmentation with biotin-, digoxigenin- or fluorescent probe-conjugated nucleotides to visualize the 3'-OH ends of cut DNA. Using ISEL in isolation, one group found evidence of apoptosis in PD,[1] while others found none.[2,3] Apoptotic nuclei have been identified in the nigras of PD brains by electron microscopy (EM)[4] but this method is laborious. We have developed a fluorescent double-labeling method combining ISEL and the dimeric cyanine dye YOYO-1 that intercalates with DNA, to ascertain whether chromatin condensation (a hallmark of apoptosis) is present in those nuclei that have been positively *in situ* end-labeled. When combined with high-resolution confocal laser imaging and deconvolution analysis, this method allows visualization of the nuclear structure and provides unequivocal identification of apoptotic nuclei.[5]

Apoptosis is postulated to consist of three phases – an induction phase in which death can be stimulated by a heterogeneous assortment of signals, an effector phase which translates the signal into the ultimate decision to die, and finally the degradation phase in which the morphological and biochemical changes characteristic of apoptosis become apparent.[6] The stimuli for apoptosis may include withdrawal of trophic support,[7,8] dexamethasone,[9] irradiation,[10] damage by toxins such as MPTP,[5,11] the

[279]

ligation of death-signal transmitting receptors such as Fas/APO-1/CD95[12,13] or TNFα.[14] In PD, mitochondrial vulnerability,[15] oxidative stress,[16] environmental toxins and even monoamine-[17] or levodopa-derived[18] injury may contribute to dopaminergic cell death, either alone or in combination. It is not yet clear whether any one or more of these factors may be the initiating signal in PD.

A fall in mitochondrial membrane potential ($\Delta\psi_M$) is one of the earliest apoptotic events in neuronal and non-neuronal systems, irrespective of the inducer.[19–23] Cells with a low $\Delta\psi_M$ proceed to DNA fragmentation. The loss of $\Delta\psi_M$ occurs *via* a sudden increase in permeability of the inner mitochondrial membrane, due to the opening of the permeability transition pore (PTP). Cyclosporin A or bongkregic acid can inhibit PTP opening and block the disruption of $\Delta\psi_M$.[20] PTP opening leads to the release of apoptosis initiating factor(s) (AIFs) which causes the nuclear stigmata of apoptosis, and also to mitochondrial generation of reactive oxygen species. Depletion of glutathione, increased cytosolic calcium and nuclear DNA fragmentation *via* endonucleases are independent events, but reflect the point of no return in the degradative phase of apoptosis. Agents which promote increased glutathione,[24] decreased oxidative free radicals[16] or nitric oxide-derived radicals[25] increase cell survival. Clearly, several different molecules can intervene in apoptotic processes and 'rescue' cells from death.

Morphological Characterization of Apoptosis

Apoptosis affects scattered individual cells rather than groups of contiguous cells.[26] Cells undergoing apoptosis have condensed chromatin, and an absence of exudative inflammation characteristic of necrosis. Chromatin marginates in coarse granular aggregates which are often confluent throughout the nucleus. The nuclear membrane undergoes convolution and the resulting protuberances separate from the main nuclear body. Condensed chromatin masses are found in the cytosol, which also condenses but mitochondria and other organelles remain structurally intact, albeit compacted together. Overall, marked cell/nuclear shrinkage is evident.

Apoptosis is difficult to recognize with routine stains because of the involvement of only scattered single cells and the rapid disposal of apoptotic bodies without any obvious inflammatory response.[26] Traditionally, the criteria of pyknosis (nuclear condensation) and karyorrhexis (nuclear fragmentation) have been accepted as evidence of cell death but both terms can be applied to certain stages in either necrosis or apoptosis. Accordingly, EM has been used to define and record ultrastructural criteria to support the recognition of apoptosis.[27–30]

The Use of *In Situ* End Labeling to Detect Apoptosis

Although DNA fragmentation is a late apoptotic event, and not always present in all models of apoptotic cell death,[31] it is a useful marker. An *in situ* method was developed which uses terminal deoxynucleotidyl transferase (TdT) to label the 3'-OH ends of endonuclease-digested DNA by nick-translation.[32] This enzyme preferentially labels single stranded DNA or double stranded DNA with 3' protruding ends. Recessive 3'-OH ends, the expected result of single strand DNA nicks, are least efficiently labeled by TdT.[33] The addition of Co^{2+} ions improves the efficiency of TdT such that it will prime any 3' terminus, although not with uniform efficiency.[34] Results suggest that double-strand nicks are likely produced in apoptosis, while single strand nicks may occur in 'normal' tissue and perhaps in necrosis.[5] ISEL alone is therefore insufficient to demonstrate apoptosis unequivocally. It has been used to determine whether apoptosis occurs in neurodegenerative conditions other than PD,[35–38] but additional methods, such as gel electrophoresis or EM, were employed to confirm the ISEL data.

COMBINED USE OF ISEL WITH FLUORESCENT DNA-BINDING DYES

New conjugates to dUTP have been made, most notably the BODIPY fluorophores (Molecular Probes) which are intensely fluorescent when conjugated to nucleotides. These fluorescent nucleotides offer the advantage of direct localization. The standard ISEL protocol is considerably shortened by the use of a fluorescent tag and allows same-day double-labeling and analysis. Moreover, the fluorescent marker is readily distinguished from nearby neuromelanin. Secondly, sections can be examined by confocal laser imaging which provides information about sub-nuclear localization of DNA fragmentation.

The dimeric cyanine dye YOYO-1 (Molecular Probes) binds to DNA by intercalation but may also have preferential base specificity.[39] YOYO-1 is a very bright fluorochrome, and confocal laser microscopy combined with deconvolution analysis reveals patterns of chromatin condensation.

IN SITU METHODS TO IDENTIFY APOPTOTIC NUCLEI CHROMATIN CONDENSATION

The metachromatic fluorochrome acridine orange intercalates with double-stranded DNA to emit maximally at 530 nm as a bright green fluorescence, and associates with single-stranded RNA to emit maximally at 640 nm as a bright orange-red fluorescence. Normal neuronal nuclei have a few bright-green strands against a relatively dull matrix and a bright orange cytoplasm.[5] In contrast, apoptotic neuronal nuclei appear as a homogeneous bright green with a dull orange or dark cytoplasm as seen with an epifluorescence microscope. However, the superior resolution of confocal laser imaging confirmed that the apparently homogeneous green DNA-acridine orange stained nucleus occurred in coarse chromatin clumps, similar to EM images seen in other models of apoptosis. Different pretreatment methods preclude the use of acridine orange staining on the same sections as *in situ* end-labeling with the ApopTag kit. We therefore developed a double-labeling method to enable both *in situ* end-labeling of DNA and visualization of chromatin condensation in the same nucleus.

USE OF FLUORESCENT DOUBLE-LABELING METHODS TO DETECT APOPTOTIC NUCLEI

The germinal plate region from the nervous system of a 23-week-old fetus was used as a positive control for the method. Approximately 100–150 serial sections of the SNc, each ten microns thick, from patients with PD, diffuse Lewy body disease and two age-matched controls were examined. Figure 1 illustrates the correspondence of YOYO-1 and BODIPY-dUTP labeling in neurons undergoing programmed cell death in the germinal cortex. The upper left hand panel shows the heterogeneous staining pattern of YOYO-1

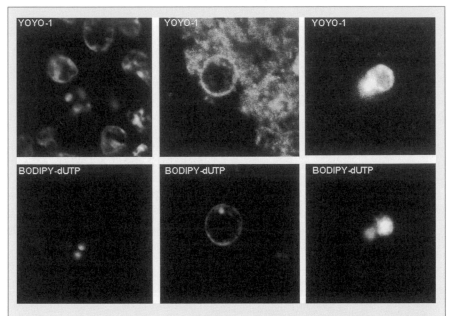

Figure 1: Confocal laser images of YOYO and BODIPY-dUTP labeled cells in the human embryonic germinal plate undergoing developmentally programmed cell death. The upper panel shows different patterns of chromatin condensation as revealed by bright fluorescent YOYO-DNA complexes. Upper left: a nucleus separating into smaller apoptotic bodies; upper center: chromatin margination at the nuclear membrane; upper right: a relatively homogeneous pattern of chromatin condensation throughout the nucleus. The lower panel shows the identical nuclei *in situ* end-labeled with BODIPY-TR-dUTP. Only those cells in the upper panel that were fluorescent bright with YOYO-1, indicating apoptotic chromatin condensation, are end-labeled with BODIPY-dUTP, indicating DNA fragmentation.

in normal nuclei which surround a central apoptotic nucleus which is separating into apoptotic bodies. In the corresponding BODIPY-dUTP image (lower left panel), only the nucleus separating into apoptotic bodies demonstrates bright BODIPY labeling. The upper central panel shows chromatin margination to the nuclear periphery. The corresponding BODIPY image, lower central panel, shows an identical margination pattern. The upper right hand panel demonstrates a relatively homogeneously bright nucleus with YOYO-1 staining. The BODIPY image (lower right) demonstrates the correspondence of bright ISEL with bright YOYO staining. We have seen similar patterns in the SNc of the MPTP-treated mouse following ISEL and acridine orange staining of sections.[5] Similar patterns have been described with EM images of apoptotic nuclei.[26]

Figure 2 illustrates confocal laser images of combined fluorescent ISEL with YOYO-1 in the SNc from human post-mortem PD brain. The upper left panel depicts by interference contrast a neuromelanin-containing neuron with abundant neuromelanin granules and the clearly-outlined smooth nuclear membrane. Using appropriate filters for BODIPY-dUTP labeling (central panel), the nucleus does not show any remarkable bright staining. With YOYO-1 staining (right panel) the nucleus does not appear bright, apart from the region immediately adjacent to the nucleolus. The lower left panel shows an interference contrast image of a neuron with neuromelanin granules that no longer appear to have a distinct granular form. The BODIPY-dUTP image (lower middle panel) of the same neuron shows a very bright, relatively homogeneous staining nucleus indicative of positive ISEL, while YOYO-1 staining (lower right panel) shows a very bright staining nucleus with a coarse granular appearance, confirming the occurrence of chromatin condensation in the same nucleus that demonstrated DNA fragmentation. Deconvolution analysis confirms that YOYO-1 staining does indeed reveal the chromatin condensation patterns of apoptosis. We could not detect any difference in background and non-specific labeling with either the BODIPY-nucleotides or YOYO-1 from tissue fixed for either 2 months or 9 months.

These techniques indicate that apoptotic neuronal death does occur in the SNc of patients with PD. Some apoptotic nuclei were detected in a single case of diffuse Lewy body disease, but they appeared to be less frequent than in PD. Finally, some apoptotic nuclei have been observed in age-matched control nigras, but in very low numbers compared to PD.

SUMMARY

- We have developed a fluorescent double-labeling method combining ISEL and YOYO-1 techniques to detect DNA changes and chromatin condensation as markers of apoptosis.
- When combined with high-resolution confocal laser imaging and deconvolution analysis, this method allows for unequivocal identification of apoptotic nuclei.

- We demonstrate the presence of nuclei in the SNc of PD patients which stain with both YOYO-1 and ISEL. Staining of individual neurons with both techniques provides unequivocal evidence of apoptosis in PD. This occurs much more frequently in PD than in age-matched controls.

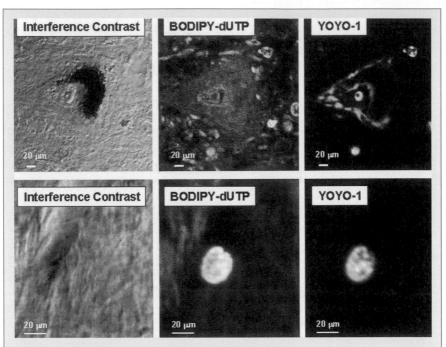

Figure 2: Combined YOYO-1 staining and BODIPY-dUTP end-labeling identify apoptotic nuclei in PD nigra. The upper panel depicts a normal neuromelanin-containing neuron from the PD nigra. Upper left: a neuron with discrete neuromelanin granules viewed with interference contrast confocal laser imaging, showing a discrete nuclear membrane and plasma membrane boundaries; upper center: the same neuron with BODIPY end-labeling, showing no significant labeling of the neuronal nucleus; upper right: the same neuron with YOYO-1 staining, showing no DNA condensation, although there is slightly more intense labeling in the area immediately surrounding the nucleolus. The lower panel depicts an apoptotic neuron from another section through the same PD nigra. Lower left: some neuromelanin remains with interference contrast but no longer in a distinct granular pattern; lower center: an apoptotic neuron brightly end-labeled with BODIPY-dUTP throughout the nucleus, indicating DNA fragmentation; lower right: the same neuron brightly stained with YOYO-1 throughout the nucleus indicating chromatin condensation and thus confirming apoptosis.

REFERENCES

1. Mochizuki H, Goto K, Mori H, Mizuno Y. Histochemical detection of apoptosis in Parkinson's disease. J Neurol Sci 1996; 137: 120–123.

2. Dragunow M, Faull RL, Lawlor P, Beilharz EJ, Singleton K, Walker EB, Mee E. *In situ* evidence for DNA fragmentation in Huntington's disease striatum and Alzheimer's disease temporal lobes. Neuroreport 1995; 6: 1053–1057.

3. Kosel S, Egensperger R, Eitzen U, Mehraein P, Graeber MB. On the question of apoptosis in the parkinsonian substantia nigra. Acta Neuropathol 1997; 93: 105–108.

4. Anglade P, Vyas S, Javoy-Agid F, Herrero MT, Michel PP, Marquez J, Mouatt-Prigent A, Ruberg M, Hirsch EC, Agid Y. Apoptosis and autophagy in nigral neurons of patients with Parkinson's disease. Histol Histopathol 1997; 12: 25–31.

5. Tatton NA, Kish SJ. In situ detection of apoptotic nuclei in the substantia nigra compacta of 1-methyl-4-phenyl-1,2,3,6-tetrahydropyridine-treated mice using terminal deoxynucleotidyl transferase labelling and acridine orange staining. Neurosci 1997; 77: 1037–1048.

6. Kroemer G, Zamzani N, Susin SA. Mitochondrial control of apoptosis. Immunol Today 1997; 18: 43–51.

7. Rossiter JP, Riopelle RJ, Bisby MA. Axotomy-induced apoptotic cell death of neonatal rat facial motoneurons: time course analysis and relation to NADPH-diaphorase activity. Exp Neurol 1996; 138: 33–44.

8. Tatton WG, Ju WY, Holland DP, Tai C, Kwan M. (-)-Deprenyl reduces PC12 cell apoptosis by inducing new protein synthesis. J Neurochem 1994; 63: 1572–1575.

9. Zamzami N, Marchetti P, Castedo M, Zanin C, Vayssiere J-L, Petit PX, Kroemer G. Reduction in mitochondrial potential constitutes an early irreversible step of programmed lymphocyte death *in vivo*. J Exp Med 1995; 181: 1661–1672.

10. Enokido Y, Araki T, Tanaka K, Aizawa S, Hatanaka H. Involvement of p53 in DNA strand break-induced apoptosis in postmitotic CNS neurons. Eur J Neurosci 1996; 8: 1812–1821.

11. Mochizuki H, Nakamura N, Nishi K, Mizuno Y. Apoptosis is induced by 1-methyl-4-phenylpyridinium (MPP+) in ventral mesencephalic-striatal co-culture in rat. Neurosci Lett 1994; 170: 191–194.

12. Chinnaiyan AM, Dixit VM. Portrait of an executioner: the molecular mechanism of Fas/APO-1-induced apoptosis. Semin Immunol 1997; 9: 69–76.

13. Micheau O, Solary E, Hammann A, Martin F, Dimanche-Boitrel MT. Sensitization of cancer cells treated with cytotoxic drugs to fas-mediated cytotoxicity. J Natl Cancer Inst 1997; 89: 783–789.

14. Polla BS, Jacquier-Sarlin MR, Kantengwa S, Mariethz E, Hennet T, Russo-Marie F, Cossarizza, A. TNF-alpha alters mitochondrial membrane potential L929 but not in TNF alpha-resistant L929.12 cells: relationship with the expression of stress proteins, annexin 1 and superoxide dismutase activity. Free Rad Res 1996; 25: 125–131.

15. Schapira AH. Mitochondrial disorders. Curr Opin Neurol 1997; 10: 43–47.

16. Jenner P, Olanow CW. Oxidative stress and the pathogenesis of Parkinson's disease. Neurol 1996; 47 (Suppl 3): S161–S170.

17. Zilkha-Falb R, Ziv I, Nardi N, Offen D, Melamed E, Barzilai A. Monoamine-induced apoptotic neuronal cell death. Cell Mol Neurobiol 1997; 17: 101–118.

18. Ziv I, Zilkha FR, Offen D, Shirvan A, Barzilai A, Melamed E. Levodopa

induces apoptosis in cultured neuronal cells – a possible accelerator of nigrostriatal degeneration in Parkinson's disease. Mov Disord 1997; 12: 17–23.

19. Wadia JS, Chalmers-Redman RME, Ju WJH, Carlile GW, Phillips JL, Fraser AD, Tatton WG. Mitochondrial membrane potential and nuclear changes in apoptosis caused by serum and nerve growth factor withdrawal: time course and modification by (-)-deprenyl. J Neurosci 1998; 18: 932–947.

20. Zamzami N, Susin SA, Marchetti P. Mitochondrial control of nuclear apoptosis. J Exp Med 1996; 183: 1533–1544.

21. Marchetti P, Castedo M, Susin SA, Zamzami N, Hirsch T, Macho A, Haeffner A, Hirsch F, Geuskens M, Kroemer G. Mitochondrial permeability transition is a central coordinating event of apoptosis. J Exp Med 1996; 184: 1155–1160.

22. Castedo M, Hirsch T, Susin SA, Zamzami N, Marchetti P, Macho A, Kroemer G. Sequential acquistion of mitochondrial and plasma membrane alterations during early lymphocyte apoptosis. J Immunol 1996; 157: 512–521.

23. Cossarizza A, Franceschi C, Monti D. Functional heterogeneity of an isolated mitochondrial population revealed by cytofluorometric analysis at the single cell level. Exp Cell Res 1995; 220: 232–240.

24. Kruman I, Bruce-Keller AJ, Bredesen D, Waeg G, Mattson MP. Evidence that 4-hydroxynonenal mediates oxidative stress-induced neuronal apoptosis. J Neurosci 1997; 17: 5089–5100.

25. Hantraye P, Brouillet E, Ferrante R, Palfi S, Dolan R, Matthews RT, Beal MF. Inhibition of neuronal nitric oxide synthase prevents MPTP-induced parkinsonism in baboons. Nat Med 1996; 2: 1017–1021.

26. Wyllie AH, Kerr JFR, Currie AR. Cell death: the significance of apoptosis. Int Rev Cytol 1980; 68: 251–305.

27. Kerr JFR, Searle J, Harmon BV, Bishop CJ. Apoptosis. In, Potten CS, ed, Perspectives on Mammalian Cell Death. Oxford: Oxford University Press, 1987: 93–128.

28. Kerr JFR, Wyllie AH, Currie AR. Apoptosis, a basic biological phenomenon with wide-ranging implications in tissue kinetics. Br J Cancer 1972; 26: 239–257.

29. Sanders EJ, Wride MA. Programmed cell death in development. Int Rev Cytol 1995; 163: 105–156.

30. Walker NI, Harmon BV, Gobe GC, Kerr JFR. Patterns of cell death. Methods Achiev Exp Pathol 1988; 13: 18–54.

31. Schultze-Osthoff K, Walcak H, Dioge W, Krammer PH. Cell nucleus and DNA fragmentation are not required for apoptosis. J Cell Biol 1994; 15–20.

32. Gavrieli Y, Sherman Y, Ben-Sasson SA. Identification of programmed cell death in situ via specific labeling of nuclear DNA fragmentation. J Cell Biol 1992; 119: 493–501.

33. Ben-Sasson SA, Sherman Y, Gavrieli Y. Identification of dying cells – in situ staining. Methods Cell Biol 1995; 46: 29–39.

34. Tabor S, Struhl K, Scharf SJ, Gelfand DH. Enzymatic manipulation of DNA and RNA. In, Current Protocols in Molecular Biology. New York: J Wiley & Sons Inc, 1997.

35. Kerrigan LA, Zack DJ, Quigley HA, Smith SD, Pease ME. TUNEL-positive ganglion cells in human primary open-angle glaucoma. Arch Ophthalmol 1997; 115: 1031–1035.

36. Petito CK, Roberts B. Evidence of apoptotic cell death in HIV encephalitis. Am J Pathol 1995; 146: 1121–1130.

37. Troost D, Aten J, Morsink F, de Jong JMBV. Apoptosis in amyotrophic lateral sclerosis is not restricte to motor neurons. Bcl-2 expression is increased in unaffected post-central gyrus. Neuropath Appl Neurobiol 1995; 21: 498–504.

38. Portera-Cailliau C, Hedreen JC, Price DL, Koliatsos VE. Evidence for apoptotic cell death in Huntington disease and excitotoxic animal models. J Neurosci 1995; 15: 3775–3787.

39. Hirons GT, Fawcett JJ, Crissman HA. TOTO and YOYO: New very bright fluorochromes for DNA content analyses by flow cytometry. Cytometr 1994; 15: 129–140.

DISCUSSION

Olanow: It appears from your mouse data that the number of cells staining with acridine orange was greater than those staining with the ISEL technique, yet one of our concerns is that ISEL produces many false positives. Does this mean that there are more false positives with acridine orange?

N. Tatton: It is probably easier with acridine orange staining to detect a very bright nucleus and it may also give us more latitude in terms of looking at chromatin clumping from a range of time points. We may be unable to mark something like apoptosis using BODIPY dUTP throughout the whole time course of the decline in apoptosis so that may be the reason for the discrepancy.

Gash: We are struggling with methods for unequivocal demonstration of apoptosis as opposed to some of the artefacts and you were illustrating both. The MPTP-treated mouse model is very dependent on strain and age If MPTP is given to young mice of the C57BL strain, the neurons are injured but they recover, and if you give higher doses you can indeed kill the neurons but you also kill the mouse. I was wondering how you control these parameters to look for apoptosis in the mouse model?

N. Tatton: We picked a dose of MPTP that we knew would kill about 30–40% of the nigral neurons in the C57BL mouse, judging by Nissl counts and alternate sections of TH-identified neurons. This was 150 mg/kg total dosage. I have since seen data from another group using a 50 mg/kg single dose and they also saw apoptosis in the substantia nigra. Achieving the right dosage can be a gamble. Other groups have used a different approach, with a cumulative amount of 80 mg/kg given as four divided doses. The outcome was what appeared to be a non-apoptotic cell death, possibly necrotic. This mimics what one would see in tissue culture, in that a high dose reduces the mitochondrial membrane potential very quickly, resulting in a necrotic type of cell death without the opportunity to respond by changes in gene transcription. A more prolonged chronic dose is effectively a slightly milder insult so one can simulate apoptotic descent.

Langston: The route of administration may be important too. Subcutaneous administration gives a stronger effect than intraperitoneal dosing, which could be an advantage or disadvantage. Can you describe the units that you used to measure apoptotic cells? Secondly, did I understand correctly that one of your parkinsonian cases did not have PD clinically during life?

N. Tatton: To answer your first question, I looked at the number of neuromelanin cells remaining per slide, and the cells I counted were those that had an obvious nucleolus on interference contrast. Secondly, there was no clinical diagnosis of the cases and the definition was based on neuropathology. Perhaps Dr. Perl can explain?

Perl: Our cases came from a nursing home because we wanted the freshest material possible with a short post-mortem interval. The first case looked like PD neuropathologically. The diagnosis had not been made in the nursing home and perhaps should be considered as an incidental Lewy body case although it is likely that the patient had PD based on chart review. We will look at more well-defined cases in the near future. One of the cases had dementia and a pathological picture consistent with dementia Lewy bodies.

N. Tatton: One of my initial concerns was to minimize the length of time the tissue was in fixative. Actually, I saw no difference in terms of non-specific labeling between tissue that was in fixative for two months as opposed to eight months. Therefore we can now look at cases that have been in fixative longer and have better characterized PD.

Hirsch: Different types of programmed cell death can be defined according to morphological criteria. For instance, what is really apoptosis and what is autophagic degeneration? With your different nuclear markers, have you seen any involvement of the cytoplasm?

N. Tatton: I have not looked closely at that yet. I have seen some bright staining which would appear to be cytoplasmic but it is very small and I have not done a double stain to identify the cells as macrophages or any other type of glia or neuronal cell. I think cytoplasmic involvement will be there.

Beal: According to cell counting with these techniques, particularly end-labeling, one might expect that with the normal rate of cell death, these brains would be degenerating much more rapidly than one could account for under normal circumstances. Do you have any thoughts on the explanation for this?

N. Tatton: We have at least two problems. Firstly, we do not know the duration of the life of an apoptotic body *in vivo*, in human tissue. A paper in *NeuroReport* reported an *ex vivo* study of dorsal ganglia from the rat which seemed to suggest that the *in vivo/in vitro* life might be about an hour. Secondly, we are sometimes looking at tissue from a very old patient and it seems that there might be a different rate of decline in the first few years of being identified as parkinsonian. That may also be reflected in the rate of cell death. There may be an early wave of apoptotic cell death that slows down by the time we see most of these specimens. Until we have a better feel for the *in vivo* lifetime of an apoptotic nucleus, it will be very difficult to extrapolate.

Riederer: Do you think that the apoptosis that you see in PD is the result of the agonal state or of the disease process?

N. Tatton: I think it is a result of the disease process.

Mizuno: We have studied about seven patients with sporadic PD by the TUNEL method and the number of apoptotic positive neurons was about 2% in the remaining nigral neurons which fits with your data of 1.7%. Therefore I believe that apoptosis is involved in PD. How long do such apoptotic bodies remain in the substantia nigra? According to the literature, it has been found that apoptotic bodies remain for only two hours in tissue culture. Do you have any idea how long they would remain in patients with PD?

N. Tatton: I think it is going to be several hours, if only for the fact that we are still seeing autophagic consumption of these apoptotic bodies. They are not disappearing immediately so there is obviously time for microglia to consume them. I do not know if there is a way to determine the actual length of time. This could be done easily in an *in vivo* animal model by staging the time of sacrifice according to the time of induction of apoptosis. We could not do that on human tissue so we need to look for markers occurring in the earlier induction and effector phases of the apoptotic process. We should not put too much emphasis on the end phase of apoptosis but right now it is a useful marker and we can look at it in a number of different tissues fairly easily.

Mizuno: We also studied six control patients and most of them had severe anoxic periods before their death. None of them showed apoptotic positive neurons, so I believe TUNEL-positivity indicates a disease process not an agonal state.

Marsden: If the apoptotic body remains for about a week and if 2% of the residual nigral neurons are lost then they should all be dead within a year. There is something seriously wrong here which raises a question. Do you know what the effect brain pH has on apoptosis? In our own brain bank we use brain pH as the best marker of a viable brain.

N. Tatton: I have not seen any published data on the effects. I think what we are seeing here is the expression of apoptotic nuclei against a very small number of remaining neuromelanin neurons and if we look earlier we see a substantially larger number of neuromelanin-containing cells in the nigra which will change our ratios significantly. Ultimately these apoptotic nuclei may not remain for more than 20 minutes, but we may be unable to answer this question.

Olanow: I think there is a possibility that what you may be seeing are vulnerable or pre-apoptotic cells that have, for example, altered mitochondrial membrane potential. During the death process, cells that might undergo apoptosis over the next months or years are pushed into apoptosis by the stresses associated with the agonal stages of life.

N. Tatton: We need to look for markers, perhaps the translocation of NFκB or GAPDH into the nucleus, which appear to occur early in the apoptotic process. That may give us a better handle on lifespan as well as being a more reasonable marker of this event.

Beal: We know from these other *in vivo* models, from your own work with MPTP and from the work with ischemia, that clear-cut TUNEL labeling can be seen and appears predominantly by about three weeks. If we are losing 2% per day we should not have many neurons left after a short period of time.

N. Tatton: You are assuming that this is a synchronous event and I do not know if this is the case in humans.

Hirsch: We are particularly aware of the problems of pre-mortem severity and in our studies in PD cases we control for that. We have an index which was published in 1984 and we have many more apoptotic features in PD patients than in controls matched for pre-mortem severity index. So if it plays a role, something else is associated with the disease in PD. Concerning the rate of cell loss, we know that in PD there is extraneuronal neuromelanin and many more than 2% of the cells must be surviving to correspond with aggregates of neuromelanin. I wonder whether these nuclei or apoptotic fragments are simply sitting in the macrophages and would take a long time to be removed. We have no real concern about the extraneuronal neuromelanin so why should we have with these apoptotic fragments?

Schapira: To respond to one point which was raised about the multifactorial induction of apoptosis by reducing the APT level, we showed that MPP can induce apoptosis in a concentration-dependent manner but switches to necrosis further up the concentration scale. Apoptotic induction by MPP+ and other complex I inhibitors can be blocked with free radical scavengers, so it is probably the release of free radicals following as a consequence of the respiratory chain inhibition that is responsible. So we have a drop in both APT and free radical generation which together combine to produce apoptosis possibly through opening of the pore. To some extent this may help explain what happens in an agonal state which might result in increased apoptosis before death, if there is a defect in the compensatory mechanisms of free radical scavenging that occur in the agonal state. If brain pH between parkinsonian and controls is controlled, there is no significant increase in apoptosis.

Marsden: The brain pH story is worth mentioning in more detail because clinical indices of the agonal state, times of post-mortem and refrigeration are very crude indices of brain viability. The brain pH does provide the best index, at least of preservation of mRNA.

Olanow: Nonetheless, it is appealing to speculate that if the nigral cells have mitochondria with reduced mitochondrial potential as we found in the PD fibroblasts that Dr. Bill Tatton showed, they may be prone to go into apoptosis under agonal conditions.

Marsden: Absolutely. One may be detecting a vulnerability to apoptosis which is seen to excess because of the agonal state.

N. Tatton: I want to recall for everyone that when we look at the appearance of chromatin condensation as well as DNA fragmentation through primary labeling, after the induction of apoptosis under *in vitro* conditions of trophic withdrawal, it takes about six hours to start to see these markers. We have to bear in mind that there is a certain lag time before any of these structural changes start to occur. If we can look at very short post-mortem times, we could lessen our chances of any kind of artifactual apoptotic events occurring.

Langston: I would point out that much of the neuromelanin is sitting in macrophages or microglia. Unless these apoptotic bodies are in glia, it is probably not the best analogy to use.

W. Tatton: There is much literature on intracellular pH in apoptosis now and one of the principal features is that marked intracellular pH changes occur with relatively little extracellular change. I would argue that the intracellular changes are important here and putting a pH meter into the tissue will reveal very little.

Marsden: Actually it reveals much about the chances of preserving mRNA. A good brain for *in situ* mRNA studies is one with a decent pH.

CHAPTER TWENTY ONE

Levodopa toxicity and apoptosis

ELDAD MELAMED, DANIEL OFFEN, ANAT SHIRVAN, RUTH
DJALDETTI, AVI BARZILAI, AND ILAN ZIV
Department of Neurology, Rabin Medical Center, Beilinson Campus,
and Felsenstein Research Institute, Petah Tikva, and Sackler School
of Medicine, Tel Aviv University, Tel Aviv, Israel

The therapeutic options for improving symptoms, motor function and quality of life of patients with Parkinson's disease (PD) include pharmacological measures such as levodopa, dopamine agonists, monoamine oxidase (MAO) inhibitors, anticholinergics and amantadines, and ablative, stimulatory and transplantational surgical approaches.[1,2] Oral levodopa remains the most effective antiparkinsonian drug[3] and its efficacy can be amplified by co-administration with inhibitors of peripheral dopa decarboxylase (DDC), MAO and, recently, catechol-o-methyltransferase. Unlike the missing neurotransmitter dopamine, orally-administered levodopa can cross the blood–brain barrier. In the striatum, it is converted to receptor-accessible dopamine by DDC in the surviving nigrostriatal nerve terminals and in non-dopaminergic cellular compartments.[4,5] Thus, exogenous levodopa can replenish the markedly reduced levels of dopamine in the parkinsonian striatum and repair the arrested or suppressed nigrostriatal dopaminergic neurotransmission. However, experience indicates that the interactions of long-term levodopa with PD are extremely complex, and its use causes persistent concern. Firstly, exogenous levodopa is not a physiological treatment for PD.[6] When given orally, it reaches and floods the entire brain and bombards not only the basal ganglia and the dopaminergic receptorial system but also the entire CNS. In addition, exogenous levodopa and the dopamine it generates are handled differently to the endogenous levodopa formed from tyrosine hydroxylation.[7] The dopamine formed from endogenous tyrosine and levodopa is stored within neurons mostly in vesicles and its release and synthesis are linked to neuronal firing rates. By contrast, synthesis and release of dopamine formed from exogenous levodopa is entirely dissociated from dopaminergic neuronal activity. In all likelihood, this dopamine is not stored within vesicles but spills into the synapse as soon as it is generated, stimulates the receptors in a non-physiological manner and is rapidly metabolized. This may explain the many adverse reactions to chronic levodopa treatment, including dyskinesias, complex motor fluctuations and psychosis. Levodopa may also be toxic to the remaining dopaminergic neurons (and perhaps to other non-dopaminergic neuronal systems).[8] Sustained administration might change the predetermined natural history of the disease and accelerate its progression by increasing the rate of nigrostriatal degeneration. If this is the case, levodopa treatment should be reserved for the more advanced stages of the illness.[9–12]

IN VITRO TOXICITY OF LEVODOPA

Levodopa is toxic to various cultured neuronal and non-neuronal cells.[13–15] This may be linked to levodopa auto-oxidation,[16] which generates toxic free radical species including superoxide, hydrogen peroxide and hydroxyl radicals, as transition metals may enhance these toxic pathways.[14,17] One product of oxidative metabolism of levodopa is the pigment dopa-melanin[18] which, together with its semiquinone and quinone metabolic intermediaries, is toxic and may itself be lethal to cells *in vitro*. Blockade of *in vitro* toxicity of levodopa by combined treatment with antioxidants (particularly the thiol-containing compounds) supports the crucial role of levodopa-derived reactive oxygen species.[19–22] Levodopa and its oxidative metabolites may kill cells by causing membranal lipid peroxidation and disruption.[23] It may poison the mitochondrial respiratory apparatus – mainly complex I,[24–26] and may cause nuclear DNA damage.[27,28] Dopamine is also extremely toxic,[14,29] being equipotent to levodopa in its effects in tissue culture.[14] Levodopa toxicity may therefore also be due, at least in part, to its conversion to dopamine.[30]

LEVODOPA AND APOPTOSIS

There are two major modes of cell death, necrosis and apoptosis.[31–33] Necrosis is the non-selective death of multiple cells, always induced by non-physiological triggers. By contrast, apoptosis involves activation of genetically-encoded cell suicide programs, and involves death of individual cells, sometimes by purely physiological stimuli. As a rule, intracellular organelles remain intact in apoptosis but are destroyed in necrosis. Apoptosis, or programmed cell death, plays a major physiological role in the differentiation and organization of the central nervous system during its normal development. The developing brain loses about 50% of its cells *via* apoptosis before achieving maturity. Apoptosis may be involved in the pathogenesis of degenerative human neurological disorders, particularly those associated with aging.

Dopamine and levodopa can exert the characteristic biochemical and morphological features of apoptosis in several neuronal and non-neuronal cell cultures.[34–36] Such programmed cell death can be inhibited by co-treatment with thiol-containing antioxidants[37] and by vector-driven expression of the apoptosis-blocking proto-oncogene *bcl-2*.[38] Inadvertent activation of intrinsic cell suicide programs in nigral neurons by levodopa or dopamine and its toxic oxidation products may therefore lead to their degeneration by an apoptotic mode in PD. Ultrastructural morphological studies have demonstrated that dopaminergic neurons are indeed undergoing apoptosis in the parkinsonian substantia nigra.[39–42] The nigra in PD is under conditions of excess oxidative stress,[43–45] which may be due to auto- and enzymatic oxidation of dopamine, the presence of iron, and synthesis of neuromelanin that generates semiquinones and quinones *en route*. Levodopa administration may also play a role as it is an extremely potent inducer of apoptosis.[46] Similar findings were reported in catecholaminergic PC-12 cells.[47] No evidence yet suggests that systemic levodopa is responsible for some or all of the apoptotic changes observed in the parkinsonian nigra.[39,40] The number of neurons undergoing apoptosis at any one time in post-mortem PD nigral tissues is small.[39–42] A systemically-administered toxin such as levodopa would be expected to result in a much higher number of apoptotic nigral neurons. However neurons are very rapidly phagocytized by macrophages and may disappear without local inflammation or other damage. At death, most of the levodopa-triggered apoptotic neurons may have already disappeared. Most plausibly, however, levodopa may not be toxic to, and does not evoke apoptosis of, nigral neurons *in vivo*, including in patients with PD, but the possibility remains.

Is Levodopa Toxic *in vivo* in Animals and Patients?

In vivo studies using long-term administration of large levodopa doses to experimental animals have not shown damage to nigrostriatal neurons.[48,49] However, levodopa treatment can potentiate the toxicity of intracerebroventricular injections of 6-hydroxydopamine (6-OHDA) in mice.[50] Long-term treatment with levodopa induced additional damage to rodent ventral tegmental (but not nigrostriatal) dopaminergic neurons surviving prior exposure to 6-OHDA.[51,52] These results were not confirmed in a study where levodopa was given for six months.[53] Likewise, no damage to dopaminergic neurons was observed following long-term daily injections of levodopa, despite systemic administration of MPTP.[54] Chronic levodopa destroyed fetal mesencephalic dopaminergic neurons grafted into striatum in rats[55] but a transplant into rat corpora striata denervated by 6-OHDA lesions was unaffected by chronic (27 weeks) levodopa treatment.[56] Repeated levodopa injections to pregnant mice did not damage nigrostriatal neurons and did not impair postnatal development in the fetuses.[57] Thus, laboratory studies do not establish toxicity associated with levodopa therapy.

Clinical studies in humans to show or disprove levodopa toxicity are difficult to perform, since PD progresses even under chronic levodopa coverage. However, since levodopa exerts a clinical benefit, it is difficult to determine whether the disease progresses at a predetermined pace or whether it is further accelerated by levodopa. Nevertheless, most studies indicate that chronic levodopa treatment is not toxic to human nigrostriatal dopaminergic neurons, and does not aggravate PD.[58–60] In addition, excellent survival and axonal outgrowth of transplanted dopaminergic neurons was observed, despite continuous post-operative levodopa administration.[61] .

POSSIBLE EXPLANATIONS FOR THE DISCREPANCY BETWEEN MARKED LEVODOPA TOXICITY *IN VITRO* AND ITS ABSENCE *IN VIVO*

Cells in culture may lack the defense mechanisms of target tissue *in vivo*, such as enzymes that scavenge toxic free radical species, other antioxidants, trophic growth factors, and the soluble calcium-binding protein calretinin.[62] A potent inhibitor of apoptosis is the proto-oncogene *bcl-2*.[63,64] PC-12 cells over-expressing *bcl-2* were immune to dopamine and also to levodopa toxicity *in vitro*.[38,65] Activity of the *bcl-2* family of anti-apoptotic proto-oncogenes in the brain, and particularly in the parkinsonian substantia nigra, may provide protection against systemic levodopa, the generated dopamine and reactive oxidation species.[66] Another crucial component are glial cells which, in pure culture, are resistant to the toxicity of dopamine, H_2O_2, MPTP and levodopa.[67] Glial cells normally present in the substantia nigra contain high levels of reduced glutathione and may neutralize environmental toxins as well as endogenous noxious compounds. Glia contain high levels of glutathione, a potent natural antioxidant. Studies looking for signs of neuronal apoptosis in the parkinsonian nigra unexpectedly reported a relatively high number of glial cells showing the morphological characteristics of programmed cell death.[39,42] Glial cells, serving as a major defense against local toxins and exogenous levodopa, may bear the brunt of the attack and die apoptotically after saving their protégé neurons.

Concentrations of levodopa in tissue culture media are typically much higher than those attainable in the CNS of experimental animals and parkinsonians *in vivo* after systemic drug administration.[68,69] Levodopa may even be protective under certain circumstances due to injury-induced upregulation of anti-oxidant and anti-apoptotic molecules.[70] Preconditioning of neurons by prior exposure to sub-lethal concentrations of levodopa renders the cells resistant against second exposure to lethal doses of the drug (unpublished observations) possibly because they contain higher concentrations of reduced glutathione.[71] Peripheral blood lymphocytes from parkinsonian patients treated chronically with levodopa are more resistant to toxicity induced by dopamine, H_2O_2 and high doses of levodopa than controls. Cells in peripheral tissues and neurons in the brain may be preconditioned by chronic levodopa treatment to develop or strengthen defense mechanisms such as glutathione content, free radical scavenging enzymes and trophic factors. Chronic levodopa treatment may not be associated with enhanced oxidative stress, at least in plasma.[72]

When more than 60% of dopaminergic neurons in the parkinsonian nigra die, remaining neurons become hyperactive and fire more rapidly than neurons in an intact nigra,[73] and this may also accelerate the progression of PD. There is no clinical proof, but exogenous levodopa would be expected to stimulate autoreceptors on striatal nerve-endings and nigral dendrites of surviving hyperactive nigrostriatal neurons and suppress their firing rates via the central production of unstored dopamine freely spilled into synapses.

Thus, it canot be established with certainty whether levodopa has any toxic effects on dopamine neurons in PD. It is hard to replicate the circumstances that are present in the PD nigra in an experimental paradigm but, for now, clinical studies do not demonstrate convincing evidence of accelerated neurodegeneration due to levodopa therapy. Nonetheless, this possibility has not been refuted and should be considered when levodopa is administered to PD patients.

SUMMARY

- Levodopa metabolism can generate reactive oxygen species through its conversion to dopamine or its autooxidation.

- Levodopa has been shown to induce apoptosis in cultured dopaminergic neurons.

- There are as yet no data indicating that levodopa induces toxicity in PD patients. Although this is reassuring and encouraging, it is still inconclusive since the susceptibility of nigral dopaminergic neurons to the toxic effects of systemic levodopa cannot be completely ruled out. Furthermore, lack of a toxic effect in the normal brain may not assure the absence of toxicity in PD where there is increased iron and defense mechanisms are compromised.

- For that reason, it would be logical to exercise caution in the treatment of early PD and use other drugs such as dopamine agonists to delay initiation of levodopa for as long as possible.

ACKNOWLEDGMENT

Supported, in part, by the National Parkinson Foundation, Miami, U.S.A.

REFERENCES

1. Marsden CD. Parkinson's disease. Lancet 1990; 335: 908–952.

2. Agid Y. Parkinson's disease: Pathophysiology. Lancet 1991; 337: 1321–1324.

3. Cotzias GC, Van Woert MH, Schiffer LM. Aromatic amino acids and modification of parkinsonism. N Engl J Med 1967; 276: 374–379.

4. Melamed E, Hefti F, Wurtman RH. Non-aminergic striatal neurons convert exogenous L-dopa to dopamine in parkinsonism. Ann Neurol 1980; 8: 528–536.

5. Hefti F, Melamed E. L-dopa's mechanism of action in Parkinson's disease. Trends Neurosci 1980; 3: 229–231.

6. Melamed E. Mechanism of action of exogenous L-dopa: Is it a physiological therapy for Parkinson's disease? In, Jankovic J, Tolosa E, eds, Advances in Parkinson's Disease and Movement Disorders. Baltimore: Urban and Schwarzenberg Inc, 1988: 87–97.

7. Melamed E. Biochemical and functional differences between dopamine formed from endogenous tyrosine and exogenous L-dopa in nigro-striatal dopaminergic neurons. Neurochem Int 1992; 20 (suppl): 115–117.

8. Fahn S. Is levodopa toxic? Neurol 1996; 47 (suppl): S184–S195.

9. Fahn S, Bressman SB. Should levodopa therapy for parkinsonism be started early or late? Evidence against early treatment. Can J Neurol Sci 1984; 11: 200–206.

10. Rajput AH, Stern W, Laverty WH. Chronic low dose levodopa therapy in Parkinson's disease: An argument for delaying L-dopa therapy. Neurol 1984; 34: 991–996.

11. Melamed E. Initiation of levodopa therapy in parkinsonian patients should be delayed until the advanced stages of the disease. Arch Neurol 1986; 43: 402–405.

12. Quinn NP. A case against early levodopa treatment of Parkinson's disease. Clin Neuropharmacol 1994; 17: S43–S49.

13. Wick MM, Byers L, Frei E. L-dopa: selective toxicity for melanoma cells in vitro. Science 1977; 197: 468–469.

14. Tanaka M, Sotomatsu A, Kanai H, Hirai S. Dopa and dopamine cause cultured neuronal death in the presence of iron. J Neurol Sci 1991; 101: 198–203.

15. Mena MA, Pardo B, Casarejos MJ, Fahn S, de Yebenes JG. Neurotoxicity of levodopa on catecholamine rich neurons. Mov Disord 1992; 7: 23–31.

16. Graham DJ, Tiffany SM, Bell WR, Gutknecht WF. Auto-oxidation versus covalent binding of quinones as the mechanism of toxicity of dopamine, 6-hydroxydopamine and related compounds towards C1300 neuroblastoma cells in vitro. Mol Pharmacol 1978; 14: 644–653.

17. Newcomer TA, Rosenberg PA, Aizenman E. Iron-mediated oxidation of 3,4-dihydroxyphenylalanine to an excitotoxin. J Neurochem 1995; 64: 1742–1748.

18. Graham AG. Oxidative pathways for catecholamines in the genesis of neuromelanin and cytotoxic quinones. Mol Pharmacol 1978; 14: 633–643.

19. Pardo B, Mena MA, Fahn S, de Yebenes JG. Ascorbic acid protects against levodopa-induced neurotoxicity on a catecholamine-rich human neuroblastoma cell line. Mov Disord 1993; 8: 278–284.

20. Mena MA, Pardo B, Paino CL, de Yebenes JG. Levodopa toxicity in fetal rat midbrain neurons in culture: modulation by ascorbic acid. Neuroreport 1993; 4: 438–440.

21. Basma AN, Morris EJ, Nicklas WJ, Geller HM. L-dopa cytotoxicity to PC-12 cells in culture is via its auto-

oxidation. J Neurochem 1995; 64: 825–832.

22. Pardo B, Mena MA, Casarejos MJ, Paino CL, de Yebenes JG. Toxic effects of L-dopa in mesencephalic cell cultures: Protection with anti-oxidants. Brain Res 1995; 682: 133–143.

23. Li CL, Werner P, Cohen G. Lipid peroxidation in brain: interactions of L-dopa/dopamine with ascorbate and iron. Neurodegeneration 1995; 4: 147–153.

24. Przedborski S, Jackson-Lewis V, Muthane U, et al. Chronic levodopa administration alters cerebral mito-chondrial respiratory chain activity. Ann Neurol 1993; 34: 715–723.

25. Przedborski S, Jackson-Lewis V, Fahn S. Antiparkinsonian therapies and brain mitochondrial complex I activity. Mov Disord 1995; 10: 312–317.

26. Pardo B, Mena MA, de Yebenes JG. L-dopa inhibits complex IV of the electron transport chain in catecholamine-rich human neuroblastoma NB69 cells. J Neurochem 1995; 64: 576–582.

27. Spencer JP, Jenner A. Aruoma OI, Marsden CD, Halliwell B. Intense oxidative DNA damage promoted by L-dopa and its metabolites: implications for neurodegenerative disease. FEBS Lett 1994; 353: 246–250.

28. Wick MM. Levodopa/dopamine analogs as inhibitors of DNA synthesis in human melanoma cells. J Invest Dermatol 1989; 92: 329S–331S.

29. Michel PP, Hefti F. Toxicity of 6-hydroxydopamine and dopamine for dopaminergic neurons in culture. J Neurosci Res 1990; 26: 428–435.

30. Alexander T, Sortwell CE, Sladek CD, Roth RH, Steece-Collier K. Comparison of neurotoxicity following repeated administration of L-dopa, D-dopa and dopamine to embryonic mesencephalic dopamine neurons in cultures derived from Fischer 344 and Sprague-Dawley donors. Cell Transplant 1997; 6: 309–315.

31. Boobis AR, Fowthrop DJ, Davies DS. Mechanisms of cell death. Trends Pharmacol Sci 1989; 10: 275–280.

32. Martin SJ. Apoptosis: Suicide, execution or murder? Trends Cell Biol 1993; 3: 141–144.

33. Cohen JJ. Apoptosis. Immunol Today 1993; 14: 126–130.

34. Ziv I, Melamed E, Nardi N, Luria D, Achiron A, Offen D, Barzilai A. Dopamine induces apoptosis-like cell death in cultured chick sympathetic neurons - a possible ovel pathogenetic mechanism in Parkinson's disease. Neurosci Lett 1994; 170: 136–140.

35. Offen D, Ziv I. Gordin S, Malik Z, Barzilai A, Melamed E. Dopamine-induced programmed cell death in mouse thymocytes. Biochim Biophys Acta 1995; 1268: 171–177.

36. Zilkha-Falb R, Ziv I, Nardi N, Offen D, Melamed E, Barzilai A. Monoamine-induced apoptotic neuronal cell death. Cell Mol Neurobiol 1997; 7: 110–118.

37. Offen D, Sternin H, Ziv I, Melamed E, Hochman A. Prevention of dopamine-induced cell death by thiol antioxidants: possible implication for treatment of Parkinson's disease. Exp Neurol 1996; 141: 32–39.

38. Ziv I, Offen D, Haviv R, Stein R, Panet H, Zilkha-Falb R, Shirvan A, Barzilai A, Melamed E. The proto-oncogene bcl-2 inhibits cellular toxicity of dopamine: possible implications for Parkinson's disease. Apoptosis 1997; 2: 149–155.

39. Mochizuki H, Goto K, Mori H, Mizuno Y. Histochemical detection of apoptosis in Parkinson's disease. J Neurol Sci 1996; 137: 120–123.

40. Anglade P, Vyas S, Javoy-Agid F, Herrero MT, Michel PP, Hirsch EC, Agid Y. Apoptosis and autophagy in nigral neurons of patients with Parkinson's disease. Histol Histopathol 1997; 12: 25–31.

41. Tompkins MM, Basgall EJ, Zamvini E, Hill WD. Apoptotic-like changes in

Lewy body-associated disorders and normal aging in substantia nigral neurons. Am J Pathol 1997; 150: 119–131.

42. Kosel S, Egensperger R, von Eitzen U, Mehraein P, Graeber MB. On the question of apoptosis in the parkinsonian substantia nigra. Acta Neuropathol 1997; 93: 105–108.

43. Fahn S, Cohen G. The oxidant stress hypothesis in Parkinson's disease. Evidence supporting it. Ann Neurol 1992; 32: 804–812.

44. Olanow CW. A radical hypothesis for neurodegeneration. Trends Neurosci 1993; 16: 439–444.

45. Jenner P, Dexter DT, Sian J, Schapira AHV, Marsden CD. Oxidative stress as a cause of nigral cell death in Parkinson's disease and incidental Lewy body disease. Ann Neurol 1992; 32: S82–S87.

46. Ziv I, Zilkha-Falb R, Offen D, Shirvan A, Barzilai A, Melamed E. Levodopa induces apoptosis in cultured neuronal cells – a possible accelerator of nigrostriatal degeneration in Parkinson's disease? Mov Disord 1997; 12: 17–23.

47. Walkinshaw G, Waters CM. Induction of apoptosis in catecholaminergic PC12 cells by L-dopa. Implications for the treatment of Parkinson's disease. J Clin Invest 1995; 95: 2458–2464.

48. Hefti F, Melamed E, Bhawan J, Wurtman RJ. Long-term administration of L-dopa does not damage dopaminergic neurons in the mouse. Neurol 1981; 31: 1194–1195.

49. Perry TL, Yong VW, Ito U, et al. Nigrostriatal dopaminergic neurons remain undamaged in rats given high doses of L-dopa and carbidopa chronically. J Neurochem 1984; 43: 990–993.

50. Naudin B, Bonnet JJ, Costentin J. Acute L-dopa pretreatment potentiates 6-hydroxydopamine-induced toxic effects on nigrostriatal dopaminergic neurons in mice. Brain Res 1995; 701: 151–157.

51. Blunt SB, Jenner P, Marsden CD. Suppressive effect of L-dopa on dopamine cells remaining in the ventral tegmental area of rats previously exposed to the neurotoxin 6-hydroxydopamine. Mov Disord 1993; 8: 129–133.

52. Ogawa N, Aganuma M, Kondo Y, Yamamoto M, Mori A. Differential effects of chronic L-dopa treatment on lipid peroxidation in the mouse brain with and without pretreatment with 6-hydroxydopamine. Neurosci Lett 1994; 171: 55–58.

53. Dziewczapolski G, Murer G, Agid Y, Gershanik O, Raisman-Vozari R. Absence of neurotoxicity of chronic L-dopa treatment in 6-hydroxydopamine-lesioned rats. Neuroreport, 1997; 8: 975–979.

54. Melamed E, Rosenthal J. Can chronic levodopa therapy accelerate degeneration of dopaminergic neurons and progression of Parkinson's disease? In, Nogatsu T, Fisher A, Yoshida M, eds, Basic Clinical and Therapeutic Aspects of Alzheimer's and Parkinson's diseases. New York: Plenum Press, 1990: 253–256.

55. Steece-Collier K, Collier TJ, Sladeck CD, Sladeck JR. Chronic levodopa impairs morphological development of grafted embryonic dopamine neurons. Exp Neurol 1990; 110: 201–208.

56. Blunt SB, Jenner P, Marsden CD. The effect of L-dopa and carbidopa treatment on the survival of rat fetal dopamine grafts assessed by tyrosine hydroxylase immunohistochemistry and ^{3}H-mazindol autoradiography. Neurosci 1991; 43: 95–110.

57. Melamed E, Rosenthal J, Reches H. Prenatal administration of levodopa is not toxic to fetal dopaminergic neurons in vivo. Neurol 1992; 42 (Suppl 3): 378.

58. Quinn N, Parkes D, Janota I, Marsden CD. Preservation of the substantia nigra and locus ceruleus in a patient receiving levodopa (2 kg) plus decarboxylase inhibitor over a four year period. Mov Disord 1986; 1: 65–68.

59. Rajput AH, Fenton ME, Birdi S, Macaulay R. Is levodopa toxic to human substantia nigra? Mov Disord 1997; 12: 634–638.

60. Blin J, Bonnet AM, Agid Y. Does levodopa aggravate Parkinson's disease? Neurol 1988; 38: 1410–1416.

61. Kordower JH, Freeman TB, Snow BJ, Olanow CW. Neuropathological evidence of graft survival and striatal reinnervation after the transplantation of fetal mesencephalic tissue in a patient with Parkinson's disease. N Engl J Med 1995; 332: 1118–1124.

62. Isaacs KR, Wolpoe ME, Jacobowitz DM. Calretinin-immunoreactive dopaminergic neurons from embryonic rat mesencephalon are resistant to levodopa-induced neurotoxicity. Exp Neurol 1997; 146: 25–32.

63. Reed JC. Bcl-2 and the regulation of programmed cell death. J Cell Biol 1994; 124: 1–6.

64. Munez G, Clarke MF. The bcl-2 family of proteins: Regulators of cell death and survival. Trends Cell Biol 1994; 4: 399–403.

65. Offen D, Ziv I, Panet H, Wasserman L, Stein R, Melamed E, Barzilai A. Dopamine-induced apoptosis is inhibited in PC12 cells expressing bcl-2: Evidence that the proto-oncogene may act as an antioxidant. Cell Mol Neurobiol 1997; 17: 285–304.

66. Mogi M, Harada M, Kondo T, Mizuno Y, Maraboyashi H, Riederer P, Nagatsu T. Bcl-2 protein is increased in the brain from parkinsonian patients. Neurosci Lett 1996; 215: 137–139.

67. Mena MA, Casarejos MJ, Carazo A, Paino CL, de Yebenes GJ. Glia conditioned medium protects fetal rat midbrain neurons in culture from L-dopa toxicity. Neuroreport 1996; 7: 441–449.

68. Olanow CW, Gauger BA, Cederbaum JM. Temporal relationships between plasma and cerebrospinal fluid pharmacokinetics of levodopa and clinical effect in Parkinson's disease. Ann Neurol 1991; 29: 556–559.

69. Durso R, Evans JE, Josephs E, Szabo GK, Evans BA, Handler JS, Jennings D, Browne TR. Central levodopa metabolism in Parkinson's disease after administration of stable isotope-labeled levodopa. Ann Neurol 1997; 42: 300–304.

70. Mytilineou C, Han SK, Cohen G. Toxic and protective effects of L-dopa on mesencephalic cell cultures. J Neurochem 1993; 61: 1470–1478.

71. Han SK, Mytilineou C, Cohen G. L-dopa upregulates glutathione and protects mesencephalic cultures against oxidative stress. J Neurochem 1996; 66: 501–510.

72. Ahlskog JE, Uitti RJ, Low PA, Tyce GM, O'Brien JF, Nickander KK. Levodopa and deprenyl treatment effects on peripheral indices of oxidant stress in Parkinson's disease. Neurol 1996; 46: 796–801.

73. Melamed E, Hefti F, Wurtman RJ. Compensatory mechanisms in nigrostriatal dopaminergic system in parkinsonism: studies in an animal model. Isr J Med Sci 1982; 18: 159–163.

DISCUSSION

De Yebenes Justo: I fully agree with your conclusions. We were concerned about levodopa toxicity and performed a number of experiments many years ago. About three years ago at the time of the European Parkinson's disease meeting, I had to review that topic. The first thing that struck me was that all the data related to levodopa toxicity were obtained in pure neural cultures – fetal neuronal cells, neuroblastoma cells, sympathetic cells – in the absence of glia. We then started a series of experiments to find out the role of levodopa in the presence of glia. We found that not only did glia protect, but if neuronal cultures were treated with levodopa with the addition of glia-conditioned medium, the toxicity disappeared. So not only are the glia able to trap levodopa but they also produce factors that block levodopa toxicity. We tried to find out what these factors were by fractionation of the glia. We compared the activity of the high molecular weight compounds – greater than 10 kDa – with smaller compounds and reached the conclusion that neurotrophic factors were not the key element in protection by glia. Of the compounds that are produced by glia, we measured their concentration in glia-conditioned medium, and the highest one was glutathione. But, more recently, in a different model involving post-natal cells, levodopa is not only toxic but is neurotrophic, so if levodopa is added to post-natal cultures which are treated simultaneously with glia-conditioned medium and levodopa, we see increased arborization and numbers of tyrosine hydroxylase cells.

Melamed: It is not impossible that levodopa might be protective. It could be protective in another manner. We think that there is wear and tear because of hyperactivity of the surviving dopaminergic neurons. The dopamine that is formed from levodopa in non-dopaminergic compartments could just as easily reach the autoreceptors on the surviving neurons and shut off the hyperactivity.

De Yebenes Justo: What I mean is that under certain conditions levodopa is neurotrophic since it increases the number of neurons and the size of those neurons.

Olanow: Dr. Cohen and Dr. Mytilineou found that both the protective effect and the toxic effect of levodopa were essentially due to the same mechanism, the difference being a matter of degree. Both effects were apparently related to toxicity. In the protective model there was minimal injury and the cells could up-regulate protective molecules. If dopamine auto-oxidation was blocked with ascorbate this prevented the minimal toxicity. To eliminate the possibility that the trophic effect is not due to a minimal injury, you should add ascorbate to your system to confirm that it is in fact a direct trophic effect.

Youdim: It is not surprising that glia are resistant to dopamine because we know that they produce radicals and glutamate and are nonetheless protected. To return to the issue of levodopa and melanin, we know that the only site in the brain that contains neuromelanin or other melanin forms is the substantia nigra. Other dopaminergic systems in the brain do not contain melanin. Do you have any comment on this? Is there a special enzyme or system that allows melanin to be formed and is it protective?

Melamed: Since I read Dr. Marsden's paper in *Journal of Anatomy* about the neural melanin content in various species, we have been asking ourselves why the nigra dies selectively but not exclusively in PD. Other systems that do not contain neuromelanin also die, a good example being the cholinergic system, both in the brain and the gut. Certainly the SNc neurons bear the brunt but in other dopaminergic systems, for instance the hypothalamic system, there is also some degeneration. Nobody has looked at the dopaminergic neuronal system in the amacrine cell layer in the retina which does not contain neuromelanin and we do not know whether it degenerates as well. Electro-physiological studies may show some disturbances in these systems. Incidentally, rats are relatively immune to MPTP toxicity, but when we injected synthetic neuromelanin into their striata and gave systemic MPTP, we could induce toxicity in these neurons. Neuromelanin is toxic to neurons in culture and may therefore have some etiological role in PD. However, large amounts of neuromelanin granules are normally present in the cytoplasm of the dopaminergic neurons in the substantia nigra pars compacta and these cells normally do not degenerate in non-parkinsonians. These are totally unprotected by a surrounding membrane and yet the neurons do not die. There appears to be a missing factor in PD that somehow may change this extremely protected environment to a hostile one in which iron, melanin and dopamine suddenly become malignant and kill dopaminergic neurons.

W. Tatton: You remarked about apoptosis and its occurrence in glial cells. The work of Drs. Hirsch and Mizuno showed clearly that there is strong evidence for apoptosis in neurons in the substantia nigra in PD. Dr. Graber, however, has recently reported evidence for glial rather than neuronal apoptosis but his results may be artifactual and should be regarded with caution.

Melamed: The methods used to detect apoptosis in human autopsy tissues from PD and other diseases are very non-specific and therefore problematic.

Mizuno: We studied the substantia nigra by the TUNEL method and, as you mentioned, nigral glial cells showed more TUNEL positivity compared to neurons. However, some neurons also showed TUNEL positivity in PD so we believe some neurons, or glial cells, are programmed to die by apoptosis due to oxidative stress or dopamine toxicity. This raises a very important question about the difference between the *in vitro* and *in vivo* situations. Levodopa given to animals is not toxic but given to cultures of mesencephalic neurons or other cells it is very toxic. When we gave MPTP or MPP+ to animals it was toxic only to the nigral neurons but when we added MPP+ to mesencephalic cultures, not only the TH-positive cells but also the TH-negative neurons died. This difference may be due to the route of entry. In living animals, levodopa is taken up through the specific transporter for neutral amino acids then very quickly carboxylated to dopamine, but in cell culture levodopa may enter by means other than the specific transporter which might explain why it is toxic in cultured cells.

Melamed: This is an important issue. We looked at the persistence of levodopa in extracellular fluid using *in vivo* electrochemistry which is quite a good method. Amazingly there was no levodopa in the extracellular fluid while large amounts could be measured in the striatum using HPLC-EC and tissue extracts. Therefore, all the levodopa rapidly became intracellular in glia, neurons or perhaps dopaminergic terminals, since these were intact animals. We should remember that MPTP undergoes conversion to MPP+ within glial cells yet the glia do not die, even *in vivo*. Glial cells are extremely resistant to MPP+ *in vitro*. There must be some mechanisms in the brain, such as the glia or other uptake systems, that are responsible for this protection.

Shoulson: There is no convincing evidence that levodopa is toxic to PD patients when given clinically, but neither is there any convincing evidence that is not toxic. Small studies on a very few patients have not shown major effects, but it would be difficult to elucidate such toxic effects against the background of the symptomatic benefits of levodopa. The Parkinson Study Group under the leadership of Dr. Fahn has just been awarded a grant from NIH to study this in a placebo-controlled trial in 340 patients with very early PD. Patients will be randomized to begin levodopa, either early on or delayed, for nine months. This study began in the first part of 1998.

Melamed: Caution should be advocated in the eternal battle between those neurologists who give levodopa immediately upon diagnosis and those, including myself, who postpone the initiation of levodopa until the disease is more advanced. We still do not know whether it is toxic to vulnerable neurons in PD. Moreover, the administration of levodopa may be associated with the development of response fluctuations and dyskinesias. The results of this trial will be eagerly awaited.

De Yebenes Justo: I would like to make a crude speculation about the putative neurotrophic effect of levodopa. If this is true, dopamine may play a role in synaptogenesis in the nigrostriatal system. Individuals with a mutation in chromosome 14, responsible for levodopa-responsive dystonia, have low TH activity. Late in life some of them develop parkinsonism which is indistinguishable from idiopathic parkinsonism and which co-exists with other, purely levodopa-responsive, dystonias in members of the same family.

These individuals develop the same complications as those with idiopathic PD. The parkinsonians that belong to the TRD families develop parkinsonism with fluctuations and so forth. Therefore, low dopamine activity in these synapses may predispose to degeneration of the nigrostriatal system in these individuals.

SECTION V

Neuroprotection

CHAPTER TWENTY TWO

Neuroprotection for Parkinson's disease

WILLIAM C. KOLLER

University of Kansas Medical Center, Kansas City, Kansas, USA

There are currently three therapeutic approaches to Parkinson's disease (PD): (1) symptomatic, (2) neuroprotective, and (3) restorative. Disruption of the nigrostriatal pathway leads to a dopamine deficiency, particularly in the putamen, and forms the basis of dopamine replacement strategies with levodopa.[1] Although these treatments can provide dramatic initial improvement, their effects are often short-lived and adverse motor and mental reactions significantly limit therapy.[2] Other approaches for PD patients are clearly needed.

Neuroprotection can be defined as an intervention that slows or stops the progression of neuronal degeneration,[3] and seeks to interfere with the basic pathogenetic mechanism of nigral cell death. Neuroprotection is not a pharmacologic attempt to eliminate or postpone the motor complications associated with chronic levodopa therapy. While not considered a cure, successful neuroprotection would have a major impact on PD. Most patients respond well to current treatment early in the course of the disease, but disability increases with progression of PD and emergence of adverse reactions to drug therapies. Moreover, the psychological burden is enormous. For example, prolongation of minimal disability from five to ten years with neuroprotection therapy would have a major impact, particularly for individuals developing the disease later in life. Neuroprotective therapy would also have a tremendous economic impact by prolonging capacity for work, delaying disability costs and reducing expenditure on hospitalization and nursing home placement.

Another form of neuroprotection is 'neurorescue' – the ability of an intervention to normalize sick cells which are injured but not yet dead. This emerging concept suggests that neurons may be dysfunctional but not irreversibly injured, and are therefore capable of being restored to normal functioning by an intervention such as a trophic factor.[4]

Neurorestoration is another category of potential treatment for PD, and involves placement of new cells such as fetal nigral neurons into the striatum of PD patients.[5,6] This approach has the advantage of replacing damaged neurons with functioning cells but, to date, has yielded only modest improvement.

APPROACHES FOR NEUROPROTECTION

A considerable amount of information on neuronal degeneration is now available, and agents that could interfere with the cascade of proposed events in nigral cell death have been identified. PD is most likely to be the result of an interaction between as yet unidentified environmental influences and genetic susceptibility factors. Simply removing susceptible individuals from environmental exposures could constitute neuroprotection. The nature of the initial insult is not clear but a cascade of pathophysiologic changes can occur in nigral neurons, suggesting many possible modes of intervention to block cell death. The safety and efficacy of a potential neuroprotective agent will have to be studied in normal subjects and in patients with PD, but the methodology for clinical trials needed to show neuroprotection has not been clearly elucidated.

Neuroprotection and selegiline

The neurotoxin 1-methyl-4-phenyl-1,2,3,6-tetrahydropyridine (MPTP) induces clinical symptoms identical to PD and causes substantia nigra cell death. MPTP is converted to 1-methyl-4-phenylpyridine (MPP+) by monoamine oxidase B (MAO-B).[7,8] Inhibition of this reaction prevents the development of nigral cell death,[8] so MAO-B inhibition is speculated to prevent the conversion of a protoxin to a toxin, or change the progression of PD. Patients receiving selegiline with levodopa enjoyed longer survival and less disability than patients treated with levodopa alone.[9] Furthermore, oxidative stress may play a major role in the pathogenesis of PD and raises the possibility that MAO inhibition could be neuroprotective by inhibiting peroxide formation consequent to the oxidative metabolism of dopamine.[10]

Later studies have shown that selegiline significantly delayed the development of disability requiring levodopa therapy.[11–13] The improvement in motor scores after the initiation of selegiline and the worsening after drug withdrawal suggests the beneficial effect may be related in part to a symptomatic amelioration of PD. However, the reduction in disability was significant compared to placebo, even in selegiline-treated subjects who initially had no improvement in motor scores, suggesting that the results cannot be explained totally by the symptomatic effects of the drug. Symptomatic deterioration may have been observed in all patients if wash-out had been performed prior to reaching end-point (disability requiring levodopa treatment), and if observed over a longer period of time.[14] If selegiline had a neuroprotective effect, the subjects who had originally received selegiline would show superior and sustained benefits after re-initiation of selegiline treatment compared with subjects not previously treated with selegiline. During an extended trial, however, 189 subjects previously assigned to selegiline reached the end-point of disability faster than the 121 subjects who had not been assigned selegiline.[15] The initial advantages of selegiline were not sustained, though firm conclusions are difficult because the selegiline patients had more severe impairment at baseline, there was a two-month interruption of therapy, and interpretation of open-label assessments was varied.

A prospective, randomized, double-blind, placebo-controlled study was designed to minimize confounding symptomatic effects in order to address the issue of neuroprotection with selegiline.[16] Patients with untreated PD were randomly assigned to one of four treatment groups: (1) selegiline + levodopa, (2) placebo + levodopa, (3) selegiline + bromocriptine, and (4) placebo + bromocriptine. After 12 months of treatment, selegiline and placebo were discontinued, and levodopa and bromocriptine were withdrawn seven weeks later, so all patients were untreated by the final visit. The primary end point was the deterioration in total Unified Parkinson's Disease Rating Scale (UPDRS) score from baseline to final visit, which was considered to be a measure of progression of the underlying parkinsonism. Patients on selegiline had significantly less deterioration in parkinsonian signs and symptoms than placebo-treated patients. Similar results were seen in the subgroup of patients receiving either levodopa or bromocriptine. It is unlikely that differences between the treatment groups were due to inadequate washout of selegiline because the magnitude of the effect far exceeded the small symptomatic effect known to be associated with selegiline and even exceeded the extent of deterioration that occurred following withdrawal of levodopa. To ensure adequacy of washout, levodopa and bromocriptine were withdrawn for an additional seven days in a subgroup of patients because so little is known about the time required for complete elimination of their symptomatic effects. An end-point analysis still showed a significant benefit favoring selegiline-treated patients despite the small sample size. These findings suggest that selegiline provides benefits in PD patients that are not readily accounted for by symptomatic effects.

The neuroprotective role of selegiline remains controversial. Clinical observations show that disease progression is ongoing while taking selegiline,[17] and the degree and duration of neuroprotection with selegiline are currently undefined. In laboratory models of neuroprotection, selegiline clearly provides a protective action. Its ability to inhibit MAO-B was initially thought to be responsible for its pharmacologic action in PD and may well be responsible for its symptomatic effect. Many animal studies indicate, however, that the protective action of selegiline is not dependent on MAO-B inhibition,[18–20] and it appears to block apoptotic cell death by inducing new protein synthesis. The putative neuroprotective action of selegiline may be mediated by a metabolite, desmethyl selegiline, which can protect cultured dopaminergic neurons.[21]

Vitamin E

Vitamin E was the first anti-oxidant to be studied as a neuroprotective agent but its effects were no different to placebo.[13] Interpretation of negative results is hampered by concerns over the adequacy of the dosage, or the ability of the drug to gain entry to the site of action. While the oxidant stress theory of the pathogenesis of PD remains the dominant hypothesis, there are no clinical data to support the use of vitamin E in the treatment of PD.

METHODOLOGICAL ISSUES

The methodology to document neuroprotection in clinical trials is not yet established. Studies that attempt to show neuroprotection are of necessity long-term, since modification of the course of the disease must be shown. The degree of nigral cell death cannot currently be quantified, so indirect measures of progression must be used. The primary outcome variable of the DATATOP trial was disability resulting in the initiation of levodopa treatment in previously untreated patients,[13] but selegiline had a symptomatic effect which confounded the results. The long-term follow-up study was also flawed.[15] Attempts to distinguish between symptomatic and neuroprotective effects of selegiline by withdrawal of the drug have been described,[16] but problems include potential worsening during drug withdrawal, length of time to follow patients in both arms of the study, and poor patient acceptance of this design. Recently, the 'randomized start design' has been proposed,[22] in which patients receive the same treatment but are randomized to begin therapy at different times, and if the separation in starting time is sufficient, the performance of the groups will be distinguishable. Besides clinical measures, other means to assess disease progression such as fluorodopa PET and β-CIT SPECT, may become available.[23,24]

PRESYMPTOMATIC DETECTION

Recent pathologic and neuroimaging data suggest that the preclinical periods of PD range from four to six years.[23,25] Numerous investigations have proposed methods for detecting early physiologic abnormalities in PD[26] and, while these approaches have often shown statistically significant differences between PD patients and normal controls, considerable overlap is also observed. Such tests, therefore, have limited value as diagnostic tools. Another approach is to combine multiple tests, such as the 'PD battery'[27] which incorporates tests of motor function, olfaction and mood (depression). This approach is currently being tested in normal elderly subjects who will be followed longitudinally for the development of PD.

Summary

Many therapeutic strategies have the potential to interfere with the pathogenesis of PD. Proper study design will be needed to show neuroprotection, particularly if the neuroprotective effect is not robust. Increased knowledge of the basic mechanisms of nigral cell death means that a neuroprotective drug for PD is likely to be found in the near future.

REFERENCES

1. Shoulson I. Protective therapy for Parkinson's disease. In, Koller WC, ed, Handbook of Parkinson's disease. New York: Marcel Dekker 1992: 301–309.

2. Marsden CD, Parkes JN. Success and problems of long-term levodopa therapy in Parkinson's disease. Lancet 1992; 1: 345–349.

3. Shoulson I. Protective therapies for Parkinson's disease. In Koller WC, Paulson GW, eds, Therapy of Parkinson's disease. New York: Marcel Dekker 1990: 352–368.

4. Shults CW. Neurotrophic factors. In, Watts RL, Koller WC, eds, Movement disorders: Neurologic principles and practice. New York: McGraw-Hill, 1997: 117–123.

5. Lindvall O, Barkland EO, Farle L, et al. Transplantation in Parkinson's disease. Two cases of adrenal medullary grafts to the putamen. Ann Neurol 1987; 22: 457–468.

6. Freeman TB, Olanow CW, Hauser RA, et al. Bilateral fetal nigral transplantation as a treatment for Parkinson's disease. Ann Neurol 1995; 38: 379–388.

7. Chiba K, Trevor A, Castagnoli N Jr. Metabolism of the neurotoxic tertiary amine, MPTP, by brain monoamine oxidase. Biochem Biophys Res Commun 1984; 129: 547–578.

8. Langston JW, Irwin I, Langston EB, Forno LS. Pargyline prevents MPTP-induced parkinsonism in primates. Science 1984; 225: 1480–1482.

9. Birkmayer W, Knoff J, Riederer P, et al. Improvement of life expectancy due to L-deprenyl addition to Madopar treatment in Parkinson's disease: a long-term study. J Neural Transm 1985; 64: 113–127.

10. Olanow CW. Oxidation reactions in Parkinson's disease. Neurol 1990; 40: 32–37.

11. Tetrud JW, Langston JW. The effect of deprenyl (selegiline) in the natural history of Parkinson's disease. Science 1989; 245: 519–522.

12. Parkinson's Study Group. DATATOP: a multicenter controlled clinical trial in early Parkinson's disease. Arch Neurol 1989; 46: 1052–1060.

13. Parkinson's Study Group. Effect of deprenyl on the progression of disability in early Parkinson's disease. N Engl J Med 1989; 321: 1364–1371.

14. Olanow CW, Calne D. Does selegiline monotherapy in Parkinson's disease act by symptomatic or protective mechanism? Neurol 1991; 42(Suppl 6): 13–26.

15. Parkinson Study Group. Impact of deprenyl and tocopherol treatment on Parkinson's disease in DATATOP subjects not requiring levodopa. Ann Neurol 1996; 39: 29–36.

16. Olanow CW, Hauser RA, Gauger L, et al. The effect of deprenyl and levodopa on the progression of Parkinson's disease. Ann Neurol 1995; 38: 771–777.

17. Findley LJ. Selective monoamine oxidase B inhibitor (deprenyl) in Parkinson's disease. In, Koller WC, Paulson G, eds, Therapy of Parkinson's disease. New York: Marcel Dekker 1990: 345–356.

18. Tatton WG, Greenwood CE. Rescue of dying neurons: a new action for deprenyl in MPTP parkinsonism. J Neurosci Res 1991; 30: 666–677.

19. Mytilineou C, Cohen G. Deprenyl protects dopamine neurons from the neurotoxic effect of l-methyl-4-phenyl-pyridinium ion. J Neurochem 1985; 45: 1951–1953.

20. Ansari KS, Yu PH, Kruck TPA, Tatton WG. Rescue of axotomized immature rat facial motor neurons by R(!)-L-deprenyl: stereospecificity and independence from monoamine oxidase inhibition. J Neurosci 1993; 13: 4042–4053.

21. Mytilineou C, Radcliffe P, Olanow CW. L-(-)-desmethyl-selegiline, a metabolite of L-(-)-selegiline, protects mesen-

cephalic dopamine neurons from excito-toxicity *in vitro*. J Neurochem 1997; 68: 434–436.

22. Leber P. Slowing the progression of Alzheimer's disease. Methodologic issues in Alzheimer's disease and associated disorders. 1997; 11: 510–521.

23. Morrish PK, Sawle GV, Brooks PJ. An ^{18}F-dopa PET and clinical study of the rate of progression in Parkinson's disease. Brain 1996; 11: 9585–9591.

24. Brooks D. Neuroimaging of movement disorders. In, Watts RL, Koller WC, eds, Movement disorders: Neurologic principles and practice. New York: McGraw-Hill 1997: 31–48.

25. Lee CS, Schulzer M, Mak E, *et al.* Clinical observations on the rate of progression of idiopathic parkinsonism. Brain 1994; 117: 501–507.

26. Koller WC, Langston JW. Preclinical detection of Parkinson's disease. Neurol 1991; 41(suppl 2): 1–94.

27. Koller WC, Montgomery CM. Issues in the early diagnosis of Parkinson's disease. Neurol 1997; 49(suppl 1): S10–S25.

Discussion

Polymeropoulos: If we were to recruit Greek subjects, who are not actually patients but were carriers of the α-synuclein mutation and therefore have an 80% risk of developing PD later, what would you propose to do with them? We can identify them at age five or ten, so this is a unique opportunity to study preclinical parkinsonian protection.

Koller: This is an issue we address with every patient, which is the benefit/risk ratio. If we had a neuroprotective therapy that we knew was safe and had no long-term toxicity, the benefit/risk ratio might suggest that we treat those patients. On the other hand, if the agent had toxicity that is a different story. The question of how early should we initiate treatment is interesting. If the pathological process has already started then the earlier we initiate therapy the better but if we wait until signs and symptoms develop, we may have lost our opportunity to prevent significant nigral damage.

Leenders: Concerning vitamin E and early neuroprotection, it seems clear that in patients who have clinical PD it has no effect. However, recent data from an epidemiological study in Rotterdam, looking at 7000 inhabitants longitudinally, showed that vitamin E could protect from PD. So there is a concept that once the disease has started, vitamin E may still have a role in long-term protection if taken in time.

Koller: It stems back to the initial definition of neural protection and neural rescue, which may be two different concepts. Even in the DATATOP study, negative data are always hard to interpret. Did we have the right dose, the right timing, did it reach the site of action?

Olanow: Would Dr. Shoulson comment about some recent data on vitamin E from the DATATOP study, suggesting that even after a long period of time levels were still increasing?

Shoulson: We have really seen no effect with vitamin E on either the primary or secondary response variable. We are now looking over a ten-year period. We can detect a two–threefold increase in CSF tocopherol levels in the patients treated with vitamin E. This is a fat in an aqueous solution, but at least we could detect that increase in an aqueous phase. We cannot say whether it is getting into the brain, let alone what part of the brain or what part of the cells.

Wood: To return to Dr. Polymeropoulos' point about predictive testing, we do not test minors under the age of 18, because there is nothing we can do about it. So if something really neuroprotective is coming out, it will be extremely important. We could have the first case in the world where we have a reason to test minors. We have to be certain that the evidence for neuroprotection is solid because we are going to get a lot of pressure from these patients.

Shoulson: In addition, in this type of paradigm, if we knew what intervention to give in a logical way, one or two families is probably too insufficient a sample size, unless the predicted effect was so robust that the magnitude of the effect was greater than 50%. We are trying to model this on Huntington's disease which one can detect presymptomatically with great reliability. It is a problem but it should not deter us from the intellectual exercise of trying to find a reasonable intervention, given our knowledge of the etiology and pathogenesis.

Koller: I think the issue is even more complex. We all believe that there are multiple etiologies for PD and theoretically an intervention might work for one sub-set of PD and not for another.

Youdim: In our Eurasian studies with Dr. Riederer on the brains from parkinsonians, we did not see any change. There was a significant amount of vitamin E and vitamin C and they were not changed in PD but glutathione was reduced. Why we would need more when the level is unchanged and when we know that the substantia nigra has the highest concentration in the brain? Moreover, we have to be very cautious about vitamin E because it crosses the blood–brain barrier freely, so we have to give much larger doses. There is a compound, lipoic acid, which is being used for neuropathy and may be considered as a substitute for vitamin E.

Jenner: Certainly the static levels of vitamin E and vitamin C in post-mortem brains are normal, but Dr. Halliwell suggests that we need to look at the cycline around these vitamins as well.

Polymeropoulos: Does anyone know what glutathione does in patients? Does it offer protection?

Jenner: No, it does not pass through cell membranes. Glutathione itself cannot enter the brain and even some of the esters and diesters do not penetrate into the brain readily or replenish glutathione in depleted animals. It is very difficult to restore glutathione. Thioctic acid or α-lipoic acid might be one way. Dr. Riederer got it to reduce co q but we have had very little luck in using it as a neuroprotectant.

Youdim: In the chronic studies that we did with lipoic acid in the 6-OHDA model we achieved protection against 6-OHDA.

Jenner: We could not see protection against 6-OHDA or against MPTP, despite performing chronic studies.

Olanow: While there are doubts as to whether selegiline has clinical effects on neuroprotection, and if it does whether these effects are long-lasting and meaningful, in the laboratory there is no doubt that it provides protection in a large number of model systems. The effect is not dependent on MAO-B inhibition and it appears to have anti-apoptotic properties. There is evidence that the active moiety of selegiline is desmethyl selegiline which is more potent in laboratory models and has a reduced tendency to block MAO-B or A. Potentially, therefore, it could be given in much higher doses in clinical trials in an effort to match the dose-dependent protection that we see in the laboratory models. The phase I trials of desmethyl selegiline will be looked at with great excitement in the hope that it will enhance the efficacy that we saw with selegiline and potentially provide meaningful neuroprotection.

Youdim: We have a drug, drasegiline, which is desmethylated and shows all the features of selegiline, but is more potent. It is now in phase III clinical studies and it will be interesting to see how this will behave.

CHAPTER TWENTY THREE

DATATOP: a decade of neuroprotective inquiry

IRA SHOULSON AND THE PARKINSON STUDY GROUP
Department of Neurology, University of Rochester, Rochester, New York, USA

How do we detect neuroprotective effects in clinical trials? Protective therapies for neurodegenerative disorders may be defined as interventions that produce enduring benefits by influencing underlying etiology or pathogenesis and forestalling onset of illness or clinical decline. In Parkinson's disease (PD), potential pathogenetic mechanisms include oxidative stress, excitotoxicity, immunogenicity, mitochondrial dysfunction, and apoptosis.[1,2] This provides us with an opportunity to interfere with these mechanisms and to develop neuroprotective therapies. In the past decade, neuroprotective clinical trials in PD have focused on oxidative mechanisms and their dysfunction. It is likely that attempts to interfere with oxidative stress and with other possible mechanisms will lead to an increasing number of trials aimed at slowing the rate of progression in PD.

DATATOP: THE PRIMARY TRIAL

In 1987, the DATATOP (Deprenyl And Tocopherol Antioxidative Therapy Of Parkinsonism) clinical trial was initiated.[3] The trial was based on the assumption that deprenyl (selegiline, a type-B monoamine oxidase inhibitor), and alpha-tocopherol (the biologically active antioxidant of vitamin E), alone or in combination, would slow disability over a two-year period of observation. Pilot studies indicated that deprenyl produced no short-term symptomatic benefits in patients with early PD,[4] which was also true for alpha-tocopherol. In the absence of symptomatic benefits, demonstrable effects on delaying the development of disability might be considered tantamount to neuroprotection.

DATATOP was designed as a 2x2 factorial, double-blind, placebo-controlled multicenter trial to determine if deprenyl 10 mg per day and/or tocopherol 2000 IU per day, administered to otherwise untreated patients with early PD, would prolong the time until levodopa therapy was required to treat emerging disability. Approximately 75% of these patients developed disability within two years of follow-up sufficient to require levodopa therapy.[5] Eight hundred patients with early, untreated PD were enrolled from 28 research sites. Following baseline evaluation and randomization to double-placebo, active deprenyl alone, active tocopherol alone, or both active deprenyl and tocopherol, subjects were re-evaluated at regular intervals (Figure 1). Clinical measures included the Unified Parkinson's Disease Rating Scale (UPDRS).[3] The primary endpoint occurred when the investigator considered that the subject had reached a level of functional disability requiring initiation of levodopa therapy.

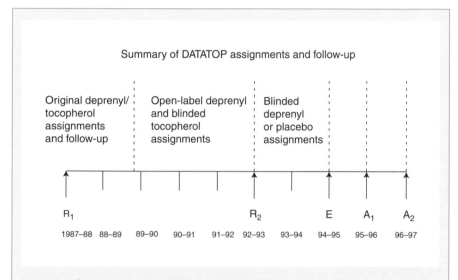

Figure 1: Summary of DATATOP (Deprenyl and Tocopherol Antioxidative Therapy of Parkinsonism) treatment assignments and follow-up. Calendar dates are not exact due to the staggered randomizations. R = randomization to treatment (R₁ was original; R₂ was to continue on deprenyl or switch to placebo for deprenyl;) E = last standard clinical evaluation; A1 and A2 = annual telephone ascertainments. Reprinted with permission.[18]

Approximately 22 months prior to the planned completion of the trial, the trial was modified because of the striking impact of deprenyl on the primary endpoint of disability determined at a planned interim analysis.[6] The trial was modified to provide open-label deprenyl to all subjects while maintaining the blinded treatment assignments for alpha-tocopherol. A separate trial on 51 early PD subjects followed for up to three years also showed a statistically significant delay in the time to endpoint of disability.[7]

The beneficial effects of deprenyl occurred largely during the first 12 months of treatment and significantly delayed, by about nine months, the onset of disability requiring levodopa therapy (hazard ratio, 0.50; 95%

confidence interval, 0.41 to 0.62; $p < 0.001$). However, the hazard ratio did not remain constant during the initial 24 months of follow-up observation, but increased from 0.35 (95% confidence interval, 0.21 to 0.58) during the first six months to 0.38 (0.27 to 0.54) during the second six months, and to 0.77 (0.52 to 1.15) during the third six months. This suggested that the initial effects of deprenyl were not sustained. Furthermore, at one and three months, deprenyl-treated patients showed significant improvement in UPDRS. In 682 subjects who completed six months of evaluation, those not assigned to deprenyl had a UPDRS decline about 10% faster than those on deprenyl.[8] Although the overall effects of deprenyl in ameliorating parkinsonian features were small by clinical standards, the observed symptomatic effects may have contributed to the slowing of disability and have been unrelated to slowing of underlying PD. There were no beneficial effects of tocopherol or any interaction between tocopherol and deprenyl.`

DATATOP EXTENSION STUDIES

Active study subjects, whether or not they required levodopa therapy, were placed on open-label deprenyl and followed for about 3.5 years (Figure 1). Concealed tocopherol treatment assignments were maintained for 3–4 years after the initial randomization. Subjects began levodopa in addition to study drug when they were judged to require therapy for emerging disability. Investigators remained blinded to individual treatment assignments and adjusted levodopa dosage to achieve optimal clinical benefits and avoid dopaminergic adverse effects. If this failed, subjects could also receive a supplemental dopamine agonist, either bromocriptine or pergolide.

During the initial mean 21 months, 310/800 enrolled subjects did not reach the primary end point. After open-label deprenyl treatment for an additional mean 12 months, 189/310 subjects originally assigned to deprenyl reached endpoint faster than the 121/310 subjects not assigned to deprenyl (hazard ratio, 1.43; 95% CI, 0.98, 2.90, $p = 0.065$). However, the former group were more severely impaired at baseline and may have been more likely to require levodopa during this extended period. Nevertheless, prior treatment with deprenyl did not appear to lead to sustained benefits[9] nor did it reduce the occurrence of subsequent levodopa-associated adverse effects such as 'wearing-off', dyskinesias or 'on–off' motor fluctuations.[10]

Cognitive performance

The DATATOP cohort was characterized by largely normal and stable cognitive performance at baseline and throughout the initial 14 months.[11] Addition of levodopa, while improving motor function, did not appreciably affect cognitive performance.[12] However, subsequent follow-up of DATATOP subjects has shown a five-year incidence of dementia of about 7%.[13] There is no evidence that deprenyl or tocopherol have slowed intellectual decline in patients with early PD, but a more extended analysis is underway to assess the long-term mental outcomes.

Gait and balance

During the initial two years of the trial, 193 (24.1%) of the DATATOP subjects developed freezing of gait, particularly those with more advanced disease at baseline. Subjects assigned to deprenyl showed a 53% reduction in the risk of developing freezing of gait (hazard ratio 0.47; 95% CI 0.34, 0.66; $p < 0.0001$), but this beneficial effect waned after withdrawal of treatment. Tocopherol treatment had no impact on the development of freezing of gait.[14] The mechanism whereby deprenyl forestalled freezing of gait remains unclear but it is the first observation suggesting an effective intervention for this disabling problem, and requires confirmation.

As levodopa therapy was required in the DATATOP trial, large proportions of the cohort developed 'wearing-off' (50%), dyskinesias (30%), and freezing (25%). Experimental treatments did not significantly alter the occurrence of these levodopa-related complications, although patients on deprenyl alone had the lowest occurrence of freezing (17%).[10]

THE SECOND RANDOMIZATION

Concerns about the sustained benefit of deprenyl[9,10,15,16] led to a second randomization (Figure 1). Subjects who required levodopa were randomized independently of their original randomization to continue deprenyl (n=191) or switch to deprenyl placebo (n=177). There were no major clinical differences between the two groups at the second randomization. During the average two years of follow-up, there were no differences in serious adverse events, cardiovascular adverse events or the first development of 'wearing-off', dyskinesias or 'on–off' fluctuations in the two groups. The results suggested that sustained deprenyl treatment heightened the risk of dyskinesias but forestalled 'on–off' motor fluctuations and freezing of gait,[17] consistent with the earlier phases of the trial regarding the beneficial effect of deprenyl on freezing of gait.

MORTALITY

After an average of 8.2 years, there were 137 deaths among the 800 enrolled subjects (17.1%, or 2.1% per year).[18] This low rate was as expected for an age- and gender-matched US population without PD.[19] Neither deprenyl, tocopherol, nor the combination affected mortality in these early PD patients. These results differ from those of an open-label UK study,[20,21] in which the subjects enrolled were slightly older, more disabled and were requiring levodopa at the time of entry. These characteristics might account for the higher overall mortality, but do not explain the increased mortality among subjects assigned to levodopa plus deprenyl.[21] In a trial more similar in design to the UK study, three deaths occurred among 51 patients assigned to deprenyl plus levodopa compared with five deaths in 50 patients assigned to placebo plus levodopa.[22]

The delay of disability after the initial randomization in DATATOP was not associated with longer life, consistent with later observations that the initial benefits of deprenyl were not sustained. These data do not support results of uncontrolled studies suggesting extended life from deprenyl treatment.[23,24] Nevertheless, an association of the overall low death rate (compared with an age- and gender-matched US control population) with some deprenyl treatment, rather than the duration of deprenyl treatment, cannot be excluded.

IS DEPRENYL NEUROPROTECTIVE?

Although deprenyl initially slowed disability by about nine months when administered to patients with early untreated PD, the therapeutic effects were not sustained or translated into enduring benefits such as reduced levodopa-associated adverse effects or extended life. For some patients and clinicians, the effect of deprenyl in delaying disability and thereby postponing the need for levodopa therapy may be important. DATATOP did not address whether delaying levodopa therapy *per se* influenced clinical outcomes and survival. This is the objective of a newly-initiated trial in patients with early, mild PD. Subjects assigned to placebo will be compared with those randomized blindly to three different dosages of levodopa. The findings should help to clarify the wisdom of delaying, sparing or avoiding levodopa therapy in patients with very early PD.

SUMMARY

- Deprenyl has been shown to delay the emergence of disability as determined by the need for levodopa in the DATATOP study. It is not clear if these benefits are due to neuroprotection or to the drug's symptomatic effect.
- There is no firm evidence to indicate that deprenyl exerts neuroprotective effects in slowing the neural degeneration underlying PD.
- Although deprenyl 10 mg per day initially slowed disability by about nine months when administered to patients with early, untreated PD, the therapeutic effects were not sustained or translated into enduring benefits such as reduced levodopa-associated adverse effects or extended life.
- Deprenyl may exert some advantages with respect to freezing of gait.
- Deprenyl did not exert any long-term deleterious effect on mortality either before or after the need for levodopa therapy.

ACKNOWLEDGMENTS

Steering Committee: Ira Shoulson (Principal Investigator), David Oakes (Chief Biostatistician), Stanley Fahn (Co-Principal Investigator), Anthony Lang, J. William Langston, Peter LeWitt, C. Warren Olanow, John B. Penney, Caroline Tanner, Karl Kieburtz (Medical Director). *Participating Investigators:* William Koller, C. Warren Olanow, Robert Rodnitzky, J. Stephen Fink, John H. Growdon, George Paulson, Roger Kurlan, Joseph H. Friedman, Stephen Gancher, John Nutt, Ali H. Rajput, James B. Bennett, G. Frederick Wooten, Peter LeWitt, Christopher Goetz, Caroline Tanner, Kathleen Shannon, Oksana Suchowersky, Mitchell F. Brin, Susan B. Bressman, William J. Weiner, Juan Sanchez-Ramos, Joseph Jankovic, John B. Penney, Anthony Lang, Margaret Hoehn, James Tetrud, J. David Grimes, Ronald Pfeiffer, Cliff Shults, Leon Thal, Serge Gauthier, Lawrence I. Golbe, Joel S. Perlmutter, Hamilton Moses III, Stephen G. Reich, Howard I. Hurtig, Matthew Stern. *Site Coordinators:* Ruth Barter, Bridget Vetere-Overfield, Lisa Gauger, Teresita Malapira, Judith Dobson, Susan Atamian, Marsha Tennis, Jennifer B. Cohen, Gena Desclos, Elizabeth Hoffman, Karen Graefe, Catherine Burke, Ari Marcus, Lena Denio, Steven Huber, Teresa Woike, Kimberly Zoog, Rebecca Mendell, Kimberly Dudte, Jill Behr, Irenita Flynn Gardiner, Margaret Lannon, Julie Carter, Susanne Northrup, Bernice Kanigan, Margaret Turk, Elke Landow, Patricia Schlick, Kathie Mistura, V. Susan Carroll, Jean A. Thelen, Carol Demong, Linda Winfield, Carol Moskowitz, Angela Ingenito, Carol Sheldon, Lisa Cornelius, Dorothy Heiberg, Cathleen Dunne, Jan Brady, Catherine Kierans, Loretta Belle-Scantlebury, Jan Duff, Helena Weber, Deborah Savoini, Paula Lewis, S. Jerome Kutner, Peggy Gray, Carolyn Glaeske, Ruth Hofman, Mary Margaret Pay, David Salmon, Frances McFaul, Donna Amyot, Mary Bergen, Lori McGee-Minnich, Patricia O'Donnell, Susie Ferrise, Kathy Shallow. *Biostatistics and Coordination Centers Staff:* Catherine Axtell, (biostatistics postdoctoral fellow), Deborah Baker (administrative assistant), Cynthia Casaceli (analyst-programmer), Shirley Eberly (biostatistician), Michael McDermott (biostatistician), Frederick Marshall (Medical Monitor), Ruth Nobel (administrative assistant), Constance Orme (information analyst), Rita M. Pelusio (program manager), Sandra Plumb (coordinator), Alice Rudolph (senior study coordinator), Heidi Randolph (data control clerk), Jenny Sotack (data control clerk), Arthur Watts (analyst-programmer).

This research was supported by a Public Health Service Grant (NS24778) from the National Institute of Neurological Disorders and Stroke, grants from the General Clinical Research Centers Program of the National Institutes of Health, and a grant from Somerset Pharmaceuticals, Inc. (Tampa, Florida, USA) for the follow-up of patients after their initial two years in the trial and for the second randomized assignment to deprenyl or placebo treatments.

REFERENCES

1. Olanow CW, Jenner P, Youdim M, eds, Neurodegeneration and Neuroprotection in Parkinson's Disease. New York: Academic Press, 1996.

2. Bar PR, Beal MF, eds, Neuroprotection in CNS Diseases. New York: Marcel Dekker, Inc, 1997.

3. Parkinson Study Group. DATATOP: A multi-center controlled clinical trial in early Parkinson's disease. Arch Neurol 1989; 46: 1052–1060.

4. Shoulson I: Protective therapy for Parkinson's disease. In, Koller WC, Paulson G, eds, Therapy of Parkinson's Disease. New York: Marcel Dekker Inc, 1990: 357–358.

5. Goetz CG, Tanner CM, Shannon KM. Progression of Parkinson's disease without levodopa. Neurol 1987; 37: 695–698

6. Parkinson Study Group. Effect of deprenyl on the progression of disability in early Parkinson's disease. N Engl J Med 1989; 321: 1364–1371.

7. Tetrud JW, Langston JW. The effect of deprenyl (selegiline) on the natural history of Parkinson's disease. Science 1989; 245: 519–522.

8. Parkinson Study Group. Effects of tocopherol and deprenyl on the progression of disability in early Parkinson's disease. N Engl J Med 1993; 328: 176–183.

9. Parkinson Study Group. Impact of deprenyl and tocopherol treatment on Parkinson's disease in DATATOP subjects not requiring levodopa. Ann Neurol 1996; 39: 29–36.

10. Parkinson Study Group. Impact of deprenyl and tocopherol treatment on Parkinson's disease in DATATOP subjects requiring levodopa. Ann Neurol 1996; 39: 37–45.

11. Kieburtz K, McDermott M, Como P, Gordon J, Brady J, Carter J, Huber S, Kanigan B, Landow E, Rudolph A, Saint-Cyr J, Stern Y, Tennis M, Thalen J, Shoulson I and the Parkinson Study Group. The effect of deprenyl and tocopherol on cognitive performance in early untreated Parkinson's disease. Neurol 1994; 44: 1756–1759.

12. Growdon JH, Kieburtz K, McDermott MP, Panisset M, Friedman JH and the Parkinson Study Group. Levodopa improves motor function without impairing cognition in mild non-demented Parkinson's disease patients. Neurol 1998, in press.

13. Panisset M. Siderowf A, McDermott M, Kieburtz K, Friedman J, Growdon J and the Parkinson Study Group. Baseline predictors of subsequent dementia in the DATATOP cohort. Mov Disord 1997; 12: 836.

14. Giladi N, McDermott M, Fahn S, Przedborski S, and the Parkinson Study Group. Freezing of gait in Parkinson's disease. Mov Disord 1996; 11 (Suppl 1): 167.

15. Schulzer M, Mak E, Calne DB. The antiparkinsonian efficacy of deprenyl derives from transient improvement that is likely to be symptomatic. Ann Neurol 1992; 32: 795–798.

16. Ward CD. Does selegiline delay progression of Parkinson's disease? A critical reevaluation of the DATATOP study. J Neurol Neurosurg Psychiatry 1994; 57: 217–220.

17. Parkinson Study Group. Clinical outcome following placebo-controlled withdrawal of deprenyl (selegiline) among levodopa-treated DATATOP subjects. Mov Disord 1997; 12: 838.

18. The Parkinson Study Group. Mortality in DATATOP: a multicenter trial in early Parkinson's disease. Ann Neurol 1998; 43: 318–325.

19. National Center for Health Statistics. Vital statistics of the United States, 1991; 11: Mortality, part A. DHHS publica-

tion no. (PHS) 96-1101. Washington, DC: Public Health Service, 1996.

20. Parkinson's Disease Research Group in the United Kingdom. Comparisons of therapeutic effects of levodopa, levodopa and selegiline, and bromocriptine in patients with early, mild Parkinson's disease: three year interim report. BMJ 1993; 307: 469–472.

21. Lees AJ (Parkinson's Disease Research Group of the United Kingdom). Comparison of therapeutic effects and mortality data of levodopa and levodopa combined with selegiline in patients with early, mild Parkinson's disease. BMJ 1995; 311: 1602–1607.

22. Olanow CW, Godbold JM, Koller W. Patients taking selegiline may have received more levodopa than necessary. BMJ 1996; 213: 702–703.

23. Birkmayer W, Knoll J, Riederer P, Youdim MB.(-)-Deprenyl leads to prolongation of L-dopa efficacy in Parkinson's disease. Mod Probl Pharmacopsychiatry 1983; 19: 170–176.

24. Birkmayer W, Knoll J. Riederer P, et al. Increased life expectancy resulting from addition of L-deprenyl to Madopar treatment in Parkinson's disease: a long-term study. J Neural Transm 1985; 64: 113–127.

DISCUSSION

Langston: Looking back at all we have been through with the DATATOP study, if we had a new putative neuroprotective agent for PD that we were confident did not have any symptomatic effect, would you use the same design as that of the DATATOP study or can you think of a better study design?

Shoulson: The design of the DATATOP study is very robust. I feel that time-related endpoints are very important in the area of neuroprotection. They accomplish two things. It is statistically powerful and it adds a time dimension, because if we have a very robust effect which is not enduring, it means nothing. The issue of performing a 2x2 factorial design is another issue. I am not sure that every time we do a trial we have to look at two interventions in the same trial, but I do think it is effective and relatively economical. In the future, I would like to have biochemical and imaging markers of the number of nigral dopamine neurons. I do feel that the time will come in the next few years when we will have relevant markers to help us interpret the primary clinical effects. It is also very important to do good phase II dosing studies before embarking on major phase III trials so that you can be sure that the optimum doses have been selected. In retrospect, I would have looked more carefully at the various doses of deprenyl and in particular of tocopherol. All the information we have on deprenyl comes from trials using 10 mg/day. We do not have any information on lower or higher doses.

Mizuno: Was there any difference in mortality between the patients who did not receive selegiline in the initial phase and later received levodopa, and those who received selegiline in the initial stage and levodopa later? Also, did all of your patients who reached the endpoint receive both selegiline and levodopa?

Shoulson: There was no statistical difference in mortality between patients who took deprenyl and levodopa *versus* levodopa alone. There were two randomizations – the initial randomization to deprenyl or its placebo, followed by a second randomization to continue deprenyl or to go onto placebo. In between, all patients were on deprenyl for approximately two years. Thus, over the course of the study, some patients were on deprenyl for eight years and some were on it for as little as three years. We did not see any statistical difference in mortality. Eventually almost all of the patients received levodopa and deprenyl therapy at some point.

Poewe: Most of the mortality studies in PD patients found an increased ratio of death over expected number of deaths in the normal population. There was a three-fold increase in the pre-levodopa era which came down to 1.5-fold after the introduction of levodopa. A review of a number of studies suggests that there is currently a two-fold increase in mortality. Now you show a ratio of 1 or less in your DATATOP population. Do you have any explanation for this? Is it a particularly and carefully selected patient group?

Shoulson: These patients were particularly healthy and the results are not generalizable to the patient population as a whole. I mentioned a study on heart disease reported in the *New England Journal of Medicine* ten years ago, where patients who were eligible for the trial but did not enter it for a variety of reasons were still followed. The patients who participated in the trial, even those on placebo, did better than the people who did not participate. This is a salutary effect of participation in clinical trials and may have relevance here. There was also a difference between our trial and the UK trial. We followed the patients every three months for almost ten years, as opposed to their study where there was an initial examination followed by sending them out and waiting for reports. We did not see any excess mortality in our patients, and in fact our mortality rate was slightly less than that seen in the general population. It is possible that some exposure to deprenyl over that period of time, whether for three or eight years, had a beneficial effect. However, we did not see the same results that Dr. Birkmeyer found in his retrospective analysis of patients who were treated with either levodopa and selegiline or levodopa alone. Here, there was a striking difference, with almost a 50% improvement in mortality. There are a variety of reasons for the fact that we have a relatively low mortality rate in our study, including the possibility that some exposure to deprenyl may have contributed to survival, patient selection, and careful follow-up with high quality care.

Youdim: I should point out that in the Birkmeyer study, we did not see a 50% difference between groups. Our data were very similar to yours. Our study was also over eight years.

Shoulson: If we look at the maximum mortality between the groups, there was a time when there was a 50% difference. Obviously the lines come together because at one point everybody dies. Your study was retrospective and not randomized, so it does not have the same predictive value.

Youdim: Perhaps the two sets of data may be very similar in that there was a beneficial effect of deprenyl and levodopa.

Shoulson: If there was a beneficial effect it was unrelated to the duration of therapy. The UK trial actually saw a deleterious effect on mortality, but not all the data have been reported, and there is a third group on bromocriptine alone. So, we have to reserve judgement until we have more information.

Youdim: The results from the UK group are complicated by the fact that some patients may have had pre-existing cardiovascular problems. Deprenyl is a vasoactive amine that can affect heart rate and blood pressure. These patients may have distorted the data and if they were excluded there may not have been any difference in mortality as they reported.

[328]

Leenders: I am concerned about this very high selection bias in the DATATOP study, and the fact that you have put them through several randomizations, and that all patients at one stage or another took deprenyl. How much does this invalidate your conclusions, because in the final analysis you are only left with patients who are willing to follow your study protocols over many years. They may be a particularly healthy group, but what about the dropouts and non-compliers?

Shoulson: Our dropout rate was between 10–15%, depending on the treatment arm. This time-related trial enabled us to determine not only how many dropped out, but when they dropped out, and it made no difference at all to our conclusions. Regarding selection bias, all clinical trials are biased in terms of selecting a group according to specific inclusion and exclusion criteria. But the power is inherent in the randomization. and this is missing from epidemiologic studies which examine several variables often retrospectively in large non-randomized populations. We control for the intervention using the power of randomization, but we have to homogenize the group in order to do this. This was therefore a relatively homogeneous group. Our conclusions therefore, in the strictest sense, only apply to a group of patients with early PD who were not seriously ill and who had never been exposed to anti-parkinsonian medications. In the UK study, the patients may have been more seriously ill, requiring levodopa therapy at the time of entry into the study. They were a year older and were not followed every three months by the investigator. These factors may have played an important role in explaining the different results in our two studies.

CHAPTER TWENTY FOUR

Dopamine agonists and neuroprotection in Parkinson's disease

C. Warren Olanow[1], Peter Jenner[2] and David J. Brooks[3]

[1]Department of Neurology, Mount Sinai School of Medicine, New York, New York, USA, [2]Neurodegenerative Diseases Research Centre, Pharmacology Group, Biomedical Sciences Division, King's College, London, UK, [3]MRC Cyclotron Unit, Hammersmith Hospitals, London, UK

Dopamine agonists provide anti-parkinsonian benefits by directly stimulating dopamine receptors, and have traditionally been used as an adjunct to levodopa in Parkinson's disease (PD) patients with dyskinesia and motor fluctuations.[1–5] More recently, dopamine agonist therapy has been used in the early stages of PD and has been demonstrated to protect against the development of levodopa-related motor complications.[6,7] Both animal and clinical studies have shown that dopamine agonists are associated with a reduced frequency of motor complications compared to levodopa, when used in early disease either as monotherapy or in combination with levodopa.[8–12] Monotherapy studies in early PD have now been performed with the new dopamine agonists, ropinirole and pramipexole, and have shown anti-parkinsonian benefits[13–15] which in one study were comparable to levodopa for patients in stage I and II of the disease.[16] Based on these observations, it has been argued that dopamine agonists should be used as the primary symptomatic agent in the treatment of PD.[17]

There has also been considerable interest in the potential of dopamine agonists to provide neuroprotection and to alter the natural course of PD. Such a benefit might derive from (a) a levodopa sparing effect, (b) stimulation of dopamine auto-receptors, (c) direct anti-oxidant effects, and (d) restoration of dopaminergic tone to suppress excitotoxic effects due to overactivity of the subthalamic nucleus (STN). Studies in tissue culture and in rodent models of parkinsonism support this concept and clinical trials to test this hypothesis in PD patients are underway. This chapter reviews the evidence that dopamine agonists might be neuroprotective in PD.

LEVODOPA AND NEURODEGENERATION

Levodopa metabolism can generate toxic oxidative metabolites that might accelerate neuronal degeneration in PD.[18,19] Levodopa can be converted to dopamine, which, when metabolized either enzymatically or by auto-oxidation, can yield reactive oxygen species (ROS) such as hydrogen peroxide (H_2O_2) and hydroxyl radical (OH). H_2O_2 is normally cleared by reduced glutathione (GSH), but excess H_2O_2 can react with iron to yield OH. Increased dopamine turnover, increased iron, or decreased GSH, as have been found in PD, can all lead to excess free radical formation, with oxidative damage to critical biomolecules and the initiation of apoptosis. Indeed, dopamine has been shown to induce an increase in markers of oxidative stress[20–22] and to be toxic to cultured dopaminergic neurons.[23–25]

Considerable evidence indicates that the substantia nigra pars compacta (SNc) is under oxidant stress in PD.[26] This is reflected by increased iron, which promotes oxidant stress, and decreased glutathione, the primary defense mechanism in the brain against oxidant stress. Biochemical markers of oxidative damage to proteins, lipids and DNA are evident in the SNc of PD patients. Further enhanced nitrotyrosine immunostaining, indicative of nitric oxide and peroxynitrite formation, has been detected in Lewy bodies in SNc neurons of PD patients.

Levodopa may, in theory, enhance oxidant stress and promote nerve or glial cell degeneration in PD patients. It can be decarboxylated to dopamine, thereby increasing the steady state concentration of H_2O_2 and the risk of OH· radical formation. Levodopa can also be auto-oxidized to form semi-quinones, levodopa radicals, and other oxidizing species. It can also form an adduct with GSH and further deplete the already reduced GSH levels in PD patients.[21] *In vitro* and *in vivo* studies demonstrate that levodopa can induce increased levels of oxidized glutathione,[27] hydroxyl radicals,[28] markers of DNA damage[29] and lipid peroxidation,[30,31] and damage to the mitochondrial respiratory chain.[32] Levodopa can also induce necrosis or apoptosis in cultured dopaminergic neurons[23,33–35] and impair the development of transplanted embryonic dopaminergic neurons.[36] Levodopa might also account for the widespread oxidative damage to DNA and proteins seen in multiple brain regions in PD patients.[37–39] Levodopa does not appear to induce degeneration of dopamine neurons in normal rodents, non-human primates, or humans,[40–43] but this may not be the case in PD where there is evidence of oxidant stress and defense mechanisms are compromised. In this regard it is noteworthy that levodopa does increase damage to dopamine neurons and markers of lipid peroxidation following 6-hydroxydopamine (6-OHDA) toxicity.[44,45] This suggests that levodopa may induce damage in previously damaged or vulnerable dopaminergic neurons.

The situation is complicated by evidence that levodopa may be neuroprotective. In small doses, levodopa induces an increase in GSH levels in mesencephalic cell cultures.[33,46] Further, cells exposed to low doses of levodopa are protected from subsequent exposure to toxins that otherwise induce neurodegeneration. Therefore, levodopa can induce either degenerative or protective effects depending on the concentration. If large numbers of radical species are formed, neuronal degeneration ensues. In contrast, if oxidant stress is minimal, molecules such as GSH which can protect the cell against subsequent toxic exposure, are up-regulated. Interestingly, exposure of cultured dopamine neurons to low doses of levodopa induces effects similar to those observed following exposure to selegiline and trophic factors (such as BDNF) which also up-regulate GSH and protect dopamine neurons from a variety of toxins.[47–52] Ascorbate, which blocks levodopa auto-oxidation, blocks both the toxic and protective effects of levodopa.[46,53] Molecules other than GSH may also be involved, as selegiline can protect neurons from GSH deficiency induced by buthionine sulfoximine,[52,54] by up-regulation of anti-oxidant and anti-apoptotic 'survival' molecules.[50,51]

In the PD patient, levodopa concentrations may differ markedly from those used in tissue culture models, particularly within critical subcellular sites such as mitochondria or the nucleus. Additionally, glial cells and other compensatory biological responses in PD patients may modulate any toxic effect of levodopa. Nonetheless, there is sufficient evidence for the toxicity of levodopa under some circumstances to warrant consideration of alternate treatment approaches in early PD.

DOPAMINE AGONISTS AND NEUROPROTECTION IN PD

There are several possible mechanisms whereby dopamine agonists might provide neuroprotection in PD.

Reduced need for levodopa

Numerous studies have demonstrated that dopamine agonists decrease the cumulative levodopa dose that a PD patient takes over the course of their illness.[4,56–56] Fewer molecules of levodopa therefore undergo oxidative metabolism, so reducing the formation of ROS. In 6-OHDA-treated rodents, levels of striatal dopamine and its metabolites are significantly greater in animals treated with levodopa compared to those treated with dopamine agonists despite comparable behavioral effects.[31]

Stimulation of dopamine receptors

There is evidence indicating that stimulation of D_2 auto-receptors on dopamine neurons decreases dopamine synthesis, release, metabolism and the formation of ROS. Pramipexole induces a dose-dependent decrease in dopamine concentration in the medium of cultured dopaminergic neurons.[57] *In vivo*, the dopamine agonists apomorphine, quinpirole, U91356A, and pramipexole depress dopamine neuronal firing[58] and bromocriptine decreases dopamine turnover as determined by the DOPAC + HVA/dopamine ratio.[59] Similarly, microdialysis studies have revealed that pramipexole and talipexole decrease the extracellular concentration of dopamine and its metabolites in healthy rats.[57] In contrast, the D_2 receptor antagonist sulpiride reversed the effects of pramipexole and caused an increase in striatal dopamine levels. D_1 receptor antagonists had no effect, supporting the notion that the dopamine agonist-induced reduction in dopamine synthesis, release, and turnover occurs through stimulation of D_2 auto-receptors.

It has recently been suggested that stimulation of D_2 receptors may be associated with apoptosis. D_2 receptor knock-out mice developed hyperplasia and increased numbers of lactotrophs within the pituitary gland.[60,61] This suggests an antiproliferative function for dopamine and dopamine agonists that is regulated through D_2 receptor activation. In support of this notion, bromocriptine inhibited proliferation of ACTH-secreting pituitary cells in the mouse.[62] This effect was inhibited by cycloheximide and actinomycin D, suggesting dependence on new RNA and protein synthesis. DNA fragmentation assays and cell cycle analysis confirm that bromocriptine induced apoptosis in these cells. The mechanism remains to be elucidated.

Direct antioxidant effects

Bromocriptine has been shown to effectively scavenge hydroxyl and superoxide radicals *in vitro*[59,63] and inhibits hydroxyl radical formation and lipid peroxidation *in vivo*.[59] Pergolide can also scavenge nitric oxide radicals[64] and induce an increase in basal ganglia levels of SOD.[65] More recently, the salicylate radical trapping technique and *in vivo* dialysis methods have demonstrated that both bromocriptine and ropinirole reduce hydroxyl radical generation in the rodent striatum following MPP^+ infusion. The hydroxylated benzyl ring structure within most dopamine agonists may bestow free radical scavenger properties on these molecules.

Inhibition of STN-induced excitotoxicity

Dopamine depletion is associated with disinhibition of the subthalamic nucleus (STN).[66,67] Output neurons originating in the STN are excitatory and use glutamate as a neurotransmitter. Unbridled STN output could induce excitotoxic damage in target structures and accelerate nigral degeneration in the SNc and induce changes in other targets that result in the development of parkinsonian features that do not respond to levodopa. Indeed, lesions of the STN protect against SNc dopamine neuronal damage and transneuronal degeneration in the SNr.[68,69] Dopamine agonists could restore dopaminergic tone and protect against the risk of excitotoxic damage due to excess firing of disinhibited STN neurons.

EVIDENCE OF NEUROPROTECTION
WITH DOPAMINE AGONISTS

Preclinical

Dopamine agonists protect cultured dopaminergic neurons from the degeneration induced by a variety of toxins. Bromocriptine, pergolide, pramipexole, and ropinirole lead to increased cell survival and dopamine uptake indicative of increased numbers of terminals. Apomorphine is a potent free radical scavenger[70] that protects PC12 cells from oxidant stress induced by H_2O_2 and 6-OHDA.[71] Pramipexole protects against levodopa-induced damage to cultured dopamine neurons,[72] while bromocriptine and quinpirole protect against glutamate neurotoxicity. These effects were not seen with D_1 receptor agonists and were blocked by D_2 receptor antagonists. In many of these models, the effect of the agonist on cell survival is U-shaped with loss of the protective effect at higher doses. This phenomenon could relate to the potential of higher levels of D_2 receptor stimulation to induce apoptosis as described above.

In animal models, intraventricular injections of bromocriptine and pergolide protect against the loss of nigral neurons and striatal dopamine and prevent the increase in lipid peroxidation induced by 6-OHDA in rodents.[59,73] Low doses of pergolide in the diet also protected against the normal age-related decline in nigral neurons and striatal dopamine terminals in Fischer rats.[74]

Clinical

Few clinical studies have addressed the potential of dopamine agonists to provide neuroprotection in PD. The SINDEPAR study evaluated the rate of deterioration in UPDRS score in PD patients randomized to either levodopa or bromocriptine.[75] There was no significant difference between the two groups, but concerns surrounded the completeness of the washout period, and possible interactions between the study drugs and selegiline, which was included in the study design. In the prospective double-blind Prado study, patients randomized to bromocriptine plus supplemental levodopa if necessary had less mortality than patients randomized to levodopa alone.[76] This outcome has not been explained nor observed in other studies.

Several clinical trials have recently been designed specifically to test the putative neuroprotective effect of dopamine agonists in PD. Clinical indices as well as striatal fluorodopa uptake on positron emission tomography (PET) are the measures of disease progression. Interim analysis of the PET scan data at the 2-year time point is available from one study comparing ropinirole to levodopa in patients with untreated PD (Brooks, personal communication). These preliminary data showed no significant difference in the rate of deterioration in putaminal Ki between the treatment groups, although there was a trend favoring ropinirole-treated patients (ropinirole 13% *versus* levodopa 17.8%). However, in a subgroup of patients with short duration disease (<2 years) who are thought to have a more rapid rate of neuronal deterioration, differences in the rate of deterioration were more striking (ropinirole 14.2% *versus* levodopa 28.2%). These differences were significantly different in the striatum with the most prominent involvement (1.4% *versus* 30.3%). No changes were detected in the caudate nucleus. Long-term data with larger numbers of patients are awaited, as are the results of similar ongoing studies testing different dopamine agonists.

SUMMARY

- A body of information suggests that dopamine agonists are neuroprotective in *in vivo* and *in vitro* pre-clinical models.

- Clinical trials to test the potential of dopamine agonists to provide neuroprotective effects in PD have been initiated. Preliminary PET studies suggest that there may be reduced deterioration in striatal fluorodopa uptake in PD patients randomized to receive the dopamine agonist ropinirole *versus* levodopa.

- While it has not been established that levodopa is toxic in PD, or that dopamine agonists will alter the natural history of the disorder, an argument can be made for the early use of dopamine agonists, particularly with the accumulating body of evidence indicating that dopamine agonists may delay the development of the motor complications associated with levodopa therapy.

- Based on these concepts, many physicians now choose to initiate symptomatic therapy in PD with a dopamine agonist, reserving levodopa for adjunctive use when the symptoms can not be satisfactorily controlled with the agonist alone.[17,77] There may even be an argument for starting agonists at the time of diagnosis if they are confirmed to be neuroprotective and to be relatively free from the risk of developing motor complications.

REFERENCES

1. Kartzinel R, Teychenne P, Gillespie MM, *et al.* Bromocriptine and levodopa (with or without carbidopa) in parkinsonism. Lancet 1976; ii: 272–275.

2. Calne DB, Burton K, Beckman J, Martin WR. Dopamine agonists in Parkinson's disease. Can J Neurol Sci 1984; 11: 221–224.

3. Hoehn MM, Elton RL. Low dosages of bromocriptine added to levodopa in Parkinson's disease. Neurol 1985; 35: 199–206.

4. Olanow CW, *et al.* A multi-center, double-blind, placebo-controlled trial of pergolide as an adjunct to Sinemet in Parkinson's disease. Mov Disord 1994; 9: 40–47.

5. McDonald RJ, Horowski R. Lisuride in the treatment of parkinsonism. Eur Neurol 1983; 22: 240–255.

6. Olanow CW. A rationale for dopamine agonists as primary therapy for Parkinson's disease. Can J Neurol Sci. 1992; 19: 108–112.

7. Olanow CW. A rationale for using dopamine agonists as primary symptomatic therapy in Parkinson's disease. In, Olanow CW, Obeso JA, eds, Dopamine agonists in early Parkinson's disease. Royal Tunbridge Wells: Wells Medical Limited, 1997: 37–52.

8. Bédard PJ, Di Paolo T, Falardeau P, Boucher R. Chronic treatment with levodopa, but not bromocriptine induces dyskinesia in MPTP-parkinsonian monkeys. Correlation with [3H]spiperone binding. Brain Res 1986; 379: 294–299.

9. Pearce RKB, Banerji T, Jenner P, Marsden CD. Effects of repeated treatment with L-dopa, bromocriptine and ropinirole in drug-naïve MPTP-treated common marmosets. Br J Pharmacol 1996; 118: 37.

10. Rinne UK. Brief communications: early combination of bromocriptine and levodopa in the treatment of Parkinson's disease: a 5 year follow-up. Neurol 1987; 37: 826–828.

11. Olanow CW, Alberts M, Stajich J, Burch G. A randomized blinded study of low dose Bromocriptine versus low dose Carbidopa/Levodopa in untreated Parkinson patients. In, Fahn S, Marsden D, Calne D, Goldstein M, eds, Recent Developments in Parkinson's Disease, Vol II. Macmillan Health Care, 1987: 201–208.

12. Montastruc JL, Rascol O, Senard JM, Rascol A. A randomized controlled study comparing bromocriptine to which levodopa was later added, with levodopa alone in previously untreated patients with Parkinson's disease: a five year follow up. J Neurol Neurosurg Psychiatry 1994; 57: 1034–1038.

13. Wheadon DE, Wilson-Lynch K, Kreider M. The efficacy and safety of ropinirole in early parkinsonian patients not receiving dopaminergic therapy – a multicenter double-blind study. Neurol 1996; 46: 159.

14. Hubble JP, Koller WC, Cutler NR, *et al.* Pramipexole in patients with early Parkinson's disease. Clin Neuropharmacol. 1995; 18: 338–347.

15. Parkinson Study Group. Safety and efficacy of pramipexole in early Parkinson's disease. JAMA 1997; 278: 125–130.

16. Rascol O. A double blind L-dopa controlled study of ropinirole in *de novo* patients with Parkinson's disease. Neurol 1996; 46: 160.

17. Olanow CW, Koller WC. An algorithm (decision tree) for the management of Parkinson's disease. Neurol, in press.

18. Halliwell B, Gutteridge J. Oxygen radicals and the nervous system. TINS 1985; 8: 22–29.

19. Olanow CW. Oxidation reactions in Parkinson's disease. Neurol 1990; 40: 32–37.

20. Spina MB, Cohen G. Dopamine turnover and glutathione oxidation: Implications for Parkinson's disease. Proc Natl Acad Sci USA 1989; 86: 1398–1400.

21. Spencer JPE, Jenner P, Halliwell B. Superoxide-dependent depletion of reduced glutathione by L-dopa and dopamine. Relevance to Parkinson's disease. NeuroReport 1995; 6: 1480–1484.

22. Chiueh CC, Krishna G, Tulsi P, et al. Intracranial microdialysis of salicylic acid to detect hydroxyl radical generation through dopamine autooxidation in the caudate nucleus: Effects of MPP+. Free Rad Biol Med 1992; 13: 581–583.

23. Tanaka M, Sotomatsu A, Kanai H, Hirai S. Dopa and dopamine cause cultured neuronal death in the presence of iron. J Neurosci 1991; 101: 198–203.

24. Ziv I, Melamed E, Nardi N, et al. Dopamine induces apoptosis-like cell death in cultured chick sympathetic neurons - a possible novel pathogenetic mechanism in Parkinson's disease. Neurosci Lett 1994; 170: 136–140.

25. Michel PP, Hefti F. Toxicity of 6-hydroxydopamine and dopamine for dopaminergic neurons in culture. J Neurosci Res 1990; 26: 428–435.

26. Jenner P, Olanow CW. Oxidative stress and the pathogenesis of Parkinson's disease. Neurol 1996; 47: S161–S170.

27. Spina MB, Cohen G. Exposure of striatal synaptosomes to L-dopa elevates levels of oxidized glutathione. J Pharmacol Exp Ther. 1988; 247: 502–507.

28. Spencer Smith T, Parker WD Jr, Bennett JP. L-dopa increases nigral production of hydroxyl radicals in vivo: potential L-dopa toxicity? NeuroReport 1994; 5: 1009–1011.

29. Spencer JPE, Jenner A, Aruoma OI, et al. Intense oxidative DNA damage promoted by L-dopa and its metabolites: Implications for neurodegenerative disease. FEBS Lett 1994; 353: 246–250.

30. Tanaka M, Sotomatsu A, Kanai H, Hirai S. Combined histochemical and biochemical demonstration of nigral vulnerability to lipid peroxidation induced by dopa and iron. Neurosci Lett 1992; 140: 42–46.

31. Ogawa N, Edamatsu R, Mizukawa K, et al. Degeneration of dopaminergic neurons and free radicals: possible participation of levodopa. Adv Neurol 1993; 60: 242–250.

32. Przedborski S, Jackson-Lewis V, Muthane U, et al. Chronic levodopa administration alters cerebral mitochondrial respiratory chain activity. Ann Neurol 1993; 34: 715–723.

33. Mytilineou C, Han S-K, Cohen G. Toxic and protective effects of L-dopa on mesencephalic cell cultures. J Neurochem 1993; 61: 1470–1478.

34. Basma AN, Morris EJ, Nicklas WJ, Geller HM. L-dopa cytotoxicity to PC12 cells in culture is via its autooxidation. J Neurochem 1995; 64: 825–832.

35. Walkinshaw G, Waters CM. Induction of apoptosis in catecholaminergic PC12 cells by L-dopa. Implications for the treatment of Parkinson's disease. J Clin Invest 1995; 95: 2458–64.

36. Steece-Collier K, Collier TJ, Sladek CD, Sladek JR. Chronic levodopa impairs morphological development of grafted embryonic dopamine neurons. Exp Neurol 1990; 110: 201–208.

37. Sanchez-Ramos JR, Overvik E, Ames BN. A marker of oxyradical-mediated DNA damage (8-hydroxy-2'deoxyguanosine) is increased in nigro-striatum of Parkinson's disease brain. Neurodegen 1994; 3: 197–204.

38. Alam ZI, Jenner A, Daniel SE, et al. Oxidative DNA damage in the parkinsonian brain. A selective increase in 8-hydroxyguanine in substantia nigra? J Neurochem, in press.

39. Alam ZI, Daniel SE, Lees AJ, et al. A generalized increase in protein carbonyls in the brain in Parkinson's but not Incidental Lewy Body disease. J Neurochem, in press.

40. Hefti F, Melamed E, Bhawan J, Wurtman R. Long term administration

of L-dopa does not damage dopaminergic neurons in the mouse. Neurol 1981; 31: 1194–1195.

41. Perry TL, Young VW, Ito M, *et al.* Nigrostriatal dopaminergic neurons remain undamaged in rats given high doses of L-dopa and carbidopa chronically. J Neurochem 1984; 43: 990–993.

42. Quinn N, Parkes JD, Janota I, *et al.* Preservation of substantia nigra neurons and locus coeruleus in patients receiving levodopa (2 gm) plus decarboxylase inhibitor over a four year period. Mov Disord 1986; 1: 65–68.

43. Zeng B-Y, Lyras L, Pearce R, *et al.* Failure of chronic L-dopa administration to cause damage to the nigrostriatal system in normal monkeys. Neurosci, in press.

44. Blunt SB, Jenner P, Marsden CD. Suppresive effect of L-dopa on dopamine cells remaining in the ventral tegmental area of rats previously exposed to the neurotoxin 6-hydroxydopamine. Mov Disord 1993; 8: 129–133.

45. Ogawa N, Asanuma M, Kondo Y, *et al.* Differential effects of chronic L-dopa treatment on lipid peroxidation in the mouse brain with or without pretreatment with 6-hydroxydopamine. Neurosci Lett 1994; 171: 55–58.

46. Han S-K, Mytilineou C, Cohen G. L-dopa up-regulates glutathione and protects mesencephalic cultures against oxidative stress. J Neurochem 1996; 66: 501–510.

47. Tatton WG, Ju WYH, Wadia J, Tatton NA. Reduction of neuronal apoptosis by small molecules: promise for new approaches to neurological therapy. In, Olanow CW, Jenner P, Youdim MHB, eds, Neurodegeneration and Neuroprotection in Parkinson's disease. London: Academic Press, 1996; 202–220.

48. Mytilineou C, Radcliffe P, Leonardi EK, Werner P, Olanow CW. L-deprenyl protects mesencephalic dopamine neurons from glutamate receptor-mediated toxicity. J Neurochem 1997; 68: 33–39.

49. Hyman C, Hofer M, Barde YA, *et al.* BDNF is a neurotrophic factor for dopaminergic neurons of the substantia nigra. Nature 1991; 350: 230–232.

50. Tatton WG, Ju WYL, Holland DP, *et al.* (-)-Deprenyl reduces PC12 cell apoptosis by inducing new protein sythesis. J Neurochem 1994; 63: 1572–1575.

51. Ogawa N, Iwata E, Asanuma M, Nishibayashi S, Iida K. Oxidative stress and transcription factors. In, Packer L, Hiramatsu M, Yoshikawa T, eds, Free Radicals in Brain Physiology and Disorders. San Diego: Academic Press, 1996: 131–140.

52. Mytilineou C, Leonardi EK, Radcliffe P, Heinonen EH, Han SK, Werner P, Cohen G, Olanow CW. Deprenyl and desmethylselegiline protect mesencephalic neurons from toxicity induced by glutathione depletion. J PET, in press.

53. Pardo B, Mena MA, Fahn S, de Yebenes JG. Ascorbic acid protects against levodopa-induced neurotoxicity on a catecholamine-rich human neuroblastoma cell line. Mov Disord 1993; 8: 278–284.

54. Kokotos Leonardi ET, Cheng B, Radcliffe PR, Olanow CW, Cohen G, Mytilineou C. L-dopa and L-deprenyl protect against L-BSO induced cell death in cultured mesencephalic neurons. Soc Neurosci Abs 1996; 22: 6786.

55. Brooks DJ, Turjanski N, Burn DJ. Ropinirole in the symptomatic treatment of Parkinson's disease. J Neural Transm 1995; Suppl 45: 231–238.

56. Calne DB, Burton K, Beckman J, Martin WR. Dopamine agonists in Parkinson's disease. Can J Neurol Sci 1984; 11: 221–224.

57. Carter AJ, Muller RE. Pramipexole, a dopamine D_2 receptor agonist, decreases the extracellular concentration of dopamine *in vivo*. Eur J Pharmacol 1991; 200: 65–72.

58. Piercey MF, Camacho-Ochoa M, Smith MW. Functional roles for dopamine-

receptor subtypes. Clin Neuropharmacol 1995; 18: 34–42.

59. Ogawa N, Tanaka K, Asanuma M, et al. Bromocriptine protects mice against 6-hydroxydopamine and scavenges hydroxyl free radical in vitro. Brain Res 1994; 657: 207–213.

60. Saiardi A, Bozzi Y, Baik J-H, Borrelli E. Antiproliferative role of dopamine: loss of D_2 receptors causes hormonal dysfunction and pituitary hyperplasia. Neuron 1997; 19: 115–126.

61. Kelly MA, Rubinstein M, Asa SL, et al. Pituitary lactotroph hyperplasia and chronic hyperprolactinemia in dopamine D_2 receptor-deficient mice. Neuron 1997; 19: 103–113.

62. Yin D, Kondo S, Takeuchi J, Morimura T. Induction of apoptosis in murine ACTH-secreting pituitary adenoma cells by bromocriptine. FEBS Lett 1994; 339: 73–75.

63. Yoshikawa T, Minamiyama Y, Naito Y, et al. Antioxidant properties of bromocriptine, a dopamine agonist. J Neurochem 1994; 62: 1034–1038.

64. Nishibayashi S, Asanuma M, Kohno M, Gómez-Vargas M, Ogawa N. Scavenging effects of dopamine agonists on nitric oxide radicals. J Neurochem 1996; 67: 2208–2211.

65. Clow A, Freestone C, Lewis E, et al. The effect of pergolide and MDL 72974 on rat brain CuZn superoxide dismutase. Neurosci Lett 1993; 164: 41–43.

66. Albin RL, Young AB, Penney JB. The functional anatomy of basal ganglia disorders. TINS 1989; 12: 366–375.

67. DeLong MR. Primate models of movement disorders of basal ganglia origin. TINS 1990; 13: 281–289.

68. Piallat B, Bennazouz A, Bressand L, et al. Subthalamic nucleus lesion in rat prevents dopaminergic nigral neuron degeneration after striatal 6-OHDA injection. Soc Neurosci Abst 1995; 74.

69. Saji M, Blau AD, Volpe BT. Prevention of transneuronal degeneration of neurons in the substantia nigra reticulata by ablation of the subthalamic nucleus. Exp Neurol 1996; 141: 120–129.75.

70. Gassen M, Glinka Y, Pinchasi B, Youdim MB. Apomorphine is a highly potent free radical scavenger in rat brain mitochondrial fraction. Eur J Pharmacol. 1996; 308: 219–225.

71. Gassen M, Gross A, Youdim MBH. Apomorphine enantiomers protect pheochromocytoma (PC12) cells from oxidative stress induced by hydrogen peroxide and 6-hydroxydopamine. Mov Disord, in press.

72. Carvey PM, Pieri S, Ling ZD. Attenuation of levodopa-induced toxicity in mesencephalic cultures by pramipexole. J Neural Transm 1997; 104: 209–228.

73. Asanuma M, Ogawa N, Nishibayashi S, Kawai M, Kondo Y, Iwata E. Protective effects of pergolide on dopamine levels in the 6-hydroxydopamine-lesioned mouse brain. Arch Int Pharmacodyn 1995; 329: 221–230.

74. Felten DL, Felten SY, Fuller RW, et al. Chronic dietary pergolide preserves nigrostriatal neuronal integrity in aged Fischer 344 rats. Neurobiol Ageing 1992; 13: 339–351.

75. Olanow CW, Hauser RA, Gauger L, et al. The effect of deprenyl and levodopa on the progression of signs and symptoms in Parkinson's disease. Ann Neurol 1995; 38: 771–777.

76. Przuntek H, Welzel D, Blumner E, et al. Bromocriptine lessens the incidence of mortality in L-dopa-treated parkinsonian patients: Prado study discontinued. Eur J Clin Pharmacol 1992; 43: 357–363.

77. Olanow CW, Obeso JA. Dopamine agonists in early Parkinson's disease. Royal Tunbridge Wells: Wells Medical Limited, 1997.

DISCUSSION

Langston: Dr. Olanow, you marshalled a series of arguments for why dopamine agonists might be neuroprotective. What are your explanations for not seeing neuroprotection in the Sindepar study?

Olanow: The Sindepar study was not designed specifically to look for neuroprotection; this was a secondary analysis. Further, the Sindepar study was not powered with respect to that particular endpoint. At the present time, the theoretical arguments and laboratory studies supporting the notion that dopamine agonists might be neuroprotective are, in my mind, sufficient to warrant performing a clinical trial specifically designed to address this issue.

Polymeropoulos: The neuroprotective effect you have shown in tissue culture was achieved with low doses of bromocriptine. Are these doses sufficiently low not to interfere with prolactin levels in young women, particularly those who might be defined as being at risk through genetic testing?

Olanow: I do not think it will be a problem from that standpoint. Bromocriptine does reduce prolactin levels but they might also be altered by the lack of dopamine. Typically we do not see many women of childbearing age with PD who are anxious to become pregnant, so we do not have much information on what it might do to pregnancy. Toxicology studies with many of the dopamine agonists have not shown specific problems that I am aware of. It is interesting though that many dopamine agonists do induce testicular adenomas in some rodents, although I am not sure what the mechanism is and have not seen this problem in PD patients.

Gash: You showed U-shaped dose–response curves in your neuroprotection studies. In rodent studies, different doses can be assessed in a number of groups, but how do you get around that in patient studies where, if the wrong dose is selected, more problems may be created than corrected? Also, do you have any idea why there is a U-shaped curve with these drugs?

Olanow: Clearly we require as much preclinical data as possible and phase II dose-finding studies are necessary in man before going into larger studies. It is a mistake in my opinion to conduct human trials at a single dose, without having previously performed a dosing study. This might preclude using doses high enough to achieve the optimal clinical effect or low enough to minimize side effects. This will help in symptomatic studies but is a problem in trials of neuroprotection and probably multiple doses will have to be tested. It is fascinating that there appears to be a U-shaped curve for neuroprotection with agonists. Recent studies suggest that dopamine agonists that stimulate the D_2 receptor can protect or induce cell death. Interestingly, cell death can be blocked by transcriptional inhibitors suggesting that this is a form of apoptotic cell death. This is an area that is going to have be examined more carefully in the future but it does appear that dopamine agonists have the potential to both protect against and to induce cell death.

Obeso: The reduction in the incidence of dyskinesias and motor fluctuations seen with dopamine agonists could also be due to neuroprotection through preservation of dopamine terminals that buffer against pulsatile stimulation of dopamine receptors, as you suggested. But, it is also possible that this could relate to differences in the pharmacodynamic properties of dopamine agonists *versus* levodopa. In trials of dopamine agonists as early therapy, we should follow the 'off' scores of motor disability as well as the incidence of complications.

Olanow: Studies are now underway in untreated patients who are randomized to levodopa, or a dopamine agonist with levodopa when necessary. The end points are motor complications, UPDRS in 'off' time, and imaging markers such as striatal fluorodopa uptake on PET or β-CIT on SPECT. There are also studies of putative neuroprotection using a design similar to that used in the Sindepar study. Here we looked at the degree of deterioration in parkinsonian signs and symptoms between untreated baseline and a final visit performed after the patient had washed out of all anti-parkinsonian medications. Until we have an unequivocal marker of dopamine neurons or a drug that markedly affects disease progression, it will be difficult to do a clinical trial to detect neuroprotection.

Bonnuccelli: You showed an *in vivo* study in rats demonstrating preservation of dopamine neurons with aging in dopamine agonist-treated animals. Rather than being due to a reduction in dopamine metabolism as you have suggested, could this be an indirect effect of dopamine agonists on something else that decreases the vulnerability of the entire dopaminergic system?

Olanow: It is certainly possible that there are other explanations for why dopamine agonist-treated animals had relative preservation of their nigrostriatal system. For example, animals that lose weight tend to live longer and in studies looking at survival, it is important that they be adequately controlled for weight. Dr. Felton has done this in his study, but this was not done in some of the earlier studies showing that levodopa- or selegiline-treated animals lived longer. There are certainly many other factors that could be contributing, but I think that the decrease in dopamine turnover is the most compelling explanation at this time.

Jenner: Dr. Brooks, I am most impressed by your preliminary PET scan data even though it is a small number of patients. Mostly, I am impressed that it now appears we have the technology to be able to do neuroprotective studies using imaging markers as end points with a reasonable expectation of being able to detect relatively modest differences between groups. More specifically, how hard do you think your data are at this point in claiming that dopamine agonists slow the rate of decline in striatal fluorodopa uptake in comparison to levodopa?

Brooks: This was an interim analysis and only a small number of patients were studied, particularly in the levodopa group. The results are intriguing and suggest that there may be a difference in the two groups in patients who have relatively short duration disease. But, it is far too early to draw any specific conclusion from this study. We need more patients and we need to follow them longer. I do agree with you that it does appear we have the technology to detect modest differences between relatively small groups followed for two to five years. Thus this type of testing is now feasible.

Olanow: Dr. Brooks, in your ropinirole *versus* levodopa neuroprotection study, the randomization was meant to be 2:1 but it appeared to be 3:1?

Brooks: That is correct.

Olanow: If the early patients responded best to agonist therapy, one might think that the less affected putamen would be the most protected. How do you account for your finding suggesting that the putamen with the lowest fluorodopa uptake to start with was the most protected if, as you said earlier, PD appears to deteriorate at a faster rate in the early stages of the disease?

Brooks: There are two arguments here. Firstly, theoretically the protection should be better in the less affected side as you say, but secondly, if the less affected side is progressing faster, it may be harder to demonstrate protection.

Stocchi: Did you show a toxic effect of levodopa or a protective effect of ropinirole?

Brooks: One cannot answer that question since there was no placebo control group. The levodopa arm seemed to progress at a very similar rate to the earlier pilot study that we performed with Dr. Paul Morrish. The ropinirole arm seemed to be progressing very slowly indeed, certainly in those patients with early disease, who normally would be expected to progress rapidly. Whether levodopa is toxic and the ropinirole arm reflects natural disease progression is impossible to say as we only have progression data on treated patients and not on untreated patients.

Leenders: You expressed the data as the percentage change, since you saw the significant effect on the worst side, which means you started with very low fluorodopa levels. Therefore a small change would have manifested itself in a fairly large percentage change, more than on the good side. Since there are different numbers in the levodopa and ropinirole groups, could this be an explanation for the effect you saw?

Brooks: The dissimilarity between the two sides is not, in fact, that great as we have seen repeatedly. While there is a big clinical difference between the two sides in early disease, the difference in dopa K_i is quite small.

Rakshi: I have a comment about levodopa toxicity. In a different study we performed 3D fluorodopa PET scans on patients at the two extremes of the disease, one group with Hoehn & Yahr stage I, and another group with advanced bilateral PD with a mean duration of 12 years. We plotted individual putamen K_i values for the least and the worst affected side for both groups and for a normal control group, and found an exponential decline, assuming that each putamen levodopa influx value represents a different stage of the disease process. A surprising feature is that, although the patients who have advanced bilateral PD have been on levodopa for ten years or more, the actual percentage difference or decline in putamen K_i is relatively small, 20–40%. One interpretation is that levodopa is not toxic. In fact, the greatest difference you see when you compare the two groups is in the brainstem and more specifically in the dorsal midbrain.

Gash: I am trying to put your data into perspective with our unilateral MPTP lesion model in Rhesus monkeys. We have been trying to study the compensatory changes seen on the less lesioned side, which are very robust and occur early on. Perhaps the hemiparkinsonian model would be a good animal to model to determine what is happening to the side that is less affected in early parkinsonism.

Brooks: I do not understand why we are not seeing an agonist protective effect bilaterally. Your MPTP lesion model may well be able to tell us whether the faster progressing, less affected side is less susceptible to the effect of ropinirole. On the other hand, it is not clear that there is any meaningful progression after MPTP treatment or that we could detect it if there was with PET scan.

Langston: I worry about levodopa confounding factors in the rapid early disease decline that you are seeing with PET. Have you looked at untreated patients?

Brooks: No, it is very difficult to find patients who can manage without treatment for 3–4 years.

Olanow: But you have done studies with levodopa before and after PET scans and shown that it did not meaningfully influence PET?

Brooks: Levodopa treatment *per se* does not alter fluorodopa uptake.

CHAPTER TWENTY FIVE

Subthalamic nucleus-mediated excitotoxicity in Parkinson's disease: a target for neuroprotection

MARIA C. RODRIGUEZ[1], JOSÉ A. OBESO[1] AND
C. WARREN OLANOW[2]

[1]Department of Neurology and Neurosurgery, HOSPITEN, and
Laboratory of Experimental Neurology and Neurobiology, Department of
Physiology, Medical School, Universidad de La Laguna, Tenerife, and
Clinica Quiron, San Sebastian, Spain, [2]Department of Neurology,
Mount Sinai School of Medicine, New York, New York, USA

The subthalamic nucleus (STN) is a key structure in the functional organization of the basal ganglia,[1,2] and inhibition of STN activity is currently being studied as a treatment for the motor effects of Parkinson's disease (PD). It is also noteworthy that STN neurons use glutamate as their primary neurotransmitter.[3] Glutamate activity is exerted through the activation of glutamate receptors – the ionotropic N-methyl-D-aspartate (NMDA) and the alpha-amino-3-hydroxy-5-methyl-4-isoxazolepropionate-kainate (AMPA) receptors localized postsynaptically and the presynaptic metabotropic receptor (mGlu) family.[4] Glutamate-mediated toxicity is a major putative mechanism mediating neuronal death[5,6] and is potentially involved in the etiopathogenesis of PD.[7] Excessive neuronal activity in the STN is a hallmark of the parkinsonian state.[2,8] A consequent increase in glutamate release could thereby be postulated to accelerate the loss of neurons in target structures which include the globus pallidus pars interna (GPi), globus pallidus pars externa (GPe), substantia nigra pars reticularis (SNr), pedunculopontine nucleus (PPN) and the substantia nigra pars compacta (SNc). STN overactivity could thus contribute to an accelerated loss of dopaminergic cells in the SNc and to the rate of progression of neurodegeneration in PD. Accordingly, blockade of the STN could be considered as a target for potential neuroprotective as well as symptomatic effects. This chapter reviews the anatomo-chemical and physiological basis for this concept.

Glutamine and the STN

In the basal ganglia, NMDA and AMPA receptors are predominantly expressed. Each is subdivided into several variants according to molecular structure.[9] This heterogeneity may be important from an etiopathogenic and therapeutic point of view, since they are distributed differently throughout the central nervous system and vary in their pre- and post-synaptic preferential location.[9,10]

Metabolic and electrophysiological studies

The glutamatergic nature of STN neurons has been elucidated by metabolic and electrophysiological studies in the rat and monkey. In the normal rat, STN ablation induced a reduction in the ipsilateral SNr and globus pallidus (GP) in the activity of metabolic markers such as succinate dehydrogenase (SDH) and cytochrome oxidase (CO) indicating that STN has an excitatory effect on these targets.[11] Similarly, lesions of the STN reduce the activity of mitochondrial complexes I, II and IV in the SNr, GP and entopeduncular nucleus (EP).[12,13] In 6-hydroxydopamine (6-OHDA)-lesioned rats, SDH and CO immunostaining are enhanced in the EP and SNr. A unilateral lesion of the STN completely reverses this effect.[14] In MPTP-treated monkeys, a unilateral lesion of the STN reduces expression of GAD mRNA[15] in the SNr and GPi. These findings suggest decreased neuronal activity in keeping with the notion that STN neurons are excitatory.

Excitatory effects of STN stimulation have been shown electrophysiologically in the SNr of the intact rat[16] while lesions of the STN regularize the firing pattern.[17] Microinjection of muscimol (a GABA agonist) into the STN to inhibit its activity, induces a reduction in neuronal firing and in 2-DG uptake in the ipsilateral SNr, EP and GP.[18,19] The opposite effects are noted with the GABAergic antagonist, bicuculline. In the monkey, lesions of the STN with kainic or ibotenic acid induce a reduction in neuronal firing in GPi and Gpe.[20] The available data therefore indicate conclusively that the efferent activity of the STN is excitatory.

Anatomy

Glutamatergic projections to the SNc

Several sources of glutamatergic input to dopaminergic cells in the SNc and ventral tegmental area (VTA) have been detected. These include the STN,[21,22] the PPN,[22–24] the cerebral cortex[25] and the amygdala.[26] NMDA receptors mediate the excitatory effect from the STN and cortex and AMPA-kainate receptors are involved in PPN projections.[27–29] There is also evidence of glutamate in STN terminals within SNc.[30–33] A proportion of PPN fibers are cholinergic but glutamate-positive boutons have been clearly identified using retrograde tracing with PHA-L.[24] There is ultrastructural evidence of synaptic contacts between glutamate-enriched terminals and dopaminergic neurons. Cortical afferents to the STN have also been demonstrated in the rat and monkey.[34] The dorsolateral region of the STN corresponds with the sensorimotor area of the nucleus in monkeys and humans[35,36] and the primary motor cortex projects mainly to the dorsolateral STN.[22]

Dopaminergic projection to the STN

There is also evidence for the existence of dopamine projections from the SNc to the STN as indicated by the presence of homovanillic acid in the STN of human brains.[37] Anatomical studies in the rat noted the presence of numerous catecholaminergic fibers and varicosities in most parts of the STN.[38] The dopaminergic nature of these catecholaminergic fibers became evident based on studies noting the expression of tyrosine hydroxylase (TH) and dopamine transporter (DAT)[39,40] in retrogradely-labeled SNc neurons of rodents. In non-rodents, the SNc projection to STN is less prominent.[41] D_1 and D_2 dopamine receptors have been documented within the STN of the rat.[42–48]

PHYSIOLOGY

STN excitatory activity and dopaminergic neurons

There is a body of evidence indicating that the STN exerts a regulatory effect on neuronal firing in the SNc. Midbrain dopaminergic neurons typically exhibit burst firing after STN stimulation, which is believed to be at least as important as firing frequency.[49] The excitatory effect of the STN on the SNc was first shown in the intact rat.[50] Electrical stimulation of the STN produced a marked enhancement of dopamine (DA) release in the ipsilateral SNc which lasted for at least 60 min[51] and a significant decrease in DA release was observed after completion of STN stimulation. Injection of acetylcholine into the STN induced similar results indicating that these effects are due to STN activation and not stimulation of fibers of passage. There is also evidence to suggest a modulatory role of STN neurons in nigrostriatal dopamine function.[51] The response of SNc neurons to activation or inhibition of the STN is not uniform,[18,52] and it has been suggested that this mixed response is partly due to collaterals from the SNr.

Burst firing in the SNc is under the direct influence of glutamatergic input[52–54] and is likely due to inputs from STN. A reduction in bursting activity without a change in the mean firing rate of SNc neurons follows inactivation or lesioning of the STN.[52] Similarly, inhibition of STN neurons by intranuclear injection of GABA in the rat regularized burst firing in dopaminergic neurons.[55] In contrast, bicuculline injections which increase firing in STN neurons augments burst discharges in some dopamine neurons.

Dopaminergic cells in SNc have been shown to fire phasically. [56] Cortical stimulation can also induces bursting neuronal activity in the SNc[57] but with a long latency.[58] Since the activity of the STN is under the direct influence of a monosynaptic projection from the sensorimotor cortex[59], it is likely that STN mediates bursting discharges in the SNc neurons after cortical stimulation.

Cortical stimulation of STN neurons has been shown to involve glutamate based on finding glutamate within vesicles of axon terminals in the cortico-STN pathway.[60] STN excitation induced by stimulation of the cortex or by microiontophoretically-applied glutamate is blocked by drugs with broad-spectrum antiglutamatergic activity (glutamic acid diethyl ester, kynurenic acid and cis-2,3-piperidine dicarboxylic acid) but not by the specific NMDA receptor antagonist 2-amino-5-phosphonovaleric acid.[61] The specificity of glutamatergic-mediated transmission in cortico-STN projections can be further demonstrated by the fact that STN excitation induced by local infusion of acetylcholine or PPN stimulation is not blocked by glutamic acid diethyl ester. Further, infusion into SNc of the NMDA antagonist CPP but not the AMPA antagonist CNQX blocks bursting-evoked activity following prefrontal cortex stimulation in the rat.[62] The PPN also exerts an excitatory action on SNc neurons[63] but without bursting activity. It does, however, send glutamatergic and cholinergic projection to STN,[64] which could indirectly produce bursting activity in DA cells.

Dopaminergic control of the STN

There is evidence that dopamine impacts on the STN. Systemic administration of dopamine agonists induces a marked increase in STN glucose utilization.[65] Iontophoretic application of dopamine into STN induces an increase in the discharge rate in a dose-dependent manner. Flupenthixol, a selective dopamine antagonist, attenuates or prevents this response. These results indicate a direct effect of dopaminergic drugs on the STN.[44,66] The experimental results are, however, difficult to interpret. The most well-established finding is that D_1 receptor agonists (SKF 38393 and SKF 82958) increase neuronal firing in the STN and that D_1 antagonists (SCH 23390) abolish this effect. D_2 receptors appear to influence the response to D_1 agonists but do not have a direct effect.

HYPERACTIVITY OF THE STN IN THE PARKINSONIAN STATE

Evidence of augmented neuronal activity

Dopamine deficiency has been shown to cause a series of functional changes in the basal ganglia characterized by increased neuronal activity in the STN and in the main basal ganglia output nuclei, namely the GPi and SNr.[2,67,68] Microrecording of neuronal activity in the basal ganglia of MPTP monkeys shows an increase in mean neuronal firing frequency in the GPi and STN.[8,69,70] Lesion or inactivation of the STN with muscimol[71] significantly reduces the mean frequency of discharge in the GPi. These studies indicate that there is increased neuronal activity in the STN in the parkinsonian state.

A more direct demonstration of the paramount role of STN hyperactivity in the pathophysiology of parkinsonism stems from behavioral studies in monkeys. Lesions of the GPi with kynurenic acid markedly alleviates parkinsonian signs[72] while STN lesion have are associated with marked improvement in mobility, posture and tremor in MPTP-treated monkeys.[15,73,74] Surgery of the STN has now been introduced for patients with PD, allowing for recording of neuronal activity and the study of the somatotopic organization of the STN in these patients.[36] Additionally, inhibition of STN by either lesions or deep brain stimulation (DBS) produces a marked amelioration of all cardinal features of PD[75,76] and improvement in premotor area activation.[77]

The origin of increased STN activity

The precise mechanisms responsible for the STN hyperactivity in the parkinsonian state are unknown. It appears that only a small change in neuronal activity in the STN and GPi is necessary to induce a parkinsonian state[8,68,69] and a relatively modest variation in discharge rate may be sufficient to shift from the normal state to parkinsonism. STN hyperactivity could be caused by reduced inhibition, increased excitation or both. The GPe exerts the major inhibitory control on the STN. In the dopamine depleted parkinsonian state, neuronal activity in the GPe is reduced which removes its tonic inhibitory effect on the STN and may be enough to produce the functional changes associated with the parkinsonian state. If this is the case, at least three mechanisms may be involved: (1) lesion or degeneration of GABA neurons in the GPe itself; (2) increased inhibition from the striatum by way of its GABA-enkephalin projecting neurons; and (3) the effects of dopamine deficiency. The last is the only well-documented mechanism.[78] Alternatively, increased activation of the STN could originate from several theoretical sources, the most important being the cerebral cortex and the PPN. At the present time, there is no evidence for increased excitatory input to the STN.

GLUTAMATE AND NEUROTOXICITY

There is good evidence that glutamate can induce neuronal degeneration.[79] Systemic administration of glutamate to neonatal rats results in retinal degeneration[80] and excitoxicity has been implicated in the pathogenesis of a variety of neurodegenerative disorders including amyotrophic lateral sclerosis, Alzheimer's disease, Huntington's disease and olivo-ponto-cerebellar atrophy as well as PD.[5,6]

Mechanism of action of glutamate-induced neurotoxicity

Glutamatergic stimulation of NMDA receptor can damage and eventually kill target neurons, a phenomenon known as excitotoxicity. Although the precise mechanisms are unresolved, excitotoxicity involves an increase in intracellular Ca^{++} *via* NMDA receptor activation and opening of ionic channels. A rise in free cellular calcium leads to excessive Ca^{++} inflow into the mitochondria. This in turn can reduce the electrochemical gradient across the mitochondrial membrane provoking opening of the mitochondrial permeability transition pore (PTP) and the release of small mitochondrial proteins that promote apoptosis.[81–85] In addition, a rise in intracytosolic Ca^{++} levels can result in an increase in the synthesis of nitric oxide (NO), free radical formation, and PARS activation.[75,86–92]

GLUTAMATE AND SNc DEGENERATION

Glutamate and PD

There are several lines of evidence indicating that glutamate toxicity contributes to cell degeneration in PD. NMDA receptor antagonists protect SNc dopamine neurons in rats from toxicity provoked by direct infusion of MPP^+ or systemic administration of MPTP.[76] $MPTP/MPP^+$ interfere with complex I of the respiratory chain and can thereby block energy metabolism.[93] Depletion of cell energy supplies can lead to partial depolarization and relief of the voltage-dependent Mg^{2+} blockade of NMDA receptor channels,[94] which permits physiologic concentrations of glutamate to induce excitotoxicity. In monkeys, co-administration of MK-801 with MPTP prevents the development of parkinsonism and reduces dopamine depletion in the putamen and caudate.[95] Glutamate-induced excitotoxicity is partially related to the action of NO. Transgenic mice deficient in neuronal nitric oxide synthase (nNOS), the enzyme that generates NO, are resistant to the effect of MPTP.[96] Further, the nNOS inhibitor 7-NI protects against MPTP-induced dopamine depletion in mice and baboons.[97] These observations stress the importance of NO formation and excitotoxicity in MPTP-induced neuronal degeneration. More recently, there has been interest in the potential of increased cellular calcium to induce cell death by way of apoptosis.[98] A fall in mitochondrial membrane potential was an early event in neuronal apoptosis, and that a rise in calcium was a key factor necessary for the induction of the apoptotic process.[84] More recently it has been shown that deprenyl protects against apoptosis induced by excitotoxicity[99] and that this benefit depends upon the drug's capacity to induce transcriptional effects[100] and to maintain levels of BCL-2 which protects against opening of the PTP. Deprenyl has been shown to slow the rate of deterioration in early PD, although the mechanism responsible for this effect remains uncertain.[101] Finally, there is evidence of excitotoxic damage in the SNc of PD patients as evidenced by the accumulation of 3-nitrotyrosine.[102]

Effect of lesioning of the STN

A direct approach to testing the role of glutamate in SNc degeneration is to assess the effects of eliminating the glutamatergic efferents arising from the STN. Cell loss in the SNc caused by 6-OHDA in the rat was significantly reduced by prior ipsilateral subthalamic ablation.[103] Ongoing experiments in monkeys appear to show that similarly STN lesions protect against MPTP toxicity (Benabid, personal communication).

Mitochondrial dysfunction and SNc vulnerability to glutamate

The problem in PD may be complicated by the observation of a complex I defect in the SNc in PD. A defect in complex I activity could lead to a decrease in ATP synthesis and a loss of the voltage dependent Mg^{++} blockade of NMDA receptors, thereby potentially making dopamine cells vulnerable to even small changes in glutamate levels. Further, a complex I defect could lead to a reduction in mitochondrial membrane potential due to impaired proton pumping and an increased risk for apoptosis. The paramount importance of mitochondrial dysfunction in the mechanisms of neuronal degeneration in the SNc is supported by studies in cultured mouse mesencephalic neurons.[104] These neurons were not damaged when exposed to either rotenone (an inhibitor of complex I) or low concentrations of glutamate, but exposure to both agents caused a marked decrease in cell survival. Dopaminergic cells were more sensitive to this synergistic effect than GABA cells.

GLUTAMATE ACTIVITY, THE STN AND THE ETIOPATHOGENESIS OF PD

The evidence described above permits the hypothesis that STN overactivity in PD contributes to the degeneration of SNc dopamine neurons and accelerates the rate of disease progression. One can further speculate that a vicious cycle develops in which degeneration of dopamine neurons results in disinhibition of the STN and STN overactivity induces further degeneration of SNc dopamine neurons. Further, STN overactivity could also lead to excitotoxic damage in GPi, SNr and PPN and thereby account for the development of parkinsonian features such as freezing, gait dysfunction, and dysautonomia that do not respond to levodopa therapy.   The origin of PD may be envisioned to result from the following sequence of events:

1. A mitochondrial defect and/or oxidant stress renders SNc dopamine neurons susceptible to noxious stimuli. Some of these cells start to degenerate spontaneously.
2. A decrease in striatal dopamine leads to disinhibition of the STN.
3. Increased STN neuronal activity leads to excess glutamate release and excitotoxic damage in vulnerable SNc neurons.
4. Increasing loss of SNc neurons leads to greater dopamine depletion and further disinhibition of the STN. Thus a vicious cycle develops in which

STN overactivity contributes to degeneration of SNc dopamine neurons.

5. Eventually there is a critical loss of striatal dopamine and SNc dopamine neurons and patients begin to experience the initial features of PD.

6. Continued STN overactivity could also lead to degeneration of neurons in the GPi, SNr, and PPN with the resultant development of the non-dopaminergic features of PD.

This chain of events need not necessarily start with abnormal energy production or oxidant stress causing degeneration of SNc neurons but could be initiated by any etiologic factor. A more radical view is that increased STN neuronal firing due to any of the causes described above is the primary event leading to the loss of vulnerable SNc neurons. There are no experimental data at present to support this speculation, but it may explain the apparent heterogeneity of PD.

SUBTHALAMIC NUCLEUS-MEDIATED EXCITOTOXICITY AND NEUROPROTECTION

A consequence of the proposed hypothesis is the possibility that therapies that inhibit STN firing might be neuroprotective in PD. There are several approaches to this goal. One is the early introduction of dopaminergic therapy. Many physicians are reluctant to start levodopa at the time of diagnosis because of the risk of motor complications and the possibility of accelerating the degeneration of dopamine neurons.[105-107] The situation may be different with dopamine agonists which are associated with a lower risk of motor complications and may provide neuroprotective effects. Clinical trials to test dopamine agonists as putative neuroprotective agents are underway and future trials could be initiated from the time of diagnosis.

A second approach is the use of agents that interfere with glutamate receptors. NMDA receptor antagonists are poorly tolerated because of psychiatric side effects but the development of agents that target specific subsets of glutamate receptors may permit the use of this strategy in the future. Alternatively, agents that inhibit glutamate release such as lamotrigine or riluzole might be effective, and preclinical data indicate they protect against dopamine cell loss in monkeys following MPTP administration. Clinical trials of riluzole as a putative neuroprotective agent are currently being initiated.

Finally, interventions that directly inhibit STN firing such as lesions or DBS might be neuroprotective in PD. Lesions may cause hemiballismus and physicians have been reluctant to employ this technique. However, DBS may provide an opportunity to functionally inhibit STN bilaterally without the risk of permanent hemiballismus. This procedure has been tested in advanced PD and shown to improve motor dysfunction. As a possible neuroprotective strategy it would be preferable to use it in the early stages of the disease where presently there are several practical limitations. Firstly, the precise mechanism of action of DBS and its long-term effects are not known. Secondly, surgery on the basal ganglia carries a low but definite risk which will have to be considered in relatively healthy patients with other symptomatic opportunities. Finally, economic factors might limit this approach.

SUMMARY

- We hypothesize that STN overactivity in PD may contribute to disease progression and the development of features that do not respond to levodopa.

- Dopamine deficiency is causes overactivity of the STN.

- The output of the STN is glutamatergic.

- The STN projects to the GPi, SNr, GPe, PPN, and SNc.

- There is a complex I defect in PD which may render SNc dopamine neurons vulnerable to excitotoxicity.

- In PD, a vicious cycle may develop in which the initial dopamine loss induces disinhibition of the STN activity and increased firing of STN neurons may induce excitotoxic damage in SNc dopaminergic neurons.

- Therapeutic approaches capable of reducing STN overactivity such as dopamine agonists, glutamate inhibitors, or surgical inhibition of the STN might slow the progression of PD.

ACKNOWLEDGMENT

These studies are supported by the National Parkinson Foundation (Miami, USA), the Lowenstein Foundation, the European Community Biomed-2 program, Medtronic Inc (Minneapolis, USA), and ASTA Medica (Madrid, Spain).

REFERENCES

1. Feger J, Hassani LN, Mouroux M. The subthalamic nucleus and its connections: new electrophysiological and pharmacological data. Adv Neurol 1997; 74: 31–44.

2. DeLong MR. Primate models of movement disorders of basal ganglia origin. TINS 1990; 13: 281–285.

3. Rinvik E, Ottersen OP. Terminals of subthalamonigral fibres are enriched with glutamate-like immunoreactivity: an electron microscopic, immunogold analysis in the cat. Neuroanat 1993; 6: 19–30.

4. Nicoletti F, Bruno V, Casabona G, Knöpfel T. Metabotropic glutamate receptors: a new target for the therapy of neurodegenerative disorders? TINS 1996; 19: 267–271.

5. Choi DW. Glutamate neurotoxicity and diseases of the nervous system. Neuron 1998; 1: 623–634.

6. Albin RL, Greenamyre JT. Alternative excitotoxic hypotheses. Neurology 1992; 42:733–738.

7. Greenberg DA. Glutamate and Parkinson's disease. Ann Neurol 1994; 35: 639.

8. Bergman H,Wichmann T, DeLong MR. The primate subthalamic nucleus. II. Neuronal activity in the MPTP model of Parkinsonism. J Neurophysiol 1994; 72: 507–520.

9. Hollmann M, Heinemann S. Cloned glutamate receptors. Ann Rev Neurosci 1994;17:31–108.

10. Standaert DG, Testa CM, Young AB, Penney JB. Organization of N-Methyl-D-Aspartate glutamate receptor gene expression in the basal ganglia of the rat. J Comp Neurol 1994; 343: 1–16.

11. Blandini F, Greenamyre JT. Effect of subthalamic nucleus lesion on mitochondrial enzyme activity in rat basal ganglia. Brain Res 1995; 669: 59–66.

12. Blandini F, Greenamyre JT. The effect of subthalamic nucleus lesion on mitochondrial enzyme activity in rat basal ganglia. Brain Res. 1995; 588: 307–310.

13. Blandini F, Porter RHP, Greenamyre JT. Autoradiographic study of mitochondrial complex I and glutamate receptors in the basal ganglia of rats after unilateral subthalamic lesion. Neurosci Lett 1995; 186: 99–102.

14. Blandini F, Garcia-Osuna M, Greenamyre JT. Subthalamic ablation reverses changes in basal ganglia oxidative metabolism and motor response to apomorphine induced by nigrostriatal lesion in rats. Eur J Neurosci 1997; 9: 1407–1413.

15. Guridi J, Herrero MT, Luquin MR, Guillén J, Ruberg M, Laguna J, Vila M, Javoy-Agid F, Agid Y, Hirsch E, Obeso JA. Subthalamotomy in parkinsonian monkeys. Behavioral and biochemical analysis. Brain 1996; 119: 1717–1727.

16. Hammond C, Deniau JM, Rizk A, Féger J. Electrophysiological demonstration of an excitatory subthalamonigral pathway in the rat. Brain Res 1978; 151: 235–244.

17. Ryan LJ, Sanders DJ. Subthalamic nucleus lesion regularizes firing patterns in globus pallidus and substantia nigra pars reticulata neurons in rats. Brain Res 1993; 626: 327–331.

18. Feger J, Robledo P. The effects of activation or inhibition of the subthalamic nucleus on the metabolic and electrophysiological activities within the pallidal complex and substantia nigra in the rat. Eur J Neurosci 1991; 3: 947–952.

19. Robledo P, Féger J. Excitatory influence of rat subthalamic nucleus to substantia nigra pars reticulata and the pallidal complex: electrophysiological data. Brain Res 1990; 518: 47–54.

20. Hamada I, DeLong MR. Excitotoxic acid lesions of the primate subthalamic nucleus result in reduced pallidal neuronal activity during active holding. J Neurophysiol 1992; 68: 1859–1866.

21. Smith Y, Charara A, Parent A. Synaptic innervation of midbrain dopaminergic neurons by glutamate-enriched terminals in the squirrel monkey. J Comp Neurol 1996; 364: 231–253.

22. Charara A, Smith Y, Parent A. Glutamatergic inputs from the pedun-culopontine nucleus to midbrain dopaminergic neurons in primates: *Phaseolus vulgaris*-leucoagglutinin anterograde labeling combined with postembedding glutamate and GABA immunohistochemistry. J Comp Neurol 1996; 364: 254–266.

23. Scarnati E, Proia A, Campana E, Pacitti C. A microiontophoretic study on the nature of the putative synaptic neurotransmitter in the pedunculo-pontine-subthalamic nigra pars comp-acta excitatory pathway of the rat. Exp Brain Res 1986; 62: 470–478.

24. Lavoie B, Parent A. Pedunculopontine nucleus in the squirrel monkey: cholinergic and glutamatergic projection to the substantia nigra. J Comp Neurol 1994; 344: 232–241.

25. Naito A, Kita H.The cortico-nigral projection in the rat: An anterograde tracing study with biotinylated dextran amine. Brain Res 1994; 637: 317–322.

26. Gonzales C, Chesselet MF. Amygd-alonigral pathway: An anterograde study in the rat with *Phaseolus vulgaris*-leucoagglutinin(PHA-L), J Comp Neurol 1990; 297: 182–200.

27. Chergui K, Charlety PJ, Akaoka H, Saunier CF, Brunet JL, Buda M, Svensson TH, Chouvet G. Tonic activation of NMDA receptors causes spontaneous burst discharge of rat midbrain dopamine neurons *in vivo*. Eur J Neurosci 1993; 5: 137–144.

28. Tong ZY, Overton PG, Clark D. Antagonism of NMDA receptors but not AMPA/kainate receptors blocks bursting in dopaminergic neurons induced by electrical stimulation of the prefrontal cortex. J Neural Transm 1996; 103: 889–904.

29. Di Loreto S, Florio T, Scarnati E. Evidence that non-NMDA receptors are involved in the excitatory pathway from the pedunculopontine region to nigro-striatal dopaminergic neurons. Exp Brain Res 1992; 89: 79–86.

30. Smith Y, Hazrati LN, Parent A. Efferent projections of the subthalamic nucleus in the squirrel monkey as studied by the PHA-L anterograde tracing method. J Comp Neurol 1990; 294: 306–323.

31. Carpenter MB, Carleton SC, Keller JT, Conte P. Connections of the subthalamic nucleus in the monkey. Brain Res 1981; 224: 1–29.

32. Parent A, Smith Y. Organization of efferent projections of the subthalamic nucleus in the squirrel monkey as revealed by retrograde labeling methods. Brain Res 1987; 436: 296–310.

33. Parent A, Hazrati LN. Functional anatomy of the basal ganglia.II. The place of subthalamic nucleus and exter-nal pallidum in basal ganglia circuitry. Brain Res Rev1995; 20: 128–154.

34. Afsharpour S. Topographical projections of the cerebral cortex to the subthalamic nucleus. J Comp Neurol 1985; 236: 14–28.

35. Wichmann T, Bergman H, DeLong MR. The primate subthalamic nucleus.I. Functional properties in intact animals. J Neurophysiol 1994; 72: 494–506.

36. Rodriguez MC, Gorospe A, Mozo A, Guridi J, Ramos E, Linazasoro G, Obeso JA. Characteristics of neuronal activity in the subthalamic nucleus and substantia nigra pars reticulata in Parkinson's disease. Soc Neurosci Abs 1997; 23: 471.

37. Hornykiewicz O. Dopamine (3-hydrox-ytyramine) and brain function. Pharmacol Rev 1966; 18: 925–964.

38. Brown LL, Makman MH, Wolfson LI, Dvorkin B, Warner C, Katzman R. A

direct role of dopamine in the rat subthalamic nucleus and an adjacent intrapeduncular area. Science 1979; 206: 1416–1418.

39. Hassani OK, François CH, Yelnik J, Féger J. Evidence for a dopaminergic innervation of the subthalamic nucleus in the rat. Brain Res 1997; 749: 88–94.

40. Aller KA, Juncos JL, Rye DB. Anatomical investigation of the dopaminergic innervation of the rat subthalamic nucleus. Soc Neurosci Abst 1997; 23: 197.

41. Rinvik E, Grofova I, Hammond C, FégerJ, Deniau JM. A study of the afferent connections of the subthalamic nucleus in the monkey and cat, using the HRP technique. Adv Neurol 1979; 24: 53–70.

42. Martres MP, Bouthenet ML, Sales N, Sokoloff P, Schwartz JC. Widespread distribution of brain dopamine receptors evidenced with [(125)I]iodosulpride, a highly selective ligand. Science 1985; 228: 752–755.

43. Yokoyama C, Okamura H, Nakajima T, Taguchi JI, Ibata Y. Autoradiographic distribution of 3HYM901512, a high-affinity and selective antagonist ligand for the dopamine D_2 receptor group, in the rat brain and spinal cord. J Comp Neurol 1994; 344: 121–136.

44. Dawson TM, Barone P, Sidhu A, Wamsley JK, Chase TN. The D_1 dopamine receptor in the rat brain: quantitative autoradiographic localization using an iodinated ligand. Neurosci 1988; 26: 83–100.

45. Mansour A, Meador-Woodruff JH, Zhou Z, Civelli O, Akil H, Watson SJ. A comparison of D_1 receptor binding and mRNA in rat brain using receptor autoradiographic and in situ hybridization techniques. Neurosci 1992; 46: 959–971.

46. Parry TJ, Eberle-Wang K, Lucki I, Chesselet M. Dopaminergic stimulation of subthalamic nucleus elicits oral dyskinesia in rats. Exp Neurol 1994; 128: 181–190.

47. Kreiss DS, Anderson LA, Walters JR. Apomorphine and dopamine D_1 receptor agonists increase the firing rates of subthalamic nucleus neurons. Neurosci 1996; 72: 863–876.

48. Allers KA. Dopamine innervation of the subthalamic nucleus. Doctoral thesis. Emory University Medical School, Atlanta, Georgia.

49. Fetz EE. Temporal coding in neural populations? Science 1997; 278: 1901–1902.

50. Hammond C, Deniau JM, Rizk A, Féger J. Electrophysiological demonstration of an excitatory subthalamonigral pathway in the rat. Brain Res 1978; 151: 235–244.

51. Mintz I, Hammond C, Guibert B, Leviel V. Stimulation of the subthalamic nucleus enhances the release of dopamine in the rat sub-stantia nigra. Brain Res 1986; 376: 406–408.

52. Smith ID, Grace AA. Role of the subthalamic nucleus in the regulation of nigral dopamine neuron activity. Synapse 1992; 12: 287–303.

53. Charlety PJ, Grenhoff J, Chergui K, de la Chapelle B, Buda M, Svensson TH, Chouvet G. Burst firing of mesen-cephalic dopamine neurons is inhibited by somatodendritic application of kynurenate. Acta Physiol Scand 1991; 142: 105–112.

54. Overton P, Clark D. Iontophoretically administered drugs acting at the N-methyl-D-aspartate receptor modulate burst firing in A9 dopamine neurons in the rat. Synapse 1992, 10:131–140.

55. Chergui K, Akaoka H, Charléty PJ, Saunier CF, Buda M, Chouvet G. Subthalamic nucleus modulates burst firing of nigral dopamine neurones via NMDA receptors. Neurophysiology, Basic and Clinical. Neuroreport 1994; 5: 1185–1188.

56. Schultz W, Romo R. Dopamine neurons of the monkey mindbrain: contingencies of response to stimuli eliciting

immediate behavioral reactions. J Neurophysiol 1990; 63: 607–624.

57. Tong ZY, Overton PG, Clark D. Stimulation of the prefrontal cortex on the rat induces patterns of activity in midbrain dopaminergic neurons which resemble natural burst events. Synapse 1996; 22: 195–208.

58. Gariano RF, Groves PM. Burst firing induced in midbrain dopamine neurons by stimulation of the medial prefrontal and anterior cingulate cortex. Brain Res 1988; 462: 194–198.

59. Kitai ST, Deniau JM. Cortical inputs to the subthalamus: intracellular analysis. Brain Res 1981; 214: 411–415.

60. Albin RL, Aldridge JW, Young AB, Gilman S. Feline subthalamic nucleus neurons contain glutamate-like but not GABA-like or glycine-like immunoreactivity. Brain Res 1989; 491: 185–188.

61. Rouzaire-Dubois B, Scarnati E. Pharmacological study of the cortical-induced excitation of subthalamic nucleus neurons in the rat: evidence for aminoacids as putative neurotransmitters. Neurosci 1987; 21: 429–440.

62. Tong ZY, Overton PG, Clark D. Antagonism of NMDA receptors but not AMPA/kainate receptors blocks bursting in dopaminergic neurons induced by electrical stimulation of the prefrontal cortex. J Neural Transm 1996; 103: 889–904

63. Scarnati E, Florio T. The pedunculopontine nucleus and related structures: functional organization. Adv Neurol 1997; 74: 97–110.

64. Bevan MD, Bolam JP. Cholinergic, GABAergic, and glutamate-enriched inputs from the mesopontine tegmentum to the subthalamic nucleus in the rat. J Neurosci 1995; 15: 7105–7120.

65. Brown LL, Wolfson LI. Apomorphine increases glucose utilization on the substantia nigra, subthalamic nucleus and corpus striatum. Brain Res 1978; 140: 188–193.

66. Kreiss DS, Walters JR. Dopamine D_2 receptor tone plays a critical role in dopamine D_1 receptor mediated excitatory effects on subthalamic nucleus neurons. Soc Neurosci Abs 1997; 23: 746.

67. Mitchell IJ, Clarke CE, Boyce S, Robertson RG, Peggs D, Sambrook MA, Crossman AR. Neural mechanisms underlying parkinsonian symptoms based upon regional uptake of 2-deoxyglucose in monkeys exposed to 1-methyl-4-phenyl-1,2,3,6-tetrahydropyridine. Neurosci 1989; 32: 213–226.

68. Obeso JA, Rodriguez MC, DeLong MR. Basal ganglia pathophysiology: A critical review. Adv Neurol 1997; 74: 3-18.

69. Filion M, Tremblay L. Abnormal spontaneous activity of globus pallidus neurons in monkeys with MPTP–induced parkinsonism. Brain Res 1991; 547: 142–151.

70. Miller WL, DeLong MR. Altered tonic activity of neurons in the globus pallidus and subthalamic nucleus in the primate MPTP model of parkinsonism. In, Carpenter MB, Jayaraman A, eds, The Basal Ganglia II. New York: Plenum Press 1987: 415–427.

71. Wichmann T, Bergman H, DeLong MR. The primate subthalamic nucleus.III. Changes in motor behaviour and neuronal activity in the internal pallidum induced by subthalamic inactivation in the MPTP model of parkinsonism. J Neurophysiol 1994; 71:521–526.

72. Brotchie JM, Mitchell IJ, Sambrook MA, Crossman AR. Alleviation of parkinsonism by antagonist of excitatory aminoacid transmission in the medial segment of the globus pallidus in rat and primate. Mov Disord 1991; 6: 133–138.

73. Bergman H, Wichmann T, DeLong MR. Reversal of experimental parkinsonism by lesions of the

subthalamic nucleus. Science 1990; 249: 1436–1438.

74. Aziz TZ, Peggs D, Sambrook MA, Crossman AR, Lesion of the subthalamic nucleus for the alleviation of 1- methyl-4-phenyl-1,2,3,6-tetrahydro-pyridine (MPTP) induced parkinsonism in the primate. Mov Disord 1991; 6: 288–292.

75. Hirsch EC, Brandel JP, Galle P, Javoy-Agid F, Agid Y. Iron and aluminium increase in the substantia nigra of patients with Parkinson's disease. An X-ray microanalysis. J Neurochem 1991; 56: 446–451.

76. Turski L, Bressler K, Rettig KJ, Löschmann PA, Wachtel H. Protection of substantia nigra from MPP+ neurotoxicity by N-methyl-D-aspartate antagonists. Nature 1991; 349: 414–418.

77. Limousine P, Greene J, Pollak P, Rothwell J, Benabid AL, Frackowiak R. Changes in cerebral activity pattern due to subthalamic nucleus or internal pallidum stimulation in Parkinson's disease. Ann Neurol 1997; 42: 283–291.

78. Gerfen CR, Engber TR, Mahan LC, Susel Z, Chase TN, Monsma FR, Sibley DR. D1 and D2 dopamine receptor-regulated gene expession of striatonigral and striatopallidal neurons. Science 1990; 250: 1429–1432.

79. Blandini F, Porter RHP, Greenamyre JT. Glutamate and Parkinson's disease. Mol Neurobiol 1996; 12: 73–94.

80. Lucas DR, Newhouse JP. The toxic effect of sodium L-glutamate on the inner layers of the retina. Arch Ophthalmol 1957; 58: 193–201.

81. White RJ, Reynolds IJ. Mitochondrial depolarization in glutamate-stimulated neurons: an early signal to excitotoxin exposure. J Neurosci 1996; 16: 5688–5697.

82. Marchetti P, Castedo M, Susin SA, Zamzami N, Hirsch T, Macho A, Haeffner A, Hirsch F, Geuskens M, Kroemer G. Mitochondrial permeability transition is a central coordinating event of apoptosis. J Exp Med 1996; 184: 1155–1160.

83. Schinder AF, Olson EC, Spitzer NC, Montal M. Mitochondrial dysfunction is a primary event in glutamate neuro-toxicity. J Neurosci 1996; 16: 6125–6133.

84. Wadia JS, Chalmers-Redman ME, Ju WJH, Carlile GW, Phillips JL, Fraser AD, Tatton WG. Mitochondrial membrane potential and nuclear changes in apoptosis caused by serum and nerve growth factor withdrawal: time course and modification by (-)-deprenyl. J Neurosci 1998; 18: 932–947.

85. Mattson MP, Zhang Y, Bose S. Growth factors prevent mitochondria dysfunction, loss of Ca++ homeostasis, and cell injury, but not ATP depletion in hippocampal neurons deprived of glucose. Exp Neurol 1993; 121: 1–13.

86. Lipton SA, Choi YB, Pan ZH, Lei SZ, Chen HS, Sucher NJ, Loscalzo J, Singel DJ, Stamler JS. A redox-based mechanism for the neuroprotective and neurodestructive effects of nitric oxide and related nitroso-compounds. Nature 1993; 364: 626–632.

87. Dawson VL, Kizushi VM, Huang PL, Snyder SH, Dawson TM. Resistance to neurotoxicity in cortical cultures from neuronal nitric oxide synthase-deficient mice. J Neurosci 1996; 16: 2479–2487.

88. Ayata C, Ayata G, Hara H, Matthews RT, Beal MF, Ferrante RJ, Endres M, Kim A, Christie RH, Huang PL, Hyman BT, Moskowitz MA. Mechanisms of reduced striatal NMDA excitotoxicity in type I nitric oxide synthase knock-out mice. J Neurosci 1997; 17: 6908–6917.

89. Stuehr DJ, Nathan CF. A macrophage product responsible for cytostasis and respiratory inhibition in tumor target cells. J Exp Med 1989; 169: 1543–1555.

90. Nakao N, Frodl EV, Widner H, Carlson E, Eggerding FA, Epstein CJ, Brundin P. Overexpressing Cu/Zn superoxide

dismutase enhances survival of transplanted neurons in a rat model of Parkinson's disease. Nature 1995; 1: 226–231.

91. Dawson VL, Dawson TM, Snyder SH. A novel neuronal messenger molecule in brains:The free radical, nitric oxide. Ann Neurol 1992; 32:297–311.

92. Zhang J, Dawson VL, Dawson TM, Snyder SH. Nitric oxide activation of poly(ADP-ribose) synthetase in neurotoxicity. Science 1994; 263: 687–689.

93. Heikkila RE, Nicklas WJ, Vyas I, Duvoisin RC. Dopaminergic toxicity of rotenone and the 1-methyl-4-phenylpyridinium ion after their stereotaxic administration to rats: implication for the mechanism of 1-methyl-4-phenyl-1,2,3,6-tetrahydropyridine toxicity. Neurosci Lett 1985; 62: 389–394.

94. Nowak L, Bregestovski P, Ascher P, Herbet A, Prochiantz A. Magnesium gates glutamate-activated channels in mouse central neurons. Nature 1984; 307: 462–465.

95. Zuddas A, Oberto G, Vaglini F, Fascetti F, Fornai F, Corsini G. M-801 prevents MPTP-induced parkinsonism in primates. J Neurochem 1992; 59: 133–739.

96. Przedborski S. Role of nitric oxid in MPTP-induced dopaminergic neurotoxicity. Proc Natl Acad Sci USA 1996; 93: 4565–4571.

97. Shultz JB, Matthews JB, Muqit MMK, Browne SE, Beal MF. Inhibition of neuronal nitric oxide synthase by 7-nitroindazole protects against MPTP-induced neurotoxicity in mice. J Neurochem 1995; 64: 936–939.

98. Olanow CW, Tatton WG. Etiology and pathogenesis of Parkinson's disease. Ann Rev Neurosci, in press.

99. Mytilineou C, Radcliffe P, Leonardi EK, Werner P, Olanow CW. L-deprenyl protects mesencephalic dopamine neurons from glutamate receptor-mediated toxicity. J Neurochem 1997; 68: 33–39.

100. Tatton WG, Chalmers-Redman RME. Modulation of gene expression rather than monoamine oxidate inhibition: (-)-deprenyl-related compounds in controlling neurodegeneration. Neurol 1996; 47: S171–S183.

101. Parkinson Study Group. Effects of tocopherol and deprenyl on the progression of disability in early Parkinson's disease. N Engl J Med 1993; 328: 176–183.

102. Good PF, Hsu A, Werner P, et al. Protein nitration in Parkinson's disease. J Neuropath Exp Neurol, in press.

103. Piallat B, Benazzouz A, Benabid AL. Subthalamic nucleus lesion on rats prevents doopaminergic nigral neuron degeneration after striatal 6-OHDA injection: behavioural and immunohistochemical studies. Eur J Neurosci 1996; 8: 1408–1414.

104. Marey-Semper I, Gelman M, Lévi-Strauss M. A selective toxicity toward cultured mesencephalic dopaminergic neurons is induced by the synergistic effects of energetic metabolism impairment and NMDA receptor activation. J Neurosci 1995; 15: 5912–5918.

105. Obeso JA, Grandas F, VaamondeJ, Luquin MR, Artieda J, Lera G, Rodriguez ME, Martinez-Lage JM. Motor complications associated with chronic levodopa therapy in Parkinson's disease. Neurology 1993; 43(Suppl 2):1459–1464.

106. Obeso JA, GrandasF, Herrero MT, Horowsdi R. The role of pulsatile versus continuous dopamine receptor stimulation for functional recovery in Parkinson's disease. Eur J Neurosci 1994; 6: 889–897.

107. Obeso JA, Linazasoro G, Gorospe A, Rodriguez MC, Lera G. Complications associated with chronic levodopa therapy in Parkinson's disease. In, Olanow CW, Obeso JA, eds, Dopamine agonists in early Parkinson's disease. Royal Tunbridge Wells: Wells Medical 1997: 11–36.

DISCUSSION

W. Tatton: Why is it not accepted that high frequency stimulation of the subthalamic nucleus (STN) at a rate of 180 cycles/second induces its functional effects by producing a depolarization block? Is there any evidence against it?

Obeso: To put it the other way around, there is limited evidence that it does produce a depolarization block. On the other hand, there is a proportion of neurons that fire spontaneously at that frequency or at even higher frequencies in the parkinsonian brain, so there is no reason why a proportion of those neurons could not be driven rather than jammed at that frequency. It is also hard to understand how chronic depolarization blockade can be maintained for months or years.

Olanow: There are other hypotheses. Some data are consistent with the idea that DBS acts through preferential stimulation of inhibitory interneurons. DeLong believes that high frequency stimulation of the STN may produce its clinical effects by back-firing with stimulation of inhibitory neurons in the globus pallidus pars externa (GPe) and consequent inhibition of the globus pallidus pars interna (GPi). It is not clear which, if any, of these mechanisms is responsible for the clinical effects observed.

Caraceni: If you record the activity in parkinsonian patients who are subjected to high frequency stimulation you can register whether or not there is depolarization block. At the end of the stimulation you can register from the globus pallidus pars interna (GPi) or perhaps also from the globus pallidus pars externa (GPe). What has been seen is a complete lack of activity. Is this not consistent with depolarization blockade?

Obeso: I have not seen these data from PD patients. There are experimental data in the rat and they do indeed show a reduction in neuronal activity, but the stimulation was only for five seconds. My point is that we have yet to prove that the same mechanism is operational chronically over days and weeks and that this is responsible for the clinical effect. Further, you can not record at precisely the same time that you are stimulating because of the stimulation artefact. While there is suppression of activity after the stimulation is stopped when recording can take place, one cannot be completely certain that there was suppression of firing during the actual stimulation itself.

Olanow: In PD, there is disinhibition of the STN with a resultant increase in neuronal firing. As STN neurons are excitatory and use glutamate as a transmitter, there is concern about their potential to induce excitotoxic damage in target regions. These include the substantia nigra pars compacta, the substantia nigra pars reticularis, and the PPN in the brain stem as well as the GPi. Benabid and his group in Grenoble have shown that lesions of the STN protect dopamine neurons in the SNc from MPTP toxicity. Based on these observations we have hypothesized that it may be reasonable to introduce dopaminergic replacement therapy immediately upon diagnosis in order to try and restore dopamine tone and inhibit STN firing so as to protect SNc neurons. Do you agree with this concept or do you think it is too theoretical?

Obeso: I agree completely and do not think it is too theoretical at all. In my mind this is a pivotal point. Once there is dopamine deficiency, it may trigger increased neuronal firing in the STN and lead to further dopamine neuronal loss in the SNc.

Olanow: It is interesting how things go in cycles. In the early days, patients were treated with levodopa as soon as the diagnosis was made. Perhaps the doses used were too high and patients experienced severe motor complications. Now, the philosophy has changed and many physicians delay the introduction of dopaminergic treatment for as long as possible, or at least until the patient has functional disability. Based on the information presented, and recent information indicating that dopamine agonists have less potential to induce motor complications than levodopa, we probably should be looking more seriously at introducing dopaminergic treatment from the onset of the illness. This question has the potential to be answered by a clinical trial, but obviously it would be long-term and expensive.

Obeso: It is an interesting idea and I think it is one worth pursuing. However, we do not know the consequences of using dopaminergic drugs in this fashion and one might anticipate considerable non-physiological dopaminergic restoration, for instance, by giving such patients standard levodopa three times a day. If we were to do such studies, I would favor using dopamine agonists because you are not looking for symptomatic effects, and these agents are associated with a much reduced propensity to induce dyskinesia compared to levodopa.

Beal: The evidence that an STN lesion can block 6-hydroxydopamine toxicity is interesting. Could one replicate that with inhibitors of either the NMDA or non-NMDA glutamate receptors? I am not aware that anyone has been able to block toxicity in the *in vivo* situation.

Obeso: That is quite a plausible approach, which leads to a number of experiments, some of which in fact we have just started in monkeys. We want to determine if increased sensitivity of neurons in the nigra can be achieved by manipulating mitochondrial function. We would then increase activity from the STN by reducing inhibition from the GPe to determine if this sensitizes for the induction of parkinsonism.

Future Directions

The causes of Parkinson's disease are being unravelled and rational neuroprotective therapy is close to reality

C. DAVID MARSDEN[1] AND C. WARREN OLANOW[2]
[1]Institute of Neurology, The National Hospital for Neurology and Neurosurgery, London, UK, [2]Department of Neurology, Mount Sinai School of Medicine, New York, New York, USA

The application of molecular genetics and neurobiology to the study of Parkinson's disease (PD) has resulted in significant progress in our knowledge of the cause, pathogenesis, and nature of the cell death process in this disorder.[1] The chapters in this volume summarize relevant background information and the important changes that have taken place in each of these areas in recent years. Together, they offer a wide range of opportunities for designing rational strategies aimed at providing neuroprotection in PD.

The clinical syndrome of parkinsonism consists of bradykinesia (including akinesia, hypokinesia and pseudo-fatigue), muscular rigidity, usually a characteristic tremor, postural abnormalities and freezing phenomena.[2] PD is the commonest cause of parkinsonism and can be diagnosed reasonably confidently when there is classical tremor, a unilateral onset, and a considerable response to levodopa replacement therapy, provided there is no early dementia or falls, abnormality of eye movements, or signs of cerebellar, pyramidal, peripheral nerve or autonomic involvement. The characteristic pathological picture is one of preferential degeneration of the substantia nigra pars compacta, with loss of melanized pigmented dopaminergic neurons, and the presence of residual neurons containing Lewy body inclusions. Hereto, the picture is somewhat obscured by the overlap that exists between PD, Alzheimer's disease, and dementia with Lewy bodies (DLB).[3]

A single gene defect can produce PD in some families, but this does not account for the vast majority of cases of apparently familial PD nor for the even greater number of patients with apparently sporadic PD. Whatever the causes of PD, all eventually lead to degeneration of the substantia nigra pars compacta (SNc) through what appears to be a common pathogenesis and mechanism of cell death. This process may involve a cascade of events that includes oxidative stress, abnormalities of mitochondrial function, excitotoxicity, inflammatory factors and glia. Death of SNc dopaminergic neurons probably occurs through the process of apoptosis. Strategies for neuroprotective therapies that can intervene at any stage in this sequence of events leading to PD can now be contemplated. We are not yet at the point where we can consider primary prevention designed to reduce the incidence of the disease in the general population. We may be closer to being able to offer secondary prevention by interfering with pathogenesis. It may be conceivable to test putative protective treatments on those with a high risk of developing PD and may be at a 'pre-clinical' stage.

ETIOLOGY OF PD

Hereditary PD

Cross-sectional surveys have shown an increased instance of a positive family history in patients with PD.[4] Most studies indicate a two to three-fold increase in the risk of developing PD in first degree relatives. However, the majority of cases of PD still appear to be sporadic. There are a small number of families in which PD is inherited as an autosomal dominant trait. Recently a single gene defect was identified in one such large kindred, the Contursi pedigree.[5] Linkage to chromosome 4q21–q23 was quickly followed by the identification of a mutation in the α-synuclein gene in this family. The Contursi family has clinical features of PD with Lewy body pathology and a good response to levodopa. Affected individuals in this family differ from the bulk of PD patients only in a younger age of onset and a somewhat more aggressive course. The same mutation in the α-synuclein gene has been found in five unrelated Greek families and it is possible that this mutation is due to a common founder effect. A second α-synuclein mutation has been discovered in a German family, thereby increasing the likelihood that the gene mutation is directly related to the development of PD in these families.[6]

α-Synuclein is normally expressed abundantly in all regions of the brain including the substantia nigra. Interestingly, the human α-synuclein protein was first isolated from plaques in AD.[4] It is found abundantly in Lewy bodies and neurites from both hereditary and sporadic cases, where its expression overlaps with that of ubiquitin. α-Synuclein is normally a soluble unfolded protein, but it can aggregate to form insoluble amyloid fibrils, particularly in its mutated form.[7] Thus, PD joins several other neurodegenerative conditions in a common theme in which neuronal death is associated with insoluble protein aggregates. It is unclear why PD should develop in humans with a mutation in the α-synuclein gene when the homologue of the mutant α-synuclein is a normal constituent of several birds and fish. Further, in the canary the homologue of the mutant α-synuclein, synelfin, has been implicated in a physiologic function, namely song learning.

The α-synuclein mutation is now known not to be responsible for most cases of familial PD, nor for sporadic cases. Studies both in Europe and the United States have shown no mutation in the α-synuclein gene in familial cases or in hundreds of sporadic examples of PD.

Another genetic cause or risk factor for autosomal dominant inherited PD has been linked to chromosome 2. Linkage to chromosome 17 has also been established in pallido-ponto-nigral degeneration. Linkage to chromosome 6 has been established in an autosomal recessive form of juvenile parkinsonism in Japan which clinically resembles PD and is associated with nigral degeneration, but without Lewy bodies. There remain other families with a clinical syndrome of PD in which genetic linkage has yet to be assigned. Finally, there is the intriguing possible role of mitochondrial inheritance in PD. For the present, gene discovery has not provided an opportunity to institute a neuroprotective therapy, but the information obtained may hopefully be used to develop better models of PD. Thus, even if an individual gene mutation only rarely causes clinical PD, it may provide an insight into the manner by which cell death occurs in the disorder.

Sporadic PD

The failure to find mutations in the α-synuclein gene in sporadic cases of PD, or any other genetic abnormalities, does not mean that none exist. There has been a belief that a number of genetic susceptibility traits may pre-dispose individuals to develop PD if combined with other susceptibility genes or exposure to environmental toxins.[8,9] For instance, inheritance of the CYP2D6 allele of the P450 complex seems to confer an odds ratio of between two and five for the development of PD. Recently it has been suggested that inheritance of a mutant allele of CYP2D6 (which is involved in the first activation step of xenobiotic detoxification) combined with a mutant allele of a second phase enzyme GSTM1 may increase that odds ratio to 10 to 14. Even more recently, the association of a mutant allele of the enzyme N-acetyl transferase 2 with the development of PD suggests that a defect in acetylation of certain toxins may result in nigral degeneration.

The likely role of an environmental factor in sporadic PD has been highlighted by the USA Veteran Twin Study.[9] In 1992, 193 cases of PD were identified among the 20,000 survivors of this twin study, and their mean age was 64 years. An increased incidence of PD in monozygotic twins would be expected if PD were solely due to a genetic cause. In this study, the ratio of PD in monozygotic *versus* dizygotic twins of the PD patients was 1.39 and did not reach statistical significance. In those with onset of PD over the age of 50 years the ratio was 1.02, implying that genetic factors are not a primary factor in the average patient with sporadic PD. Conversely in PD with onset under the age of 50 years, the ratio was 6.00 in favor of the monozygotic twin. This implies that genetic factors are more likely to be involved in young-onset cases of PD where environmental factors, with or without genetic susceptibility, are more likely to be an important factor in sporadic PD in those with disease onset over the age of 50 years.

The MPTP story has shown that environmental toxins can induce a clinical and pathological picture strikingly similar to PD.[9] However, no such toxin has yet been identified. Epidemiological studies searching for environmental factors have yielded tantalizing clues, but none have given entirely robust or reproducible findings. Nevertheless, rural living, farming, herbicide use, exposure to pesticides, and well-water consumption may all increase the risk of developing PD. Indeed, there have been a few reports of increased concentrations of pesticide/herbicide compounds in the brains of patients with PD, but these are neither consistent nor common. It is also intriguing to consider that some endogenous toxins are formed via dopamine metabolism and other endogenous metabolic routes.

Current information suggests that most cases of PD are likely to result from a combination of both genetic and environmental factors (the so-called 'double hit' hypothesis), and that these might differ among individuals. In support of this concept, nigral degeneration with parkinsonism has been reported in the SOD mutant mouse following small doses of MPTP where neither the toxin nor the genetic defect acting alone is sufficient to induce these findings. Similarly, GSH depletion does not by itself induce neurodegeneration but enhances the dopaminergic toxicity associated with MPTP or 6-OHDA.[1]

Insight into risk factors for the development of PD is likely to identify at-risk patients for clinical trials of neuroprotective therapies and an opportunity to remove environmental risk factors or facilitate metabolic pathways, thereby preventing the development or progression of the disorder.

THE PATHOGENESIS OF NIGRAL DEGENERATION

Whether PD is initiated by a genetic aberration, an environmental toxin, or a combination of both, there follows a sequence of events culminating in the destruction of pigmented brainstem catecholaminergic neurons, particularly the dopaminergic neurons of the SNc. Several interacting themes appear to form a cascade of events culminating in nigral cell death, including oxidant stress,[1] mitochondrial dysfunction,[10,11] excitotoxicity with excess nitric oxide formation,[12] and glia and inflammatory processes.[13] It is now believed that these events culminate in the induction of apoptosis in nigral dopaminergic neurons.[14]

The role of oxidative stress in nigral neuronal degeneration

The SNc is particularly vulnerable to oxidative stress. Dopamine metabolism by monoamine oxidase or through auto-oxidation leads to the formation of hydrogen peroxide which can react with iron to form the cytotoxic hydroxyl radical. In addition, dopamine auto-oxidation can lead to the formation of superoxide radical, and reactive quinones and semiquinones. Neuromelanin in dopaminergic neurons binds ferric iron and has the potential to reduce it to its reactive ferrous form. Thus, the SNc, because of its dopamine, neuromelanin, and iron content, appears to be prone to develop oxidative stress.

Studies in the SOD mutant model of amyotrophic lateral sclerosis indicate that the presence of neurofilament and the absence of calbindin confer vulnerability on nerve cells that participate in the neurodegenerative process.[15] This selective neuronal vulnerability in the SNc in PD is evident from several lines of evidence.[13] The meso-striatal dopamine pathway is more affected than the mesolimbic pathway which originates from the ventral tegmental region. The loss of dopaminergic neurons is greatest in the SNc (76%) in comparison to the ventral tegmental area (55%), the peri- and retro-rubral region (31%), and the central grey matter (3%). Even within the SNc there is selective vulnerability with the ventral tier, particularly the lateral region, being more affected than the dorsal tier. Dopamine cell loss appears greatest in those cells of the SNc with the least amount of calbindin suggesting that absence of this protective mechanism may confer additional vulnerability on dopamine neurons as has been found in the SOD mutant mouse model of neurodegeneration.[15]

There is abundant evidence for oxidative stress in nigral degeneration in PD.[1] In studies of the substantia nigra from post-mortem PD brains there is evidence of increased malondialdehyde and hydroperoxides suggesting lipid peroxidation, increased carbonyl proteins suggesting oxidized proteins, increased 8-hydroxy-2-deoxyguanosine suggesting DNA degradation, increased iron without a corresponding increase in ferritin, diminished reduced glutathione with no change in oxidized glutathione, and increased γ-glutamyl transpeptidase activity. The findings of excess iron, decreased GSH, and widespread oxidative damage in the substantia nigra of PD patients suggests that the nigra is in a state of oxidant stress and that oxidative damage has occurred. Oxidative stress can directly damage critical biomolecules and can signal for the initiation of apoptosis.[16]

The possibility that oxidant stress contributes to cell death in PD offers many therapeutic opportunities for neuroprotection. These include free radical scavengers, glutathione enhancing agents, iron chelators, and drugs that interfere with the oxidative metabolism of dopamine. Clinical trials to date have largely focused on vitamin E and deprenyl.[17] Vitamin E in oral doses of 2000 IU was found to have no effect. Deprenyl slowed the emergence of disability and the progression of signs and symptoms but the drug's symptomatic effects confounded interpretation of the results. Further clinical trials are warranted to test other anti-oxidant agents. Levodopa undergoes oxidative metabolism and has been shown to induce apoptosis in cultured dopamine neurons.[18] Studies are accordingly being performed to determine if levodopa accelerates the rate of disease progression. Alternatively, there is evidence indicating that dopamine agonists, which do not undergo oxidative metabolism, may be neuroprotective,[19] and studies to assess their effects on the natural history of PD are underway.

The role of mitochondrial dysfunction in nigral neuronal degeneration

A robust finding has been the reduction in the activity of complex I of the mitochondrial respiratory chain in PD.[10] Complex I deficiency is not found elsewhere in the brain in PD, nor in other disorders that affect the SNc such as multiple system atrophy so it cannot be simply due to nigral degeneration. A number of different abnormalities in the mitochondrial genome in the parkinsonian brain have been described, but these are difficult to interpret because similar changes are found with aging.[11]

At first, it seemed unlikely that mitochondrial inheritance plays a role in PD. Most cases are sporadic, but so too are most cases of classical mitochondrial encephalomyopathies. Overall, there has been no suggestion of a maternal inheritance pattern in PD as would be expected with an inherited mitochondrial defect, although occasional such families have been reported, but this again is often the case in the mitochondrial encephalomyopathies.

The role of possible mitochondrial inheritance of susceptibility to PD has been highlighted by recent discoveries related to platelet mitochondrial function in the illness. The activity of complex I in platelets from patients with PD is reduced, indicating that the mitochondrial defect found in PD is generalized and is not confined to the brain. The platelet mitochondrial abnormality might be due to the impact of an endogenous or exogenous toxin or to a mitochondrial gene defect. Recently, cybrid technology has been employed to explore this issue.[10] Cybrid cell lines in which mitochondrial DNA has been destroyed can be re-populated with mitochondrial DNA from the platelets of patients with PD. It has been discovered, and independently replicated, that cybrids re-populated with mitochondria from PD platelets exhibit the same defect of complex I activity as was found in the original platelets. Furthermore, such cybrids show increased susceptibility to MPP+ toxicity, dying by way of apoptosis. This defect of mitochondrial complex I is transferred in subsequent divisions of cybrid cell lines, indicating that it must be due to transmission of abnormal mitochondrial DNA. The cause of the defect remains unknown, but could be due to an inherited defect in mitochondrial DNA or a mutation in the mitochondrial genome induced by a toxin. In either case, it would appear that some patients with PD may have a mitochondrial DNA defect which renders them susceptible to other exogenous or endogenous toxins.

Another biochemical abnormality found in the substantia nigra in PD is a reduction in α-ketoglutarate dehydrogenase.[11] A reduction in both complex I and α-ketoglutarate dehydrogenase could combine to increase the risk of neurodegeneration due to compromised mitochondrial energy metabolism and weak excitotoxicity.[12] This theory suggests that impaired mitochondrial ATP production results in a loss of the voltage dependent magnesium blockade of NMDA receptors and enhances their susceptibility to excitotoxicity. Here, physiologic concentrations of glutamate could stimulate the NMDA receptors and induce an influx of calcium into neurons and mitochondria. This could result in additional mitochondrial damage and increased free radical production. Further, a rise in free cytosolic calcium activates nitric oxide synthase (NOS) that generates nitric oxide (NO) and calpains that promote the formation of superoxide radical. The interaction of NO with the superoxide radical generates the highly oxidizing substance peroxynitrite which can oxidize proteins, lipids and DNA and is marked by the accumulation of nitrotyrosines due to its propensity to nitrate tyrosine residues on proteins.

Evidence that such a sequence involving NO may play a role in PD is illustrated by the finding that transgenic mice with knock-out of NOS are resistant to striatal injections of MPP+.[12] Such knock-out mice are also resistant to NMDA excitotoxicity. Furthermore, there is evidence that NOS inhibitors block both glutamate excitotoxicity and MPTP neurotoxicity. Finally, there is a marked increase in nitrotyrosine staining in the PD nigra[1] which interestingly is primarily localized to Lewy bodies.

There is also increasing evidence that mitochondria play an important role in the initiation of apoptosis and that apoptosis could be induced by a defect in mitochondrial function.[16]

These findings suggest that bioenergetic agents such as co-enzyme Q10 or creatinine, drugs that prevent NO formation such as NOS inhibitors, and agents that block calcium entry into the cell or mitochondria might be neuroprotective. It is also noteworthy that dopamine depletion induces disinhibition of the subthalamic nucleus (STN) with a resultant increase in its glutamatergic output.[20] This in turn could result in excitotoxic damage to areas innervated by the STN, such as the globus pallidus pars interna, the substantia nigra pars reticularis, the pedunculopontine nucleus in the brainstem, and the SNc itself. It also suggests that agents or surgical procedures that inhibit STN output might be neuroprotective.

The role of inflammation in nigral neuronal degeneration

A consistent pathological finding in the SNc of patients with PD is astrocytosis, which includes activated microglia expressing HLA-DR antigens. Activated microglia (the macrophages of the central nervous system) can produce cytokines and NO, leading to oxidant stress and apoptosis.

A possible role of inflammation in the pathogenesis of PD has been highlighted by the discovery that the SNc contains markedly increased levels of interleukin 1β, interferon γ, and tumor necrosis factor-α (TNF-α).[13] In addition, TNF-α has been shown to induce transient free radical formation, nuclear translocation of NFκB, and apoptosis in cultured dopamine neurons. While it is impossible to replicate these experiments in human patients, it is noteworthy that the increase in TNF-α in the PD nigra is associated with a 70-fold increase in nuclear NFκB, suggesting that a similar mechanism may be applicable to the cell death that occurs in PD.

Glial involvement in the origin of PD is also suggested by a number of other observations. The extent of the depletion of reduced glutathione and complex I activity (around 30-40%) in substantia nigra homogenates from patients with PD cannot be explained solely by dopamine cell loss in PD, since dopaminergic neurons probably account for only about 2% of tissue in such samples.[1] Additionally, the most affected area of dopaminergic cell loss, the SNc, contains the lowest density of glial cells in controls as indicated by staining with glial fibrillary acidic protein.[13] Furthermore, the number of glial cells containing glutathione peroxidase, an index of anti-oxidant capacity, is least in the SNc, suggesting that these neurons are relatively lacking in protective mechanisms afforded by neighbouring glia. Indeed, there is a fairly good correlation between the propensity of dopaminergic neurons to undergo degeneration in PD and the melanin content, neuronal calbindin expression, density of glial cells, and density of glutathione peroxidase-containing glial cells. All this evidence raises the possibility that a major problem in PD may reside in the glial cells in the SNc. Those regions of the SNc containing the least protection by glia against oxidative stress may be the most susceptible to the disease process. Alternatively, alterations in glia could contribute to the neurodegeneration process through an inflammatory process involving activated microglia.

A role of glia in neurodegeneration suggests that anti-inflammatory agents, specifically those which can interfere with cytokines or NO formation, might afford neuroprotection in PD. Conversely, there is evidence that glial cells can produce trophic factors that support dopamine neurons in response to local injury. There are now data indicating that trophic factors can rescue dopamine neurons in tissue culture and animal models of PD.[21] Small molecules that induce the release of trophic factors or direct intracerebral administration of trophic factors into the brain might provide benefit in PD patients and clinical trials of glial-derived neurotrophic factor (GDNF) have begun.

THE TYPE OF NIGRAL CELL DEATH IN PD

The final consequence of these events is the death of nigral dopaminergic neurons, now generally believed to occur by apoptosis.[14,22] Evidence of apoptosis of neurons has been described in the SNc in the brains of patients with PD using *in situ* end-labelling (ISEL) techniques such as TUNEL to mark the 3' ends of DNA that have been cut by endonucleases. These results are somewhat controversial because of the relatively large number of apoptotic nuclei that have been detected and question the reliability of the ISEL techniques. More convincing are reports of apoptotic changes in the SNc in PD brains using electron microscopy or concurrent staining of individual neurons with both an ISEL technique and a dye that marks chromatin clumping. These results are less ambiguous and indicate that the number of apoptotic nuclei in the SNc in PD far exceeds that seen in normal aging (approximately 2% *versus* 0.2% of nuclei). Further evidence that apoptosis is occurring in PD comes from the finding of nuclear translocation of NFκB in nerve cells in the SNc in PD,[13] an observation that is associated with apoptosis in cultured dopaminergic nerve cells.

The sequence of events underlying nerve cell apoptosis is rapidly emerging and mitochondria appear to play a critical role.[16] Increasing evidence indicates that a fall in the mitochondrial membrane potential and a rise in intramitochondrial calcium are the earliest events leading to the development of apoptosis. These are in turn associated with the opening of a mitochondrial megapore and the release from mitochondria into the cytoplasm of small proteins known as apoptosis initiating factors (AIFs) that signal for the initiation of apoptosis.

Complexes I, III, and IV of the mitochondrial respiratory chain pump protons from the mitochondria and play an important role in maintaining the mitochondrial membrane potential. A defect in complex I, such as is seen in PD, might lead to a defect in proton pumping, a fall in mitochondrial membrane potential, and an increased risk of apoptosis even if the complex I defect is insufficient to induce a reduction in ATP production. That such a scenario might be relevant to PD is supported by the recent finding of a defect in mitochondrial membrane potential in fibroblasts derived from PD patients,[16] which might also account for the large number of apoptotic nuclei found in the SNc of PD patients. Apoptotic nuclei are thought to be present for only a matter of hours, so if such a large number of cells are found to be in apoptosis at any one time, theoretically in a matter of months there should be no further cells left in the nigra. However, if SNc neurons are vulnerable to apoptosis then they might enter apoptosis in response to agonal events.

Evidence that apoptosis plays a role in cell death in PD offers another series of targets for neuroprotection in PD. These might include agents that preserve the mitochondrial membrane potential, that maintain closure of the pore, or that prevent AIFs from signalling for the initiation of the apoptotic process. It is now believed that the anti-apoptotic effects of BCL-2 and cyclosporin A are related to their capacity to prevent opening of the pore, while the selegiline metabolite desethyl selegiline is thought to block apoptosis by binding to GAPDH, preventing its nuclear accumulation and preventing its inhibition of BCL-2 formation.[7,16,23]

THE FUTURE OF NEUROPROTECTION IN PD

It can be seen from this overview that there are many potential targets for neuroprotective therapy in PD. The problems are which factors to target, which agents to concentrate on, and which patients to study. This complex web of factors must be disentangled and the roles played by oxidant stress, mitochondrial dysfunction, excitotoxicity, and inflammatory factors in the cell death process must be determined. Whether each of these factors is a primary event or develops secondary to an alternate etiology must also be determined. Further, an understanding of the sequence of the events is crucial if a rational attempt to interfere with the pathogenic cascade is to be designed. For example, oxidative stress can cause mitochondrial dysfunction and *vice versa*, so the timing of these events must be resolved in order to understand which event should be preferentially targeted in an attempt to obtain neuroprotection.

A rational argument can be made for investigating a large number of different drugs. Agents that protect against oxidative stress and/or reduce the generation of reactive oxygen species from the metabolism of dopamine, those that enhance mitochondrial energy metabolism, those that protect against calcium entry into the cell, those that protect against excitotoxicity and NO production, those that reduce the inflammatory process, trophic factors, and agents that block the apoptotic process might all be worthy of trial. The problems of choice are formidable.

So too are the problems of trial design. The DATATOP study was a remarkable model of our capacity to perform a large multi-centre trial of a possible neuroprotective treatment for PD.[17] Unfortunately, because of a mild, confounding symptomatic effect, a true neuroprotective effect of the drug could not be established by this huge and costly venture.[24] However, DATATOP indicated clearly the nature and size of the operation required to test a single drug for a modest neuroprotective action in PD. Given the large number of possible approaches to neuroprotection highlighted in this summary, let alone those yet to come, it is inconceivable that large multi-centre trials modelled on the DATATOP paradigm could be mounted for each possible agent. Other strategies must be considered.

Perhaps it would be better to select sub-sets of patients with PD who are most likely to respond to a given therapeutic approach in order to test a specific hypothesis. One such starting point could be treating at-risk individuals who carry the α-synuclein mutation with the agents most effective at blocking cell death in models of α-synuclein-induced toxicity. Another approach would be to utilize cybrid technology to identify a sub-set of PD patients with a defect in the mitochondrial genome. Such individuals and their families could be candidates for clinical trials using agents designed to enhance mitochondrial function such as coenzyme Q10 or creatinine. Yet another approach might be to identify PD patients or their relatives who have fibroblasts with a defect in mitochondrial membrane potential for testing of agents that inhibit apoptosis, such as desmethyl selegiline. These strategies would aim to identify those patients most likely to benefit from a specific type of putative neuroprotective therapy in the hope that such a benefit could be detected with a relatively small numbers of patients.

A complimentary strategy would be to identify individuals in the pre-clinical stages of PD. Hitherto, there has been no satisfactory marker of pre-clinical PD that satisfactorily discriminates affected patients from controls. However, advances in the technology of positron emission tomography (PET) utilizing ^{18}F-dopa with 3-D registration of images have increased signal-to-noise ratio six-fold. Such 3-D PET technology can now discriminate PD patients from controls and detect individuals who presumably have pre-clinical disease.[25] This has been shown in asymptomatic relatives of families with autosomal dominantly inherited PD and in apparently unaffected monozygotic and dizygotic twins of patients with PD. PET technology is not widely available and is too expensive to use as a simple screening test for pre-clinical PD. However, it appears that similar results can be obtained with the more widely available technique of single photon emission computed tomography (SPECT) using ligands which bind to the dopamine transporter in striatal nigrostriatal nerve terminals. This technology may bring such an approach into the general clinical arena.

PET and SPECT techniques can now provide a biological marker of the rate of nigral cell degeneration in PD, and it has been estimated that the rate of decline in striatal dopaminergic activity in patients with PD is approximately 10% per annum. Drugs thought to exert a neuroprotective action might slow this rate of decline, and such deceleration might be detectable in relatively small groups of patients at reasonable cost using SPECT technology.

Another important point is that the earlier a neuroprotective therapy can be evaluated in the course of the disease, the better the chances of detecting the benefit of an effective agent.[2,24,25] Both PET and SPECT techniques and neuropathological evidence suggest that the rate of progression of PD in the early phases is more rapid than in the more advanced stages. This offers a therapeutic window for rescuing nigral neurons and preventing nigral degeneration before symptoms have actually developed. In addition, it should be easier to see small neuroprotective effects when the rate of disease progression is more rapid.

Another approach would be to use a cocktail of drugs with the potential to block cell degeneration from a number of different vantage points, a strategy that has found success in clinical trials of treatments for various cancers and AIDS. Drug cocktails can be tested and modified in an empirical program to identify the optimum combination to slow or halt the progression of PD. Such a programme is daunting, but feasible, even if it might require international collaboration.

Thus, there is a philosophical issue concerning the approach to the next generation of clinical trials looking for neuroprotection in PD. Advancements in science have provided us with a rather daunting list of potential neuroprotective agents, any one of which might provide benefit for PD patients. It is evident that conventional approaches to trials which examine one agent at a time in unselected patients in search of subtle incremental benefits are costly, time consuming, and utilize large numbers of patients that are often difficult to identify. As such, it will be virtually impossible to test all of the potentially valuable neuroprotective agents that are now at hand, let alone those that will emerge as our knowledge increases and as better models of PD become available. Further, it may be important to test a cocktail of drugs with different therapeutic targets.

We suggest that rather than performing a limited number of costly clinical trials that test single agents in large numbers of unselected cases in search of small and incremental benefits, it may be preferable to perform a large number of clinical trials to test a large number of agents in a small number of selected patients in search of a more robust neuroprotective effect. Thus, a larger number of agents and combinations of agents can be scanned for putative neuroprotective effects, reducing the risk of missing a powerful neuroprotective treatment through lack of time, money, or patients.

[375]

REFERENCES

1. Jenner P, Olanow CW, this volume.

2. Poewe WH, Wenning GK, this volume.

3. Perl DP, Olanow CW, Calne D, this volume.

4. Gasser T, this volume.

5. Polymeropoulos MH, this volume.

6. Krüger R, Kuhn W, Müller T, *et al.* Ala30Pro mutation in the gene encoding α–synuclein in Parkinson's disease. Nat Genet 1998; 18: 106–108.

7. Borden KLB, this volume.

8. Wood NW, this volume.

9. Langston JW, this volume.

10. Schapira AHV, Gu M, Taanman JW, Tabrizi SJ, Seaton T, Cleeter M, Cooper JM, this volume.

11. Mizuno Y, Yoshino H, Ikebe S, Hattori N, Kobayashi T, Shimoda-Matsubayashi S, Matsumine H, Kondo T, this volume.

12. Beal MF, this volume.

13. Hirsch EC, Hunot S, Damier P, Faucheux B, this volume.

14. Tatton NA, Maclean-Fraser A, Tatton WG, Perl DF, Olanow CW, this volume.

15. Morrison BM, Hof PR, Morrison JH, this volume.

16. Tatton WG, Chalmers-Redman RME, this volume.

17. Burke RE, Kholodilov NG, this volume.

18. Shoulson I and the Parkinson Study Group, this volume.

19. Brooks DJ, this volume.

20. Koller WC, this volume.

21. Melamed E, Offen D, Shirvan A, Djaldetti R, Barzilai A, Ziv I, this volume.

22. Olanow CW, Jenner P, Brooks D, this volume.

23. Rodriguez MC, Obeso JA, Olanow CW, this volume.

24. Gash DM, Zhang Z, Gerhardt G, this volume.

25. Olanow CW, Tatton WG. The etiology and pathogenesis of Parkinson's disease. Ann Rev Neurosci 1998, in press.